French Women in Politics

# French Women in Politics

*Writing Power, Paternal Legitimization, and Maternal Legacies*

By
*Raylene L. Ramsay*

Berghahn Books
New York • Oxford

First published in 2003 by

**Berghahn Books**
www.berghahnbooks.com



**Library of Congress Cataloging-in-Publication Data**
Ramsay, Raylene L., 1945–
French women in politics : writing power / Raylene Ramsay,
p. cm
Includes bibliographical references (p. ) and index.
ISBN 1-57181-081-1 (hardcover : alk. paper). -- ISBN 1-57181-082-X (pbk. : alk. paper)
1. Women in politics--France--History. 2. Women public officers--France--History. 3. Women in politics--France--Biography. 4. Women public officers--France--Biography. 5. Women authors, French. I. Title
HQ1235.5.F8R38 1998
320'.082--dc21 97-45098
CIP

**British Library Cataloguing in Publication Data**
A catalogue record for this book is available from the British Library.

ISBN 1–57181–081–1 hardback
ISBN 1–57181–082–X paperback

*Female MPs in the French National Assembly, June 12, 1997.*

# Contents

# List of Illustrations

# Foreword

The situation of French women in relation to political power must be puzzling for historians. Women in France obtained the right to vote much later than in most Western countries and, years after they had acquired this right, their representation in parliamentary assemblies and in positions of power was still so limited that they demanded—and finally obtained—a "parity" law, guaranteeing the equal representation denied to them by party traditions and masculine ambitions. And yet, for centuries, they had hardly been slow in putting forward their claims for equal rights within the couple and the family (spearheaded by Georges Sand, the wonderfully scandalous nineteenth-century writer), in the social and political spheres (beginning with Olympe de Gouges, an early martyr to the cause, who perished on the scaffold in 1793 after publishing her "Déclaration des Droits de la Femme et de la Citoyenne" in 1791), with the suffragettes, and then continuing on with the women politicians of the twentieth century. Not to mention as well the steps taken with respect to economic rights, first to manage one's own property, and subsequently, non-discrimination with respect to earnings and qualifications, and the rights over one's own body through birth control, access to contraception and abortion. These battles, ranging from very real material inequalities to sexist uses of language, which, little by little, have gained ground over a chauvinistic vision of the world, are altogether too numerous to be listed here.

As Dr. Ramsay suggests, such a historical situation cannot be fully accounted for by rational argument alone. Hence the utility of her method, which brings together both facts and the perceptions of women from different fields and with varied opinions. Dr. Ramsay provides an illuminating and comprehensive way of approaching these more obscure realms of French history. Where militant discourse and even sociological argument struggle to provide an account of the real, such an exploration of the discourses of fiction and of intimacy may well provide a way forward.

I am convinced that part of the reason for the delays surrounding the entry of women into politics that have marked these last years lies within the expression of an important truth. A truth that has remained in the realm of the unsaid: the judgment made on the vanity of certain forms of political power, the rather too vague expression of hope of seeing politics modified by women's presence. It is my hope that women's fuller integration into political life, by means of the parity law, will not see them abandon the goal of changing the rules of a game that still put the conquest of preeminence before the search for excellence.

Huguette Bouchardeau
Former Minister and Presidential Candidate

# Preface and Acknowledgements

This study grew out of a powerful reading experience, that of Huguette Bouchardeau's autobiographical work of fiction, *Choses dites de profil* (Speaking Indirectly), a book that I was invited to review in 1992. At that time I was working on the "new autobiographies," self-reflexive texts, mostly French, incorporating a critical analysis of the way in which our histories and life stories are prestructured and given meaning by the narrative conventions that give voice to them: for example, beginning and closure that suggest linear movement toward a resolution, chronology that also constitutes causality and progress, and characters that conform to the notions we have of psychological unity and coherence. The assumption that language simply mirrors or recovers the real, inherent in the realist aesthetic, is questioned by these literary "autofictions." Language is seen to construct rather than reflect reality. In contrast, most literary narratives, like political texts, continue to draw on traditional conventions as if these were somehow natural, and to situate themselves predominantly within the realist aesthetic as a mirror to the world.

Bouchardeau's novel is a seemingly mainstream fictional narrative about ten days in the life of a woman environment minister. Yet, the writer, herself a minister of the environment like her character, is at the same time a woman in search of the meanings of her own life. As in her earlier pioneering political histories of women, Bouchardeau layers aspects of her personal experience with her depiction of the public life of political women in France, creating portraits that resemble the decentered and multiple subject found in the "new autobiographies." Behind the representation of the political world "out there" by a self-knowing, fully self-present, unified traditional subject, Bouchardeau's writing reflects the complex political and social contexts at play when the writer puts pen to paper. These include language, other people's texts, and the forces of the personal and collective unconscious. Examined across a number of different genres, the political experience of women turns out to be as much about gaps, incompatibility and lack as about self-fulfillment and political achievement.

If Bouchardeau's writing lends itself productively to new kinds of political readings, it also echoes the process by which contemporary theory, and more specifically, narrative theory, has been breaking down barriers between both genres and disciplines. Interest in the role of literature in the production of political representations and in a narrative approach to politics to capture plurality and uniqueness is becoming evident in networked political studies women's groups. Many of the texts in the emerging new body of studies by and on political women—a term that is still something of an oxymoron in traditional language—share aspects of Bouchardeau's exploration of subjective understandings (or fictions) of political life from the particular perspective of a woman. They focus on values, emotions, or identity. I argue that these texts work to constitute and legitimate a rethinking and a "rewriting" of traditional political history and help to construct the unique and yet multiple identity of the political woman.

The present book examining the emergent body of writing on the experience of French women in political power has a dual purpose. The primary and largely descriptive goal is to illuminate women's changing roles in French life. The more theoretical goal is to seek to understand what is new and significant in the content and in the modes of writing by which this body of knowledge is being constituted.

As Gayatri Spivak reminds us: "It is a truism to say that the law is constituted by its own transgression."[1] Like the law, power is constituted both by adherence and by transgression. In asking whether this predominantly female writing on women in power "makes a difference" (how it reinforces the notion of power or deconstructs the power in place), this study must consider why the idea of "feminine difference" has become central to all the genres of the new writing. This reflection opens up onto a number of other questions: does feminine difference serve to conserve or subvert the social and narrative status quo? History and story (both words referred to as *histoire* in French) turn out to have a closer relationship than was imagined, within the ready-made narrative and reading conventions by which they are structured. If these texts can be said to constitute "new" writing, does this go as far as realizing the abstract ideals of feminine writing or of feminine power concretely? Or do the latter remain ideals? Is a women's history really possible?

The situation of women in the political arena has become a focus of studies across disciplines. It is the question of gender difference that creates the backbone of the new body of texts; a distinctive body that conducts its own debates, on values such as feminine difference, for example. I argue that reaching a critical mass, these various disciplinary texts now feed into and strengthen one another. However, it is also the case that political histories, sociopolitical surveys, interviews, autobiographies, biographies, and fictions do investigate women and power in very different ways. Examined chapter by chapter, each of these genres reveals its own conventions for producing knowledge. Each offers scope for a different kind of understanding of the political possibilities for women.

Over two decades of research by women historians is now available. Constructing political history since the Revolution from the perspective of women, these histories do appear to be recovering a new history (of the franchise for women and of women's representation) and are thereby rewriting the old political stories. As historians' accounts are shaped by their national, ideological, and disciplinary contexts, so too, in the case of women's histories, are the stories also shaped by the historian's particular position on debates about feminine difference and parity. The teller and his/her (gendered) contexts turn out to be part of any tale told.

Alongside these new, explicitly gender-informed histories, two decades of work by political and social scientists (most notably the publications of Janine Mossuz-Lavau and of Mariette Sineau) provide a solid backbone for the description of most aspects of the contemporary relation between women and power. These texts, too, have the strengths and the limitations both of their respective disciplinary-based methodologies (opinion polls and surveys, for example) and of the writer's own political and gendered positions.

A series of interviews, both my own and the recent proliferation of published interviews with political women, provides information in this quite distinctive genre. The comparison of a body of interviews published in 1986 and interviews given some ten years later shows major changes in content as in contexts and the growing sense that women do have a legitimate place in politics. Despite the personal character of the interview, the questions asked, and the experiences recounted, what is most striking is the similarity of many of the opinions offered and of the discourse in circulation. Conventionality and intertextuality mark these interviews as if certain contemporary concerns and ideas, those present in *l'air du temps*, are being recycled, constituting something like a shared women politicians' discourse.

Along with the interview, the political autobiography has been traditionally used in history and political studies as a representation of life in politics. In autobiographical texts by political women (a genre growing rapidly as I was researching and writing) I found something rather different, the private and public intimately interwoven in a recurring and quite central structure. Again, there was some evidence of intertextuality in the circulation of similar stories among writers seeking to understand and define their place as women in the political world.

The few existing biographies of political women also contain the new hybrid structure in which the private and the public faces of the subject are referred to simultaneously. Biographies tell us as much about the biographer as about the object of his/her study and in this respect, biographies written by women in politics about other women can be particularly revealing. Nonetheless, it is in fiction, in particular that of Françoise Giroud and Huguette Bouchardeau examined in the last two chapters, that some of the personal yet deeper "truths" about women and power are detectable. These are truths about the desire for paternal legitimization and the progressive movement toward maternal legacies or truths of a feminine self not made for a masculine political life. These literary texts contribute a more intimate, fluid, and multilayered reflection on women's relations to power than the other genres, and as such can only be told indirectly.

Where should knowledge be located and power situated in the various writing projects of/on political women? The larger questions that lie behind my summaries of this corpus of texts and the constitution of an ancillary body of information from oral interviews became clearer as I followed the spurt in publications on political women and the unfolding of the parity debate from week to week in Paris. My study concludes that there is a correlation between the emergence of this body of texts on and by political women and the adoption of the parity discourse in France. The texts on political women have made a difference. This difference is most immediately manifest in the textual symbolic reshaping of the (masculine) power in place, a reshaping of a political scene in which feminine difference is at the core and the needs of women are addressed. Such a re-inscription is present in all the textual genres that incorporate and consider the difference brought by women in politics. It has an effect in the real world where women have new and major political roles and where there has been an astonishing interest in the parity debate. The traditional French "exception"—the distinctiveness of French culture marked by masculine *galanterie* and feminine mystique, alongside apparently contradictory masculine *gauloiserie* and feminine autonomy —now astonishingly coexists with a further French exception in the form of the "parity" law voted on 2 June 2000 in a country that has generally seen American-style "affirmative action," translated into French as *discrimination positive*, as a form of discrimination.

In the final instance, I suggest that what has nudged France into accepting a principle as revolutionary as parity democracy or equal representation for men and women in all political assemblies is the discourse on feminine difference circulating in the new body of writing on women in politics and constituting something like a female writing tradition. French women in politics are indeed examining, and in many cases, rewriting power. In a small number of exceptional cases, as in Jean-Paul Sartre's well-known literary autobiography *Les Mots*, such a celebration of the power of words may also be accompanied by a critical deconstruction; the critique of the apparent power of (women's) language, and the attempt to map and make explicit what it conceals—the very real limitations of the new discourse and its modes of re-presentation. Even if many of these women's texts continue to manifest very conventional realist origins that may sometimes be regressive, such texts are rewriting power by a simple politics of presence.

The project of identifying, describing for an English-speaking readership, and analyzing the new body of political writing is an ambitious one, perhaps particularly so for a student of literary theory. The attempt made to examine texts from different disciplines without established credentials in all of their methodologies—those of history, or political and social science, for example—will leave this study open to criticism. It is justified only by the conviction that the scope for cross-fertilization across disciplines is increasing and collaboration is now necessary. Participation in an eight-week seminar on modern French political history with historians and political scientists at the Institut d'Etudes Politiques in Paris, funded by the National Endowment for the Humanities and run by Bernard Brown, professor of political studies at the CUNY Graduate School, gave me a sense of the differences in disciplinary approach and background, but also of the real possibilities of interdisciplinarity. During this period, Janine Mossuz-Lavau and Mariette Sineau generously discussed their work and their methods with me. I would like to thank these colleagues for their time and their (sometimes cautious) interest in this project beyond disciplinarity.

To the many ministers and former ministers who gave me their time in hour-long interviews or more, I express my gratitude: to Huguette Bouchardeau in particular for her always encouraging and productive discussions; to Véronique Neiertz, Roslyne Bachelot, Christiane Taubira-Delannon, Michèle Barzach, Simone Veil, and Edith Cresson, former prime minister. Generous with her time, the sociologist Françoise Gaspard allowed me to ask her difficult questions between a seminar and an appearance before a senatorial committee at which she would present the cause for legislation on parity. Personal contact with these women added a further level of discourse to their stories in the form of body language and performance. A number of ministers and former ministers of the Juppé government also responded to a written questionnaire I sent to them in late 1996: Anne-Marie Idrac, then transportation minister, and Elisabeth Dufourcq, assistant minister for research in 1995, among others.

I owe many thanks to the library staff of the Institut d'Etudes Politiques and the impressive Bibliothèque Nationale de France, newly inaugurated on 15 December 1996. I am also grateful to the University of Auckland for leave to complete much of the manuscript, which I did perched in an apartment overlooking the rooftops of Paris, with the heart of that political center beating around me. I am indebted to my friend and former colleague in Boston, Terese Lyons, for her ability to spot gallicisms in my summaries of the French texts and point out references to French institutions that might have left an Anglo-Saxon reader perplexed. Her help in reworking the first draft was invaluable, as was the editorial assistance provided by Sandra Grey, now completing a Ph.D. in political studies at the Australian National University.

My interest in the experience of these political women derives in part from my own life as a woman entering the academy as a member of that one half of humanity traditionally classed with "minority" groups. The need to both celebrate and deconstruct my own situation will certainly have some bearing on my readings. In the early seventies, I received invitations to receptions at Cambridge University, stipulating that dress should be black tie and academic gown, pointedly addressed by the porters at Jesus and Magdalene Colleges as "madam" rather than "doctor." Terrifyingly anxious to conform, to be perfect, it took a number of years before I came to realize that the canonical texts of French literature I was teaching, their images of women, were male-centered; that I was perpetuating scholarly studies of "enlightened" Rousseau that had somehow missed critiquing Book Five of *Emile* with its unenlightened treatise on the (non)relation of women to the social and the naturalness of the non-education of women. To bold feminist theorists and to women's writing as it came to modify the canon and inform my thinking, I owe a debt of personal emancipation.

The interdisciplinary and comparative aspirations of this work are reinforced by my somewhat itinerant career: seven years in the French system (in Poitiers, Paris, Toulouse, and Aix-en-Provence), three years in the Cambridge University tradition in Britain, eight years at Massey University in New Zealand, eight years at American universities (Tufts, Clark, and Simmons, and as visiting professor at Brown University). A return to Auckland in New Zealand to a Chair in French has coincided with the period that saw the first elected female Labor Prime Minister Helen Clark take over the reigns of government from the first female National Prime Minister Jenny Shipley. I dedicate this book to the many gifted, hard-working teachers and scholars, and the women in politics encountered along my path whose commitment, talents, generosity, and openness have enabled me to dare to engage with vital contemporary questions about women and power across territories beyond my own.

## Note

1. Gayatri Spivak, *A Critique of Postcolonial Reason: Toward a History of the Vanishing Present* (Cambridge, Mass.: Harvard University Press, 1999), p. 113.

# Writing and Power: Introduction and Overview

France is a country with a strong human rights tradition, where women have a very high level of education, civil rights, and independence, but it is a country in which women did not win the right to vote until 1944. This belated vote for women in France is puzzling in the light of the suffrage won more than fifty years earlier in the new egalitarian frontier states of the U.S. or the pioneering colonies such as New Zealand and Australia. Not only did universal suffrage come late in France, but levels of female representation in successive national assemblies have been low. Until mid-1997, women represented less than 6 percent of those who had sat in the French National Assembly and fewer than 5 percent of those who had been in the Senate. The proportion of female representation had barely altered since women were first elected to the national assemblies in 1945 when women occupied 5.9 percent of the seats in the National Assembly. Indeed, even in 1999, with a bare 11 percent of seats in the National Assembly held by women (59 out of 577 deputies and 19 out of 321 senators), France was ahead of only Great Britain and Greece in terms of female representation levels in Europe. The low level of representation stands in striking contrast to the over 40 percent female representation in some Protestant countries in Northern Europe.

Why did female suffrage come so late in France? Why was it granted by De Gaulle as a reward for women's efforts during the war and more particularly, as a barrier to the Communists, rather than as a result of constitutional process? What might account for the proportionally fewer women in high political office in May 1997 than in 1945 when women first voted? How can France's distinctive trailing position in Europe with respect to female representation until mid-1997 be explained? Or indeed, the parity law and the major increase of women candidates in the March municipal elections in the new millennium? This book asks whether there are culturally and politically specific factors constituting the "French exception" with respect to female political rights.

## Setting the Scene

In the half-century of change since women's enfranchisement in 1945, French women have been forming new images of themselves as they take up new roles in society. Women have come to constitute 45 percent of the work force, their religious practice has declined, and they have surpassed the results of their male counterparts at the level of the Baccalauréat. Women have gained access in increasing numbers to the positions of prestige offered by entrance to the competitive institutions of higher learning in France, such as the Grandes Ecoles and in particular, the school that trains the civil service elites, the ENA (Ecole Nationale d'Administration). L'Ecole Polytechnique opened its doors to women in 1972, but the prestigious and competitive educational tracks in mathematics and science and the economic and administrative professions are still largely dominated by men, seemingly due at least in part to a choice made by women who are less willing to enter a male arena so driven by competition and "excellence," preferring to maintain breadth and interest in their studies and lives. A law passed in 1965 allowed women to work, open a bank account and dispose of their own property without the consent of their husband. There has since been a plethora of major new laws for equal pay (1972) and workplace opportunity and equality (1982, 1983), divorce by mutual consent (1975), civil equality, repression of workplace harassment (1992) and antisexism. These new laws come to stand alongside the traditionally generous paid maternity leave and pre- and postnatal financial and medical benefits, job protection while on maternity leave, help with child care, and family allowances. As part of the expansion of the traditionally strong measures to support maternity and therefore increase France's birthrate, there has been legislation on parental leave (1977) and more recently a "Family Bill" providing financial incentives for those who elect to stay home with their children. In another move to support the maternal role, a child can now bear (although not pass on) the name of his/her mother. Most of these changes in law and in women's lives have been documented and analyzed in texts written by women.[1]

The most significant of social changes for political women writers have been the major laws passed since 1967 that favor new sexual freedoms. These include the legalizing of contraception and contraceptive information in 1967 and of termination of pregnancy (IVG or *interruption volontaire de grossesse*) in 1975, the introduction of sex education, penalties for sexual violence, harassment, rape, and abuse, and greater freedom of sexual practice. As Janine Mossuz-Lavau points out in her 1992 study *Les Lois de l'amour* (Laws on Sexuality), the younger generation has now come to consider their individual right to choose or reject motherhood as perfectly normal, "a child: when I want one, if I want one, in the manner I choose." Changes in biological constraints and in the sexual landscape are dramatically altering the social and psychological situation of women. These changes have also begun to modify certain traditional personal relations of power between the sexes. A recent survey, for example, shows that 50 percent of younger men consider parenting to be a priority in their lives. These men consider availability, not authority or security, to be their most important contribution to the family unit. However, between 1986 and 1999, as Michelle Perrot points out, the share of household tasks assumed by men increased by only 3 percent (from 32 to 35 percent, according to INSEE polls). This means an excessive load is placed on women's shoulders, with women between the ages of twenty-five and forty-nine representing 73 percent of the workforce (82 percent for men), and 75 percent of them with two children.[2]

Along with the dramatic social and psychological changes for women in France, the political landscape has also changed. These changes are highlighted in the major surveys of the political scientist Janine Mossuz-Lavau. Women in France now represent a majority electoral force (53 percent of the population), voting in more or less equal proportions to men. As the abstention rate by women declined to become the same as that of men by 1988, the conservative orientation of women's vote also changed substantially.

It was the women's vote that denied power to Mitterrand, first favoring "the father" De Gaulle in 1968 and then in 1974 "the aristocrat," Giscard d'Estaing. A movement in the female vote finally brought the left and its Common Program (Programme Commun) to power in 1981. In 1988, for the first time, a majority of women (51 percent) voted for the Socialist government to enable it to regain power after a period of cohabitation. Again in 1993 the women's vote shaped French political leadership when female voters turned away from the Socialist government. Unemployment, a general crisis of confidence in the workings of government and in the traditional ideological distinctions between left and right turned women voters toward favoring the opposition. The landslide against the Socialists, whose traditional social platform and values of solidarity were seen to have been superseded by liberal economic policies practiced by the right, by the left, and by the center, was also a call for a change in the nature of politics. Since 1993, the dynamic and talented young women ministers and advisors who had appeared under Mitterrand's patronage were no longer in the limelight of high political office and their ideas impinged only from the political periphery. This absence from office motivated the writing of a number of the pioneering political memoirs spoken of in this book. The social and attitudinal changes played a part in the unearthing of women's political histories from buried archives.

## Gender Matters

The analysis of portraits, self-portraits, and surveys from France highlights those same significant patterns as can be found in women's own explanations for their astonishing absence from the scene of high political power.[3] If the relative newness of the right to hold office, ideological affiliation, class and generational difference are accounted for, does gender matter? The response by women in politics is most often affirmative. Even when they accept the political world they enter into as necessarily governed by hierarchy, party loyalties, and confrontational debate, their very presence appears to bring issues of gender relations to the surface. By putting forward the idea of a value added to politics by women's difference, the parity movement has been attempting to counter this deeply seated and widely shared sense of illegitimacy.

As absent mothers, unavailable wives or as successful politicians, women in politics are seen or see themselves as guilty intruders or usurpers of natural male prerogatives.[4] They are put back where they belong by longstanding French traditions whether they be *galanterie* (from the medieval tradition of knightly chivalry toward the idealized Lady) or the more earthy *gauloiserie* (the locker-room humor that reduces a woman to her sexual function). Yann Piat, Front national deputy in 1986 and the Front's only elected representative in 1988, wrote of a world decidedly not conceived to correspond to the needs of women. There was the minor material detail of lack of suitable accommodation for women provided in the Assemblée Nationale buildings, and the more troubling lack of room for her own political authority within the paternalistic party where she was expected to continue to play the role of Le Pen's goddaughter and supporter. On the private level, too, her husband, a fighter pilot, was finally unable to reconcile his self-image with the public importance of his wife, bringing up the issue of lack of any provision for political husbands as opposed to the place of honor reserved for political wives. Yann Piat's entry into politics led to divorce.

Many women in political office still prefer to think of themselves in the traditional feminine mode of having an indirect influence rather than direct personal power, defined as virile and threatening to the "femininity" so vital to the unconscious of French culture. It has been argued persuasively that women prefer to be *femmes d'influence* (women of influence) rather than *femmes de pouvoir* (women of power). An example of this can be found in the legend of the *éminence grise* created around Marie-France Garaud, a former advisor to President Georges Pompidou. Physical attractiveness and elegance are considered to be of importance even into the 1990s. Paradoxically, these qualities have often served as pretext for women's disqualification as serious politicians.

Male discourse—such as Giscard d'Estaing's observation in his memoirs on Alice Saunier-Seïté's feline legs, noted in Adler's popular study of political women, or Chirac's condemnation of Michèle Barzach's dissidence for which she deserved "a spanking"—reveals the deeply entrenched paternalist and sexualized frames of reference within which political women are often still situated by their male colleagues. The media is still constantly guilty of trivializing or gender-typing women.

While appearing on the evening news to argue that France should ratify its full membership of the European Union, Elizabeth Guigou, minister for Europe in Mitterrand's government, was asked to watch and comment on a fashion collection that made up the following news item. There seemed to be little awareness that this switch might trivialize Guigou's political message. The study of the biography of Edith Cresson in chapter 7 will support the argument that the media was partly responsible for the destruction of the politician's image by reducing her to a sexual feline body.

The need for the paternal legitimization that Julia Kristeva sees as so vital for the psychic survival of women plays a discernible role at the heart of much women's "political" writing, which is as concerned with individual needs for security and autonomy as with issues of political policy. In any event, when women hold high political office, they do not appear to attract or impress the opposite sex at least in the sense that Henry Kissinger declares "power" to be the most powerful aphrodisiac. Women are attracted to powerful men; men tend to be less than comfortable with powerful women.

In Françoise Giroud's autobiographical account of her sojourn in the land of power, *La Comédie du pouvoir* (The Comedy of Power), the former politician pleads with the French electorate to stop expecting democracies to provide all-powerful father figures. A majority of women voters had supported De Gaulle from 1945 to 1968, less as a vote for the right than as a vote for a paternal figure, father of the Nation, who could be seen as above party. Giroud's texts reveal that this need for (and refusal of) paternal legitimization is deeply rooted in her own experience and unconscious. She writes against but is also influenced by these narratives of paternal authorization. Her autobiography, *Leçons particulières* (Private Lessons), combines the journalistic style of her articles on public politics (editorials in *L'Express* or diary entries in *Journal d'une Parisienne*) with the private confession of an attempted suicide and subsequent analysis with Lacan that revealed the wound left by her need to be as good as the son her father had so desired.

In Bouchardeau's political histories, the former Socialist environment minister and *députée* (deputy or elected representative to the Lower House of the National Assembly) analyses the predominance of the phenomenon of women entering public office with male patronage. Women *conseillères adjointes* or local councilors and women ministers, if appointed and not elected, then owe a debt of gratitude to those male politicians who nominated them. Legitimacy conferred by other women—in the sense that Luce Irigaray theorizes female authority, in a frame of sisterhood—seems to hardly exist. The parity movement, however, has seen the development of increasing solidarity among women and across parties, strengthening further under the Jospin government.

It is clear that the phenomenon known as *le fait du prince* (patronage or protection by the prince) is still symbolically significant in the traditionally virile world of politics. Here, it is claimed, women, predominantly defined by the seductive and the sexual, wait, like Cinderella or Beauty to be chosen by the prince, or attempt to please the father. Power, it seems, may well be inseparable from sexuality and the body; power relations exist in the unconscious much as the unconscious is present in the exercise of power. Giroud and Bouchardeau's literary texts intimate that most women still struggle with deep feelings of illegitimacy and unease about assuming masculine power despite their own public success.

## Writing Difference

Another prominent topic in texts written by French political women is their "difference." This appears at first sight to have little to do with the theories of feminine writing or *écriture féminine* elaborated by the new French feminist intellectuals in the seventies, Irigaray, Cixous, and Kristeva. Yet, Irigaray's latest work (despite its abstraction and philosophical/psychoanalytical character and, indeed, its essentialism) is curiously attuned to women's focus on their political difference and the arguments developed in parity texts from this gender difference. In *Le Souffle des Femmes* (Women's Spirit, 1997), Irigaray writes of the need to reconstruct the world from a basis of the two subjects—otherwise, she claims, the risk of one subject alienating the other is too great. She prefers the notion of equivalence to that of equality because it better "protects difference." However, in its attempt to break down the binary oppositions of the masculine language in power, Irigaray's experimental writing from a fluid and desiring feminine body itself suggests that *écriture féminine* may be, as yet, an unrealized ideal.

Any argument based on difference between the genres or the sexes arising from their relationships with the public and private, with traditional, limited, taxonomic "masculine" fields of knowledge and "feminine" boundary-crossing, with transparent political discourse and a multilayered or dialogic literary discourse that brings different arguments into relationships, should be embarked upon with great caution. I approach it with a series of disclaimers that include the now well accepted need to acknowledge the very significant differences (of race, class, party, sexual preference) within feminine difference or feminisms, the problematic existence of any such single thing as "women's experience," the need to situate and historicize all accounts of women's writing, and the constructed nature of the relationship between gender (sociocultural) and sex (biological and genetic).

It is nonetheless the case that the argument most often encountered from men and women alike, regarding women's presence in circles of power (power defined as decision making or having influence on public events), is a differential one: the life experience of women gives them a pragmatic sense of everyday realities that their male counterparts seem often to lack. Both biology and social conditioning (both nature and nurture) can play a determining role in the fashioning of a woman. Although I may seem to argue that the complex, opaque discourse allowing the presence of anxieties and a sense of illegitimacy in relation to power is "feminine," while the transparent text of political reminiscence and objective non-gendered analysis is "masculine," it is not evident that the two are necessarily or naturally gender marked.[5]

Paradoxically, political women's claim to difference as, for example, greater concern for morality, for future generations, and for the public good, has been argued to have its origins in theoretical concepts of republican universalism. The American historian Joan Scott claims that from Olympe de Gouges to Madeleine Pelletier, feminism has specifically served to reveal the central contradictions in the republican discourse. Feminism was produced within these discursive contexts and its paradoxes do not then reflect the limitations of the feminist imagination but rather the very contradictions and the practices of representative democracy (universalism as the exclusion of women and women's singularity) within which it is seeking a voice. Feminism has attempted both to recognize sexual difference and to deny it any relevance. The moral of Scott's work on the "paradoxical citizen" is that the parity arguments must formulate differences between the sexes differently so as not to reproduce that particular sexed difference of the citizen that had led to women's exclusion at the dawn of the Revolution. Michelle Perrot sees this task of changing internalized and persistent symbolic representations of gender difference as central to the contemporary feminist enterprise: "Incorporating difference, thinking it differently, being able to make it disappear and reappear, being at once both the same and the other in a subtle game of changing identities, such is the horizon of the new century… Utopias do sometimes help to change the world."[6]

## Not the Public or the Private, but Both

A major gendered difference appearing within French stories and histories is the treatment of the public and private realms. French politics has traditionally exemplified the principle of the separation of the public and the private. In his memoirs, the two-volume *Le Pouvoir et la vie* (Power and Life), traditional in content and in style, former President Giscard d'Estaing (1974–1981) recalls noteworthy public political events and individuals in relation to his own encounters, political battles, exploits, and observations. In this conventional and seemingly universal story, the only private matters discussed are the anecdotal dinner parties given with significant political characters against the dimly lit backdrop of the natural and unfailing wifely support of Anne-Aimone.

An acceptance of this separation for those in public office in France is demonstrated in the events following Francois Mitterrand's death in

1995. Revelations by the popular magazine *Paris Match* about Mitterrand's secret second family had caused an outcry of protest in the reputable press. The public appearance of wife and mistress, sons, and newly recognized daughter Mazarine together at Mitterrand's funeral mass in Notre Dame cathedral reinforced the principle of the separation of the public and private spheres for those in positions of public leadership in France. While the media and d'Estaing struggled to keep the public and private separated, in many of the women's texts, the two spheres are curiously intertwined in a manner that transgresses traditional genre boundaries and can be seen as specifically "feminine." In her account of ten days in the life of an environment minister in Mitterrand's first Socialist government, *Choses dites de profil*, Huguette Bouchardeau focuses on the repressed psychological effects and philosophical questions that arise with the holding of ministerial office. Her story is told from the particular perspective of a woman's life experience; both the personal and the public are present and deeply connected. The essential questions are those of personal responsibility (in relation to her silence on the sinking of the Greenpeace protest yacht, *Rainbow Warrior*, the compromise on reducing car pollution levels in Europe, and the accommodation with hunters to avoid a total shooting ban on wood-pigeons crossing the Pyrénées, for example), family demands, and the jealousies inherent in personal relationships. Giscard's memoirs, centered on a public self with clearly drawn ego boundaries and on political male rivalries, may be more authoritative but they are no closer to the truth than Bouchardeau's fictional autobiography, marked by greater fragmentation, more fluid ego boundaries, and with an emphasis on the importance of relationships and intimacy.

## Women Writing Up on Power

Any reading of women's exclusion from the public scene in terms of the politico-economic inferiorization effected by their relegation to the private feminine sphere of family must see gender as a primary field of the articulation of power inequality. The parity movement has been seeking a new language that will create a post-equality space allowing for gender complementarity and the modification of the masculine mechanisms governing the political world. Feminine legitimacy is being forged politically by increasing occupation of territory but also by the kinds of representations of difference elaborated by the parity movement. These new differences, as theorized by the literary feminist critic Teresa de Lauretis, are contextual rather than essential but do not require renouncing feminine specificity. They give access to a specificity and to an agency that enable women to modify their situation through choices and style (something like a "care of the self" in the later Foucault). Writing and rewriting constitute a form of remaking or taking of power, or, at the least of asking what it means to speak of power in the feminine. Empowerment, then, may derive at the simplest level from the new knowledge of women's political roles, as this is being researched and made public in published texts.

If one remains skeptical about any power that does not substantially inflect the world of material rewards, or feels concerned that any argument for feminine difference risks sliding back into traditional essentialism, new power may be seen to lie in the call for a new kind of political practice: one that Simone Veil describes in terms of ideas and feminine praxis, of pragmatics rather than discursive practices (speech-making), of action rather than ego-flashing and antler-crashing words; a political morality less isolated from affect and more directly concerned with experience.

The power in place, however, both linguistic and institutional, as Foucault so convincingly argues, involves the shaping of preferences and desires, conscious and unconscious. This would explain the unease felt by many women in politics, their feeling of being on the defensive, and the problem of remaining "feminine." This is perhaps why many women do not vote for or accept other women in positions of high power and why political women are expected to pass the test of being "real" women—feminine women, mothers, non-feminist.The relation of women to political power can be excavated at different levels, across the direct and seemingly transparent interviews, manifestos or autobiographical accounts of political life as well as indirectly within the multilayered narratives of the imagination, that is, in fiction. Literary narratives, such as Huguette Bouchardeau's *Choses dites de profil* or Giroud's new subjective journalism, allow for a more contradictory relation to power to surface. A hidden fear of illegitimacy and ancient taboos of paternal interdiction or need for paternal authorization emerge, along with interest in maternal legacies and new aspirations.[7] What the writing by and about political women in France does reveal is that the "collective unconscious" and its incorporation of traditional feminine essentialism has consistently constituted a major impediment to the acceptance of women holding power.

In the presidential elections of April 1995, Le Pen and his extreme right-wing paternalist party drew on such a collective consciousness to total almost 16 percent of the vote. In that same election De Villiers' right-wing aristocratic and nationalist party won another 5 percent. Both of these political groups have family programs and ideas of order, security, and nation that require the expulsion of difference (the foreigner) and the return of women to "their" bedrooms, nurseries, and kitchens to protect the identity of a certain kind of (French)man. In the second round of the 1995 elections, won narrowly by Jacques Chirac, parties left of center held the balance of power in a political situation in which the traditional French parties had lost much of their dominance. This trend was reversed in 1997 with a return of the Socialists to a cohabitation government with Jacques Chirac as president. But the extreme right and its appeal to a certain collective unconscious—of the nation and of the gender roles that constitute it—continues to have a significant following. The male following outnumbers the female.

Much of the new women's political theory conceives power differently than can be found in male writing. Women see power in terms of empowerment, "power to" (exercise civic responsibilities or change society) rather than "power over." Women are most generally characterized as cooperative and practical, civic-minded, non-personally ambitious, and, in a sense, non-political. Success in the careers of these political women is presented not so much as a question of climbing the ladder, getting to the top, or winning political power in order to exercise control, as in the ability to relate in meaningful ways to events and to others. But this conception of feminine power is of course elaborated in opposition to the competitive discursive power embodied by their male colleagues.

Beyond the feelings of illegitimacy and the debate on the redefinition of a system of power and a democracy that has been established without women, most of these texts express a lived frustration with the organization and nature of the political world: the vanity of partisan debates, phrase-making rituals, the bubble decried by Giroud separating the powerful politician from the common mortal in France (the chandeliers, chauffeurs, motor-cycle escorts, special airport lounges), and the connections necessary to establish oneself as a political identity that leave no room for family obligations. Almost all women in politics are critical of the party system as closed, non-democratic, highly competitive, and dominated by a discursive (male) power. These are irritations that have come to be shared by an often-disillusioned electorate of both men and women.

In feminist writings "empowerment" is presented as a non-hierarchical kind of counter-power. Yet as Bouchardeau points out, in practice, without power over, it is impossible to act effectively. This fact is reiterated by Giroud in her 1999 study *Les Françaises*, where the journalist echoes Elisabeth Badinter in declaring that women will need to develop a share of "virility" (taste for risk, sense of utopia) if they want to succeed in the public world. Both of these writers doubt that women's presence will make politics a paradise. At the same time, both argue that it will introduce a different way of looking at the other and at a time when men are seeking a new contract with women.

Whereas Foucault leaves gender out of his analysis, feminism observes the gendered and different nature of women's control that makes real equality (equality in fact as well as in law) so difficult. If the source of power is to be found in the common knowledge of society and not in a juridico-political system or hierarchy, legitimacy and reputation are vital prerequisites to having and commanding confidence. Feminist theorists argue that Foucault and feminism come together in an understanding of the importance of the local networks of power relations as these function at the micro-levels of the society, in the control of the body in sexuality, in the family, in everyday experience.

Our study suggests that women's legitimacy to exercise public power has not been fully embedded in the shared knowledge of French society but that this situation is changing. Whilst recognizing that power may be concentrated in a given political function and certainly in the state, one also has the option of "fictioning" power, as Foucault so neatly expresses the capacity of creative language to capture or manufacture something that does not yet exist. Many of our texts that begin to seek such a "fictioning" transmit the sense that change must derive from the specificity of women's lives as much as from the "equality" implicit in the "universal" human rights that managed to exclude half of humanity. Change must come from "insertion" (standing alongside or intermingling) rather than assimilation (disappearing into).

Political theory has, until recently, given little place to the specificity of women and has largely ignored questions of emotion, sexuality, and private life. This writing on power and re-writing of power by French women represents a description of a new women's political history in the making: from the Revolution through the power to vote and then on toward the power to represent, and perhaps to represent differently, at the very highest levels.

Chapter 1 outlines the histories of the franchise for women and briefly analyzes these narratives on the difficult accession to the vote and to a civil equality. The parliamentary debate on women's franchise had less to do with claims for equality than with arguments about different representations of female identity and feminine difference. Those in favor of the right to vote depicted women as mothers who could bring caring qualities to a kinder, gentler politics; those opposed to female suffrage saw women as hysterical or irrational wombs, or gracious, fragile creatures not equipped for public life.

Chapter 2 is an introduction to the statistics on and stories of women's representation from the franchise to the present. Ideas on how constructions of difference and power have affected women's history are traced through these early chapters that argue that these new histories did make a difference. Two of the early versions of the story of access to the franchise and civic equality were written by politicians; by the conservative *député* Jean Pascal (published in 1990), and by the president of the former left-wing party Parti Socialiste Unifié (PSU) and *députée* Huguette Bouchardeau (through an unpublished manuscript written in the late 1980s).[8] A comparison of these accounts by political figures from very different backgrounds highlights the importance of the writer's personal itinerary, historical contexts, and, indeed, gender. The contexts of the teller alter the tale of the past, as in post-Einsteinian physics the instrument of observation itself alters the phenomenon observed. Pascal represents a long tradition of conservative thinking on feminine difference. The left-wing Bouchardeau is more influenced by changes in the contexts in which questions of difference are being articulated—by the 1968 implosion of the authoritarian, centralized structures of French society, the beginning of French feminist movements (notably the MLF, or Women's Liberation Movement in 1970), and the plethora of legislative changes that were revolutionizing the legal status of women. Any analysis of these texts must also concur with contemporary narrative theory in concluding that the past is always reconstructed as a function of present frames of reference and of what has happened since. The past cannot be recovered in some kind of pristine purity.

The distinctive French parity movement for the equal representation of men and women in all political assemblies and its contribution to the reflection on the nature of citizenship and democracy is outlined in chapter 3. This chapter can offer only a brief introduction to the impact of the media and political writing in helping parity to become politically successful. The question of the conservative or subversive power of texts opened up in the study of the narratives of franchise, representation, and parity is developed in chapter 4, which looks at women's political power and legitimacy as this is partially transformed from the protective but inhibiting *fait du prince* (will of the prince) to the claim of French women's political legitimacy in their own right.

Following the new histories of women, the social and political surveys, and the writing on parity, the second major source of this book is the body of texts by women who have themselves held high political office in France over the past two decades. Chapters 5, 6, and 7 present portraits of the most important women to have held political office, through interviews, autobiographies, and biographies respectively. The corpus of autobiographical writing summarized in chapter 6 is fairly comprehensive, at least through June 1997 when, with the return of the Socialists to office under Jospin, the number of women in high political office doubled overnight.[9] Chapter 7 examines three major published biographies and the limited kinds of "truths" the biography is able to tell. With Edith Cresson, the first female prime minister in France, the aim is to understand which discourses caused her popularity to plummet after an initial period of high approval ratings. The example of Simone Veil provides the portrait of a very different political "destiny": Veil, who had the experience and moral authority of a survivor of Auschwitz and held the only position of real female influence in Edouard Balladur's center-right government that replaced the Socialists in 1993, has been a determined advocate of respect for human dignity and freedom for women, and a leader in the movement for parity democracy. But, like many of the appointed women ministers of her generation, Veil never stood for elective office in France. In Veil's interview with me, the politician contests the "truths" of her life as these are revealed by her biographer. In fact, biography turns out to be what Janet Beizer has called "bio-auto-graphy," revealing as much about its writer as its subject. This is also the case for the co-authored journalistic biography of the woman who was second to the prime minister in Jospin's Socialist government in the late 1990s, Martine Aubry. These chapters ask questions about the origins of our disciplinary conventions and the perspectives and limitations inscribed within the different genres.

Finally, chapters 8 and 9 continue the reflection on writing across the literary explorations of two key figures of the French political and intellectual world, Huguette Bouchardeau and Françoise Giroud, who were both prolific writers. The close relation between the constitution of knowledge and power that also preoccupied Michel Foucault is at issue here. Does knowledge function as power and simply shore up the institutions it models? Does it always remain within these institutions and disciplines, within traditional power, as Foucault suggests? Or can women's writing break the frame and rewrite power? We will argue that it can.

## Notes

1. For example, in March 2000, the historian Michelle Perrot pulled together a number of texts for the official French documentation service in Paris (La Documentation Française) in a volume entitled *An 2000: Quel bilan pour les femmes*? (The Year 2000: What is the Balance Sheet for Women?). La Documentation Française now devotes a section of its website www.ladocfrancaise.gouv.fr to articles on the contemporary situation of women.
2. Michelle Perrot, *Quel bilan pour les femmes?*, p. 7. Unless otherwise noted, all translations from French into English throughout this chapter and throughout this book are my own.
3. Gender is used most generally in this study in the sense of a cultural construction of the "feminine" and the "masculine" as conceptual configurations and identifications that can, of course, be common to both male and female discourse. However, in some cases, it does refer to biology or sex (male and female).
4. This summary draws on the journalist and historian Laure Adler's detailed but very readable exploration of attitudes toward political women in *Les Femmes Politiques* (Paris: Seuil, 1993).
5. Although the scope of this study does not permit such detailed comparative analysis, it would be of interest to compare Giroud and Bouchardeau's biographical and autofictional texts with male-authored texts: Giscard's 1994 novel or Mitterrand's many autobiographical and biographical accounts in which he positions himself as the "hero" of a novel (complete with second, secret, illegitimate family, hidden right-wing political past, and contested posthumous glory), or Alain Juppé's 1996 autobiographical work that attempts to convince the French public that despite his unpopularity and his reputation for being dry and unfeeling, this prime minister is a sensitive human being.
6. Michelle Perrot, *Quel bilan pour les femmes?*, p. 8.
7. Such a return to that which is kept repressed in the cultural unconscious, a movement that opinion polls, surveys, statistics, laws or knowledge of the institutional structures of a culture cannot predict, appears a legitimate object of study in a world in which archaic forms of ethnic, religious, and sexual exclusion continue to resurface from within seemingly rational political orders (as in Somalia, Rwanda, Bosnia, Kosovo, East Timor, Afghanistan).
8. I use the feminine form of *députée* except where *député* is used by authors I am quoting. Despite the recommendations of the commission formed by Yvette Roudy on the feminization of professional names, *députée* has not long been in common use in

France. The masculine form *député* is still used in the Cabinet lists in the 1996 *Encyclopédie des femmes politiques sous la Vième Rébublique* (Paris: Patrick Banon, 1996), nonetheless prefaced by "Anne-Marie Couderc, Ministre *déléguée* pour l'Emploi, *Chargée* des Droits de la femme." Although these feminine adjectives denoting adjunct status appear on the front cover, *Madame le ministre* remains the term of address for the minister. For the list of members of Cabinet, this becomes *ministre auprès du premier ministre, chargée des Droits de la Femme.* Consistency and coherence fall victim to the psychological difficulty of accepting the morphologically inoffensive form (*la*) *ministre* in official lists. Anne-Marie Couderc was also responsible for restoring the term of *Les Droits de la femme* (Woman's Rights), a regression in relation to Roudy's title of *Ministre des droits des femmes* or Wom*en*'s Rights, stressing the plural rather than single nature of women. By the end of 1997, Martine Aubry, Elisabeth Guigou, Catherine Trautmann, and Dominique Voynet—who finish in the top five of an *IPSOS-Le Point* (*Le Point*, 15 November 1997, p. 13) survey on approval ratings for the actions of political leaders, with a 59 percent approval for the leader, Martine Aubry—are using the title of *Madame la ministre.*

9. By 1996, one hundred and seventy-six women had sat in high political office. Although it seeks to be as comprehensive as possible, this study cannot pretend to be exhaustive; apart from the examination of the work of Jean Pascal, it does not examine in any detail the recent texts by male politicians (Jack Lang, for example) or the texts of male journalists in sympathy with the cause of women and with parity, although they are mentioned in passing.

# Part I

## Writing Women's Political History

# 1

# From the Revolution to the Franchise

## Pioneering Political Histories: Pascal and Bouchardeau

In writing *Pas d'histoire, les femmes?* (So Women Don't Have a History? 1977), Huguette Bouchardeau sets out to contest Simone de Beauvoir's claim that women have no history, based on the lack of published texts by women or on women in history. Bouchardeau's book represents one of the earliest attempts to write on the little explored history of the struggle for the civil equality of women. Huguette Bouchardeau was a forerunner as a presidential candidate, minister, and *députée* who retired from French national politics in 1993. Bouchardeau observes that, until recently, women's history has been obscured by official political histories, or by traditional political memoirs and political biographies, held to be the norm. Since Bouchardeau's first book there has been much academic debate on whether it is indeed possible to write a history of women and what it means to do so.[1] Bouchardeau's 1977 book was followed in 1979 by a political autobiography, *Un Coin dans leur monde* (A Corner in Their World), and in 1984 by the manuscript of *Les Femmes et le pouvoir* (Women and Power), a pioneering recovery of the story of women's struggle for the right to vote and hold political office.[2] Then in 1990, there came another exception in French literary history. Jean Pascal, a former *député*, published his own scholarly study, *Les Femmes députés de 1945 à 1988* (Women Deputies from 1945 to 1988), the first history of political women written by a male politician.

A comparison of these two early political histories on women in politics by political insiders reveals major differences both in their sources of documentation and chosen content. The ideological or interpretative contexts within which the two authors write result in quite dissimilar readings of women's political representation in France. In sympathy with the contemporary feminist project to recover "her story" from history, Bouchardeau sets out to expose the workings of the bias in history that keep certain interests (women's interests) from being heard. She grapples with the traditional shaping of preference for masculine representatives, and brings complex questions of feminine legitimacy to the surface for analysis. Her thematic focus on the exclusion, silencing, or mere absence that deny women's political existence is stated up front in the manuscript's opening quotation extracted from the 1795 Constitution: "No one is a good citizen if he is not first a good son, a good father, a good husband" (*Nul n'est bon citoyen s'il n'est pas bon fils, bon père, bon époux*). Despite other gains of the Revolution, such silencing by the powers in place meant that it would take another 150 years for women to accede to the rank of "French citizen."[3] Pascal's work is not so much concerned with such issues as with documenting the male franchise debates in the assemblies and the later presence of women and their portfolios.

Since Bouchardeau, there is increasing historical data to support the conclusion that women's situation of exclusion stemmed from the creation of a republican virtue based on the hierarchical (or patriarchal) family, a virtue born with the Revolution. This conclusion was adopted by the parity democracy movement of the last decade of the millennium. Such virile republican virtue was presented as being counter to a feminized and decadent *ancien régime*.[4] A similar silencing of women's public voices, seen as disorderly and radical, would occur again in reaction to the revolutionary movements in 1848. Bouchardeau's story concludes with an account of the repressive *Code Civil* (Napoleonic Code of Civil Law) at the beginning of the nineteenth century making women minors. For more than a century, in both France and Quebec, this code would suspend the hope that women had placed in the civil and political freedoms promised by the Revolution.

These two major works on suffrage and political representation also differ in form. Pascal's description of women parliamentarians is methodologically genealogical, devoted to the short politico-biographical sketches of the 141 women who held legislative office in France before 1988. An excerpt follows each portrait from a speech considered to be representative of the particular causes of that parliamentarian. A profusion of statistical charts on their party affiliations and the legislative effects of their presence make up the description of the female *députées*. If power is defined as the capacity to produce intended effects in others, such legislation can be taken as a crude measure of the extent of their power.[5] The apparently objective study is flanked by a long historical introduction and conclusion in which the franchise for women is justified by women's difference, defined as the need to extend the traditional virtues of the wife and mother, the "womanly woman" to the public forum, a relatively traditional view of the public role of women. On the other hand, Bouchardeau's texts invent a new structure. In *Un Coin dans leur monde*, for example, Bouchardeau alternates between a chapter that narrates her own experience as national secretary of the PSU party (Parti socialiste unifié) and a chapter that looks at the experience of women in political parties in general. What is implied by the alternating first and third person chapters is that her understanding of political power is based on interactions between the private and public spheres of life.

## *The Revolution*

The political histories constructed by Pascal and Bouchardeau do begin in the same place—with the Revolution, its challenge to existing power relations and the subsequent reaffirmation of patriarchal power. Pascal's story opens with a reference to Condorcet's enlightened support, from 1787 to 1789, for the right of women property-owners to vote. As a number of women historians will subsequently point out, certain women already enjoyed this right in the pre-Revolutionary era. Madame de Sévigné voted in Brittany in the seventeenth century on the basis of property. In Pascal's story, groups of feminists led by women such as Théroigne de Méricourt and Olympe de Gouges, called vociferously for equality of the sexes under the law—addressed in the *Déclaration des droits de la femme et de la citoyenne* (Declaration of the Rights of the Woman and Citizen) to Queen Marie-Antoinette in 1791—and they organized a women's delegation in 1792 asking for the right to equal education, majority at twenty-one, political equality, and divorce. Pascal's evocation of the heady agitation of the revolutionary period notes the fears aroused by disorderly women. The daring of the market women who marched on Versailles to force the royal family to return to the Louvre in Paris, the 154 groups of *amazones* ("women warriors") that formed around the country, and the Parisian women who joined the National Guard, are all presented as elements of subversion. Pascal focuses on these disorderly women but to conclude that ultimately they provoked negative reactions and repression. His study provides no analysis of this backlash. While Pascal does not focus on martyred heroines or provide a feminist analysis of the events and their backlash, his reading does still concur with Bouchardeau's insofar as he demonstrates that the Convention felt increasingly threatened by women's interference in the public sphere, by their vociferous contributions in the National Assembly, and by their presence at the foot of the guillotine. What the Convention wanted was to quickly send women home to their families and their domestic duties.

Huguette Bouchardeau's account of the Revolution is concerned with the analysis of what caused the backlash to female activism: women out of their place provoke anxiety, disorderly women arouse fears and subsequent fantasies of repression in both men and women committed to the status quo. Bouchardeau observes that in 1793 the Convention closed access to political clubs for women, forbade them to bear arms or wear the *cocarde* (significantly the symbols of equality, freedom, and citizenship) and ordered them to not congregate in groups of more than four or five or face imprisonment. Along with such limitations imposed upon women by the Convention, the backlash toward women predetermined, for example, the fate of Olympe de Gouges whose "disorderly" public speaking and writing of the *Declaration des droits de la femme et de la citoyenne*, lead to her death in 1793.

Most women historians since Bouchardeau have commented on the phenomenon of recurrent historical backlash against female activists, who were seen as especially dangerous when they aspired to independent political authority. For example, Laure Adler's 1993 journalistic history of women's political history, *Les Femmes Politiques*, summarizes the actions against disorderly women with perceptive humor. She finds that to ensure the status quo, the heads of a number of "dangerous" women (with social and political backgrounds as different as the too manipulatively "feminine" Queen Marie Antoinette and the too "masculine" Olympe de Gouges) were destined to fall into the baskets of so-called revolutionary Terror in 1793. Backlash also followed the defeat of the libertarian women of the Commune in 1871 and similarly characterized the authoritarian government of Vichy France in 1939, which again sent women back to their kitchens.

## The Impact of the Suffragists

According to Bouchardeau, claims for women's suffrage remained tenacious throughout the nineteenth century, even during the long period now defined by feminist writing as "Democracy without Women."[6] Once again, women's voices were heard most particularly at moments of revolution, in 1830, in 1848, and in 1870. Although Bouchardeau concedes that the demonstrations organized by French women throughout this period were less spectacular than those of the English suffragists, she insists on their importance. In contrast, Pascal sees little of real political importance happening for women in the nineteenth century. Pascal and Bouchardeau both make a reference to the *suffragette*, Eugénie Niboyet, who presided over the *Club des Femmes* and created the feminist newspaper *La Voix des Femmes* in 1848. Both writers also note the militant action of Jeanne Deroin who ran for office in the legislative elections of 1849, but it is only Bouchardeau who points out that Deroin's candidacy was illegal and therefore dangerous. While Pascal may make mention of Niboyet and Deroin, his attention is caught only momentarily by stridently militant feminism and is not captured at all by feminist activism. He is more concerned with the political import of new social movements, such as Fourier's utopian egalitarian community and his focus is on its idealization of feminine values. Pascal paints an optimistic picture of humanist or enlightened male support for women in the mid-nineteenth century. He quotes Victor Considérant's argument in parliament that, in a constitution that gives the right to vote to beggars and servants, it is illogical and unjust not to grant this right to women.

Pascal concedes that a decree passed in 1848—the year that men in France received "universal" franchise—was far removed from any attempt to advance the women's suffrage debate. The decree formally debarred women, identified as minors, from joining political groups or clubs of any kind and seems indicative of majority opinion. Two examples stand out in this regard: the forced closure of the newspaper *La Voix des Femmes* and the subsequent imprisonment of the editor Eugénie Niboyet and the introduction of the female suffrage debate into the Chamber in 1851 by Pierre Leroux. Pascal notes that the introduction of the debate was met by general hilarity, resulting in his observation that "even the socialists cannot agree on whether to distract women from their housework."[7] It would take a more feminist critical frame than that of Pascal's to later observe that revolutionary change for one (male) sector of the community has often created a correspondingly greater insistence on the maintenance of power relations within the traditional family.

Jean Pascal's research into the saga of legislative procrastination and misogyny that surround the suffrage issue is prefaced by his own eulogy to the difference that he sees as women's principal contribution to politics.

> The most basic reflection recognizes what women can bring to public life, their sensitivity, their unique approach to things and people, their passion, their transparent lack of self-interest, and their adherence to convictions. Reading their speeches gives an understanding of the wide range of their competence: any issue concerning women, the family, health, education, social conditions, relief of poverty.[8]

In 1990, this politician, sufficiently sympathetic to women's contribution to public life to write their history, still took the particularity of women's spheres of action for granted. Bouchardeau's analysis, on the other hand, situates the power of the first wave of feminism precisely in their recognition that, to use the words of Evelyn Sullerot, private life (like public life), far from being a matter of individual choice, has been organized for women by men. This covert conservative ideological frame is as much part of Pascal's story as the recovery of feminist activism and heroism is part of Bouchardeau and Adler's left-wing tales.

The moves to recover "herstory" from history result in Bouchardeau reconstructing the life of Georges Sand from the writer's diaries and publishing this in the form of a biography, in investigations into the life of Madeleine Pelletier, and in the publication of the story of Hélène Brion, a trade-unionist and pioneer in education. In their individual persons and places, these recovered figures come to embody the difficulties, the hostilities, and the contradictions faced by pioneer women prepared to attack male fortresses and thereby place themselves outside the boundaries of the prescribed feminine roles of their time. Many of the self-sacrificing heroines that feminist scholarship is bringing back to life from the documents of newly opened archives are portrayed as developing new qualities and attributes of power in their struggle for emancipation and equality.

A similar recovery of "herstory" is found in Adler's work. The journalist's text brings together as martyrs to an exalted if sometimes excessive cause, Louise Michel, the "Red-Virgin" on the 1870 barricades, the heroic figure of the crusading Flora Tristan, and the energetic, male-attired, self-educated doctor, and militant Madeleine Pelletier. Adler goes on to devote half of her book to creating a gallery of portraits of the different contemporary political women whose lives illuminate aspects of the story of women and power.

## The Concept of Difference and the Stories of Suffrage

Since the two studies by Pascal and Bouchardeau in the late 1980s, the relation of women to political power and feminine difference has begun to interest many different commentators on the French scene. From right and left, feminist and antifeminist perspectives, these writers usually focus their analysis on questions of gender difference. It is argued that the "difference" that lead to sex-role separation between public and private and that served as the central argument for the exclusion of women from public office throughout the period of the franchise debate is an eternal difference. A difference fixed in and justifying unequal and hierarchical relations between the genders, and the division of the social world into masculine and feminine spheres. This conception of difference was largely unchallenged in the work of conservative writers until many of the recent left-wing or feminist histories set out to show this concept of difference to be an abusive one and to construct other more useful conceptions of feminine difference and use of power. This chapter will now begin to develop the argument that these texts constitute a form of empowerment or, at the least, a potentially productive form of counter-power.

The parliamentary debates in the first half of the twentieth century provide many examples of the ways conventional images were used and the concept of difference was constructed to keep women out of politics. Bouchardeau echoes claims found within Michelle Coquillat's study of women of influence, *Qui sont-elles? Femmes d'influence, Femmes de pouvoir* (Who Are They? Women of Influence. Women of Power) and Michèle Sarde's *Regards sur les Françaises* (Looking at French Women) that it is the premium placed on being feminine that most dissuades French women from entering the masculine world of politics. The monstrosity of iron maidens who usurp direct power or sirens who exercise occult power is omnipresent in cultural representations, although the ideological shaping implicit in these representations is hidden.[9] The conventions (courtly love, *galanterie*) that celebrate women's traditional qualities or idealize her as angel of the home can also be used to argue against any extension of her roles. On the one hand it was claimed in the Assemblies that women would bring their caring feminine sensibility and charitable disposition, their "treasures of patience and gentleness" (*trésors de patience et de douceur* according to A. Gourgu, Socialist, 1922) to the political arena enhancing the role of the mother in the education of men. On the other, it was argued that female fragility and instability were a danger to public life just as the scalpel would be dangerous in the hands of a woman doctor.

The concept of merit also enters the debate. Men, claimed one speaker, bear the responsibilities of military service and women do not; therefore, men deserve political representation in recognition of their efforts whereas motherhood is a "woman's joy and reward." The right to bear arms is clearly equated by this speaker with citizenship. Both sides of the debate use women's difference and not rights as their argument for or against women's right to equality with men. In 1932, E. de Las Cases argued that women were attaining a respectable cultural level and would perhaps catch up with and become the educational equals of men. To support his claim he cited the existence of 3,442 women students in the humanities in 1929, 974 in the sciences, 1,430 in medicine, 1,637 in pharmacy, 1,686 in law and 300 women lawyers!

To combat the argument that most other Western democracies allowed women to vote, French women are presented as a special case, as objects of adulation. As Dr. F. Labrousse stated in 1922: "Latin women, more honored than women in the North, do not have the same reasons for making demands" (*La femme latine, plus honorée que dans le Nord, n'a pas les mêmes raisons de réclamations*). If Latin women expect to remain prized and honored creatures, they must accept the non-public role that this entails. The sex-war threat is implicit: "Women keep their prestige, all their beauty and influence, they are happy, when they remain womanly."[10] The unnaturalness of non-feminine women was depicted by one parliamentarian as a biological danger for the survival of the race. If women are given political power, reproduction becomes impossible. The arguments are reported by Pascal, but he stands at an objective distance and provides no comment or analysis. In contrast to Pascal, Bouchardeau looks critically at this position in which feminine virtues are held up, traditional images of femininity drawn on, sex-roles established to subsequently serve to justify the exclusion of women from politics.

Pascal's neutral silences and the dire predictions quoted below from Proudhon, an influential nineteenth-century politician, suggest the anxiety provoked by female suffrage. Moves to change power structures seem to have struck fear in many men and, indeed, in many conservative women in the nineteenth century:

> The leveling of the sexes leads to general desolation. Unless there is a radical difference in their spheres of action, there is neither family, nor marriage.

> The heart of man must be full of the will to command in his home: without this man will disappear.[11]

The 1901 bill proposed by the republican Jean Gautret, giving the right to vote to unmarried, widowed, and divorced women, suggests that the deepest fears provoked by votes for women were those concerning men's potential loss of authority and dominance in the stable home. Excluding married women would also make a female electoral majority impossible and limit the possible influence of the Church. It is the threat to the family hierarchy that continues to be the central concern in antisuffrage discourses, even though women have a seemingly protected place, a place naturalized and internalized by socialization. Most of the accounts by the contemporary feminist historians deconstruct the supposed naturalness, safety, and equality of this traditional place for women, while arguing for positive benefits from the justice and equality gained in the "leveling of the sexes."

## *Beyond Difference?*

A number of questions are implicit in all of the new research and writing on the franchise. Did the French concept of the republican family and of the complementarity of the sexes work for women? Did women's activism make a difference? That is, did women capture power or was this power withheld and then granted regardless of their efforts? Which leaders, or movements, radical or conservative, male or female, were most effective? Could suffrage have eventually come from within a party? Most generally, all the histories of women claim that the decrease in the importance of dowry, major changes in the workplace, women's campaigns and discourses disturbed and influenced both the private and the political scene throughout this period. All this happened against the backdrop of the legalizing of divorce passed by the Assembly in 1882 but blocked for two years by a Senate generally hostile to women's rights.

In the France of the 1930s, although they could not vote or be elected, women could be appointed to government service. As the first woman to hold high political office under such conditions, Cécile Brunschvicg was herself clear in her criticisms of the political system. Hers were the arguments on difference that would later be so commonly repeated. Women's greater civic pride, commitment to action, and lesser political ambition would bring something new to the political scene. In this respect, Brunschvicg echoed the claims of her predecessors and, indeed, of her male supporters. In the male political arena, women witness verbal and rhetorical idealism on the one hand and, on the other, political and electoral opportunism.

> For us women, who see things in simple and practical terms, and who, fortunately, still have a new spirit in political matters, it seemed that achieving

> a program of social progress and national interest was the precise goal of every party and that only the different methods of bringing this about explained the multiple groupings. But we discover that a party program is scarcely more than an indication of the general tendencies of the party and that the central question is not how it will be put in place but who will put it into place. In other words, exercising power has taken such an important place in the parties' preoccupations that they seem sometimes to completely forget the precise goal that first brought them together.[12]

Aspects of Brunschvicg's criticism of the political world, framed in terms of the absence of positive feminine difference, more practical, less self-interested, more moral, more patriotic and less sectarian, still dominate the corpus of interviews with both nominated and elected political women in the second half of the twentieth century.[13]

Pascal observes that the Republic was, in fact, not put in danger by the granting of women's right to vote and to hold office in 1945. Mariette Sineau's secular account insists rather on the fact that the Catholic Church retained a strong hold on the hearts and minds of women into the 1950s and that women's votes remained conservative until 1981. Bouchardeau's story, for its part, concludes that French women had to accept political rights imposed from above without their own direct efforts appearing to bear fruit. This would continue to be a constant and specific phenomenon in French politics, she claims, with its tradition of the *fait du prince*. That is, the male legislator or politician would always prefer to "grant as reward what ought to be recognized as a right."[14] The central theme of Mariette Sineau's *Mitterrand et les Françaises: un rendez-vous manqué* (Mitterrand and French Women: A Missed Rendezvous) is justly about this deeply entrenched character of paternalism persisting in the modern French state. Françoise Giroud's analysis is also one of a paternalistic state and an as yet imperfect democracy. Ideology (left or right positioning) is clearly a significant factor in these readings.

## *The Problem of Gender*

We belong to history before we write it; the particularity of time, place, and gendered experience affects what is written. As this chapter follows the story of the suffrage, it also attempts to trace the way in which ideology, class, nationality, and readership feed into and modify the various texts that write the story of the suffrage. But might the choice of texts itself be open to criticism? Does Pascal's non-feminist approach make him an easy target, a straw man set up merely to be shot down again? Should Pascal's work be allowed to serve implicitly as a model for a male text?

Given the relative lack of interest of male politicians and historians to date in focusing on the story of women's suffrage, Pascal's work is one of the rare examples available for study. His is the only study of women in politics by a male politician before the 1990s and the earliest scholarly study devoted to French women's suffrage by a man. Pascal's statistically useful research on women in politics follows other work by this former *député* on the French political scene that also makes rigorous use of the parliamentary archives—most notably a history of clerical political representation. Moreover, Pascal's book lends itself remarkably well to mapping the contrast between right-wing and left-wing, and traditional and non-traditional approaches to writing on women and power. Pascal documents the entry of 141 women into the world of politics using a traditional public source, the parliamentary archives. In contrast, Bouchardeau is writing a new history of a democracy without women. Her story, like most of the feminist women's histories that followed, is a story explaining and attempting to remedy their own major absence from histories. Bouchardeau's sources are often less official, less traditional than those of Pascal: she relies on unpublished documents, autobiographies, police records, and the women's press.

Women's texts, we have observed, integrate both private and public histories to write about the struggle for franchise. In its choice of local sources and attention to the small personal details, women's history in general, and more particularly, Adler's journalistic *Les Femmes Politiques*, more resemble annals than they do traditional/formal grand history. Adler personalizes her story and acknowledges her own gendered investment in its telling, as does Bouchardeau. In contrast, Pascal's authoritative scholarly neutrality, his charts and encyclopedic structures efface the personal agenda (Catholic religion) and politics (conservative) behind the writing of his history/story. The main protagonists of the two histories of the franchise are also different—male politicians and their debates in Pascal, the suffragists and suffragettes as heroines and martyrs in the women's writing. Pascal's text is shaped by his desire to affirm the Christian values inherent in a traditional kind of gender specificity—he presents as an absolute given the fact that no women would wish to leave her children for the abstraction of parliamentary debate. In fact, in Pascal's description, the most striking difference that a woman's participation introduces into the political arena is their elegance and agreeable physical appearance (*quelques élégantes silhouettes*). The well-intentioned hit parade of women's names that follows concludes with the comment "among others who will surely excuse us for their absence, and not forgetting the spectacular metamorphosis of Huguette Bouchardeau." Such unselfconscious and double-edged *galanterie* suggests Pascal's implicit belief that, as Duverger put it to me in a personal discussion, sex will always interfere to create noise in communication between politicians of different sexes.

Another difference evident in texts on political women in France is found in the divergent treatment of knowledge. The form of Pascal's work reflects his belief in, and the traditional understanding of, knowledge as objective, neutral, and universal. The "new histories" of political women, of which Bouchardeau's work can be seen as a kind of model or prototype, are most generally constructed in reaction both against the history in place, and against certain traditional and apparently objective ways of writing it. Bouchardeau and Adler's writings both deconstruct Pascal's premise that women have a natural and universal instinct for mothering and for homebound activities. Elisabeth Badinter's studies demonstrate that women have not always and everywhere been naturally devoted mothers, citing, for example, the eighteenth-century practice of aristocratic and middle-class mothers sending their babies to a wet-nurse in the country, very often to die.[15] The contemporary subversion of the absolute imperative of the maternal function is somewhat in the tradition of Simone de Beauvoir. This questioning occurs alongside a new preoccupation with respecting differences in women's lives as well as the affirming of the urgent need to help those who so desire to reconcile motherhood and political activity.

Bouchardeau's history makes clear that consciously or unconsciously women have long used the system (and traditional gender difference and discourse) by turning the system against itself. For example, one suffrage argument was that men should be subject to the rules of fidelity, chastity, control, and temperance that were imposed on women. This argument was made alongside the traditional claim made by many women that votes for women would improve the situation of the orphaned, the poor, the neglected, and mistreated.

Pascal's story is one of linear progress. Bouchardeau and Adler are more cautious about progress and victories are seldom presented as linear. History in their accounts shows a clear, repeating pattern. Women's increased place in public life in times of crisis is followed by their subsequent exclusion as the established order reasserts itself. Whereas the current of modernization and globalization is favorable to the penetration by women into the old patriarchal hierarchies of power, the structures of prestigious male institutions, parties, and what has been called a techno-bureaucracy, in particular, are still largely closed to women. Bouchardeau and Adler suggest that backlash is still as probable as progress.

If there are claims to truth in Bouchardeau's stories or the later feminist accounts, it might be argued that this truth does not derive from the discovery of any total and coherent, unchanging or essential history. The woman-centered frame and its largely female audience become consciously part of the story it investigates. It creates a narrative that does not attempt to conceal its origins in a political project of rewriting knowledge and is also a project for the construction of a new place for women in the public forum.

In his *Esthétique et théorie du roman*, Mikail Bakhtin has argued that any text is constructed as a mosaic of quotations and involves the absorption and transformation of other texts to which it responds. The writer adopts discourses already populated by the social intentions of others and uses them to suit his/her own purposes. In Bakhtinian literary theory, such a "dialogic" text involves an interaction with the inner alterity that inhabits any text. This intertextual character of the text, absorbing, rereading, and displacing other texts, is evident in the writings discussed in this book. It is found in Pascal's interaction with Christian texts, and in the writing of women's political histories, both in response to and the rewriting of the established voices of men, and in the discovery and rereading of the lost voices of women of an earlier generation.

Gérard Genette, a French narrative theorist has argued that the *récit* or narration (effacing any reference to the source that produces it) that characterized a nineteenth-century and traditional twentieth-century literary narrative striving to replace the subjective speaker/writer by a third-person impersonal and objective discourse, has been largely replaced in the twentieth century by the first-person *discours*, or speech (assumed by a real or by a fictive speaker).[16] The narrative voice, he claims, no longer manages to conceal itself behind an anonymous narrative but is progressively becoming a subjective or personally organized discourse. Pascal's text seeks to be a *récit*, or narrative of absolute objectivity; the new women's texts tend to move away from the traditional third-person omniscient narrative to a situated, first-person story (*discours*).

The non-traditional narratives are constructing themselves in interaction with other recent versions of women's history as these begin to appear publicly in interviews and media programs and in libraries. Themes such as the recovery of lost voices, of unsung heroines, of the debt owed to unruly women and the celebration of women's achievements through political activism circulate from text to text along with the sense of writing as a surrogate political action or as empowerment. Many of these themes remain present even in the texts by conservative women.

Returning to our initial question of whether these differences can be seen as deriving in part from gender or whether they should simply be ascribed to the conservative versus radical paradigms, to the extent that gender is always a determining factor among a set of others, it will certainly play some role. It would, of course, be quite imprudent to take Pascal as representative of the whole male gender, or indeed Bouchardeau as representative of the female, but what both have to say is affected by their gender contexts. Further investigation of women's political histories continues to show the impact of different contexts upon the teller and thus on the told tale.

## *The French Twist in the Woman Question*

Just as period, party or ideology, reading influences, gender and class affect the narratives surrounding women and power, so too do national and culture-specific contexts inflect the writing and reading of the suffrage story. The work of American historians introduces one such particular perspective to the history of suffrage in France. Joan Landes, for example, has described the very distinctive manner in which the

French bourgeois Republic was constituted in, and through, a discourse on gender relations: "Whereas in France educated women of the upper-class of the *ancien régime* could hold their own in the formulation of debate about the future character of the nation, in the absence of any organized women's movement in America, there was no debate on women's rights before the writing of the Constitution."[17]

Karen Offen finds a "French twist" in the fact that the issue of votes for women's rights was articulated earlier in France than in virtually any other nation in reaction to the forum/*foyer* (public/private) separation and women's disengagement from civil or property rights, and yet suffrage came very late[18]: "The Constitution of 1791 effectively dismissed women from political life" and Talleyrand "framed his program for national education accordingly, insisting on the necessity of women remaining in domestic roles for the common good."[19] The Jacobins repressed any remaining petitioning, speaking, publishing, or political activity by women. The explicit exclusion of women in 1848 confirmed the profound (masculine) gendering of the notion of citizenship in France[20]: "The electoral law we have made is the broadest that any people on the earth has ever made to convey on the people the exercise of *the supreme right of man*, his own sovereignty. We have only respected the exclusions that exist in all other nations."[21]

Offen finds that in the 1890s, Hubertine Auclert's newly invented term *féminisme*, used to affirm the rights of the feminine gender, had become common currency. This attested to the existence of a burgeoning debate. But after 1900, the suffragist movements were predominantly characterized by a traditional concept of femininity, the refusal of militancy, and the insistence on ladylike campaigning. Progress, then, is not linear. Offen believes that the existing regime of maternal protection in France, in contrast to the quasi-absence of any government support in the U.S., stems from the post-revolutionary notion of citizen-mother. This maternal protection was at its apogee when the suffrage bill became a casualty of the outbreak of the First World War.

Some form of suffrage had seemed accessible after a massive public rally held in 1913. The hierarchy of the Catholic Church, seeing its own possible advantage, had somewhat ambiguously lifted its opposition to female suffrage in 1919. But even the conservative feminine platform of maternity and family protection issues was not sufficient to overcome the intransigent resistance to the suffrage movement of the anticlerical, socially conservative Radicals in the republican Senate during the interwar years. Quoting the historical work of Klejman and Rochefort, Offen concludes that none of the very varied strategies of a large, organized, and active suffrage movement, paid off, at least in the shorter term. The final irony was an enfranchisement that came about to preserve republican institutions against a communist threat.

The parliamentary story of the first half of the twentieth century (1901–1945) on which Pascal's history of women in politics is centered, is portrayed by him as a drawn-out, unproductive, and somewhat discomforting affair. Debate in the Assembly began in 1901 on the principle of women's right to vote in local elections. It continued until 1919 when a majority consensus was reached at that point. The Senate then refused the bill. Proposals were again put forward in 1922, 1925, 1932, 1935, and 1936, but women's suffrage would continue to be blocked by the hostility and delaying tactics of the Senate for another two decades.[22] Pascal presents the debate on women's enfranchisement as this unfolds within the male parliament in some detail but without analysis. His choice and orchestration of these parliamentary arguments, which stretch over almost half a century, do, however, reveal much about the ideological climate of the period within the two houses of parliament.

If Offen and Pascal cast some doubt on the immediate or practical efficacy of French suffrage movements, other European suffrage historians paint a different story. Bard and Reynolds, for example, argue that by changing perceptions and political conditions it was the prewar movements that made the postwar granting of suffrage possible.

The well-known French feminist historian, Michelle Perrot, also seeks explanations for the paradox of France—pioneer in the development of democracy, engaged early in the discourse on gender relations, yet laggard in respect to full democracy for women. The reasons given for this paradox include the Latin character of French culture, the Catholic influence, and the very nature of the individualistic democracy adopted in France, as opposed to the more group-oriented democracy in Anglo-Saxon countries. Perrot's overview of women's history, in which she situates the roots of the present political "deficit," enumerates the factors that shaped the nineteenth-century social and political situation, including "bio-politics," the divine order of things, and the division of labor. Perrot asserts that the concept of social necessity and complementarity of the sex roles strengthened the domination of women by men in that century.[23]

In the twentieth century, the new proletarian heroes were of little help to the women's cause. Perrot claims the men of iron and marble made feminism bourgeois, isolating the movement from large numbers of women. The collective superego discouraged the majority of women from interest in the public forum. Despite this, Perrot concludes, an active feminist movement claiming political rights continued to strengthen in the twentieth century and this movement was a factor for change.[24]

## Writing as Activism

### *The Revolution*

The new body of texts on women in France takes on very different forms—some are academic histories, others are journalistic pieces for a general or a female public, others again are political manifestos. Many have explicit didactic or political purposes, notably Françoise Gaspard's 1992 history of the franchise *Au Pouvoir, citoyennes! Liberté, Egalité, Parité* (To Power, Citizens! Liberty, Equality, Parity).[25] The former Socialist mayor of Dreux and present academic, in collaboration with the militant Anne Le Gall and with Claude Servan-Schreiber, wrote this piece as a feminist manifesto for parity democracy. Whether it be the women's petition to the Queen in 1789, the march to Versailles, women's assemblies in the streets and clubs, or Olympe de Gouges's proclamation of the *Droits de la femme et de la citoyenne* in 1791, all the events discussed in the book are evoked in terms of heroism. Gaspard's analysis of the Revolution, along with her portraits of martyrs and heroines, functions to support her ideological campaign for parity.[26] Her critical feminist history of the Revolution concurs with both Adler's and Bouchardeau's theses on the impact of the revolutionary activity of women. Although the Revolution did grant the major rights to marry freely, to divorce, and to inherit, Gaspard argues that such changes occurred less to advance women's rights than in the name of antidespotism, secular society, and anti-aristocratic inheritance. Gaspard situates women's civil inequality in what she presents as a failed Revolution, which forced women to be represented by men and left "old maids" or widows deprived of legal status.

The writing of women's history has been inspiring other rewritings in a snowballing process. *Femmes et Citoyennes* (Women and Citizens), coauthored in 1995 by Patricia Latour, Monique Houssin, and Nadia Tovar again celebrates the heroines of the history of women's accession to citizenship.[27] Like Adler's book, *Femmes et Citoyennes* is divided into a history of the franchise and a series of interviews with contemporary women decision-makers. The work identifies itself and its projects explicitly as being women-centered. Elisabeth Weissman's 1995 *Les Filles, on n'attend plus que vous!* (Young Women, We're Waiting Just for You!) with its brief introduction to the history of women's representation is similarly pedagogic and addressed particularly to women but in the place of portraits from the past, it presents extracts from interviews with contemporary political women, particularly from the left wing.

The earlier writings of Louise Michel, the heroine of the barricades of the 1870 revolution, illustrate the complexities of "the woman question" even among women. For the messianic Louise Michel, class was of greater import than gender, although her refusal to identify with gender causes did not stop attacks on her feminism. Known as the "Red Virgin," Michel believed that the two sexes, whose union she sought in the liberation of the people, had different relations to power: "Men would have palavered until the end of the world, women didn't ask if something was possible but if it was useful."[28] Closer to reality, better at organization, more attuned to feeling, women govern without sound and fury. Louise Michel refused to run for a specific office, preferring to concentrate her energies on the universal revolutionary struggle.

The constancy with which even the most exceptional and non-conformist of women internalize certain of the conceptions of femininity of their time is striking. Yet writing out of her own experience, Michel is far from many of the received truths about women. She confessed to a love of danger and risk, arguing that (for special reasons) women may well enjoy revolt and revolution. According to Adler, Michel behaved "like a man" on the barricades. She later became a leader of the deported *Communards* in New Caledonia. There Michel was involved in both writing and transcribing Melanesian myths and helping set up local schools for Melanesian children—very much in a feminine tradition of caring and educating. It was to ward off criticism for what was considered a somewhat reprehensible and masculine attraction to power, as much as from idealism, that Michel added an observation that most contemporary women politicians will repeat in their writings: "It is true, perhaps, that women like rebellions. We are no better than men in respect to power, but power has not yet corrupted us."[29] In women, the argument goes, moral ends temper the use of power.

The boldness of the *pétroleuses*, the revolutionary women who were active participants in the Paris Commune of 1870, that is, in the first proletarian revolution, resulted in their imprisonment, deportation or execution. The dominant accusation made against them as against Michel was that their public disorderly behavior "profaned" the "honor of their sex." The charge, as during the Revolution, was that women were out of their place, the appeal is to a conservative position on feminine honor. Adler notes a split that the Commune opened between revolutionary working-class women and the middle-class activists: the middle-class activists rejected the extreme character of their attempted social revolution but responded to the discourse of honor and the accusation of lack of "womanliness."

## *The Conservative Patriarchal Order Threatened*

Further evidence of different approaches to the "woman question" is seen in the years immediately prior to enfranchisement. Despite its three women *secrétaires d'Etat*, Cécile Brunschvicg, Suzanne Lacore, and Irène Joliot-Curie, the short-lived left-wing coalition Popular Front government of 1936 clearly had political doubts about female suffrage and women in power. Although the time was ripe and the SFIO (section française de l'internationale ouvrière, a precursor of the Parti socialiste) found itself in a position of sufficient political and moral strength to overcome the resistance of the Senate for the first time, no one insisted that Léon Blum put the vote for women on his agenda. Blum, himself the author of a radical study on women and marriage, was clear in his pronouncement that "Women must accede to power not from the bottom but from the top." Adler's suspicious reading of this period is that, although Blum's appointment of three women to his cabinet is symbolically important, it may, in fact, have served as the half-measure (strategy or indifference? she asks) that allowed him to avoid addressing the issue while claiming credit for his tokenism.

Besides citing the enviable position of French women and the charm and superiority of French manners in defense of the status quo, the Senate debates on women's franchise brought more pragmatic concerns to the surface. Not only did women not have the preparation or the capacity to vote but, as voters, they would dangerously outnumber men. The minority would become the majority. For this reason, out of fear for their survival and that of their kind, many of the Senate members supported only those propositions that required women to be of a certain age or status to be eligible for voting rights.

Arguments for and against women's political participation were often both rooted in women's traditional roles. On the one hand, it was claimed that women's practical good sense would be beneficial (for the balancing of budgets, for example), and that far from disparaging their new voting partners, husbands would come to listen to their wives and learn to appreciate them more. On the other hand, it was feared that wives would usurp paternal authority altogether or no longer be fully committed and available to their husbands and families. Political life would turn woman, the natural guide and consolation of man, away from her normal family role, which could provoke violent disagreements and, ultimately, the rejection of marriage. According to this argument, giving the vote to women would threaten both the family and the race.

Other less consciously articulated fears of losing male privileges and power or losing security and protection for the female include the argument in the Senate that the family, not the individual, was the foundation of society. A significant group favored the family vote, arguing that the father should be given as many votes as he had children. The fear was expressed that in the proposed new order, the father would play only an episodic role in the life of his child, and the child's name would become that of the mother. Whereas woman is a divine creature of instinct and intuition. If she were to become equal to less refined men, traditional *galanterie* would vanish and "feminism would kill femininity." The patriarchal order, threatened, would retaliate, creating a situation detrimental to women and children and to the progress of the human race. Beyond the conservative reaction against any weakening of the traditional patriarchal relationships, many of the general anxieties were that women's presence in public places would bring disorder, or that the "promiscuity" of the sexes would bring domestic gender war into ordered public life. These arguments appear retrospectively to be emotionally based rationalizations based on self-interest and fear of change.

In the first half of the twentieth century, a period that saw the determined secularization of the state, the influence of the Church on women was widely considered to be a major obstacle to their enfranchisement. Bouchardeau's text concurs with Pascal's that one of the great ironies of the battle for the ballot is that both left-wing politicians (more sympathetic to the cause of women's suffrage) and right-wing politicians (generally negative toward the women's movement) recognized the probable conservative voting propensities of a female electorate. Although the crusaders for women's votes argued that there was no reason for women not to be good republicans equal to their fathers, husbands and brothers, women's enfranchisement does appear to have been seen as a real threat to hard-won secular republican institutions.

The parliamentary debate on female suffrage was couched mainly within a conservative male political discourse based on a particular conception of sexual difference and on self-interested concerns to protect the status quo. The issue of women's human rights or of a universal right to equality and social justice had little place in the debate. Legally, married women were still under the tutelage of their husbands. Even the pro-suffrage lobby based its case for equity strategically on the positive aspects of womanliness or good housekeeping: the uniting of the mind of man and the heart of woman would make for the best government.

## *Nineteenth-Century Women Writers*

Laure Adler discusses a number of woman writers who had a distinct impact on the nineteenth century. These include Pauline Roland, who died in exile in Algeria despite protest by Victor Hugo, and Jeanne Deroin who helped found, write, and direct the first women's newspaper, *La Voix des femmes*. This publication argued for women's economic independence, equality of wages, and free secular education for all. Jeanne Deroin was an active feminist who sought signatures in favor of the appointment of women ministers and helped Désirée Gay and Eugénie Niboyet produce their newspaper advocating women's right to vote. Adler includes the texts of another middle-class supporter of Saint-Simon's movement, Eugénie Niboyet and the aristocratic and solitary Flora Tristan who well before Marx tirelessly proselytized for the class struggle in her travels across France as a self-appointed spokesperson for the poor and disinherited. There was also Georges Sand, who worked with the Provisional Government and promoted social revolution in her articles in *Le Bulletin de la République*. These women, like the journalist and historian who recovered their texts, recognized the importance of writing. Of Sand's activism through writing, Adler writes: "She knew that the word establishes rights that violence could not by itself win."[30] Although Sand was later written out of a literary history focused on Realism as an "Idealist," she was a very widely read and a popular writer in her own time. And Sand has recently been rediscovered, largely by women's literary scholarship and her idealism reassessed positively. Sand's mixture of carefully articulated practicality and idealism would appear to have inspired contemporary women's work and she has been claimed both as a literary and a political mother.[31]

Georges Sand argued that women cared little for power politics, internal party competition, abstract causes, long speeches, polemics, vanity, and winning for its own sake. Rather, women wanted greater liberty, social justice between classes, and a fairer distribution of wealth. Women, she claimed, sought to reconcile interests and make concrete improvements. Sand finally renounced masculine politics in favor of writing: "I will never have what is called a passion for politics. My only passion is for ideas."[32] This interest in the higher moral ground or the indirect power of ideas and writing prefigures a common contemporary reaction by women to the disillusionment with, and limitations of, public office and reappears in the discourses around parity. Huguette Bouchardeau, who adopts Sand as a "mother," also ultimately withdrew from politics to devote herself to writing and founded her own small publishing press (Editions HB) with the same belief as that of Sand and Adler in the empowering value of the recovery and dissemination of women's stories.

## Empowerment Theory and Counter-Power in the Writing of New Histories

Given the traditional prestige of ideas and literature in France, male politicians, of course, also write, but mostly about their political memories upon leaving office. François Mitterrand, a passionate reader and author of numerous autobiographies, professed to have been tempted to give up politics for writing, although he never did so. A small number of male academics and authors have followed in Jean Pascal's footsteps in writing histories of women. They include, among others, the historians and political scientists Georges Duby and Maurice Duverger, the politician Jack Lang, and the journalist Maurice Maschino.[33]

How useful, then, is the term of "empowerment" for our understanding of the stakes of writing women's history? Much of the theorizing in political science, social science, history, philosophy, and, indeed, literary studies has turned on the measurement, distribution, and meaning of power. Feminist theorists have generally critiqued the "androcentric" aspects of theories of power and attempted to rewrite power closer to what Foucault might call the "subjugated knowledge" of women's experience.[34] A recent feminist theory of "empowerment" presents gender roles as the primary model for relations of domination-subordination. Joan Scott summarizes a version of empowerment theory as follows: "because men and women do not have the same access to resources that are associated with power and because they are socialized to use their power differently, gender becomes implicated in the conception and construction of power itself."[35] Nancy Hartsock, Janet Flammang, and Jane Jacquette[36] define feminine empowerment as "power to" rather than "power over", seeing traditional power as an unacceptable zero-sum game where one person's gain is another's loss.[37] Like the work of Bouchardeau, the "empowerment" models demonstrate a will to modify and particularize the public frame of definition of power. Sarah Hoagland, for example, argues her preference for a "power-from-within" version, defined "as a matter of centering and remaining steady in our environment as we choose how we direct our energy" in a personal frame of self-transforming.[38] Hilary Lips's evocation of the mistrust felt by women toward powerful people or institutions that impose their will on others (top down) repeats concerns prevalent in the writings of many of our politicians.[39] Luce Irigaray goes further with her theory that liberation lies in women's "breath" or spirit, the rich interiority or spirituality that allows empathy and the ability to welcome the other while staying different and separate.[40]

In its assumption that women use power differently than men, empowerment theory appears to diverge significantly from postmodern constructionist theory. But even in a Foucauldian analysis, power can give rise to counter-power. This is the organization within established power or knowledge and often at the local level or at the level of the body of a resistance to power and a new knowledge. Foucault sees counter-power, like power, as a historical and culturally relative construction that develops in relation to established power and, like power, is potentially both oppressive and productive.[41] Counter-power is not gendered but it is peculiarly open to minorities. Although the scope of this study does not allow for anything more than a very schematic discussion of these concepts, both feminine empowerment and Foucauldian counter-power can be argued to be at work in the new histories of women.

But, if the content of the new body of texts is sufficient to give them the status of counter-power, what would determine whether this content is oppressive or productive? Is the traditional conception of feminine difference oppressive and the difference given value by Sand or Bouchardeau productive? Political women have recognized the power inherent in the distribution of knowledge in their attempt to create new knowledge through their writing. Like Bouchardeau's political writing, many write from within the institution but aim to change the routined, habituated mode, seeking to subvert the norms, the old apparently objective and non-gendered universal knowledge. Although the process was ongoing throughout the nineteenth century, the critical mass of writers (and readers) appears never to have been sufficient to inflect social knowledge, enough, for example, to bring about women's suffrage. The groups of French literary feminists who attempted to work outside a male-dominated society in the 1970s and later in the women's studies departments at the Universities of Paris VII and Paris VIII, also failed to reach a wide enough public to change perceptions.

The new histories are challenging the content of traditional masculine history, rewriting the Revolution, the rise of democracy and the implementation of civil and political equality from the perspective of women, that is, the voice/the vote excluded. The discourse of political history is becoming increasingly transparent and what is beginning to show itself is the power of story—the narrativizing strategies that construct continuous, coherent, meaningful new narratives from the documents discovered. The theorist Hayden White has argued that in traditional historiography, narrative is what signals the objectivity, seriousness, and realism of historical texts and serves to make moral judgments. These stories about women in the public forum also narrativize (make realistic) and moralize (make true) as they inscribe a new story into the webs of established history and give it authority. The events are real and true, less because they occurred (although this matters) than because they are selected and ordered in a plot that gives them significance and allows the reader to perceive "the end" of the feminist moral as necessarily already inscribed from the beginning. And if, as Foucault claimed, power is synonymous with knowledge, then the new knowledge, incorporated as particular configurations into these new histories—figures for example, of women's rationalized exclusion, of her protest, her martyrdom, of heroic change, of parity—is beginning to compete with the old content for power and authority. A study on the transformation of historical consciousness[42] argues that "historical narratives no less than fictional narratives serve, in one way or other, to legitimize an actual or ideal social reality," suggesting that the truth of history is to be found less in its ability to produce a faithful record of some single past than in its own internal system of describing and structuring events in such a way as to transform our view of experience.[43]

The next part of our saga follows the stories surrounding the difficult passage of French women from winning the right to vote, to the right to represent and hold high political office. Narrative theory makes a case for the view that history and society are interpreted or "read" through the interpretative paradigms of our culture much as we read texts. Within this emerging body of texts and the new interpretative paradigms it seeks to establish, may lie the power to re-read and perhaps to remake history.

## Notes

1. See the work of M. Perrot, J. Scott and S. Reynolds who have addressed the question of women's history with specific reference to France.
2. In 1993, Huguette Bouchardeau gave me a photocopy of her virtually completed book manuscript, *Les Femmes et le pouvoir* (Women and Power), which she had abandoned in the 1980s. Pascal's book, *Les Femmes députés de 1945 à 1988* (Women Deputies from 1945 to 1988, Paris: Pascal, 1990), was published by the author himself. Laure Adler's journalistic history, *Les Femmes politiques* (Women in Politics, Paris: Seuil, 1993), which also contains a long section of interviews with female figures about whose lives there was considerable public curiosity, evidently responded to a growing public and popular interest. *Ces Femmes qui nous gouvernent* (These Women Who Govern Us, Paris: Albin Michel, 1991), published by Catherine Mangin

and Elizabeth Martichaut, an even more popularizing and personalizing work, was based on a series of interviews with women in the political spotlight. Bouchardeau's study would now require considerable updating before it could be published but it is an interestingly written and pioneering piece of research into what was still, at the time, virgin territory. I am indebted to Huguette Bouchardeau for her generosity in lending me this manuscript.

3. Bouchardeau, *Les Femmes et le pouvoir*, p. 9.
4. In the recent *Femmes et pouvoirs sous l'Ancien Régime* (Women and Power under the Old Regime), collection directed by Danielle Haase-Dubosc and Eliane Viennot (Paris: Rivages, 1991), cited by Laure Adler, the Revolution is seen as a male revolt against the powers and knowledge of the aristocratic women of the *ancien régime*.
5. In Barry Barnes, *The Nature of Power* (Cambridge: Polity Press, 1988).
6. Christine Fauré, *La Démocratie sans les femmes* (Paris: PUF, 1985). Translated as *Democracy without Women: Feminism and the Rise of Liberal Individualism in France* (Indiana University Press: Bloomington, Indiana 1991).
7. "les socialistes eux-mêmes ne sont pas d'accord pour distraire la femme de son ménage." Pascal, *Les Femmes députés*, p. 15.
8. "La réflexion la plus élémentaire reconnaît ce que les femmes peuvent apporter à la vie publique, leur sensibilité, l'approche particulière qu'elles ont des choses et des gens, leur passion, leurs convictions sans arrière-pensées. La lecture de leurs interventions délimite le large secteur de leurs compétences: toutes questions se rapportant à la femme, à la famille, à l'éducation, à la santé, à la condition sociale, au soulagement de la misère." *Les Femmes députés*, p. 7.
9. The well-known former book discussion television program *Apostrophes* devoted an evening to the history of French women by Michèle Sarde, the portrait of political women by Michelle Coquillat, and a novel by Henri Troyat. What all three works had in common was the study of the fear (and fascination) aroused by feminine power. Troyat's novel focused on the "monstrous" females who had held political power, and by extension portrayed the monstrosity represented by powerful women. But, the political power seen as "usurped" by women behind the throne, may exist only in the cultural imagination, as the female historian Françoise de Chandernagore demonstrated in her rehabilitating study of the role of Madame de Maintenon in *L'allée du roi* (The King's Way, Paris: Presses Pocket, 1989). The companion and, later, wife of Louis XIV in fact wielded little influence on the politics of the kingdom and certainly possessed no real political power.
10. "La femme conserve son prestige, toute sa beauté et toute son influence, très heureuse, lorsqu'elle veut bien rester femme," Lefebvre du Prey, Socialist, 1932, in Pascal, *Les Femmes députés*, p. 30.
11. "Le nivellement des sexes aboutit à la désolation générale. Sans une disparité radicale d'attribution il n'y a ni famille, ni mariage. Le coeur de l'homme doit être plein de la volonté de commander chez lui: sans cela l'homme disparaît." Proudhon, *La Pornocratie. Les Femmes dans les temps modernes* (1875) (Pornocracy: Women in the Modern Period), quoted by Adler, *Les Femmes politiques* (Paris: Seuil, 1993), p. 67.
12. "Pour nous femmes, qui voyons simple et pratique, qui avons encore heureusement un esprit neuf en matière politique, il nous semblait que la réalisation d'un programme de progrès social et d'intérêt national fut le but précis de chaque parti et que seules les méthodes de réalisation pussent expliquer la multiplicité des groupements. Et nous apprenons qu'un programme n'est guère qu'une indication des tendances générales du parti et que la grande question n'est pas de savoir comment on le réalisera, mais qui le réalisera. Autrement dit, la participation au pouvoir a pris une telle place dans les préoccupations des partis qu'ils semblent parfois oublier complètement le but précis qui les a tout d'abord réunis." Cécile Brunschvicg, quoted by Joy Cooper, *Cécile Brunschvicg; L'évolution de sa vision dans le cadre de l'histoire de la France et du féminisme français*, (Ph.D. thesis. University of Sydney, 1996).
13. After the French legislative elections in 1993, I asked the political scientist René Rémond whether he saw any differences in the political behavior of men and women

in the center-right parties in power. He responded, after reflection, that women were more supple and less likely to be partisan.

14. Bouchardeau, *Les Femmes et le pouvoir*, p. 11.
15. Elisabeth Badinter, *L'amour en plus: Histoire de l'amour maternel XV11–XXième siècle* (Paris: Flammarion, 1980). See also, *X,Y de l'identité masculine* (Paris: Editions Odile Jacob, 1992).
16. Gérard Genette, in "Frontières du récit," *Figures II* (Paris: Editions du Seuil, 1969).
17. In Joan B. Landes, *Women and the Public Sphere in the Age of the French Revolution* (Ithaca, N.Y.,: Cornell University Press, 1988). Quoted in Mim Kelber, ed., *Women and Government: New Ways to Political Power* (Westport, Conn.: Praeger, 1994).
18. Karen Offen presented her work in a paper at a meeting of the Center for European Studies, Cambridge, Massachusetts, which I attended in late 1995.
19. Karen Offen, "Women, Citizenship and Suffrage with a French Twist," in Caroline Daley and Melanie Dolan, Suffrage *and Beyond: International Feminist Perspectives* (New York: New York University Press, 1994), p. 152.
20. Offen analyzes the historical antecedents that contextualize the origins of such a supposedly natural and universal exclusion: the exclusion of women from the succession to the throne at the end of the sixteenth century (in a revival of the Salic Law), the reappropriation of a Roman law that identified virility with public authority (David's revolutionary painting of the *Serment du Jeu de Paume* bears witness to such classical inspiration), and the "demonization" of the queens Catherine de Médicis and Marie-Antoinette.
21. Karen Offen, "Women, Citizenship and Suffrage with a French Twist," p. 153. Offen quotes this explanation given by the provisional government from Marthe Louise Lévy's "L'émancipation politique des femmes: rapport présenté à la première conférence nationale des femmes socialistes 4–5 June, 1933" (Paris: Librairie, 1934).
22. In 1936 the principles of universal suffrage without consideration of sex and of women's eligibility for all elective assemblies was again approved unanimously (495 votes to none with ninety-three abstentions) by the Lower House (*Chambre des députés*) but consideration of the bill was once again deferred by the Senate.
23. Elizabeth Sledziewski points out the significance of the lesser-known clause in the first article of the Declaration of Rights: "social distinctions may be founded only on social usefulness" (*les distinctions sociales ne peuvent être fondées que sur l'utilité commune*). In the relative domain of social obligations, she claims, certain limits are necessarily imposed on the absolute rights of the individual. Exclusion of the poor, of foreigners, and of women from the political forum can then be justified by this distinction between human rights (individual rights) and the citizen's rights (political rights). Elizabeth Sledziewski, "L'Universalité trompeuse de la Révolution de 1789" (The Deceiving Universality of the Revolution of 1789), in Gisèle Halimi, *Femmes: Moitié de la terre moitié du pouvoir* (Women: Half of the Earth, Half of the Power, Paris: Gallimard, 1994), pp. 49–58.
24. Michelle Perrot, "La Démocratie sans les femmes: histoire élémentaire d'une spécificité française," in Gisèle Halimi, *Femmes: Moitié de la terre moitié du pouvoir*, pp. 33–40.
25. Françoise Gaspard, Claude Servan-Schreiber, Anne Le Gall, *Au Pouvoir, citoyennes! Liberté, Egalité, Parité* (To Power, Citizens! Liberty, Equality, Parity, Paris: Seuil, 1992).
26. Gaspard's feminist reading of the Revolution has met opposition. The historian Elizabeth Sledziewski argues that the achievements of the Revolution and its efforts for women should not be underestimated. In compensation for a loss of political rights, women's civil rights were reinforced, in the very midst of the Terror and at the risk of destroying the traditional family—the granting of equality in divorce, for example. In 1793 the democrats Condorcet and Guyomar refused to accept Talleyrand's distinctions between *les droits de l'homme* (human rights) and the rights of citizens. But Sledziewski's analysis agrees with Gaspard's premise that the majority of the leaders of the new revolutionary society were clearly unable to assimilate the enormity of

such a dangerous proposition as women's political rights. *Les droits de l'homme* were quite a "heady enough" proposition.

27. Patricia Latour, Monique Houssin, Madia Tovar, eds., *Femmes et Citoyennes: Du droit de vote à l'exercice du pouvoir* (Women and Citizens: From the Right to Vote to the Exercise of Power, Paris: Les Editions de l'atelier, 1995).
28. "Les hommes auraient palabré jusqu'à la fin du monde, les femmes ne se demandaient pas si une chose était possible mais si elle était utile." Quoted by Adler, *Les Femmes politiques*, p. 47.
29. "Il est vrai peut-être que les femmes aiment les révoltes. Nous ne valons pas mieux que les hommes envers le pouvoir, mais le pouvoir ne nous a pas encore corrompues." Quoted in Adler, ibid., p. 47.
30. "Elle savait que la parole fonde un droit que la violence ne saurait se donner elle-même." Adler, ibid., p. 22.
31. Adler quotes Sand, in ibid., p. 42. In a 1989 literary study, *The Mother/Daughter Plot: Narrative, Psychoanalysis, Feminism*, Marianne Hirsch notes that black writers have been insisting on the connection between their decision to write and a sense of self as being part of a link in generations of women. They attempt to piece together the story of a viable female culture in which a "mother" passes on knowledge and the authority of authorship to a "daughter" and thereby provides a model for a (black) woman's literary presence. The rediscovery of nineteenth-century political "mothers" works in similar "genealogical" fashion increasing the presence of political daughters, and particularly of writing daughters. Marianne Hirsch, *The Mother/Daughter Plot: Narrative, Psychoanalysis, Feminism* (Bloomington: Indiana University Press, 1989).
32. Adler quotes Sand, in *Les Femmes politiques*, p. 33.
33. Among the male-authored histories of women or women's movements are the following: Mattei Dogan and Jacques Narbonne, *Les Françaises face à la politique, comportement politique et condition sociale* (Paris: Albin Colin, 1955); Alain Decaux, *Histoire des Françaises* (Paris: Perrin, 1972); Georges Duby and Michelle Perrot, eds., *Histoire des femmes en Occident: XXe siècle*, 5 volumes (Paris: Plon,1992,); Albert and Nicole Du Roy, *Citoyennes! Il y a cinquante ans, le vote des femmes* (Paris: Flammarion, 1994); Roger Garaudy, *Pour l'Avènement de la femme* (Paris: Albin Michel, 1981); Jack Lang, *Demain les femmes* (Paris: Grasset, 1995); Maurice T. Maschino, *Après vous, messieurs. Les Femmes et le pouvoir* (Paris: Calmann-Lévy, 1996).
34. Political and social science have argued that power relations are based on a contract or on two-way relations between the ruler and the ruled in which there is neither total domination nor complete subordination. Some feminists theorize that this reciprocal influence between dominator and dominated limits the extent to which women are victims. Others have paradoxically argued that the subordinate or marginal feminine positions are to be valued. Doris Kadish argues, for example, that the allegorized, domesticated, sexualized, and diminished nineteenth-century woman was paradoxically imaginatively empowered as was the "feminized" French hero of Romanticism in his relation with the absent father, Napoleon. In Doris Kadish, *Politicizing Gender. Narrative Strategies in the Aftermath of the French Revolution* (New Brunswick: Rutgers University Press, 1991).
35. In Joan Scott, "Gender: A Useful Category of Historical Analyses," *American Historical Review* 91 (1986), p. 1069. Also quoted in Iva Ellen Deutchman, "The Politics of Empowerment," *Women and Politics* 11, no. 2 (1991), p. 3.
36. The following is quoted by Deutchman: Nancy Hartsock, *Money, Sex and Power: Toward a Feminist Historical Materialism* (Boston: Northeastern University Press, 1983); Janet Flammang, "Feminist Theory: The Question of Power," in S.G. McNall, ed., *Current Perspectives in Social Theory*, vol. 4, (Greenwich, Connecticut: JAI Press, 1983); Jane Jacquette, "Power as Ideology: A Feminist Analysis," in J.H. Steihm, ed., *Women's Views of the Political World of Men* (Dobbs Ferry, New York: Transnational, 1984).
37. In her book, *Money, Sex and Power: Toward a Feminist Historical Materialism* (Boston: Northeastern University Press, 1983), Nancy Hartsock's conception of gen-

dered power is not "domination but as capacity and as capacity of the community as a whole" (p. 4). She considers that women's experience of connection and relation have consequences for understandings of power. Deutchman notes in "The Politics of Empowerment" that the early social movements of the 1960s and many non-feminist thinkers have also promoted this non-hierarchical model, including Bachrach and Baratz (1962), and Foucault.

38. Sarah Hoagland, "Lesbian Ethics: Some Thoughts on Power in Our Interactions," *Lesbian Ethics* 2 (1986), p. 5.
39. Hilary Lips, *Women, Men, and the Psychology of Power* (Englewood Cliffs, NJ: Prentice Hall, 1981), p. 5.
40. Irigaray argues in *Le Souffle des femmes* written in 1999 that the liberation of women must come through "breath." Women need to accept difference within themselves in love and in maternity. They are thus better prepared to accept the other in the world. Men use breath for doing and constructing, whereas women use it for engendering life, protecting difference, and the spirit within. By means of breath/spirit, relations can be woven beneath and above language between the diverse traditions of the Book, between West and East and between men and women. Women can be mediators in dialogue between traditions and between genres/genders. Irigaray proposes a new reading of the Virgin Mary, no longer sacrifice or self-effacement before the Father, and of Virginity as the conquest of a feminine soul. Virginity is the possibility of a return to the self, to the silence of one's interiority, one's own spirit/breath that both allows attention and fidelity to the other and maintains the difference between self and other (Irigaray interviewed on her new book by Laurence Monroe in *La Croix* 11 February 1999).
41. Counter-power in Foucault's skeptical formulation is both oppressive and productive, that is, it is as potentially double (positive and energizing or normalizing) as power itself. There is, as the writer Alain Robbe-Grillet puts it, always the danger that Stalin might replace the Tsar.
42. Robert Anchor, "Narrativity and the Transformation of Historical Consciousness," *Clio* 16, no. 2 (1987), pp. 121–137.
43. Ibid., p. 134.

# 2

# From Suffrage to Representation (1946 to Today)

Women's political power was finally accepted in 1944, based on a vote in the *Assemblée consultative d'Alger* after lively dispute (fifty-one Communists and Socialists in favor, sixteen Radicals against). It had been promised by the father of the nation, De Gaulle, and was delivered not by democratic process but by an ordinance from Algiers. The Consultative Council that met in Algiers was made up principally of representatives of Resistance organizations whose role was to plan the organization of public administration in France after the Liberation. A series of proposals for half-measures in which women could vote but not hold office was finally followed by a decree formulated around Grenier's proposal that "women shall vote and be eligible for political office under the same conditions as men" (*les femmes seront électrices et éligibles dans les mêmes conditions que les hommes*). This was signed by De Gaulle as the president of the Provisional Government and women voted for the first time in municipal elections in 1945. Equal rights were written into the Constitution in 1946. Women's suffrage, then, came to be upon recognition of women's role in the Resistance, as a reward and fulfillment of commitments made by De Gaulle in his Free French speeches as early as 1942, and as part of a Gaullist political strategy to weaken the growing strength of the Communists. Adler observes that it was not a major concern of the time, nor seen as in any way inevitable.

This chapter surveys the changes in women's political representation since the suffrage. It also considers the modes of representation by which the knowledge of these changes has been and continues to be constructed and disseminated. Opinion polls, directed interviews, political histories, the language of the press and the discourse of politicians not only disclose but also construct the new political phenomenon of women in politics; the ideological positions and the experiences of the researcher, writer, or speaker influence the outcomes. Gender, as we have argued, matters. Even in the texts by right-wing women,

women's own discourse on their adventures in politics is influenced by their gendered personal experience. Right-wing women in fact show an unexpectedly positive response to the idea of parity, justified by their belief in the value of traditional women's roles and feminine difference. I argue that the new subject matter itself also makes a difference: the appearance of both scholarly studies and a popular discourse on public women is changing the political world. The new discourses in France (surveys, opinion polls, histories, media-programs and debates, such as the debate around the legitimacy of "Juppé's girls") are modifying perceptions about women in politics and constitute in and of themselves a form of political action.

## Writing and Reading the Figures

Both Bouchardeau's and Pascal's histories present statistical charts and carefully documented descriptions of the female candidates who have won political office. The more recent *Encyclopédie des femmes politiques sous la cinquième République* (Encyclopedia of Political Women in the Fifth Republic) lists the 176 women who have held office as *ministres*, *secrétaires d'Etat*, *sénateurs*, and *députées* up until early 1996. The encyclopedia includes the dates, administrative details of their mandates, and a short biographical description of each of the female politicians. The very existence of this major published work, produced under Chirac's conservative government, bears witness to the growing interest in women's history and a change in what is published about politics in France. Within this apparently neutral and traditionally configured reference work (particularly in the entries for Edith Cresson and Simone Veil) the text slides toward a heroic narrative. Gender is not absent from the fabrication and the address of this study.

As we observed in relation to histories of the suffrage, knowledge is a function not only of the object observed but also of the position of the observer and the assumptions brought to bear on the observation. Literary reception theory is based on the recognition that the message depends on "who speaks" and "to whom." The choice of discipline or genre, too, modifies the "horizons of expectation" of the reader, and thus the meanings gleaned. This is also true with the numbers. In most cases, this is the first time the figures have been broken down and made available by gender, potentially modifying the reader's "horizons of expectation."

The figures in the texts do show numerical underrepresentation of women in French politics. After the initial high points of 1945 and 1946 when the Communist party in particular made it a point of honor to nominate women, and thirty-three and thirty-five women were elected respectively, numbers of women in political office in France have declined. Over the five legislative elections during the Fourth Republic, from 1945 to 1958, women averaged only 11 percent of the total candidates. A few candidates from the Christian parties joined the rather select group of Communist women already in central politics, and the Mouvement républicain populaire (MRP) had a relatively high proportion of women while it remained an independent group until 1958. The minority Protestant church also produced many more than its share of female candidates. The right-wing parties trail. In 1958 when General de Gaulle abandoned proportional representation at the level of the *département* (administrative region), the subsequent reduction in the number of seats and the return to first past the post elections provoked an abrupt decline in female representation. In general, the system of "first past the post" appears to lessen the chances of election for women.

The Parti communiste (PC) was the leader in female representation through the late 1970s, until 1981 when the Socialists came to power. Political scientist Janine Mossuz-Lavau working in collaboration with social scientist Mariette Sineau defines these years positively as the years of women's political "apprenticeship."[1] Bouchardeau and Sineau (both of whom are Socialist by political affiliation) insist on the fact that female representation from 1945 to 1988 was very much a phenomenon of the left. Pascal draws from his charts the lesson of the static nature of the percentage of women's representation and of the numbers of women, seen as less than interested in politics.[2] In mid 1996, thirty-two women constituted 5.5 percent of the seats in the Lower House, putting France in last place on the chart of Europe, tied with Greece. (Italy had 9.5 percent representation, and Great Britain, 10 percent). With eighteen women in the Senate (5.6 percent), France was again bottom of the list among the countries with an Upper House, behind Britain, Italy, and Ireland. In the 1997 return of the Socialists in an election imprudently called early by President Chirac, women constituted more than 10 percent of elected national representatives for the first time in French history.

Even though the numbers of women in politics had increased in the 1990s, there were few women in strong political positions. Appointed prime minister in 1990, Michel Rocard had six women ministers in his cabinet (13 percent). All were either *ministres déléguées* (junior ministers) or *secrétaires d'Etat* (assistant ministers). Three of the six women ministers under the next prime minister, Edith Cresson, held full ministerial responsibilities. Things would not get much better until the return of the Socialists in 1997 and the appointments for the first time of two women to key ministerial positions (Martine Aubry as labor minister and Elisabeth Guigou as justice minister).

In Prime Minister Edouard Balladur's center-right government from 1993 to 1995, there were three tried and true women ministers: the dowager Simone Veil, the conservative Lucette Michaux-Chevry from Guadeloupe, and Michèle Alliot-Marie, daughter of a well-known political family. Although these women all had political weight in their own right and remain significant figures in the political world in the new millennium, three swallows did not make a summer.[3] The journalist

Natacha Henry notes that in April 1994, Balladur showed no interest in organizing festivities to commemorate the fiftieth anniversary of the women's right to vote.[4] If Marie Curie found a place in the all-male Panthéon that year, it was thanks to the president, Mitterrand.[5]

Not only are there changes in the number of female candidates and female representatives in France, there are also changes in regard to voting behavior. Mariette Sineau and Janine Mossuz-Lavau's gender-differentiated surveys show that the initially higher rate of voter abstention among women declined until, in 1974, male and female voting patterns had become relatively similar. The only difference in 1974 was the fact that women tended to be less supportive of the Front national than men were. Their work also charted changes both in the attitudes of women toward politics and from all voters toward female politicians. A survey at the beginning of the 1950s had shown that only 58 percent of French women considered the right to vote a good thing. Mariette Sineau's 1983 study demonstrated that 75 percent of women thought politics were as much their business as men's. An even higher proportion considered it normal to appoint a woman prime minister, but the majority still balked at the idea of a woman president. By 1996, Janine Mossuz-Lavau was able to demonstrate that more than 80 percent of those questioned had no objection to a woman president.[6]

The statistical change in voting pattern and attitudes to women in politics was narrativized within the new texts and the conclusions they drew. Bouchardeau, for example writes that antisuffrage fears had been largely unfounded. All the initial differences between female and male voting—the female vote as more reactionary, more interested in the candidate's personality than program and with a tendency to follow the vote of husband or father—had disappeared in younger generations and in the higher socioeconomic groups by 1975. With some reservations, Bouchardeau argues that women voters resemble men, and their political choices seem to have less to do with being a woman than with level of education and work outside the home. Sineau concludes that, in 1985, only the group of so-called non-active women showed significant differences in their political choices relative to males of the same age and socioeconomic background. Janine Mossuz-Lavau uses her data to show that women have become a vital sector of the electorate and that younger women are now out-voting younger men.[7]

Another set of figures,[8] published mainly by women researchers, established the shift to the left in the women's vote.[9] The new narratives use the figures to make the claim that in the 1990s women showed voting patterns that were no less progressive than men's.[10] In general, the texts that rigorously compile information on women's voting patterns and on women's levels of satisfaction with the political process serve also to assert the significance of these questions. What the figures show—increased acceptance of a woman as president, for example—is a strengthening belief that politics is a legitimate activity for women. Interestingly, Jean Pascal's reading of the figures challenges this legitimacy, concluding that women do not rush in large numbers to run for office. (Were women, he implies, really at home in politics?) In contrast to Pascal's implicit claim that women are not interested in politics, Janine Mossuz-Lavau situates any problem in the unsatisfactory character of the political world for a number of women and creates the concept of "political deficit." This is based on a methodologically rigorous analysis of the material she collected in 1993 and 1994 on ordinary French people's attitudes toward politics and their understandings of differences between parties. Mossuz-Lavau's work has authority in the world of political science.[11]

Mossuz-Lavau's surveys and "non-directive" interviews introduced the critical notion of women's "political deficit" to French political history in 1994.[12] From the sixty interviews Mossuz-Lavau conducted with French women, what had previously been labeled "political indecision" was identified in four women. Mossuz-Lavau examines these women's apparent lack of interest in politics and concludes that all four are in fact very concerned by the problems of society such as education, immigration, or the marginal position of certain groups. These concerns are labeled as *le politique* (political concerns) by Mossuz-Lavau, as opposed to the traditional *la politique* (politicians' politics). These non-voting women are not apolitical, claims Mossuz-Lavau, but symptomatic of "a lack of political identity" (*un déficit d'identité*). In other words, they do not identify with the right or with the left and have no particular affinity with the ecologists. This "deficit" is traced back by Mossuz-Lavau to their lack of a sense of belonging to a community or to the established political parties that fail to correspond to their aspirations.

Political deficit is a situation, Mossuz-Lavau claims, that women are more likely to find themselves in than men. For although the voting patterns of women are now similar to those of men, she claims fewer are really interested in politics as these are practiced.[13] The conclusion of the female political scientist is that this deficit is due to women's long exclusion from the political scene, their uncertainty about the legitimacy of an interest in politics, and concern about accepting rules laid down by a political class that is predominantly male. The political "crisis" of the 1990s has thus less to do with any lack of awareness of or interest in political problems in a voting population that Mossuz-Lavau characterizes as informed and sophisticated, than with a possible deficit in political identity arising from disaffection with the traditional political game of alternating male-dominated parties.[14] Implicit in her notion of *le politique* is the idea of a non-partisan, public interest politics less concerned with party and political caste and more inclusive of women.

## The Mitterrandian Era

### *Mitterrand's Failed Rendezvous with Women*

An analysis of Mitterrandian history by Jane Jenson and Mariette Sineau provides an understanding of why women experienced the political deficit identified by Mossuz-Lavau. Their book *Mitterrand et les Françaises: un rendez-vous manqué* (Mitterrand and French Women: A Missed Rendezvous) constructs a story of the partial failure of Mitterrand to keep his 1995 promise to extend the rights of modern republican citizenship to women. It is the only major account of the Mitterrandian era written from a feminist perspective.

The quotations that open the work position the writers as Socialists and feminists and shape the book as a whole. The first line is by the nineteenth-century statesman Léon Gambetta: "What constitutes true democracy is not the recognition of equals but the making of them" (*Ce qui constitue la vraie démocratie, ce n'est pas de reconnaître des égaux mais d'en faire*). The second is from Yvette Roudy, who was *Ministre delégué chargée des Droits de la femme* (minister of women's rights) from May 1981–1985 and then *Ministre des Droits des femmes* (women's rights minister) from May 1985–March 1986 on 8 March 1983: "If France is the land of Men's Rights, let us make it also the land of Women's Rights" (*Si la France est le pays des droits de l'Homme, faisons qu'elle devienne aussi le pays des droits de la Femme*).

Jenson and Sineau characterize modern citizenship as resulting from changes brought about by the rise of capitalism and the sovereign nation-state in the wake of the revolutions of 1776 and 1789. The authors argue that both political revolutions take the masculine as the norm for citizenship. The trilogy of the French Revolution, *liberté, égalité, fraternité*, is distinguished by the fact that it does not limit its claims to political equality but links such claims to liberty. Not only is political equality linked to liberty, but also equality is inextricably tied with the claim to fraternity. Jenson and Sineau argue that "fraternity" introduces a new element—the right to the well-being of all citizens and the corresponding social duty of solidarity. But *fraternité* (brotherhood) and the accompanying social rights have again been conceived with the male as reference.[15] For this reason, the benefits accorded women, such as family allowances and maternity leave, have still not been defined as rights: at best, they are protections for the family.[16]

In Jenson and Sineau's reading of history, the model of the male as head of the family unit holding the political and civil rights of its constituent members in his rational hands (developed by de Tocqueville) continues to be authoritative in the collective consciousness in France. More seriously, it is found in the unconscious of France, even in the present period. A survey carried out before the 1974 elections among women who had declared they would not vote for Mitterrand had revealed that the major fears were that this "communist" wanted to "kill the father." To allay such concerns, Mitterrand adopted a family-centered image and approach to politics. Campaign photos showed Mitterrand with his two sons and his wife, Danielle. Only after his death would the presence of his second family at his funeral belie the public front of thirty years of marital bliss. Our authors note that Mitterrand claimed that he wanted to make the family more equal but never shared their feminist perspective on the family as "a place of possible oppression."

Mitterrand, concedes Sineau, does seem to have understood the growing significance of women, increasingly part of the new professional middle-classes that had replaced the old France of autonomous small producers and small merchants. One of Mitterrand's projects for modernizing France and extending democracy within the family, the workplace, and the city was the *Mouvement démocratique féminin* (MDF, or Women's Democratic Movement), a "laboratory of ideas" for Mitterrand presided over by his close friend Marie-Thérèse Eyquem. Unusually for France, a shadow cabinet was formed, with a Ministry for the Promotion of Women. Jenson and Sineau note that Mitterrand also declared himself in favor of birth control but presented it in the form of the "happy motherhood", which he would always see as the "right to have children" in the right conditions, not the right *not* to have children. In the absence of a papal decision on the pill, Mitterrand's moderate approach to birth control was well received by the new and significant group of working women. The lack of any explicit mention of sexuality is critiqued by the authors but they recognize that, at the time, sex was not considered to be a political question. Despite the absence of any recognition of feminist body politics, Mitterrand's program promised to do for women what the Socialists of 1936 had done for workers. It brought forth proposals for a maternity leave of fourteen weeks at full rather than half pay, and measures for professional equality. Although Mitterrand lost the 1974 election by a very small margin, playing the woman card had proved productive according to Jenson and Sineau. Since his battle against De Gaulle, he had gained seven points in the supposedly conservative female electorate and only two points among males. The conservative tendency of the women's vote seemed to be crumbling away.

In 1978, a manifesto on the rights of women won support at the National Convention of the Socialist party. At the same time, recount Jenson and Sineau, party women were becoming increasingly unhappy with their exclusion from winnable seats in what they were becoming convinced was an exclusive male club. In 1978, the electoral situation resulted in only one Socialist woman, Marie Jacq, being elected, and it lead to the defeat of both Edith Cresson and Yvette Roudy, both central figures within the Parti socialiste. In reaction, Françoise Gaspard proposed the formation of a women's group called the "third grouping" (*courant trois*), or again, *Mignonnes, allons voir sous la rose* (Darlings, let us go and look underneath the rose), in a clever pastiche of Ronsard's "gather your rosebuds while ye may" poem. (The rose is also a symbol of the Socialist party.) Although the group did not get the 5 percent party support necessary to constitute itself as a *courant,* or official, grouping, it was evidence of discontent among Socialist women.

Jenson and Sineau's story dramatizes the threat posed by separatist feminist groups to Mitterrand. In 1978, the political group *Choisir*, which had presented its own candidates in the first round of the legislative elections, declined to call for a vote for the left in the second round. Mitterrand attempted to fight such separatism with the verbal artistry for which he was renowned, declaring "feminism" to be the "pre-history" of his own "feminine action." Sineau notes a change in Mitterrand's language as he prepared for the European elections and began to make reference for the first time to concepts and vocabulary that are feminist in origin. He referred to a "patriarchal" society and to the "exploitation" of women.

On the electoral home straight in 1981, between the two rounds of voting, argues Sineau, Mitterrand realized the need to strike a deal with the activists of the *Programme commun des femmes* (Women's Common Program). After his "One Hundred and Ten Proposals for Women" in 1981 and a public debate with the group *Choisir*, he finally managed to bring both the wave of separatist feminism of the late seventies and the party feminists over to his side. According to Jenson and Sineau, even Simone de Beauvoir and *Choisir* gave up the conviction that all political parties are equally patriarchal. The call by the MLF to vote for Mitterrand was all the more surprising, as Sineau sees it, given that Huguette Bouchardeau was representing the rival PSU (Parti socialiste unifié) party in the presidential election. Bouchardeau had declared that although she had no mandate to speak in the name of women, she was running for president as a woman so that women would no longer feel outside politics. In the 1981 election, Mitterrand gained the support of 49 percent of women voters.

There were attempts by both male and female politicians to engage with women's issues during Mitterrand's first presidential term. It was during this time that Yvette Roudy, described as the first egalitarian feminist to be a minister (for Women's Rights), would attempt to bring about the promised equality, autonomy, and dignity for women. Sineau omits any sustained account of action within the legislature or the executive. Perhaps this was because Roudy's egalitarian approach, which evoked the principle of equal pay for equal work, otherwise tended to eliminate gender demarcations and difference. As a "state" feminist, Roudy preferred to avoid the risks inherent in the argument of equal pay for "comparable" work, which is grounded in an understanding that men and women differ in their working situations. This debate will dominate the decade in women's associations and continue in the parity movement. Sineau notes that Roudy told *Le Monde* in 1994 that Mitterrand was a genius, a great romantic of politics, who "proposed an adventure" and "allowed us women to participate actively." In her autobiographical writing, however, Roudy admits that constant struggle and unrelenting vigilance had been needed for her new Women's Rights Ministry to be even partially effective. The mere seventeen women (plus the independent Gisèle Halimi), out of the 285 Socialist deputies elected in 1981 to the *Assemblée* shocked many feminists, claims Sineau. Yvette Roudy, too, in *La Femme en marge* (Women Marginalized), one of her autobiographical manifestos, concludes that women were dispossessed of their share of this historic 1981 victory. Nonetheless, in 1982, the "international women's day" was celebrated on the 8th of May, and Mitterrand entrusted *Madame le ministre des Droits de la femme* with translating women's rights into reality. Yvette Roudy had a budget at her disposal ten times the sum available to Françoise Giroud as *secrétaire d'Etat* for Women's Status in 1976. The positive profile for the Ministry, however, did not last.

After 1983, economic austerity narrowed the possibilities of the movement toward a more egalitarian republicanism. Although the law on professional equality was passed in 1983, Sineau sees this as having little practical effect as competition, unemployment, and private-sector development began to dominate the economy. Sineau's perspectives also underscore the gap between the Socialist militants who were pursuing an equality politics and the MLF, whose more radical critique of the sexism that pervaded institutions was filtering only very slowly into the political parties.

Michèle André's reduced budget for the Women's Status department in 1988 corresponded to Mitterrand's second seven-year term. André's stature was not that of Roudy's, particularly under Rocard as prime minister whose priority discourse was the need for jobs for men. The portfolio continued to slide in the 1990s. Véronique Neiertz presented herself to me in an interview as something of a frustrated token woman when she took over the portfolio in 1993, despite some positive measures such as subsidies for home help in 1991 and the professional equality law of 1993.

By the end of Mitterrand's term, the discourse had turned toward neo-liberalism, globalization, competition, and equal opportunity—a movement from a discourse of rights to one of aspirations, argues Sineau—and no progress had been made on narrowing the wage gap, the unemployment rate for women was twice that for men, and women constituted 85 percent of France's part-time workers.[17] Sineau and Jenson argue that the new economic discourse involved a rejection of both a social project and any recognition of particular obstacles facing women.

For these researchers, Mitterrand walked a fine line between a politics in favor of women and children's rights, and a family politics conforming to the need for more French children, not to mention his personal predilection for large families. Sineau's narrative concludes that Mitterrand's story is one of electoral strategizing. This view is also found in

Gisele Halimi's autobiographies. Mitterrand was not a feminist: for him, sexist discrimination per se remained an abstraction. The loss of status and prestige of the women's ministry accompanied a process in which a discourse focusing on modernization of a market economy overtook discourses about social justice, equality of opportunity, and equal rights. The French state moved from an all-powerful stance to stress its dependency on the economic situation in Western democracies, but continued to be based on male monopoly, on the tutelary model of "pater familias," with all the dated and authoritarian connotations inherited from the Napoleonic *code civil.*[18] The market and modernization discourses had not fundamentally altered this conception.

## *The Political and the Personal*

What emerges between the lines of Sineau and Jenson's scholarly study is regret regarding a missed opportunity under socialism and nostalgia for an independent political feminist politics. Despite the authors' awareness that Mitterrand had to be a man for all seasons in order to be elected, their work points to a symbolic battle of the sexes and to the fact that women had been put in visible places only to cover up their lack of true representation. Jenson and Sineau write that even when the radical lawyer and feminist Gisèle Halimi succeeded in passing a bill requiring 25 percent female representation, this "outsider"—this "disturber of the peace"—could not be seen as "representing" the nation, and was not given credit for her bill. Such choice of words betrays their personal feelings. In their discussion of the subsequent constitutional annulment of the 25 percent quota for women, the authors insist on the underground resistance operating to undermine the surface acceptance of women's rights by the government. The Assembly, they claimed, was secretly relieved that the Constitutional Council found the quotas unconstitutional, a relief similar to that found in the Assembly when the Senate refused to vote for women's enfranchisement.[19]

Left-wing politics and second-wave activist feminist convictions color Sineau's studies. These are evidenced by her dismissal of middle-class philanthropy, her sympathy for the independent women's groups, her disillusion with the legislative process, and her critique of paternalism in all its forms, including traditional models of the family. Sineau's views on the translation of changes for women from the new legislation into collective consciousness, or *mentalité*, as we also observed, are pessimistic. Nonetheless, she invested long hours researching and writing (on Mitterrand and gender, and indeed on women and political power) as if her publications might make a difference. The methodological rigor of her work has made it an acceptable building block for a number of other women researchers. Its focus on women's questions and body politics in itself constitutes a challenge to the canon of political writing. In re-evaluating the Mitterrand era, it rewrites a major period in contemporary history from a feminist perspective. Jenson and Sineau break the frame and invite reaction and interaction.

## *Other Women's Voices*

Although Jenson's and Sineau's work is academically rigorous, it could be argued that their radical feminist consciousness is out of step with mainstream political discourses. The writings of the many women in ministerial cabinets and in the Elysée generally refute the Jenson-Sineau thesis of Mitterrand as an obstacle to women's progress. The autobiographies of Elisabeth Guigou and Ségolène Royal in particular present Mitterrand as a mentor and a protector. His appointment of Edith Cresson as prime minister in 1992 broke a very old French taboo. Martine Aubry, the first woman labor minister in 1992, followed the injunctions of a European court by attempting to lift the long-standing ban on women's night work. Yvette Roudy's courage and integrity in her fight against injustice of all kinds are revealed in her own autobiographical work and can be seen as emblematic of the Mitterrandian era. The 1982 laws that provided for equal access to jobs in the public sector, for an employment and retirement status for the wives of shopkeepers and artisans separate from that of their husbands, and for reimbursement of abortions, along with the 1983 law on professional equality, and the 1984 law enforcing payment of child and wife support, all constituted major women's rights legislation.

Other women's accounts show that by the end of its term, Mitterrand's government had come closer to the acceptance that in the private domain, sexuality and sexual violence were at least somewhat within its purvey. One example of this came in 1988 when the government forced the pharmaceutical company, Roussel-Uclaf, to put the so-called abortion pill, RU486, back on the market. RU486 made surgery for abortions unnecessary; it was also an effective treatment for a number of serious medical conditions. The company had withdrawn the product in the face of a *Laissez-les vivre* (Right to Life) threat of commando actions and boycotts. The government's threat to take away the patent if this product of vital public usefulness was not made available relieved the company of any moral responsibility for the release of the drug. In 1991, a law allowing advertising of AIDS protection initially vetoed by Pierre Bérégovoy was passed and reimbursement for the new generation of the contraceptive pill was accepted. Then in 1992, Roudy finally managed to get a sexual harassment law voted in. This mandated one year of imprisonment and fines for using a position of power in the workplace to obtain sexual favors. (Harassment was not considered to be possible among "equal" colleagues.) European feminist imperatives of equality prevailed over the French tradition of protection of women's traditional difference and, in particular, of their maternal function supported by Mitterrand.

A comparative study by American scholar Dorothy McBride Stetson also comes to very different conclusions on the Mitterrandian period. Stetson notes the difficulty of a comparison between a decentralized federal American system and a very centralized French government; between a political culture of limited government with reservations about legislating on social protections and a culture of full public acceptance of the welfare state; and between a pluralistic society with a puritan heartland and a secular state with long-standing Catholic and pronatalist traditions. Despite reservations about comparative difficulties Stetson makes strong claims for major progress in the Mitterrandian period:

> The Ministry of Women's Rights and its predecessors really made the difference between United States and French policy in the last few years. From within the government, Yvette Roudy and her staff held fast to their feminist vision: they evaluated all policy according to their goal of changing the patriarchal sex role pattern to achieve equal rights and participation of women in the economy, society, and politics.[20]

Stetson declares that between 1981 and 1986 the ministry became the most important political and organizational resource for women's rights in France, noting the very high profile of Roudy's public presence and discourse. Where are the government feminists in the United States? asks the pragmatic Stetson, less concerned than Sineau with the deeply entrenched prejudices still lying below the surface in France.

## The 1990s

### *Conservative Discourses Resurface*

There may have been some limited policy successes for women in the Mitterrandian era, but conservative attitudes are still evident in the France of the 1990s. In the 1990s, advances for women could be affected by the European parliament and its policies as well as from within France. Despite this, the prospects for the rapid legitimizing and success of women candidates continued to be limited. A 1994 interview with Hélène Gisserot, who had become one of the highest ranking civil servants in France after serving as *déleguée à la condition feminine* (Junior Minister for Women's Status) from 1986 to 1988 in the center-right government, is characteristic of the moderately conservative tenor to much of the discourse on and by public women of this period.[21] Gisserot presented French women as vulnerable economically, but nonetheless as more fortunate than their male counterparts because women were part of family and social networks. By implication, men, who are less well integrated into society, have more need of the increasingly rare jobs than women. Gisserot's language transmits a traditional valuing of women's "difference." She supports the proposal for a six-month paid family leave on the occasion of the birth of a third child arguing that women are still generally associated symbolically with the domestic sphere in most countries. She stated that Latin countries, and Germany in particular, still hold firm to the belief in the value of keeping wives and mothers at home. What is surprising in Gisserot's discourse is her subsequent support for a system of quotas for political representation as in Scandinavia, on the pragmatic basis that "quotas work." In her valuing of "value-added" feminine difference and in her support for parity, Gisserot speaks for an increasing number of right-wing women.

Further evidence of conservative and traditional attitudes within French politics is found in the 1994 Family Act. As Véronique Neiertz, former Socialist minister and deputy, pointed out to me in an interview, the Family Act passed by Simone Veil was a deeply conservative piece of legislation. Neiertz herself voted for the legislation in the most immediate material interest of their female constituents. In essence, the bill provided a salary for working mothers who preferred to remain home to care for a third child. It appeared to give some choice to very low-paid mothers for whom staying at home with young children brought allowances and tax breaks almost equivalent to a salary. But given that these women were unlikely to find another place in the workforce once their children had entered school, it was considered by most feminists to be part of an attempt to reduce unemployment by sending women home to make babies. Mitterrand had stated that the principle of parental allowances used as anti-unemployment measures was unacceptable. However, Mitterrand's discourse on the conciliation of home and work without disadvantage for women in the workplace did not inspire confidence in women who were struggling already with the credibility gap between his discourse, the law, and their lived realities.

## *"Feminization" of Government*

The mid 1990s saw public and political acknowledgement across the political spectrum of the need for women to be better represented in the political arena. Catherine Pégard, a political journalist for the news weekly *Le Point*, claims that it took thirty thousand people out on the streets on 25 November 1995, in a demonstration fuelled by concern at leaving women's issues in right-wing government hands, for Jacques Chirac to become more attentive to the voice of women. In the press, Giroud presented this as a demonstration against *l'ordre moral*, or the new conservative ethical order, in favor of a "secular and social republic."[22] The women's organizations linked together by the militant left-wing Maya Surduts at the head of the umbrella organization for women's rights, Coordination pour le droit à l'avortement et à la contraception, or CADAC, had surprised even themselves by the degree of popular support they attracted, in particular, among young people. The march protested against the planned presidential amnesty for those responsible for attacks on abortion clinics and the non-reimbursement of the new "third-generation" pill. When Chirac looked around him for a more acceptable discourse on modern politics, "parity" was on hand. In fact, public disillusionment with male politicians had been growing sufficiently for Jacques Chirac to find it expedient to campaign in the 1995 presidential election on a platform that called for the "feminization" of government.

The pressure for feminization led to the appointment of "Juppé's Girls" in 1995. According to Catherine Pégard, the hours that preceded the forming of Prime Minister Alain Juppé's first cabinet were described by political observers as a "desperate" hunt for women. This last-minute search turned up a centrist, Anne-Marie Idrac, a candidate supported by the Giscardian group, Christine Chauvet, and ten other women said to have been "catapulted, without real legitimacy, into the most feminized ministerial team in history."[23] Although these new women were given mainly minor portfolios (there were only four full ministerial options), they represented 28.6 percent of the French government. The average for Europe at that time was only around 16 percent. On 19 October, Juppé denied to the press that he had chosen these women "simply to put touches of color into the much publicized photographs taken on the steps of the *palais nationaux* (the Palais Bourbon and the Senate). Then, on 7 November, in a restructuring that eliminated thirteen ministers, eight of the twelve women were dropped from the cabinet.[24] The press dramatized the issue of the demise of the women ministers by dubbing them *les juppettes* (Juppé's Girls, or Juppé's Skirts). The choice of the term *les juppettes* suggested that old habits of thinking on women's legitimization by the "Prince" lurked in the social unconscious. In Giroud's analysis, the political gesture was "wounding" for the women: "There couldn't have been a better way to show the level of esteem in which they were held."[25] What happened to the *juppettes* (as opposed to the relative success of "Blair's Babes" in Britain) suggests that the legitimacy of female representation remained somewhat superficial in France.

In the press, Françoise Giroud presents the sacked ministers both as humiliated women and as victims of the false positions created to give more women a place in politics.[26] Alain Juppé, for his part, defended his action on the grounds that although all the women he dismissed had real qualities, they were not politically representative and had no personal weight in the parties. The party bosses and the structures were at fault and certainly not him, according to Juppé, for not preparing women for political positions. For the future Socialist education minister, Ségolène Royal, certain ministers may have lacked experience, but they were no less competent than were the men. The dismissal left a general sense of unease or indignation among women of all parties and among the public. The actions also created a backlash, a mix of sympathy for the victims and a call for justice.

In part to redeem his error, Juppé proceeded to set up a new institutional body, *L'Observatoire pour la parité*, to examine parity at all levels of public life, review bills concerning women before these went to parliament, prepare proposals for a revision of the constitution, and explore the idea of linking government subsidies to political parties with the number of positions they give women. The *Observatoire pour la parité*, led by Roselyne Bachelot (RPR, or Rassemblement pour la République), was made up of eighteen members, including the left-wing Evelyne Sullerot and Gisèle Halimi.

## *The "Juppettes" Speak*

Both Anne-Marie Idrac, who remained in government, and Elisabeth Dufourcq, who was dismissed, responded to a questionnaire I sent to the twelve ministers in December 1996. Their responses are generally representative of the group at large. Asked if she supported the parity movement, Anne-Marie Idrac answered that insofar as it sought a more open political life closer to the expectations of society, she was in favor of parity. However, Idrac listed the reform of the state, the reconciliation of the French with the new hope offered by Europe, and the fight against unemployment as more urgent political tasks. The response of Elisabeth Dufourcq was also couched in the moral language of ethical commitment. Parity was not the paramount political issue and Dufourcq too made claims for women's practicality and efficacy. Observing that she was in favor of political parity "as she would be in favor of world charity!" she stated that she wanted rather more practically to help women and young people to run for office, and to separate unethical concerns of personal conquest of power from the ethical exercise of power.

Anne-Marie Idrac felt that men had not shown the listening skills and the conviction that the public desired, that in general women are less interested in power for the sake of power, have more of a sense of humor, and are more tenacious and practical, given their daily family responsibilities: "I sometimes think that politics is like bringing up children: lots of attention, day-to-day affection, persuasion with respect to one's vision of what is important, and hope for the future." Elisabeth Dufourcq, too, considered that women had more humor, realism, and were more disinterested than men. Both women claimed nonetheless to feel completely at home in the political world.

In fact, measures for women taken by Anne-Marie Couderc, who survived into Juppé's reformed government in November 1995 as junior employment minister with responsibility for Women's Affairs, were mainly symbolic and without economic cost. They included an attempt to remove illustrations in school textbooks that might tie women to traditionally feminine roles (7 March 1996) and a study of the salary gender gap, found to be around 15 percent, even in the public sector. Anne-Marie Couderc remained silent on the abortion issue.

*Elisabeth Dufourcq.*

*Anne-Marie Idrac.*

## The Battle of the Texts: Language and Power

The women's stories discussed in this chapter, which "break the frame" at least in terms of subject matter, do not take form independently of one another. New concepts such as "political deficit" and "parity" begin to circulate; the private-public distinction is broken down as sexuality, the body, and the detail of daily living acquire greater political significance. Interviews and testimonial become important for self-definition. At the level of the telling of the story, a movement between personal testimony and political critique and project comes to characterize most particularly the political autobiographies considered in chapter 6. These autobiographies by women are different in form and focus from the political memoirs of their male counterparts.

Sineau's thesis concerns the masculine over-coding of the symbols, values, and belief systems that constitute political culture in France as this is being altered by women's presence in politics and in political writing.[27] Quoting Louise Weiss's *Mémoires*, Sineau observes that the suffragist movement at the beginning of the twentieth century was already marked by the strong belief that women could modify civil and political life. Given their horror of blood in the streets, wrote Weiss, women would give a humanity overly inclined to engage in conflict, a chance of survival.[28]

In contemporary political life, it is also generally felt that women have their own language—a simpler and more direct language of daily experience, efficiency, and pragmatism. Sineau cites the work of the political scientist, Georges Lavau, stressing the significance of language in tracing the boundaries of a given political space or culture. The language of the private world of the body seen as profoundly political by many women, and the idea of renewal through women, had begun to infiltrate the political arena. It has begun to reach a critical mass through women's speech and writing covertly subversive of the masculine coding of politics in power and overtly presented as a positive force for change.

In the judgment of American historian Karen Offen, there has been a major readjustment in the balance of legal and economic power between the sexes as a result of new discourses. It is the ongoing battle over knowledge and language that Offen places at the center of the struggle: the reluctance of mainstream historians to acknowledge the significance of women's suffrage and the revolution in women's status. Offen's writing incorporates many of the current trends in the American academic experience, including the premise that power resides in the (masculine) domination of language as power and the examination of the limitations of the traditional discipline of history.[29] Citing the work of Cécile Dauphin as representative of the work of the "very few" French women historians addressing "the woman question," Offen's thesis is that the neglect of women's history in France needs to be countered by a new focus on the way authority has been gendered over the centuries.[30] This has been happening if the significant sales of the recent women's histories by now well-recognized researchers such as Michelle Perrot and Geneviève Fraisse can be taken as an indication.

## *The Diversity of Women's Voices*

Women, of course, have had differing positions on political culture, and different views regarding its transformation. In an overview of contemporary women's movements in France, Jenson and Sineau[31] give an account of the diversity of these groups beginning with revolutionary feminists (generally still referred to as the MLF) and their attempt to re-imagine a separate, purely feminine space outside the masculine political culture.[32] The radical feminists wanted to construct new social and sexual relations, creating the group Psych. et Po. (Psychanalyse et Politique) in order to re-imagine women's difference in terms of sexuality using psychoanalytic theory, a group nonetheless considered by Jenson and Sineau as a "sect" and thus implicitly rejected for its separatism. The feminist activists, on the other hand, engaged rather in (chaotic) public meetings in the early 1970s, the celebration of the "Unknown Wife" at the "Tomb of the Unknown Soldier," symbolic assaults on the centers of power, disruption of public events. The "non-aligned" (that is, the non-political left) or *lutte des classes* (class-struggle) feminists with links to the Trotskyist and Maoist groups, along with the trade union or syndicalist feminists, pushed unions to accept the specificity of women within capitalism, acknowledge the impact of sexuality on the workplace, and provide wider access to contraception and abortion.[33]

At the other extreme, the egalitarian feminists, such as the *Ligue du Droit des Femmes* (League for Women's Rights) led by Simone de Beauvoir and Gisèle Halimi's *Choisir la cause des femmes* (Choice: the Cause of Women) worked with men within the system to change it in egalitarian ways. De Beauvoir systematically refused to give in to what she called the "temptation" or the "ghetto" of difference. All of these groups develop their own language.

The telling of the stories of French politics by women also uses the range of discourses in place, as tools of investigation and as strategic political instruments. Karen Offen observes that the language used by Cécile Brunschvicg to protest against women's absence on the political stage is not merely the language of feminine difference and women's potential contributions.[34] Brunschvicg co-opted a conventional discourse, that of nationalism, to serve her cause. Present writings advocating parity democracy, such as Gaspard's *Au Pouvoir, citoyennes*, also appeal to nationalist sentiments, for example, when they argue that one would not expect to see the land of Jeanne d'Arc and the daughters of the Revolution lagging behind so many of its less advanced neighbors, including the countries of the Mediterranean. This line of reasoning resonates curiously with the language of the British suffragettes from 1866 to 1874 as analyzed by Jane Rendall.[35] Rendall argues that the claim of British women to citizenship was located within the proud national history dating from the early Anglo-Saxon women, and in the progressive movement of British civilization, differentiated from parts of the world still marked by savagery and despotism. This discourse, then, sets up a hierarchy of sociocultural development in which the civilized societies of Western Europe represent the highest point. According to Rendall, women of this period were caught up in the limitations of the discourses of their time (the ideal of individuality, the science of society, and the history of civilization), restricted by a nervousness about democracy and an ethnocentricity that they shared with male liberals. She argues, however, that they used this language strategically to accommodate sexual difference.

The discourses of difference and national honor that we followed earlier in Pascal's work on the suffrage debate and observe in the debate on representation have often been converted to new ends by women. In the pioneer countries that obtained suffrage early, what proved to be politically persuasive was the story backed up by the campaign of the Women's Temperance Union of the civilizing woman, pure wife and mother, antidrinking, bulwark against male lawlessness and disorder in the forging of a new country. By comparison, the discourse of rights for women has never been very effective. In our study of the movement toward full citizenship and political representation, women have typically turned the traditional "difference" argument to advance their own cause and establish their legitimacy. The work of political scientist Maurice Duverger

*Questions for Government at the National Assembly.*
*Front row: Martine Aubry, Bernard Kouchner, Elisabeth Guigou;*
*Behind: Claude Allègre and Dominique Voynet.*

articulates this difference as an antagonism between the sexes. In spite of his eulogy to traditional feminine difference, Pascal also believes that a battle of the sexes is being waged at some deeper level within the battles for women's suffrage and for women's representation.

> The conclusion to all these reflections is the observation of a fundamental antagonism between men and women that is not open hostility but that carries within it the seeds of an impasse at the level we have seen for more than forty years. The door of Parliament is still only half-open to women in 1989. It will take time.[36]

Pascal's arguments on women's traditional difference are shared by many women. He claims men desire to leave traces of themselves in their public achievements while women find this less imperative; their more natural "traces" are their children. Women "who enter the political game controlled by men leave aside part of the qualities that constituted their singular character."[37] Such a necessary abandonment of women's distinctive character in exchange for political power would not be justified. Pascal's notion of difference is based on essential characteristics. On the other hand, most of the women writers we have studied so far are concerned to ground their definitions of difference in lived experience and in the specificity of women's life-contexts. These writers imagine making changes to accommodate this lived difference in the conditions of the political world.

Bouchardeau's work eschews the notion of a battle of the sexes and promotes rather the ideas of freedom and diversity. If she notes the privileged centers of interest in the home, and the self-identification of many women as caregivers, her autobiographical work, *Choses dites de profil*, reveals how personally limiting she found these "natural" roles. When women in politics argue in favor of state-funded daycare or support for children and families, this is not to reinforce the traditional division of tasks. In the words of Yvette Roudy, this is rather a lightening of women's present burdens, a liberation for women for activities other than child care.

The difference arguments, stressing women's more pragmatic orientation and women's life experience, are being used in the parity cause. So, too, is the conservative argument of national honor. France, presented as having a much prouder and more unique democratic heritage than other countries, is portrayed as lagging here behind the world's least "developed" nations. The crucial contemporary questions for women in French politics, then, have crystallized around a new concept: parity. This change is indicative of a major revision of thinking on women in power effected by the new discourses at the level of the mainstream. It also signals a shift within feminist politics itself. At the end of the century, Michelle Perrot will argue, following Joan Scott, that equality is not in fact the opposite of difference (inequality is its opposite). The opposite of difference is identity and difference does not, of course, exclude equality and the opposition equality/feminine difference is a false one. Women are defined by their multiple self-identifications. The next chapter is devoted to the texts that mark the parity debate in France and demonstrate these shifts in power.

## Notes

1. Report by Janine Mossuz-Lavau from the Second National Congress of the "Association Française de Science Politique" held at Grenoble from 25 to 28 January 1984.
2. In 1945, there were 33 women or 5.63 percent of the total elected representatives; 40, or 6.48 percent in 1946; 22, or 3.50 percent in 1951; 9, or 1.55 percent in 1958; 9, or 1.86 percent in 1962; 21, or 4.27 percent in 1978; 28, or 5.7 percent in 1981; 35, or 6.06 percent, with the restoration of the "list" of candidates, that is, of a system of proportional representation apparently more favorable to women, in 1986. The figures do not improve in the following years.
3. In 2001, Michèle Alliot-Marie was successfully maintaining her position as president of the RPR party. In March 2000, Lucette Michaux-Chevry was still in office in Guadeloupe as mayor and Senator (*Senateur maire*) of the Basse-Terre *département* but had come under some attack. "La taxe de Lucette" by Thierry Fundéré (*Le Point* magazine, no. 1436, 24 March 2000, p. 18), reports that the president of the Regional Council is the object of an investigation, begun in June 1998. The mayor had allegedly raised an illegal tax on building permits to create resources for her community of Gourbeyre between 1987 and 1995. Michaux-Chevry had denied the charge and countered with the announcement of the transformation of her movement, Objectif Guadeloupe, into a political party. In "La Chute de la dame de fer" (*Le Point*, no. 1445, 26 May 2000, p. 14), Thierry Fundéré, again notes that there is a possibility that the court may strip Michaux-Chevry of her office. The journalist gives expression to popular symbolic representations of strong women politicians and ambivalence toward them by designating Michaux-Chevry as "the iron lady of Guadeloupe."
4. Natacha Henry, "Gender Parity in French Politics," *The Political Quarterly* 66, no. 3 (July-Sept 1995), pp. 177–180.
5. The autobiographical writings of Françoise Gaspard and of Gisèle Halimi acknowledge the positive aspect of Marie Curie's entry into the Panthéon, as does Giroud in her *Diary*, although Halimi comments with irony on Marie's "great solitude." Doesn't she need some company? The commemorative plaque might otherwise need to be changed to: "To its great men and one woman, with gratitude from the nation" (*Aux grands hommes et à une femme, la patrie reconnaissante*). The case of the Pantheon as an all-male home for France's great "men" recalls other instances of women's absence: the 1946 list of the resistance heroes, the "Compagnons de la Libération," which included 1024 heroic men and six women; or indeed the single woman writer in the *Académie Française* until recently, the Belgian, Marguerite Yourcenar.
6. Janine Mossuz-Lavau, *Les Français et la politique* (Paris: Odile Jacob, 1994).
7. Among young people aged between twenty-five and twenty-nine, for example, 53 percent of men and 60 percent of women vote for the left; between eighteen and twenty-four years of age, 49 percent of the female population and 44 percent of the male electorate. The zones of strength for the Socialist party among the female population are the young, the active, the well educated, and students. Among white-collar executives, 55 percent of women and 40 percent of men voted left, and among the liberal professions, 66 percent of men and 40 percent of women. Sineau indicates that 1988 was also a bumper year for women's votes for Mitterrand.
8. In 1965 in the first presidential election under universal suffrage, only 39 percent of women versus 51 percent of men voted for Mitterrand, who was running against De Gaulle. In the 1981 parliamentary elections, 54 percent of women and 58 percent of men voted for left-wing candidates. The year 1986, then, marked a high point of the

shift in women's votes toward the left as 44 percent of men and 44 percent of women overall voted for the Socialists. In the first ballot of the 1988 presidential election, 46 percent of both sexes again supported left-wing candidates, with women supporting Mitterrand more than men and Le Pen, less than men.

9. At the end of the 1980s, dissatisfaction among the electorate with the Socialist governments could be read in the unusual drop in voting numbers. A rise in interest in the ecologists, and the influence of the right-wing aristocrat, Philippe de Villiers, and the businessman Bernard Tapie, *l'intégriste* (the fundamentalist) and *l'affairiste* (the tycoon), to use the words of the political scientist Olivier Duhamel, confirmed this dissatisfaction. Support for the right-wing Front national, which rarely fell below 10 percent and reached 18 percent in the 1997 election, was a further sign of disaffection, although women were less supportive of this extremist grouping (18 percent men and 11 percent women in 1998). The anti-contraception and anti-abortion program and the call for a return of women to their home (with maternity salaries) along with the cult of aggressive virility and male authority appears to have particularly alienated younger women between eighteen and twenty-eight. A survey indicated that 15 percent of men and 10 percent of women declared that they had voted for the Front national in 1993. A SOFRES poll showed a lesser gap of 14 percent men and 13 percent of women. Twelve percent of women and 19 percent of men voted for Le Pen's Front national in 1995. This had hardly changed in 1997. In Mossuz-Lavau, "Les Femmes font de la résistance," *Le Monde Diplomatique*, May 1998.
10. Janine Mossuz-Lavau, "Le Vote des Françaises dans les années quatre-vingt-dix," *French Politics and Society* 12, no. 4 (Fall 1994), p. 65. Even in the year of greatest disaffection, 1993, women and men were equal supporters of the Socialist party, with scores of 21 percent. Rocard's 1994 parity-based list received 16 percent of female votes and 14 percent of male votes, a very much lower score than Mitterrand's first round score of 35 percent of the female vote and 31 percent of the male vote in 1988.
11. Although the electorate was disaffected and unhappy with the antagonistic left/right party structure of government, and with policies on the right and left that had become indistinguishable from one another, political commitments themselves were still strong and still organized along clearly identifiable left/right ideological axes that included both men and women. The right is characterized by the traditional conservative values of nation, family, and the morality of work in a hierarchical, authoritarian organization. The extreme right is characterized by its exploitation of social discontent and anti-immigration fury (symptomatic of the wish to abolish difference), nostalgia for the return of the family in the sense of a hierarchy of paternal authority and full-time maternal caregiving, and desire for the restoration of "moral" order. Those on the "left," according to Mossuz-Lavau's analysis, characterized by a concern to help others, a solidarity that includes the reduction of social inequalities, opposition to xenophobia (and tolerance for difference), and a desire for greater democracy, maintain strong traditions of political identity. The ecologists, characterized by their refusal of the reigning non-egalitarian system of government, and the defense of the environment, come both from the right and the left tradition and include many women.
12. Janine Mossuz-Lavau directed interviews from 1992 through 1993 and published *Les Français et la politique* in 1994.
13. A study carried out by SOFRES in 1988 points to 36 percent of women who declare that they are interested or quite interested in politics compared to 49 percent of men.
14. Janine Mossuz-Lavau has been challenged in relation to her new methodology. Interviewed for *Télérama* 2566 on 17 May 1999, the sociologist was asked whether her three-hour-long program of testimonials tracing the revolutions in work, sexuality, and political participation was really adequate to trace the evolution of the feminine condition. Mossuz-Lavau justified her decision to spend five weeks of filming ordinary women's lives and to carry out second interviews with exceptional women from her earlier studies as the most informative way of defining the complexity of women's situations.

15. Anne Phillips, *Engendering Democracy* (Oxford: Oxford Polity Press, 1991), also discusses *fraternité*, or "brotherhood," at some length.
16. Sineau notes that 1848, and not 1944, continues to be the reference in French history for universal suffrage. Sineau is quoting here from Siân Reynolds's work.
17. Twelve percent of workers were employed part-time and 8.8 percent had limited term contracts or were without full employment rights
18. Mariette Sineau, "Pouvoir, modernité et monopole masculin de la politique: le cas français, *Nouvelles Questions Féministes* 13, no. 1 (1992), pp. 40–61.
19. In 1992, Noëlle Lenoir was the first woman to be appointed to the *Conseil Constitutionnel*, one member out of nine, but a move forward symbolically that offered the possibility of a different input into future decisions. In 2001, Monique Pelletier replaced the disgraced Roland Dumas.
20. Dorothy McBride Stetson, *Women's Rights in France* (New York: Greenwood Press), p. 205.
21. "L'Express va plus loin avec Hélène Gisserot," *L'Express*, 20 October 1994. Gisserot gives an account of her talk at the international conference on women she had just attended in Vienna. Addressing delegates from fifty-four industrialized countries, she had described progress for women in France.
22. Françoise Giroud, *Chienne d'année. Journal d'une Parisienne 2* (Paris: Seuil, 1995), p. 272.
23. Catherine Pégard, "Femmes politiques. "Juppettes" les illusions perdues," *Le Point*, no. 1236, 25 May 1996, p. 68. In her column in *Le Point* on 27 May, Catherine Pégard again describes the departures and the new arrivals. The details she chooses are telling. François Bayrou, for example, greeted his three secretaries of state, two women and a man—Elisabeth Dufourcq (research), Françoise Hostalier (secondary education), and Jean de Boishue (higher education)—declaring that he alone would assume responsibility for their respective offices. He pronounced Françoise Hostalier's name incorrectly several times and the following day, on a visit to the CNRS, introduced himself as the person who was responsible for research with Elisabeth Dufourcq, who was "charming," to assist him.
24. Corinne Lepage, a lawyer, remained as minister of the environment, Anne-Marie Couderc as *ministre déléguée à l'emploi* (assistant employment minister), Anne-Marie Idrac as *secrétaire d'Etat aux transports* (junior transportation minister), and Margie Sudre as *secrétaire d'Etat chargée de la Francophonie* (junior minister for relationships with Francophone countries).
25. "On ne saurait mieux montrer la considération dans laquelle on les tenait." Françoise Giroud, *Chienne d'année*, p. 262.
26. Françoise Giroud, "Femmes, ministres et humiliées," *Le Nouvel Observateur*, 16 November 1995.
27. Mariette Sineau, *Vingtième Siècle, Revue d'histoire*, no. 43 (juillet–décembre 1994), pp. 72–78.
28. Sineau quotes Louise Weiss, *Mémoires d'une Européenne: Combats pour les femmes* 1934–1939, volume 3 (Paris: Albin Michel, 1983), pp. 18–19.
29. Offen quotes Siân Reynolds, "Marianne's Citizens? Women, the Republic and Universal Suffrage in France," in *Women, State, and Revolution: Essays on Power and Gender in Europe since 1789* (Amherst: University of Massachusetts Press, 1987) to note that 1945 is a non-date in male histories in all of the traditional histories of the French Republic.
30. Cécile Dauphin, "Culture et pouvoir des femmes," *Annales: Economies, Sociétés, Civilisations*, no. 2 (March–April 1986), translated as "Women's Culture and Women's Power: Issues in French Women's' History," in Karen Offen, Ruth Roach Pierson, and Jane Rendall, eds., *Writing Women's History: International Perspectives*, pp. 107–133.
31. "The Same or Different? An Unending Dilemma for French Women," Jane Jenson and Mariette Sineau, in *Women and Politics Worldwide*, ed. Barbara J. Nelson and Najma Chowdhury (New Haven and London, Yale University Press, 1994), pp. 244–260.

32. In 1979, the organization founded by Antoinette Fouque, Psychanalyse et Politique, legally appropriated the label as MLF déposé.
33. Sineau claims that internal conflicts and the severe decline of the far left, combined with a growing indifference to electoral politics, virtually eliminated this revolutionary feminism, which had "rejected ideas of statist change and sought to develop more spontaneous and less hierarchical forms of organization" within two decades.
34. Karen Offen, "Women, Citizenship and Suffrage with a French Twist," in Caroline Daley and Melanie Dolan, *Suffrage and Beyond* (New York: New York University Press, 1994).
35. Jane Rendall, "Citizenship, Culture and Civilization: The Languages of British Suffragists, 1866–1874," in Daley, *Suffrage and Beyond*, pp. 127–150.
36. Jean Pascal, *Les Femmes députés*s (Paris: Pascal, 1990), p. 353.
37. "La conclusion de toutes ces réflexions, c'est la constatation d'un antagonisme fondamental entre l'homme et la femme, qui n'est pas une hostilité déclarée, mais qui porte en lui-même le germe d'un blocage de la situation au niveau que nous venons de voir depuis plus de quarante ans. La porte du Parlement n'est encore qu'entreouverte aux femmes en 1989. Il faut laisser le temps au temps." Ibid., p. 352.

# Part II

## Feminine Discourses:

## The Bumpy Road Toward Progress

# 3

# Parity: Rewriting Democracy in France

From June of 1997 to March 1999, the issue of parity was a constant preoccupation in the French media, replaced only by the Kosovo crisis. By mid 2000, equal access for women to political mandates was written into French electoral law. There is little in the history of the parity debate in France to predict such success in both parliament and senate. In 1884, Hubertine Auclert's demand for half of the seats in the National Assembly had fallen on very deaf ears. Other proposals for quotas followed and largely failed.[1] Even proposals that fell short of full parity met resistance. In 1982, the deputy and feminist lawyer Gisèle Halimi introduced a bill proposing a 75 percent maximum of either sex in municipal elections. Halimi made the proposition in the name of the equality of all citizens before the law guaranteed by the *Déclaration des Droits de l'homme.*[2] But, as Halimi reports, when she launched her crusade for quotas in 1982, most of her colleagues responded benevolently but evasively with the argument that a fairer representation of women in government would come naturally with the change of attitudes. Her insistence on the need for a law led people to rush to avoid her: "Watch out, here comes Halimi-Quotas." Although the law she proposed was finally passed in the Assembly, certain clauses were then examined by the *Conseil Constitutionnel* (Constitutional Council) that struck down the amendment providing for quotas. The *Conseil* argued that the clause divided the sovereign French people into categories and was thereby contrary to Article 3 of the constitution that protected the indivisibility and universality of citizenship. Halimi, and later many of the parity advocates, counter-claimed that members of classes or categories could choose to change their category. Women, like men, cannot. As half of the world's population, encompassing all categories, women do not constitute a category. Halimi detected a misogynist motivation behind the legal opinion of the then all-male conservative *Conseil Constitutionnel* whose average age, she notes, was seventy-five.

Despite these early setbacks, on 11 March 1999, the Senate finally accepted the modification of Article 3 of the Constitution, the universality article. The addition to Article 3 read: "the law is to facilitate equal access for all women and men to elected office and political life" (*la loi favorise l'égal accés des femmes et des hommes aux mandats électoraux et fonctions électives*). Article 4 of the Constitution was to include the principle that political parties should contribute to the goal of parity. In December 1999, articles 3 and 4 finally went to Cabinet for consideration with the proposal that in 2001, electoral lists should include 50 percent female candidates and funding be withheld from parties where the lists have a gender gap greater than 20 percent.[3] What the acceptance of parity meant most immediately was that legislation for affirmative action was now possible and was protected from the censure of the Constitutional Council. The feminist historian Geneviève Fraisse (who had served as an inter-ministerial advocate for Women's Rights in the Jospin administration) warned that the legal text was not a panacea; the need to change the wider relations of power remained. But, even interpreted as a general principle of greater equality rather than as a stepping stone to a numerically equal National Assembly, the fact that parity, or at least "equal access" was written into law made France something of an "exception" once again.[4] A positive exception this time, claimed Nelly Furman, a professor at Princeton University, and one that American women might well imitate. So, how had the unexpected happened? How had France, a country slow in granting full franchise to women, suddenly leapt ahead in formalizing parity of representation? Genevieve Fraisse labeled parity a Trojan horse. If this were the case, why would the public be taken in by it and who, indeed, would take it in?

The previous chapters argued that women's texts and voices were slowly achieving a critical mass and helping to effect a change in consciousness in France. Like the legislation against sexual harassment or the feminization of names of professions, parity seemed to be benefiting from a change in public opinion long resistant to feminism and to any modification in the balance of power. One indication of altering perceptions toward women in politics may be found in the increasing presence of women in the National Assembly. In 1996, six percent of the National Assembly was female, by 1999 this presence had risen a further 5 percent, although France still trailed the European Community except for Greece. There are changes in public attitudes apparent in the 1997–2000 opinion polls that show the female ministers (Martine Aubry, Elisabeth Guigou, Catherine Trautmann, Ségolène Royal, Dominique Voynet, Marie-Georges Buffet) consistently at or near the top of the popularity ratings. At the end of the 1990s women even rated highly in polls for the presidency. In a 1999 poll, 47 percent of French people declared they were in favor of Martine Aubry and 45 percent in favor of Simone Veil as the next President of the Republic. The parity case also drew its support from the sociopolitical context: the disillusionment provoked by the scandals and corruption in the French government and the general desire for a reformed political system.

Changes in the media coverage of women's representative levels are further evidence of a change in attitudes in France, although the language used by a number of male media commentators certainly still frames the parity issue as part of a battle of the sexes. Somewhere between irony and analysis, one journalist, Pierre Georges, observes that the campaign to feminize government is not war, but nor, he adds, is it peace, and it will inevitably provoke some grinding of teeth. After all, Socialists are men too—enlightened in their writings but often sexist at their core. They will thrill at the necessary and just cause of parity and then proceed to send women back to their home "sections" (local political branches) and continue to exercise their own privileges at a central level in the *fédération*. Pierre Georges concludes with tongue in cheek that men know that a woman is stronger, more seductive, more of a fighter, more of everything. They have no good reason at all to give up their places since she would accept with alacrity and hold on to the place given up. And even homo socialistus loves winnable electoral districts.[5] Despite this framing by the traditionally antifeminist if humorous rhetoric of "the battle of the sexes" and mythology of the superwoman ready to vanquish man, Georges's article is a typical response to the changing political scene and one that is not totally unsympathetic to women's cause.

Not only were there changes in the French media, but pressure from Europe was being felt on the issue of women's representation in legislative assemblies. In 1989, the Council of Europe held a seminar on *la démocratie paritaire* as a program that would allow both sexes to play an equal role in political life without necessarily insisting on an equal number of elected men and women. At a European conference in Athens in 1992, an initiative of the Commission of the European Community adopted a final declaration that called for equality of men's and women's participation in all public decision making. This support for the parity movement from Europe would continue and increase.

Despite these changes in public opinion and visibility in the media, in *Les Femmes et leur histoire*, the historian Geneviève Fraisse stops to wonder whether it is really enough for women to believe they have the authority to speak and write in order for them to make themselves heard. Her skepticism derives from the historical invisibility of women and deafness toward the feminist voice and inclines her to argue that the parity debate of 1997, initially something of a flop, was revived only by the political action and successes of the Parti socialiste and Jospin in the spring of 1997. In this respect, it was still a kind of *fait du prince*, or top-down operation. But parity is nonetheless a word that relaunches the feminist debate in 1993, crystallizing an awareness and a revolt, according to Fraisse. For her, the acceptance of parity accompanies a general recognition that women's political exclusion was less an effect of simple individual "machismo" than of political networks that are "virile" in character and do not attract women, self-protective, and unlikely to be changed from within by the parties. In fact, the parity texts are seen by a number of women as strategic and political texts, not glorious but necessary: texts that are a pragmatic instrument in the struggle for their "half" of power. Notwithstanding these reservations, this chapter will argue that, compounded with the new texts in circulation on women's experience in political life, the discourse that argued for the necessary presence of women in the public forum, disseminated and popularized by the media, and accompanied by political action, was nonetheless falling on fertile ground and producing major political effects.

## Action on the Political Front

Quotas, like all forms of affirmative action, are a temporary mechanism of redistribution, notes Bouchardeau. Belgium requires by law that no more than two-thirds of candidates on electoral lists may be of the same sex. In Sweden, parties have been put under pressure by competition to impose their own internal quotas. But given the stakes of power, Bouchardeau further observes, the quota system has never been fully and honestly implemented in any party in France, not even in the ecological parties that have recently tried to structure themselves to achieve a complete internal parity. Nonetheless, parties across the political spectrum in France began to make moves toward greater female representation from the 1970s onward.

In 1974, the Socialist party put forward the principle of a 10 percent minimum presence of women at all levels of the party organization (*Comité Directeur, Bureau Exécutif, Fédération, Section*). The Socialist party was the first French political party to write female representation into its rules. The percentage, to be revised at each National Congress to take account of the actual proportion of women in the party, was raised to 30 percent in 1993. Confirmed at the Socialist party's convention at Lyon in July of 1993, the quota was not entirely respected either for the legislative elections or for the leadership offices of the party. In 1993, women occupied 18.5 percent of the *Bureau Exécutif* and 7.7 percent of the *Comité Directeur*. Even though female representation in the Socialist party continued to lag behind the set goals, the principle of parity was accepted as the ultimate goal. Another positive change by the Socialists was the fact that good, mediocre, and bad electoral districts were to be equitably distributed between male and female candidates. This was a break from past elections when non-winnable electorates or impossible positions on a list had been occupied predominantly by women.

In the 1990s, other French political parties followed the Socialists with respect to female representation at all levels. In the European elections of 1994, Gisèle Halimi accepted a position on Chevènement's list of candidates on the condition that his new *Mouvement des Citoyens* agreed to support a law on parity. For these European elections, both the Socialist Rocard and Chevènement alternated men and women on their party lists. This measure was met with as much derision as interest. Fun was poked at the idea in the form of the theme song from the classic Lelouch film *Un homme et une femme*, "Chabada bada," and the list was also qualified by the press as a *partouze* (a sex party). The implications of sexual promiscuity derive of course from archaic beliefs about the sexual disorder occasioned by women when they are not confined to the home. The ecological union led by Marie-Anne Isler Béguin also applied the now traditional Green principle of equal representation. By 1994, even the business tycoon Bernard Tapie's *Energie radicale* group contained 25 percent women, including Antoinette Fouque, who was president of the feminist parity group *Alliance des femmes pour la démocratie*.

Within the Socialist party a national commission worked for three months in conjunction with local federations to ratify an agreement on 21 September 1996, reserving 30 percent of electoral districts—160 in all—for women candidates in the upcoming parliamentary elections (scheduled for 1998, but moved up to 1997).[6] Forty of these seats, all held by the majority, were argued to be winnable.[7] The scores of the women in the legislative elections of 1997 were as good if not better than those of the men, and public opinion conceded that the Parti socialiste showed a certain courage in insisting that 30 percent of candidates were women. In the government announced on 4 June 1997 by Jospin, eight out of twenty-six *ministres*, *ministres délégués*, and *secrétaires d'Etat*, that is, more than 30 percent, were women. The spectacular and unexpected return of the Socialists to power thus brought six women ministers and two *secrétaires d'état* to government and doubled the number of women in the *Assemblée* (62).

Parity was not just a topic within individual political parties. In the early 1990s, Halimi's parity group, *Club Parité 2000*, Roudy's *L'Assemblée des Femmes*, and *L'Alliance des Femmes pour la Démocratie* organized in 1989 by Antoinette Fouque as the successor to the MLF (Mouvement de libération de la femme, or Women's Liberation Movement) joined forces to form the national group *Demain la Parité* (Parity Tomorrow). Over the following two years, more than thirty-five forums were organized by *Demain la Parité* around the country to help women run for office as municipal councilors. Feminist and women's groups of very different origins united around the new cause of political power. In December 1996, Halimi was asked to present a proposal for a constitutional amendment to the government.

The question of female representation within political parties and women's own raised voices were increasingly amplified by the media in the late 1990s. For example, the midday news on Thursday 3 October 1996 concluded with a short debate between the former Socialist Minister of Culture Jack Lang and the junior labor minister, *ministre déléguée à l'emploi*, Anne-Marie Couderc.[8] Jack Lang praised the boldness of the recent Socialist decision to impose quotas for the legislative elections, to support a parity law, and the plan to incrementally achieve a 50 percent political representation for women. Anne-Marie Couderc, speaking as a government representative, responded very carefully against a law imposing quotas but agreed that the situation for women needed to be changed and would be changed, soon, by "political will." The parity cause and its polemical potential had seized the interest of the media and all parties were on notice. In June 1999, women won thirty-five seats out of eighty-seven (a symbolic 40 percent) in the European Parliament. These political advances were in part a result of the parity discourse, which they further reinforced.

## The Impact of Parity Manifestos

A small number of texts were written and used to specifically support women's political action. In 1992, the first parity manifesto, *Au pouvoir, citoyennes! Liberté, Egalité, Parité,* was published in France. In their book, feminist authors Françoise Gaspard, Anne Le Gall, and Claude Servan-Schreiber called for as many seats in political assemblies for women as for men. Parity was to be a new right, as necessary a foundation of democracy as universal suffrage or the separation of powers. The book proposed a new institutional and constitutional program.[9]

The radical reading and rewriting of women's political history that underlies the arguments of *Au Pouvoir citoyennes!* turns once again on the question of how democracy came to be confiscated by the masculine sex in the very cradle of the *Droits de l'homme.* For these three writers, a problem of language had existed since the Revolution, which had given rights to *tous les Français* ("all Frenchmen"). In 1992, however, in response to the argument that "all men are born and remain free and equal in rights and responsibilities," the Constitutional Council had riposted that "women are not men." So "Frenchmen" was not a universal category after all. Given the quasi-monopoly of political representation by men, Western democracy would need to be reinvented. In 1993, in what was also a media attention-seeking gesture, Gaspard organized a group of journalists and lawyers around the "Manifesto of the 577 for a popular democracy."[10] Her arguments would circulate widely.

In the introduction to the papers published after the colloquium held in Paris by UNESCO on 3 and 4 June 1993, Gisèle Halimi advances arguments that will feed into the new parity discourse.[11] Halimi claims that given that equality had served as a perverse camouflage for the inequality of women, equality of the sexes needed redefinition.[12] Women's difference should be the determining force of a new democracy, but not in the way that difference was used to found women's inferiorization. "Would a parity law make the world better?" asked Halimi. At the least it would bring a different and more just world. The progress of women, moreover, had always coincided with the development of democracy, and regressed in the darkest periods of history (under Hitler, Franco, Pétain, Pinochet).[13] In response, the historian Michelle Perrot gave voice to the concerns of many French intellectuals and wondered whether it was really wise to abandon French-style individualistic democracy for an "interest group" (*communautariste*) approach.[14] The term *communautarisme* denoting the development of separate communities would come to stand in opposition to universalism throughout the parity debate in the media. Its connotations of diversity and multiculturalism, potential agents of fragmentation and break-up of the single shared community, are largely negative and redolent of a suspect (imperialistic) North-American culture.[15]

Following a television documentary in 1995 on women in politics (part of the series *Polémiques* or Polemical Issues), Yvette Roudy proposed the establishment of a cross-party coalition involving women who had occupied the highest positions in French politics, who had been involved in the electoral process, and who were familiar with party commissions and offices. Six political women who had appeared in the *Polémiques* documentary took up Roudy's idea: Edith Cresson, Véronique Neiertz, Catherine Tasca, Hélène Gisserot, Catherine Lalumière, and Simone Veil. The manifesto the group produced began with figures: thirty-two *députée*s out of 577, eighteen *sénatrices* out of 303. The measures proposed in the manifesto were wide ranging. The group wanted concerted action by parties, women's associations, and government in favor of the introduction of a system of voting by proportional representation; an initial goal of one-third of the places in all political bodies for women; limits on the number of political posts that could be held at the same time by a single person; state financing of parties in relation to their practical commitment to the parity principle; nomination of women to executive positions; legislation on sexism comparable to the legislation existing on racism; and a referendum on the modification of the constitution to permit affirmative action.

The text of the manifesto was published in *L'Express* in June 1996 with an introduction by the journalist Elisabeth Schemla and a form allowing readers to respond with their suggestions. *L'Express* received more than 8,000 replies.[16] Subsequently, the government organized a parliamentary debate on female legislative representation and announced its intention to field 30 percent women in the coming national elections. Again, text and political action went hand in hand.

The ten women who signed the manifesto claim to have personally faced condescending indifference, scorn, or open hostility from within the world of politics. Using the arguments developed by women historians, they write that their exclusion derives from the outdated Jacobin tradition at the heart of republicanism. Centralizing and hierarchical, rhetorical, and rational to abstraction, Jacobinism concentrates virile qualities "as only a period immersed in a mythical Antiquity could imagine them."[17] Real human relationships, sensitivity, and concrete, everyday preoccupations were cast out from the field of politics, and women with them, according to this increasingly shared analysis. The characters presented as significant in the French republican imagery—such as the mayor, the teacher, the soldier, or the judge—were essentially masculine figures. Women were outside republican imagery and their vision and experience did not contribute to lawmaking. This exclusion made it necessary to develop a place for women's contribution, and the women politicians behind the 577 Manifesto aimed at doing just that.

The 577 Manifesto did create direct response from a number of male political leaders. Like Tony Blair and Jean Chrétien before him, Lionel Jospin promised to feminize parliament while he was in opposition and approved the campaign for parity, to be applied immediately in local and regional elections. Jospin also approved moves to double the percentage of women in the legislature with each election, and he supported the introduction of proportional representation. Prime Minister Alain Juppé argued defensively that proportional representation in the regional and European elections of 1986 and 1992, and in the legislative elections of 1986, had not given any advantage to women candidates.[18] Juppé nonetheless promised to significantly increase the number of Gaullist women running in the forthcoming regional elections. Dominique Voynet, who subsequently became a Green party environment minister was in favor of the 577 Manifesto, but with a reservation. She wanted to ensure that what was being asked for was not affirmative action (identified linguistically in France somewhat negatively as positive discrimination (*discrimination positive*) but recognition that men and women are different and that this difference is positive. Robert Hue (of the PCF, or Parti communiste français) supported all proposals in the Manifesto except the withholding of state financing from non-representative parties. Not all parties supported the parity moves the Manifesto proposed. The Union démocratique française (or UDF) was not sympathetic and Le Pen (of the Front national or FN) was against everything except a limit on holding multiple offices. Nonetheless, a political revolution was under way, which included men and women from across the traditional political spectrum.

Ségolène Royal, deputy for the department of Deux-Sèvres to the southwest of Paris, had sent an open letter to the president of the Assembly presenting the results of a survey of school children in 577 classes who were asked to elect their own representatives to the parliamentary body. They had come out spontaneously in support of parity, as Elisabeth Schemla observes in *Le Nouvel Observateur*, sending 305 girls to sit on the parliamentary benches. At the same time as the Taliban in Afghanistan closed the private schools for girls set up after public education for women had been forbidden, the Catholic paper, *La Croix*, took a position in favor of the justice of the parity cause. For their part, the right-wing papers—*Le Figaro*, for example—claimed that the reform was oblique and ambiguous, raised fears of feminine takeover, and also played on the suspicion that the government was using parity to bring in proportional representation. Echoing the leader of the Senate, the right-wing papers argued that parity was a humiliation for women, who were to be protected as a weaker species.

Despite this, a critical mass of support was clearly emerging for parity, a concept that was vague enough to be inclusive. The often contrasted conceptions of feminine difference (as discussed in chapter 1, innovative with Bouchareau and conservative with Pascal) seem to fuel the topic of women in power, such that the debate alone constitutes a kind of counter-power. Whereas it is implied that Bouchardeau's vision of a new and positive feminine difference (a difference that did not yet exist, a difference to be actualized or invented) constitutes a form of "empowerment," Pascal's essentialist conservative difference seems hardly to qualify. Yet, what seems to give parity power and some potential for empowerment is precisely that it can accommodate both conservative and left-wing readings of gender difference along with principles of equality.

## For Which Parity Were Women Arguing?

*Le Monde* had published the 577 Manifesto in December of 1993. Yvette Roudy, a principle writer on the parity issue as president of the Commission for Equal Opportunity for men and women of the Parliament of the Council of Europe, made a strong claim in that publication that parity debates had brought about a general awareness of France's "scandalous" position created by the French "exceptions." She pointed to the position created by the Salic law, the Revolution, the Napoleonic Code, the Catholic Church, the unwillingness of closed male clubs to share the real power that resides in politics in France. But what did Roudy mean by the word "parity"? Parity has varied meanings in the various academic and political texts. Differences of meaning were evident, for example, in a seminar on parity that I attended in December of 1996, organized by the *Ecole Nationale des Hautes Etudes en Sciences Sociales*. The discussion highlighted the astonishing sense of solidarity toward political parity, while at the same time showing there was major divergence in its definition. In the opinion of the principal speaker, Simone Veil, parity should not mean a strict and prescriptive 50/50 division of seats between men and women, but should leave space for the distinctive character of local assemblies and aspirations. On the other hand, Anne Le Gall argued that only in politics did women still feel humiliated and spoke eloquently for parity as strict gender division of the number of places in all political assemblies. Some speakers at the seminar considered that the quantitative and constraining aspects of parity were important; others were more concerned with qualitative issues such as how to keep out the "difference" of National Front women. Simone Veil concluded the seminar by asserting her confidence that, despite the differences, misunderstandings, and the major questions still hanging over the mechanisms for implementation of the parity principle, the parity movement would strengthen the cause for increased female representation.

This divergence on the understanding of parity and its possible electoral mechanisms is also found in media reports. As the parity movement gained popular support in the late 1990s, a number of prominent women were pressed by the media to take a public position on women's political representation. Martine Aubry admitted to the press that she had been "naive about parity" for a long time, believing it unnecessary and expecting women's improved education to make the difference (*Evénement*, 11–17 February 1999). The wife of Lionel Jospin, the philosopher Sylviane Ajacinski, argued the case in the media that it was not difference but the devaluing of difference that needed to be addressed. She claimed that universalism ignored the social organization of sexual difference that made women incomplete and inferior beings. Women on the right joined in with public pronouncements of support for parity. The Rassemblement pour la République (RPR) *députée* Nicole Catala wrote that although she was not in favor of 50 percent representation, she accepted the parity principle. Françoise de Panafieu (*députée* RPR) added her voice to the cause with *Vive les femmes... et la parité* (*Le Parisien*, 8 March); Anne-Marie Idrac explained that she too had changed her mind in favor of parity. Even the author of a new book on de Beauvoir—Françoise Rétif, *L'Autre en miroir* (The Other in the Mirror), jumped on the bandwagon, insisting that the mother of first-wave egalitarian feminism would have approved of parity according to her principle that a human being is both man and woman, identical and different in each one of us.

Divergent opinions about the usefulness of feminine difference to the parity debate and the equality movement are also to be found within academic texts. Tracing the reasons for the exclusion of women from modern political life and the case for parity, historian Michèle Riot-Sarcey examines documents from the revolutionary period in France in order to argue that sovereignty resided in the single and indivisible community of active citizens. These active citizens were defined as separate from the multitude of individuals: the dependence or passivity of the latter (women and children... ) determined the independence, the freedom, the right to represent of the former.[19] Another prominent feminist historian, Geneviève Fraisse, hypothesizes that the Salic law forbidding the transmission of the crown to a woman and written into law in 1791, reveals the struggle between the sexes and the importance of biological

*Françoise de Panafieu.*

difference that continue to characterize the political arena.[20] Both women historians point to the political importance of the biological difference between the sexes in the long and incomplete process of women's inclusion in the political realm, and to the concealment of this exclusion by the supposed neutrality appealed to by universal citizenship.

In defense of the republican principle of "universality," the philosopher Elisabeth Badinter writes that despite external signs of femininity, in order to exercise power, women need to be virile, authoritative, and combative, like Elizabeth the First, Catherine the Second, Margaret Thatcher, and Indira Gandhi. At the same time, according to Badinter, Mrs. Thatcher was not simply the "only man in the government," as the press labeled her; she was also a more complete woman and a more complete human being than her male colleagues—able to express her virile side without repression: "How could we have believed for so long that women were not endowed with the same virtues and vices as men: the will to power, toughness, etc.!"[21] Badinter criticizes the parity movement's emphasis on women's difference as consecrating the most traditional of feminine characteristics.[22] Its dominant tendency is to describe women as practical and sensitive to others, as more human and more effective; men as cerebral, hierarchical, and ambitious. Badinter argues that this is a question of individual temperament and development of potential rather than gender.[23]

The limited scope of this chapter does not allow us to cover the rich and extensive academic debates on parity within feminism, political science, and women's history in any depth. One example of the different thinking on parity is found in two issues of the journal *Les Nouvelles Questions Féministes*, edited by Christine Delphy. These volumes, *For*

*Parity* and *Against Parity*, provide a brief glimpse of the range of positions and arguments. In the 1994 issue entitled "For Parity," Green party member Alain Liepetz makes the claim that the ideal of sexual difference within equality, expressed by the concept of parity, had transformed political relations in the Green movement and attracted new followers. In the same volume of essays, Françoise Gaspard attempts rather to preempt the arguments of opponents.[24] Would the distinctive character of the French Republican tradition be lost in the fragmentation that might result from any emphasis on difference or multiplicity? Equality, in any case, is already based on the implicit recognition of difference. If individuals were all the same, there would be no need for a principle of equality. Eliane Viennot's case for parity also showcases the (separatist) traditions and arguments of the academic opponents of parity in order to refute them.[25] Viennot argues that it is probable that a "feminine" style exists simply because women constitute a minority in political bodies. In an ideal situation, it would be differences between individuals rather than between the sexes that would become more important, or perhaps men would increasingly adopt "feminine" styles. Parity, she claims, would provide a new path for feminism and a much-needed renewal. Eliane Viennot and Françoise Gaspard argue that there is no possibility of sectarianism or interest-group separatism (*communautarism*) because women cross all social classes and communities. Yet they also suggest that women's projects could be seen in terms of shared commonalties (of lifestyle, condition, biology).

The prosecution put its case against parity in a sequel issue of the journal. The feminist philosopher Michèle le Doeuff argues against placing confidence in patrician women.[26] Le Doeuff cites the fact that the largest women's group in France, *Action Catholique Générale Féminine* with its 35,000 members, followed the Pope on issues of contraception. She attacks the parity cause as non-feminist. For Elena Varikas, group representation reduces citizenship to the expression of single social identities and hides the diversity amongst women.[27] In a later article, Varikas adds that a social analysis of the structures and institutions of domination (the family, the sexual division of labor, the division between public and private, institutionalized heterosexuality) of the kind that had given rise to the declaration that "the personal was the political" was, in fact, no longer sufficient.[28] Parity must be discussed in the context of an examination of political principles such as representation and the link between politics and relations of power. However, it is not clear to her whether parity democracy seeks to re-found democracy according to new definitions of community, justice, and power, or whether it aims to reform the existing founding principles of democracies. In Varikas's analysis the present principle of representative democracy defines elected assemblies as deriving from the nation and makes no claim to represent the nation's demographic and sociological composition. Citizens vote not on the basis of belonging to particular interest groups but based on their responses to the larger political, economic, and social questions of their time. It is ideas rather than persons who count, although the geographical notion of an electoral district incorporates some degree of special interests. There is no reason, then, her analysis concludes, for elected women to be necessarily representative of women. Elected men, too, come from particular kinds of backgrounds. Like many of those who write against parity, Varikas concludes that only a left-wing project could conceivably attack the very foundations of domination and re-found democracy.[29] Josette Trat, like many women from the Communist left, sees the alliance of women around parity as irrelevant in the face of the absence of a project for society that challenges social inequalities and the sexual division of labor at all levels.[30]

In *Le Monde* on 11 February 1999, Evelyne Pisier and Elisabeth Roudinesco, along with fourteen other prominent women, said "no to parity," claiming that 150 years of struggle based on the universalism of rights is being betrayed. Elisabeth Badinter and her husband, the well-known left-wing lawyer, libertarian, and Senator, Robert Badinter, publicly defended the principle of universality and of citizenship as an erasure of all distinctions. In *Libération* on 18 June 1998, Elisabeth Badinter again critiques parity on the grounds that the biological is being introduced into the political. Reviewing the recently released books that speak to parity by well-known figures—*La cité républicaine* (The Republican City) by the philosopher Blandine Kriegel, *Politique des sexes* (Gender Politics) by the philosopher Sylviane Agacinski, *Femmes-hommes. Pour la parité* (Women-Men: Toward Parity) by the political scientist Janine Mossuz-Lavau—Alain-Gérard Slama, journalist for *Le Figaro,* claims stridently that parity arguments (on both sides of the debate) announce the totalitarianism of the next century (*Le Point*, 2 May 1998).

The parity debate has now had an international resonance, feeding into the production of a body of theoretical research and writing outside France. Two examples are found in the work of British academics Catherine Hoskyns and Anne Phillips. In her book-length study of *Women, Law and Politics in the European Union* (1996), the British political scientist Catherine Hoskyns observes that significant numbers of the European Union states are beginning to move toward preferential treatment of women in the process of political representation. (Paradoxically, at the same time, the European Court ruled on two occasions that such positive action was contrary to European equality law as it discriminated against men. The court rulings have since been reversed). In favor of parity democracy, Hoskyns points out its ability to spark intellectual debate, its appeal to both traditional and feminist women, and its easy-to-understand persuasive message. Against parity, she notes its prioritizing of the sex-gender division and the danger of imposing rigidity on the process of political representation.

Another example of British writing on parity comes from the work of political scientist Anne Phillips. I will touch only briefly on this theoretical work to avoid truncating complex arguments on representation and the relation between politics and power, all of which would be better pursued by reading the original text.[31] While Phillips is wary of institutionalizing women's representative levels, she sees changing the gender composition of government as an enabling condition. She advances discussion of the notion of a "politics of presence": positive action to create a participatory democracy that allows for a rough equality between all social groupings. Such measures, she argues, have made a difference in India, where local governments have been obliged since 1993 to set aside quotas for different castes, as is the case for South Africa's first democratic elections, and for Northern Europe, where one third of parliamentary seats have been mandated for women.

Phillips is not alone in her deconstruction of universal citizenship, political representation, and in advocating group representation. There is a growing body of literature developing around the concept of a "politics of presence" (Lani Guinier, Iris Marion Young, Charles Taylor, Will Kymlicka, among others). This literature focuses on the need to ensure that all societal groups are represented in decision-making bodies, but the groups that require representation and the method for ensuring their incorporation into public decision making varies.

## The Press, Public Personalities, and Polemic: The Propagation of Parity Discourse

The debate on parity, polarized in the media, popularized as Trojan horse, sex-war, cat-fight, totalitarian feminism, or campaign for rights and justice for women, or tic-tac/zipper list, had all the elements of a popular drama. The debates were rapidly disseminated. The press took advantage of the polemical aspects of the parity debate and orchestrated fights between well-known women to enliven and to sell the story according to well-worn commercial and popularizing principles. For example, the introduction of the bill on 17 June 1998 led the newspaper *Libération* to ironically pit the center-right Roselyne Bachelot against the left-wing Elisabeth Badinter. The former supported parity and regretted that the verb "guarantees" had not been used in place of "facilitate" (equal access) in the constitutional amendment. Elisabeth Badinter denounced the parity moves as "false progress" and a "blow to the Republic." The newspaper report read like a "Who's Who" in the world of public women: Gisèle Halimi regretted the absence of a referendum but echoed Martine Aubry, Marie-Georges Buffet, and Elisabeth Guigou in their sense of being in the presence of a historic moment. Edith Cresson, Elisabeth Sledziewski, Yvette Roudy, Françoise Gaspard, Janine Mossuz-Lavau, and many other well-known women then picked up and responded to other criticisms—addressing notions of "humiliation," "nature," "difference," "exception"—and giving them a positive parity spin. For example they argued that women's under-representation is more humiliating than special measures. Accused of reverting to feminine nature or difference, a dangerous essentialism that has been the pretext for women's exclusion from public life, they made the argument for a different kind of difference, the difference inscribed in that "half of humanity" that cannot be assimilated to a social, ethnic or cultural category. Other women wrote in favor of pushing for an extension of the principle of parity to the social and economic arenas, noting, for example, the 12 percent difference in salaries between men and women that cannot be accounted for by any factor other than an inherent gender bias.

On 18 June 1998, *L'Humanité* observed that it had taken fifty-five years since the franchise to add a line on parity to the Constitution, for a prime minister to feminize Marianne (the symbol of the Republic) and make a commitment to generalized equality between women and men. The public seemed receptive to this simple argument for greater immediate political justice for women. An earlier IFOP poll had showed 71 percent of respondents in favor of the modification of the Constitution to allow parity democracy. Polls attested to an astonishing 80 percent public support for political parity in February 1999 (79 percent women and 81 percent men).

A more sophisticated analysis of public opinion by the social scientist Mariette Sineau points out that a poll presenting a number of different options for the advancement of women with respect to representation in the political arena provides evidence that there is a greater degree of support for parity to be achieved by women's own actions, party action, and natural evolution than by act of law. This feeling against legislation was surprisingly found particularly among the "feminist" minded population. Sineau's findings appear to have gone largely unread, perhaps drowned out by the media circus surrounding parity. It could be argued, however, that in popularizing the texts on women and power, it was the media who pulled the Trojan horse inside the walls!

The parity debate was enlivened by a small number of male voices. Both those in favor and those opposed were given a hearing in the media. Reviews of *La Domination Masculine*, by well-known left-wing sociologist Pierre Bourdieu, add to the polemic. Bourdieu's 1998 book provocatively compares the gender-role and power distribution in France and in Berber villages. Bourdieu throws his considerable academic weight behind the feminist thesis of masculinist domination and subsequent exclusion of females from the public arena, but also critiques parity for addressing only the question of public space and not the inevitable connection between the domestic and the political spheres. This sociologist and critic of dominant Western institutions concludes that the little strategies to deny legitimacy to women in political office—"Speak up, I can't hear you"—will not disappear with the inclusion of more women in politics. Despite the socially constructed character of the masculine vision of the world, which justifies gender difference, we remain unconsciously its products. The achievement of a parity constructed according to dominant principles, for Bourdieu, could, like many "revolutions" also produce perverse effects.[32] Bourdieu's work was critiqued as presenting a static view of an unchanging history and undervaluing women's agency. In another academic genre, Jean-François Kesler, a professor from the Université de Paris, follows in the footsteps of Mariette Sineau and Janine Mossuz-Lavau, compiling statistics to support the case for parity in the top ranks of public administrators (*Le Monde*, 4 July 1998). Kesler notes that 56 percent of employees in a given administration are female but the number of women in upper-level positions is still relatively low.

Male voices on parity from the center or right of center of the political spectrum most often have an edge. Luc Ferry, historian and author of a deconstruction of the revolution of May '68, is representative of a conservative academic response to the 1980s as the period during which the French discovered with repulsion and irony the American fashion for the "politically correct." He regrets that, little by little, attitudes have since changed. Somewhat comforted by the universalist arguments of Elisabeth Badinter and the lawyer Evelyne Pisier, Ferry comes to the conclusion that "the true victory of women" lies not in a "biologization of politics," but elsewhere.[33] The reader is expected to have little difficulty identifying the nature of this "elsewhere" that Ferry does not make explicit. Even a book published in 1996 by Maurice Maschino, which records the results of the journalist's major popular survey on the relationship of women to power and concludes in favor of parity, *Après vous messieurs. Les femmes et la politique*, asks, somewhat like Pascal, whether a certain power in the home means that women do not really need public power. For his part, the well-known conservative male journalist, Alain-Gérard Slama, represents feminine quotas and parity as "Pandora's box" (*Le Figaro*, 16 March 1997). The last two chapters of this book will unveil similar doubts and fears about women in power but expressed in greater intimacy and complexity in the literary texts of Françoise Giroud and Huguette Bouchardeau.

An examination of the French press coverage of feminist activity and discourse across the 1990s reveals how all-encompassing and dominant the parity discourse had become. About 80 percent of the press articles devoted to women's contemporary history in major French magazines and newspapers between 1994 and early 1999 concern some aspect of parity democracy.[34] Even where the gender patterns in French journalism are respected (male journalists focusing on important figures of the political caste, institutional party power struggles, or fulfilling their watchdog (or "gotcha") role, and female journalists insisting more on the relation between personal experience and social issues), during this period, both male and female journalists came back to the new questions posed by women's presence in or absence from positions of political power. An analysis of the headlines and titles of articles in the press gives a sense of the way the parity debate became a serious discussion across society—between feminists, politicians, journalists, political and social scientists, and the public.

The response of the press to parity even in the early part of this period was surprisingly lacking in the characteristic irony that most often works against women. With a number of notable exceptions, women were writing in favor of and men against parity democracy, but even the right-wing papers were giving parity a hearing. Given the power that the press has to decide what is important and what is not, the media stories on the new concept of parity clearly helped to promote the political movement. The access to broadcast media given to feminist leaders such as Yvette Roudy and Gisèle Halimi, the impact of interviews with women journalists such as Françoise Giroud, helped the concept of parity to gain ground. The headway was first made under a conservative government that was itself modifying its discourse, then continued in the euphoria of a Socialist regime with a new, more feminine face.

The media discussions on political change, their dissemination of the political manifestos and academic studies, also make the new body of histories and autobiographical writing by women more visible.[35] A large number of the articles on women and politics in the print media are journalistic reviews or discussions of recent books (by Gisèle Halimi, Geneviève Fraisse, Monique Pelletier, Yvette Roudy, Mariette Sineau, etc.). There are also responses to the publication of conference papers and manifestos, such as the review in *Le Monde* (16 June 1994) of the conference papers from the 1993 parity colloquium ("La démocratie pour les femmes: un pouvoir à partager," Paris, Unesco, 3 and 4 June) published in *Femmes: Moitié de la terre; moitié du pouvoir* (Women: Half of the World: Half of the Power). This review put into headlines Stendhal's conviction that "the admission of women to perfect equality would be the clearest sign of a civilized society" (*L'admission des femmes à l'égalité parfaite serait la marque la plus sûre de la civilisation*).

## From Texts to Practice

Jospin estimated ten years for parity to happen. In an interview with me in December 1996, Bouchardeau's prognosis was twenty years. Changing the Constitution takes a two-thirds majority of both houses (or approval by referendum). Any immediate change in political practice in France at the time seemed unlikely. But events suddenly accelerated after the election of the new government. The unpredictable happened, and supported by the new government, a parity law, a new French "exception" was enacted, enabled in part by the critical mass of discourse on parity, amplified by the media and understood by different people in different fashions.

On 28 June 1999 the French Constitution was modified to integrate the political and philosophical principle of "equal access of women and men to political office." In January 2000, the bill on parity was voted almost unanimously by the National Assembly on its first reading (with only Christine Boutin, UDF, dissenting on the grounds of non-respect of the "unity" and "indivisibility" of the Republic). The reform required that 50 percent of the candidates presented by political parties in elections observing a system of proportional representation (municipal, regional, European, and senatorial) be women. Financial sanctions would be imposed on parties who did not respect parity in legislative elections. In the March 2001 municipal elections, the numbers of women entering politics at the local level increased dramatically. Still, all issues of feminine representation, including the question of political legitimacy, had not, of course, been resolved.[36]

## Notes

1. In 1975, Giroud proposed 15 percent quotas for women in municipal elections in her "100 measures for women," but the text was later modified to read "at least 20 percent of candidates of both sexes." The Green party presented an egalitarian list of candidates in 1977. Quotas ensuring that 20 percent of candidates for local elections were women were proposed by Monique Pelletier in 1979.
2. *Le Figaro* of 17 March 1999, tracing the history of parity, presents this bill as the work of the *député* Alain Richard.
3. In December 1999, there were 60 woman deputies out of 577 and 19 senators out of 320 in government. The Parti socialiste had 28 percent in its National Secretariat, the Union démocratique française, 8.3 percent, and the Executive College of the Greens, 53.3 percent. The Rassemblement pour la République had just elected a woman as its leader, Michelle Alliot-Marie, nicknamed MAM by the press.
4. Belgium passed a law requiring 25 percent of candidates to be women. In 1999, the percentage was increased to 33.33 percent. Many parties in the North of Europe have imposed quotas or impose a "tic-tac" alternation of a man, then a woman on their lists.
5. Pierre Georges, "La Femme à la section," *Le Nouvel Observateur*, 25 May 1994.
6. In a surprising move from the right wing, Nicole Ameline, the center-right Union démocratique française-Parti républicain deputy for the Calvados, proposed a bill in 1996 for no more than two-thirds of candidates of either sex on all electoral ballots decided by proportional representation. (Municipal elections in large towns, regional elections, and European elections use this electoral system.) The bill received fewer than sixty signatures and was subsumed in the right's new project of "political modernization" announced in October 1996. But October also saw Ameline featured on the television news protesting the fact that there were only eight women out of 206 in the right-wing majority.
7. *Le Monde*, 22/23 September 1996, p. 8.
8. October 3, Chaîne 2/Channel 2, French Television.
9. Female citizens, they argue, now vote for the legislator but they do not make laws. In 1992 women constituted 17 percent of local representatives but only 5.6 percent of mayors. At the level of the *département*, where there was one single candidate ("scrutin uninominal"), women constituted only 5 percent. There were 5.4 percent of women in the Assembly and 3.9 percent in the Senate (6.8 percent in 1946 and 5.9 percent in 1986; 33 *députées* in both 1945 and 1988). Women's early average of 11 percent of candidates (13 percent in 1946) dropped to 2.31 percent in 1958 when the electoral system changed and jumped to 24.69 percent in 1986 with a proportional representation system (*scrutin de liste*) replacing the majority vote or "first past the

post" system (*scrutin majoritaire*). Women were not uninterested in politics according to Gaspard, but they usually remained at the bottom of the list and few had any chance of being elected. Male candidates had a five times greater chance of being elected. Gaspard quotes other "shocking" figures for 1991, the 2 percent of women in the U.S. Senate and 6.4 percent in the House of Representatives. In 1991 there were 11 percent of women parliamentarians in the world, the lowest figure since 1975. May 1991 saw one woman prime minister in France, but Edith Cresson was appointed and not elected. The only comforting figures are for representation in Finland (38.5 percent) and Sweden (38.1 percent).

10. The "Manifeste des 577 pour une démocratie populaire" signed by those who supported parity democracy is reproduced in *Futur Antérieur* 19–20, nos. 5–6 (1993), pp. 9–13.
11. Speakers at the influential two-day conference ranged from American academic feminists, Palestinian grassroots organizers, and new feminist theorists such as the philosopher Luce Irigaray, to religious leaders defending and questioning traditional Christian, Jewish, and Islamic views of women's place. The Reverend Lois Wilson, president of the (Protestant) Council of Churches, for example, was critical of the establishment, speaking of the new feminist theology that is rereading founding texts and recovering a positive image of women from a misogynist past. The proceedings of the colloquium were published in Gisèle Halimi, ed., *Femmes: Moitié de la terre moitié du pouvoir: Plaidoyer pour une démocratie paritaire* (Paris: Gallimard, 1994).
12. Ibid.
13. Gisèle Halimi, "Plaidoyer pour une démocratie paritaire," in *Femmes: Moitié de la terre*, pp. 11–22.
14. Michelle Perrot, "La Démocratie sans les femmes: histoire élémentaire d'une spécificité française," in *Femmes: Moitié de la terre*, pp. 33–40.
15. In an interview in 1999, Ezra Suleiman, an American political scientist from Princeton, well-known in Paris, responded that "Republican equality" is now only an ideal and an anachronistic way of thinking; France, he argues, is in fact, a multicultural country. Suleiman appears to take issue with parity on the grounds that it singles out a single category for advancement, a privileged socioprofessional group—that of political women.
16. Elisabeth Schemla, "Une nouvelle révolution française: la parité," *L'Express,* 6 June 1996, pp. 29–31.
17. "Le Manifeste des dix pour la parité," *L'Express,* 6 June 1996, pp. 32–33.
18. Although Britain, the U.S., and France, countries with single-member electoral districts, have a much lower female representation than those with a system of proportional representation, at the 1993 colloquium on parity, Sineau had warned against the expectation of an automatic causal link between proportional representation and numbers of women elected. The results, she had argued, depend on how and where the system is applied. When proportional representation is organized in small electoral districts and in a large number of districts, as in the *départements* for the legislative elections of 1986, the system favors well-known local figures or incumbents, and women have almost as little chance of being selected as candidates as in a majority vote system. Sineau also notes that March 1986 saw a plethora of women running for office (25 percent), but with only 5.9 percent elected. In larger electoral districts or in a single one, as in the European elections in 1979 when universal suffrage was introduced, the situation becomes more favorable. Women obtained more than 20 percent of the seats in the 1979 election. Mariette Sineau, in Halimi, *Femmes: Moitié de la terre*, p. 187.
19. Michèle Riot-Sarcey, "La démocratie représentative en l'absence des femmes," *French Politics and Society* 12, no. 4 (Fall 1994), pp. 53–63; see also *Futur antérieur* 19–20, nos. 5–6 (1993), pp. 7–17.
20. Geneviève Fraisse, "Quand gouverner n'est pas représenter," *Esprit*, March–April 1994, pp. 103–114.
21. Elisabeth Badinter, "Tout pouvoir est viril," *L'Histoire* 160 (November 1992), pp. 14–16.

22. Elisabeth Badinter, "Non aux quotas de femmes." *Le Monde*, 12 June 1996. Badinter does recognize the obstacles to women in France and proposes a change to the system whereby leaders and candidates would be elected by the party base in a primary rather than appointed by the party leader.
23. Badinter also critiques United States feminism, which she has defined as a "war of the sexes" that has created a society of hyper-victimization on the one hand and hyper-virilization (as seen in the movie, *The Terminator*) on the other, while preventing the passing of a long-fought-for constitutional amendment stipulating equality of the sexes. Badinter presents American feminism as characterized by the three stages, or principles—Diana, or revenge; Saba, or control by money and power; and Nike, the "Just do it" principle—and refuses these for France on the grounds that a relative harmony exists between the sexes in that country.
24. Françoise Gaspard, "De la parité: genèse d'un concept, naissance d'un mouvement," *Nouvelles Questions Féministes* 15, no. 4 (1994), pp. 29–44.
25. Eliane Viennot, "Parité: les féministes entre défis politiques et révolution culturelle," *Nouvelles Questions Féministes* 15, no. 4 (1994), pp. 65–89.
26. Michèle Le Doeuff, "Problèmes d'investiture (de la parité, etc.)," *Nouvelles Questions Féministes, "La Parité 'contre,'"* 16, no. 2 (1995), pp. 5–80.
27. Elena Varikas, "Une Représentation en tant que femme? Réflexions critiques sur la demande de parité des sexes," *Nouvelles Questions Féministes*, "La Parité 'contre'" 16, no. 2 (1995), pp. 81–127.
28. Eleni Varikas, "Refonder ou raccommoder la démocratie? Réflexions critiques sur la demande de la parité des sexes," *French Society and Politics* 12, no. 4 (Fall 1994), pp. 1–34.
29. Ibid. The parity debate continued with Catherine Tricot interviewing three women. Gaspard's arguments are familiar. Now that education and public life are open to both sexes alike, the marginalizing of women in the domain of decision making can only be attributed to a process of exclusion. Women's presence is essential precisely because women do not have exactly the same point of view or needs as men. Michèle Riot-Sarcey put forward a view closer to that of Le Doeuff. Parity would simply legitimate the present social construction of woman as other and would not hide the absence of the real representativity of those elected. Politicians are professionals, she claimed, trained in and obedient to the laws of the market and relations of power. The possibilities for the advancement of women were proportionally inverse to their feminist commitment. As one slogan putting the case for parity—"81 percent of fathers and 19 percent of mothers"—made evident that it was "mothers" among women who would continue to be appointed. Françoise Duroux, for her part, considered the project utopian, and saw quotas to be both fairer and more realistic. Whereas the principal of "the personal is the political" had concerned all women, in her view, the principle of parity did not.
30. Josette Trat, "La loi pour la parité: une solution en trompe-l'oeil," *Nouvelles Questions Féministes*, "La Parité 'contre,'" 16, no. 2 (1995), pp. 129–139.
31. Anne Phillips, *The Politics of Presence* (New York: Clarendon Press, 1995). Phillips examines the arguments that more women in politics create more role models and that women share a distinctive experience calling for greater representation. She ultimately rejects these arguments on the grounds that it is precisely because women are not a static or a homogenous group with unified positions, and because the sexual division of labor is not accepted as natural, that active intervention to include such an underrepresented group does not institute group representation.
32. See also, Pierre Bourdieu, "L'Homme décide, la femme s'efface," *Télérama*, no. 2532, 22 July 1998, pp. 22–24 and "Il manquera toujours la moustache," *Télérama*, no. 2533, 29 July 1998, pp. 25–27.
33. Luc Ferry, *Le Point*, 4 July 1998, pp. 74–80.
34. These articles are collected in the library of the Fondation Nationale des Sciences Politiques on the rue Guillaume and held in La Salle des Dossiers under the classification of "Féminisme."

35. See, for example, appendix 3, "Parity in the Press", for a presentation of press articles between February and October 1996.
36. In particular, while quotas or parity lists do not pose problems for proportional representation—regional and municipal or European elections—the question of what to do with single member constituencies (divide them into two member constituencies fielding a man and a woman?) remains unresolved.

# 4

# Women's Political (Il)legitimacy

Concern about legitimacy is one of the central and recurring themes circulating in the writing of political women in France. Ever since the first three women were appointed to serve in the administrative branch of government in 1936, the entry of women into high administrative positions has been considered a problematic top-down political matter. As early beneficiaries of what came to be known as the "protection of the prince" (*le fait du prince*), these women, appointed by Léon Blum to tutelary ministries, and notably Cécile Brunschvicg as leader of a major women's movement, invoked the issue of tokenism and the degree to which their loyalty to their selector and protector constrained their actions. At the same time, public reluctance to recognize the legitimacy of women in high places without a male sponsor has been an issue for all women nominated to office in France.

The research and writing considered in this chapter begins to explore the unconscious need for paternal legitimization found within academic and journalistic discourses. (The final chapters will examine this need in literary texts by Huguette Bouchardeau and Françoise Giroud at more intimate and more complex levels.) Awareness of the need for a Father's approval is a necessary prerequisite for the development of a resistance or a counter-discourse strong enough to take hold in the unconscious. This is the difficult process of women's recognition of their own legitimacy, of the power of the maternal legacy, of their need to change politics if they wish to successfully accommodate their difference. The present chapter touches on the various attempts to productively formulate a discourse of legitimacy in mainstream political texts.

## Delegated Power and Legitimacy and the Unconscious Creation of Desires, Identities, and Norms

Michel Foucault provides a theoretical model of the sources of legitimacy and power which goes beyond the conventional analysis of centralized repressive forms of power, that is, the juridico-discursive model that postulates a legitimate authority (masculine) codified in law and framed by a theory of rights. This model shows how certain cultural practices have produced identities and individuals. The institutional power of schools, barracks, hospitals, prisons, and everyday practices (along with political parties and parliaments) takes hold, Foucault claims, and the work of feminist theorists like Lois Mc Nay also emphasize, not through threat but through the creation of desires, identities, and norms against which individuals and their behaviors are judged and against which they police themselves. As do many feminist theoreticians, Foucault considers that the juridico-discursive model does not capture the myriad of power relations in sexuality and the family at micro-levels of society, including the relation of the daughter with the father. Focusing on this power in the network of bodily and local relations (sex, kinship, knowledge, and technology), his theory suggests that power works most profoundly from the bottom up rather than the top down. Indeed, the vital need for women to understand and work with their own often-buried sense of illegitimacy at the deepest and the most everyday levels is often discussed in political women's writings. As *le fait du prince* takes hold, it seems that freedom can only come from being aware of, and rebelling against, the ways in which we are defined and categorized by others within the constraints of the society within which we grew up.

## *Legitimacy from the Father*

A critique of the patriarchal nature of French politics is found within the writings of the emblematic socialist feminist Yvette Roudy, women's rights minister from 1981 to 1986. In her autobiographical texts, Roudy recounts the impossible battles for nominations to winnable seats. She explains that she finally had no option but to pack her bags, leave Paris and centralized politics, and go off to fight for the difficult position of mayor of Lisieux, a conservative bastion in Normandy. Roudy's texts recognize that without the support of the president and the prime minister, an arrogant and entrenched masculine administration would have blocked her projects one after another, in a war of attrition. Women, in Roudy's view, have only ever held delegated power and have usually been selected as a function of their usefulness for someone else's project. She notes the political preference for obedient women:

> A political woman is always dependent on a man... There are women who get into the halls of power and do not disturb anything. Men in power who put women into political positions often choose women estranged from women's causes. They do not do much for progress.[1]

Although Mitterrand expressed respect for women and their difference, he did not include them among his closest advisers. Roudy argues that women's struggle for legitimacy had not gone far enough before everything halted and fell into hibernation, or worse, into regression accompanied by a backlash against feminist groups and a shift in institutional support toward ecological movements.[2] The plain-speaking title and subtitle of her 1995 testimony and political manifesto, *De quoi ont-ils peur: Un vent de misogynie souffle sur la politique* (What Are They Afraid of? A Misogynist Wind is Blowing over the Political World), is indicative of her frustration, as is her generally polemical tone. Roudy's retrospective analysis of the Mitterrand era echoes something of the disillusion of Mariette Sineau's work on gains for women in this period, published in *Mitterrand et les Françaises*.

## *Power Delegated by the Father: The Widow/ Daughter Track*

Roudy's conclusion—that women have held power only by delegation—is shared by most of the women writers in my corpus. Historically, women have been legitimately mentored by men and have also stood as surrogates or substitutes for them. Adler quotes from her interview with Gilberte Brossolette, a Resistance fighter and the widow of the Resistance hero, Pierre Brossolette:

> At the beginning of my term of office, when I defended the rights of women, people would say to me: "Yes, but you're an exception as you're not really a woman." Men were very accepting. I was Pierre's widow, they all greatly respected that, they projected onto me all the affection and the admiration that they had for Pierre. I was a kind of spirit of Pierre Brossolette.[3]

But even the prestige of a dead martyr was insufficient to protect Gilberte from mutiny by the Socialists of her regional section. She nonetheless went on to become the first woman president of the Senate.

Reflecting on the acceptability of widowhood in politics, Sineau comments that it is as if a succession brought about by the death of the husband somehow canceled out the otherwise transgressive inversion of roles. Sineau writes about the legitimacy of the war widows Mme. Gabriel Péri (of the PC, or Parti communiste), Mme. Pierre Brossolette (SFIO, or Parti socialiste, section française de l'internationale ouvrière), and Mme. Cardot (MRP, or Mouvement républicain populaire), among the 25 percent of women deputies in 1946. A Gaullist party candidate in 1951 is still described as "Irène de Lipkowski, widow of a deportee who died for France" (*Irène de Lipkowski, veuve d'un déporté mort pour la France*). Hélène Missoffe began her career as deputy as the *suppléante* (replacement) of her husband, François Missoffe and she was later appointed *secrétaire d'Etat* in the Barre government. The veteran politician Jacqueline Thomé-Patenôtre, describes the beginning of her career when she stood in for her sick husband in 1945, very conscious of the advantage of her husband's reputation for her succession.

The "widow path" is still a significant one in France in the 1990s. Suzanne Sauvaigo, *députée* for the Alpes Maritimes in Juppé's government, is the widow of the *député* Pierre Sauvaigo. Margie Sudre, *secrétaire d'Etat* for Francophone countries in Juppé's government, replaced her husband in 1993 as regional president for the overseas département of La Réunion when he was declared temporarily ineligible to stand for re-election. The widow track is not only a French phenomenon—in the years from 1965 to 1982, 21 percent of women elected to the American Congress were widows of significant political figures. Four of the early New Zealand Members of Parliament were elected to seats held previously by their deceased fathers or husbands.

Political legitimacy granted through the widow track has since been broadened to include the increasingly common father-daughter succession. Besides the seven women presidents or prime ministers worldwide who have stepped into the shoes of their deceased male relatives, there are numerous others who carry on the paternal political tradition in the developing world.[4] In France, father and daughter successions abound, particularly on the Socialist side. Frédérique Bredin's father is the former vice-president of the left-wing Radical party (Radicaux de gauche), a famous Paris lawyer, and a member of the Académie Française. In a variant on this pattern, *Le Figaro* spells out Frédérique Bredin's *raison d'être* in the political world: "As her father, the lawyer Jean-Denis Bredin, former associate of Robert Badinter, had been vice-president of the movement of the left, it was quite natural she should be interested in politics."[5] Michèle Alliot-Marie, the daughter of Bernard Marie, a deputy for the RPR (Rassemblement Pour la République) party, mayor of Biarritz, and former highly visible international rugby referee, was elected to her father's seat in the Pyrénées-Orientales, later nominated to a ministerial position, and became mayor of St. Jean de Luz in 1995. In December 1999, she became the first woman to head the RPR party. Martine Aubry is the daughter of Jacques Delors, who was the president of the European Council until 1995, and early Socialist hope for the 1995 presidential elections. She is often referred to as the "daughter of Jacques Delors." Aubry's biographers suggest that the close relationship she enjoyed with the director of the Péchiney factory and with other competitive and successful men with whom she worked in the political world corresponds to her image as "the daughter" they would have liked to have had.

Sineau believes that a certain Oedipal relation to the Father as object of admiration or identification serves as a motivation for daughters of political men to enter politics, citing an interview with a representative of the center-right RPR who preferred to remain anonymous: "We were three girls, to my father's despair… and I said to myself that I would show my father that, even though I am a girl, I would be able to carry on his work."

Martine Buron pays homage to the father who passed his passion for politics on to her, his only child, and Christiane Papon expresses admiration for the Resistance heroism of the father she too would follow into the political world. Sineau argues that in these cases, obedience/sacrifice to the father would take precedence over the sacred duty of devotion to husband and children. In the Gaullist party and its offspring, the RPR, De Gaulle has also been an inspiration. Roslyne Bachelot who replaced her father as deputy for Maine et Loire in 1988 in a surprise last-minute candidacy that outwitted a RPR management hostile to her candidacy, explains that her desire to enter politics stemmed from her family's strong allegiance to De Gaulle, as Father of the Nation.[6] A number of women in the National Front are also standing in for ineligible or deceased husbands; Jany Le Pen, who claims to know and care nothing about politics and Catherine Mégret, the wife of the deputy chairman, both straw women, were elected in place of their husbands as a front, but also the widowed Marie-France Stirbois, who became an accomplished campaigner in her own right. Laure Adler's history quotes a number of cases where a sense of legitimacy is gained by working with or in place of a paternal figure or spouse.

In an interesting new variation on political dynasty, Françoise de Panafieu who was the *suppléante* and successor to her mother in the *Conseil de Paris* (Council for the City of Paris), became an *adjointe au maire* (assistant to the mayor) to Chirac and a short-lived tourism minister when Juppé sought out the women he had promised to include in his first government.

## *Cécile Brunschvicg and Patriarchal Protection*

A rare article on Brunschvicg by Paul Bastid situates this first woman minister in the shadow of her significant spouse and describes her action as "continuing the thought of the master." Léon Brunschvicg was an enlightened rationalist philosopher and a member of the *Ligue des Droits de l'Homme* like his wife.[7] From a wealthy, middle-class Jewish background, Léon shared his wife's goals for social and public action. In her own writing Cécile states that it was Léon who had suggested to her that political office would be the surest way to further the cause of female suffrage. His prestige and support helped her to pass legislation allowing women to participate in the competitive entrance exams to ministries and later to the *agrégation* exams, the path to university teaching careers. Léon's support seems to have been a condition of Cécile's own willingness to enter the political establishment. My own readings of her texts find a mix of the charitable idealism characteristic of her milieu, a deeply felt personal sense of the injustice of women's condition, and an intuitive awareness of the need to strike a non-threatening compromise in order to avoid any backlash.[8] However. the principles shared with her husband, and the authority derived from the prime minister's (Blum's) support, would certainly have assisted in giving this first appointed woman minister the confidence to believe that women can play a political role beyond traditional philanthropic social action.

If Cécile's reformist "good intentions" are presented as suspect because they are too close to nineteenth-century good conscience philanthropy, Léon presents a very modern "husband problem." Cécile Brunschvicg was attacked in 1936 France through the ridicule cast on her husband who was presented as overshadowed and emasculated by his wife's success. Joy Cooper quotes Odette Pannetier in the *Nouvelle Ménagerie Politique* and the ambiguity of the journalist's words is surely intended: "There aren't all that many men who can boast of being the husband of a minister."[9]

The difficulty of taking feminist initiatives from within an antifeminist party and the contradictions inherent in her position as both a radical minister in Blum's government and as the leader of the apolitical Union Française pour le Suffrage des Femmes (UFSF) left Brunschvicg open to accusations of being on the one hand a radical agent and on the other, a reactionary bourgeois. If Brunschvicg's action did push the state toward increased attention to the social domain, did her loyalty to the Radical party and Popular Front government inhibit progress on the suffrage issue? Blum prohibited a demonstration for suffrage and Brunschvicg did not support Louise Weiss's militant suffrage action. Perhaps for that reason, she would not be at all well treated in Weiss's memoirs. Laure Adler considers that in the final analysis, Brunschvicg's high political position helped to reconcile the bourgeoisie with controlled feminism. Women's groups of the time supported Brunschvicg's "protector," Blum. To support his claim for the need to improve the situation of women from the top down, Blum had stated that women "don't seek a change in their condition" and will not "sit among us" any time soon. If these declarations were in part political, they also reflected reality. No major social movements supported women's suffrage, and relatively few women wished to be full members of the UFSF suffrage group.

## *"To Appoint a Woman is to Take a Legitimate Place Away from a Man"*

The roles played by political parties and patronage with respect to women's entry into the world of politics include the covert or overt exclusion of women, and the judicious foregrounding of women to strengthen electoral operations. There were also some genuine attempts to ensure a more democratic and balanced representation. In many cases, this has involved molding women for distinctive party purposes and often elevating them to a political position for which they did not fight their way through the ranks. The quid pro quo was the expectation that these women would represent the party, the prime minister, or the president who had proposed them for office, and not focus on women's causes. Simone Veil points out that these women were, in a sense, more carefully selected for their loyalty than men.

"To appoint a woman is to take a legitimate place away from a man" (*Désigner une femme, c'est ôter une place à un homme*), writes the political scientist Maurice Duverger, highlighting the competitive impulse that governs party nominations and the seemingly natural exclusion of women from dominant or prestigious positions coveted by men.[10] Within political parties women have been seen as outsiders, ignorant of the codes, and too direct. In a political group whose *raison d'être* is the capture and control of power before any defense of a political platform or action, women are an encumbrance in a game ruled by fierce competition for limited places. This is a game of "you lose, I win," as Ann Richards, the former governor of Texas, has characterized such competition. Bouchardeau makes the point by inverting the formula to produce the incongruity: "to appoint a man is to take a place away from a woman."

After Blum's three women ministers, Andrée Viennot was appointed as *sous-secrétaire d'Etat* for the department of youth and sports and in 1946 Germaine Poinsot-Chapuis was made the first woman cabinet minister for public health and population under the Fourth Republic. Madame Poinsot-Chapuis was an eminent lawyer and mother of two young children, member of the Resistance, vice-president of the first *conseil municipal* (town council) in Marseille, and secretary of the conservative MPR (Mouvement populaire républicain) parliamentary group. She defended measures for the integration of the physically handicapped. She also worked for government assistance to private schools in the form of subsidies to parents. Germaine Poinsot-Chapuis's action was motivated by Christian-right principles and her discourse was conservative in tone. Her conservatism did not save her, however, from attacks on her irascibility and authoritarianism. In interviewing the veteran *députée* Marie-Madeleine Dienesch, Adler discusses comments on the characteristics that caused the minister's elimination from the government: Poinsot-Chapuis's irascibility and authoritarian character, according to Dienesch, "didn't go over well with her male colleagues."[11] Such criticism of authoritarianism in women in the highest positions, from both male and female colleagues, the press and the public, is curiously constant in the writing on and by political women. Some decades later, Martine Aubry's biographers present her as authoritarian and stubborn, even autocratic. Simone Veil wonders publicly whether she herself does not resort to authoritarianism to conceal a sense of being illegitimate. A whole series of media articles attribute the title of *la dame de fer* (the Iron Lady) negatively to women who appear to have entrenched themselves in positions of power. In *Le Point* (May 2000), Madame Lucette Michaux-Chevry, former minister and Senator and mayor of a small town in Guadeloupe, is labeled *La dame de fer de la Guadeloupe* in an article entitled "The Fall of the Iron Lady," observing that she stood accused of nepotism and of raising an illegal tax. (The court subsequently found Madame Michaux not guilty.)[12]

## *Legitimacy from the Party*

What have been the general conclusions for France? Adler quotes Monique Pelletier's verdict on appointed women: "Women ministers before 1981 were token ministers. I myself was a token."[13] Christiane Scrivener (a member of the European Parliament from 1979 to 1988) observes that the political jealousy occasioned by her selection and protection by Giscard in 1981 led her own party to bring about her defeat in the legislative elections.

Summarizing her experience in an interview with Adler in 1992, Françoise Giroud reiterates the impossibility of a normal career for a woman in the face of the male chauvinism of the parties: "The party system is the most misogynist, the most allergic to women. No woman has succeeded in making a place for herself in a party."[14] It is impossible, she claims, to move anything in the hidebound civil service unless you are either a very important person within the party or have the support of the president. Giroud had presidential support and she notes the incomparable interest of the experience, the first small steps taken despite the closed system with its rites and codes. Over the seven-year period covering Valéry Giscard d'Estaing's office and then François Mitterrand's first term, a number of laws and decrees were passed that redressed inequalities between men and women in professional and family life, and modified the modes of education and work structures that had traditionally reinforced the division of roles. The laws most often pushed through by the women's-rights ministries allowed Françoise Giroud to be somewhat effective. Pioneers like Bouchardeau, who led the PSU (Parti socialiste unifié) and Martine Aubry, who has become influential in the Socialist party and has the full support of Jospin, are beginning to change the situation in the parties through their presence and their discourse, although this progress has been painfully slow and other more misogynist traditions remain at work.

Laure Adler presents the case of Jeanne Vermeersch, one of the seven *députées* in 1946 representing the important Communist women's organization, L'Union Française des Femmes (The Union of French Women, or UFF), as personifying the contradictions inherent in the roles played by "activist" women within the Communist party. Adler claims that in the 1950s, when the number of women representatives was in steep decline, only the Communist party remained true to its doctrine, presenting about 15 percent women candidates. This active representation of women continued until the abandonment of proportional representation in 1958 dramatically reducing their numbers to the advantage of notables and incumbents. There was a strong core within the Communist party that saw woman's place as taking care of her husband in the kitchen and the bedroom, and rocking the cradle. The party also contained a masculinist group who would jealously protect privileges and political places from female "meddling." Adler nonetheless notes the significant number of women candidates imposed by the party in the post-1945 years and its strong commitment to the widows of those party members killed or deported. She concludes that women were, in fact, often nominated to electoral lists precisely because they were women and seemed to have the winds of history blowing in their favor.[15] Later, as the party went into steep decline with the breakup of the Soviet Union, this tendency accelerated.

In the early 1960s, when "Jeannette" Vermeersch entered the Parti Communiste Français (PCF) political directorate, creating some discomfort as the wife of the eminent General Secretary Maurice Thorez, the Communist party was still very influential. Adler evokes Vermersch's spirited defense of political and economic equality and her attack on the "bourgeois" notions of women (as dolls, as servants) that was shared by many men, Communist and non-Communist alike. Jeannette Vermersch, a colorful and strong woman, did not see herself as a "feminist." Her legitimacy in the party came from using the women's movements in the cause of creating equal (communist) political beings through the class struggle.[16] Her early arguments against the reform of the archaic penal law on contraception information, contraception, and abortion are evidence of the fact that she was dispossessed of her autonomy in order to serve the party apparatus and current orthodoxy rather than the cause of the women of the party. Jeannette Vermersch appears in Janine Mossuz-Lavau's 1991 study of the vital changes in the French laws governing sexuality, *Les Lois de l'amour*, which over two decades led to a socially transforming liberation of female sexual behavior. Here, Vermersch was speaking against the legalizing of both contraception (presented as a "bourgeois vice") and abortion, holding to the Communist party line on "happy motherhood" inherited from Stalin and still the Socialist doctrine of the moment. Liberation would mean women's return from the factory to home and children. By 1967, the party had realigned its position and the Communists supported the contraception bill of that year and, subsequently, a woman's right to voluntary termination of pregnancy (interruption volontaire de grossesse, or IVG).

At the same time, the disciplines and the oligarchic structures of the Communist party—its very ideology—functioned to some extent as a source of legitimization for Vermersch's position of female power. This was strengthened by the legitimacy that came to her from the authority of her partner, the Communist leader and minister, Thorez. Citing an interview with the politician Marie-Claude Vaillant-Couturier, Adler says that the confidence placed in them by the Communist party, which gave them legitimacy, was ultimately of great psychological importance to these women, more important than the limits this imposed on their real political power.

## Women of Influence: The Many Faces of Legitimacy

### *A Collective Fantasy: The Case of Marie-France Garaud*

Most of the histories of women in politics appear fascinated by the stories woven around a woman who was never an elected representative but was credited with great influence in circles of power. Françoise Giroud writes of Marie-France Garaud's influence, perceived as feminine and seductive, but also as threatening and illegitimate by many of the male politicians seeking to move close to the seat of the sovereign and at the mercy of the barrier constituted by her and her fellow adviser, Pierre Juillet. The collective myth elaborated around this attractive adviser to George Pompidou was that of a contemporary "Rastignac in petticoats," cruel priestess of secret decisions, and adviser of the night. The tales of the power behind the throne, of a modern-day Marie de Medicis or Madame de Maintenon (as Edith Cresson was also called) appeared to correspond to some very old myths about women. Were these stories pure fiction, as Marie-France Garaud herself claimed?[17]

The aura surrounding Garaud may well correspond to a collective political and historical fantasy, generated out of the fear and fascination of a female *éminence grise*. The stories may also reflect Garaud's own idea of what was legitimate feminine behavior—one that operated through powerful men. Michèle Sarde argues in her book, *Femmes de pouvoir: Femmes d'influence* (Women of Power: Women of Influence) that the only exercise of power that French women have internalized as feminine is that of hidden or indirect power. If, like Garaud, they exert charm and pull strings from behind the scenes to manipulate the "little boys" (as Garaud called male politicians), thereby corresponding to the myths of women, they thereby further exacerbate doubts about women's political legitimacy.

### *The Legitimacy of the First Ministers for Women's Affairs*

Many women-activist authors question the legitimacy of Giroud's new ministry. Was it the result of women's actions and demands or of the will and interest of benevolent or politically opportunist men? In terms of creating precedents and increasing legitimacy, the outcomes of Giroud's ministry were considerable. Giroud herself concludes in *La Comédie du pouvoir* (The Comedy of Power) that, although its impact was not as great as she had hoped, her program, One Hundred Measures for Women (*Cent mesures pour les femmes*), adopted in part by the cabinet was generally a success.

The Socialists went further than Giscard with the feminist-socialist Yvette Roudy as full minister (1981 to 1986) and a substantial raft of legislation in favor of women's civil rights. Catherine Lalumière, minister in Mauroy's government and elected deputy in the Gironde in 1986, described Roudy's influence: "I have never belonged to any feminist movement, but I owe them a debt, for they opened the doors for me. I got here just after them. Before me, there was Yvette Roudy."[18]

Interviewed by Adler in 1992, Mitterrand himself, who had always personally intervened in favor of a measure of representation for women, still seemed uncertain about whether women were important in politics, or indeed could be. However, he reaffirmed the principle that women should have access to positions of responsibility and command if they wished. The problem, he argued, was not just the misogyny in the Socialist party, as in all parties, but the limited number of women competent to assume political responsibilities, as a result he believed, of their lack of preparation or taste for such things.

## *Women's Difference as Legitimacy*

Although he also admitted to irritation at what he called the "suffragette" argument for parity, Mitterrand stated the much-repeated credo that women are closer to the concrete and the humanitarian. He continued to act on his idea of equality within traditional difference. This is demonstrated by a certain feminization of his administration, including the bold moves of designating a woman, Simone Rozès, as President of the Cour de Cassation (The Court of Appeals), the appointment of Edvige Avice as junior minister for defense and the armed forces, and the strategic appointment of Edith Cresson as prime minister to replace the increasingly unpopular Rocard, with whom Mitterrand had serious rivalries.

> I didn't expect any more of women than of men but there is a difference. Their concerns, their experiences are much closer to the real world, to the concrete, to real suffering, than are those of men. They make a unique contribution to politics, since they are concerned with the nature of reality, with the nature of society and people's difficulties within it. Women have a predisposition for all of these things that men do not have. I would have been elected in 1965 had there been only male voters. At that time, women elected General de Gaulle.[19]

A shift occurs here, from an apology of women's place in politics to a very direct, self-interested, electoral consideration. This may not constitute direct political progress for women, but such considerations of political advantage, linked to the increasing public visibility of women representatives, indicate the changed contexts in which the debates on legitimacy were beginning to be written and read more attentively. In the long term, this does indeed constitute progress.

In *Un Coin dans leur monde* (A Corner in Their World), Huguette Bouchardeau's analysis of the character and stakes of woman's difference in relation to her legitimacy is not the same as that of Mitterrand. For her, women stand for office when there are several people working as a group but they withdraw as soon as there is a question of competition. From her own experience of working with men and women in politics, she is convinced that there are just as many women competent to hold high office as men and quite enough to fill the places available. Bouchardeau's definition of "different" also differs. The problem of lack of participation, she writes, is not so much due to women's lack of taste or disposition for work in the public forum as to their difficulties with political action defined largely as the conquest of power. We recall Cécile Brunschvicg at the beginning of this chapter, who initially sought involvement in charitable or social reform movements and had to be convinced by her husband that a ministerial position would be a more productive (and equally legitimate) forum for such action. By the end of the term of her office, Brunschvicg admitted that she had come to enjoy the exercise of power.

## *Legitimacy from Reconciling the Masculine and the Feminine*

At the end of any political meeting, it is always, in Giroud's analysis, a woman who asks, "What should we do?" The flip side to this perception of women as generally more practical, she adds, is that they may be considered lacking in imagination or having no utopian dreams or visions of future societies. Political vision, a passion for truth, and achievement are, however, there for the finding in the writing by women. In the work of Georges Sand, for example, such a passionate idealism can coexist with a pragmatic rootedness in the earth and everyday living. In her biography of Georges Sand, *La Lune et les Sabots* (The Moon and Wooden Clogs), discussed again in chapter 9, Bouchardeau attempts to show how this peculiarly feminine mix of idealism and practicality shaped that nineteenth-century woman writer's daring life and original work.

There is a different value given in the public forum to masculine heroism and to such feminine mixes of idealism and practicality. Parity however, would permit a certain *mixité*. "It is the combination of the particular solutions of men and of women that seems to be the best one," says Giroud.[20] Both would be legitimate. For Giroud, as for Bouchardeau, women's connection to the earth in their daily lives has to do less with an immutable feminine essence than with a difference derived from a lived experience and an outsider status that can be altered or lost. Giroud comes to the conclusion that the authority that powerful women have always exerted indirectly from within the family circle without necessarily having "a taste for power," as Mitterrand might put it, could change to become a desire for the pleasure of public power, a pleasure that "gnaws away at the hearts and minds" of men and women alike. Whether or not men and women will come to exercise power in exactly the same range of ways and with the same kind of pleasure is still an open question. But for the moment, according to Giroud, women are still less fooled by political appearances and what she calls "the comedy of power."

In her 1995 autobiography, *Il y a deux sexes* (There are Two Sexes), Antoinette Fouque, the founder of the Mouvement de Libération de la Femme, or MLF, identifies the name of the women's movement she created and led Psychanalyse et Politique (Psych. et Po.) with her relationship to both her parents. The psychoanalysis side is associated with her "illiterate" and "wonderful" Italian mother and her experience of dreams and the unconscious. Politics is identified with her working-class Corsican father and his public commitment.[21] It is only recently that Fouque and the women's liberation movements have come to accept the legitimacy of working from inside political structures after three decades of separatism. On her return from the United States to set up L'Alliance des femmes pour la démocratie to work for parity, Fouque realized that she has passed from the idea of liberation (the MLF founded in the 1960s) as separation from the male-dominated political structures to a further stage, one of "democracy" that now permits integration. She explains her acceptance of the vice-presidency of the Commission for Women's Rights in the European Parliament both in terms of a woman's duty to make a difference where this would be most possible and of a continuing anti-authoritarian revolt from within political institutions that is made in the name of radical difference between genders. Her entry into politics, in her own analysis, thus corresponds to a new *parti-pris*, conceiving feminine difference and equal rights together; reconciling the tension in Psych. et Po. (both psychology and politics, feminine and masculine).[22]

## *Brunschvicg's Legitimacy*

Two pieces of work on Cécile Brunschvicg have recently appeared. As the unpublished Ph.D. thesis by Joy Cooper observes, this reformist of the Radical party and first woman minister has been virtually omitted in traditional political histories and side-lined in feminist histories because of her moderate approaches and her middle-class connections.[23] Cooper argues that Brunschvicg deserves the status of stateswoman for her major contribution to both French and international political and social causes. Cooper's thesis draws on the recent archival research for a *DEA mémoire* by Juliette Aubrun, supervised by René Rémond, a professor at the Institut d'Etudes Politiques. This is one of the first graduate dissertations on political women supervised by a male political scientist in what remains a very traditionally male-dominated elite French institution.

Cooper's account focuses on Brunschvicg's struggle for improvement in the conditions of women and children, and for justice and humanity. She notes the historical contexts that exerted influence on Brunschvicg's life: in particular the Dreyfus affair, the rise of fascism, and the coming to power of the Popular Front against fierce right-wing opposition. Brunschvicg's legislative contributions are tabulated. Many of the measures are consistent with traditional notions of the feminine sphere, such as the provision of hot lunches in the workplace and 1,700 school canteens, medico-pedagogical help for the handicapped, homes for delinquents, financial aid for large families, the provision of day-care, nursing rooms, and female superintendents in the workplace, home economics education, and career counseling for girls. Brunschvicg did move to change the political realm with the passing of legislation in 1935 enabling women to become *conseillères municipales adjointes* (assistant municipal councilors). Cooper points out that Brunschvicg tirelessly promoted the inclusive universalistic philosophy of an educated society with the right of all to have access to the traditionally male domain of governance and the world of paid employment.

On the other hand, Juliette Aubrun's reading of Brunschvicg's legitimacy from a feminist perspective takes little account of a recent more favorable contemporary reappraisal of philanthropy among women historians. For Aubrun, Brunschvicg's actions derived from a middle-class culture "imbued with late nineteenth century good intentions" (*pétrie des bonnes intentions de la fin du siècle*).[24] In contrast, Aubrun sees Flora Tristan's lonely proselytizing crusade for female education and a feminist socialism that would destabilize reigning power structures and Madeleine Pelletier's male dress and feminist declarations as more the stuff of which heroines are made for the Second Wave feminists. Nonetheless, Aubrun's young and feminist critique and Cooper's more mature positive recovery of Brunschvicg's political legitimacy both raise the same question: Did Brunschvicg's acceptance of Blum as "prince," and the existing rules of the political realm, legitimate these rules and further the prince's policy, at the expense of the political legitimacy of women?

Brunschvicg's reformist discourse against the "evils" that "kill our race" and prevent population growth, such as alcohol and infant mortality, closely resembled the successful arguments of those suffragists who worked through the Women's Temperance Union in the countries that first granted suffrage to women. When the discourse of women's rights met opposition, the line of women's nurturing and moral contribution to society became more politically expedient. The moral reform line might appear to sit a little uncomfortably with Brunschvicg's arguments for the necessity of a role outside the home for many women and for state provision of child care. Brunschvicg, it would seem, had no qualms accommodating the two. Early women politicians such as Brunschvicg appear to have turned conventional discourses to serve their own and other women's day-to-day purposes. Brunschvicg's own writing rejected a "ridiculous battle of the sexes" or women's participation in the army: "Our feminism is too feminine to dream of fighting and killing. We are able to serve our country without parades and uniforms."[25] Her unwillingness to become an "imitation man," and her claim to a distinctive feminine social mission drew upon a very traditional gender-role discourse. At the same time, she used this discourse of feminine difference to justify her legitimacy as a politician.

## Legitimacy through and beyond Traditional Roles

Brunschvicg's four children and traditional respectability, and particularly the support of a prestigious husband were necessary factors for legitimating her presence in political office in the 1930s. Despite criticism by the suffragist Louise Weiss, and Aubrun's negative reading of this first-wave feminist, Brunschvicg's visibility in the 1936/37 Popular Front government as *sous-secrétaire d'Etat* for education, her non-confrontational feminist activity, and her insistence on the positive but specific role of the feminine in governance—the right of women to play both maternal and public roles—was pragmatically and symbolically effective.

In the 1980s and 1990s, the so-called younger generation of Socialist female politicians did not shrink in the face of challenging portfolios new to women but nor, indeed, from foregrounding their feminine roles in public. Amidst great publicity, Ségolène Royal and Frérérique Bredin gave birth two days apart to the first children born to a minister in office, Royal virtually under the blaze of television lights. Bouchardeau notes that this was Ségolène Royal's fourth child, although the minister was barely in her forties. In fact, in their public affirmation of the right to bring the private and the feminine (pregnancy and birth) into the masculine political domain, Ségolène Royal and Elisabeth Guigou go beyond the affirmation of equality toward imposing the acceptance of feminine difference as a source of their legitimacy. It could be argued, of course, that somewhat paradoxically it was the need to find paternal legitimization, both as women politicians and as mothers, and lovers, which continued to characterize this "Mitterrand" generation. The need for legitimization certainly influenced women's decisions to enter the elite male-dominated schools of administrators and technocrats (the Ecole Nationale d'Administration, or ENA, in particular) but, again, paradoxically, it is also the Mitterrandian women politicians' foregrounding of family obligations and caring roles that mark them as feminine and different. All of these politicians have also expressed a certain guilt in relation to the conflict between their political commitments and their obligations to their children and family.

## The Power of Discourse and the Media: Using and Transforming Legitimacy

Huguette Bouchardeau remarked to me in a 1992 interview that the young women who entered politics in the 1980s and early 1990s, the so-called Mitterrand generation, followed the same educational path as their male counterparts and therefore have a greater confidence in their right to their political roles than did their mothers and grandmothers. These women include Ségolène Royal, education minister, Frédérique Bredin, minister of youth and sports, Martine Aubry, labor minister, and Elisabeth Guigou, justice minister. Using L'ENA as a springboard, women were slowly making a number of different itineraries acceptable. Originally in an appointed and paternally protected position in Mitterrand's Cabinet in 1981, the ecologist and feminist Ségolène Royal, for example, re-entered the political arena in 1988 to win an elected position as *députée* for the *Deux Sèvres* area. She became a minister again in Jospin's government in 1997. The prestigious intellectual itinerary of these women, their increasing numbers, and their determination to play both the maternal and the professional cards (as if this were quite normal) seem to have overcome some of the fears and prejudices of many of their male colleagues and the electorate. In another interview with me in 1995, Bouchardeau admitted that she had some difficulty accepting the discourse of this new generation who assume equality is a *fait accompli*—"as if there no longer exists any gender difference that could be a cause for discrimination or bias and no need to adopt feminist positions." She applauds the self-confidence and self-assertion, the apparent strength, and the assertion of legitimacy of women who can state calmly that having children and being a politician is simply a question of organization, but admits that she remains somewhat skeptical about good organization being a sufficient answer to a successful combination of the two roles.

If discourse, as Foucault has put it, is not simply that which translates struggle or systems of domination but the place of struggle itself, and the power one seeks to lay hold of, then the representations of women politicians and their work (or the absence of representations) are of great significance.[26] In a research dissertation completed at the Ecole des Sciences Politiques on the representation of women in journalism throughout the Mitterrand decade, Jane Freedman remarks on the absence of any reference to legislation for women or by women ministers in the recent monumental political study on Mitterrand by P. Favier and M. Roland-Martin, *La Décennie Mitterrand* (The Mitterrand Decade).[27] Even Roudy's 1983 law for equality in the workplace did not receive a mention from these authors. This observation helped Freedman define her topic. Freedman worked from the premise that communication has the power to construct political legitimacy (politicians are dependent on the media for transmitting their political messages and creating their image).

Freedman discovered that none of the twenty-four legislative measures of Roudy's ministry—including government-funded paid maternity leave for the self-employed, reimbursement of abortion, equality in the workplace, protection of the spouse in case of divorce—were mentioned in the eleven works on the Mitterrand era she studied. One exception was the story of the passing of the law on the reimbursement of abortion procedures recounted in *Histoire de la première République Mitterrandienne* (History of the First Mitterrandian Republic) by Solange and Christian Gras.[28] This account is not totally unsympathetic to women but it is told from inside the establishment, looking out at minority (female) behavior according to the journalistic principle of "visualizing deviance."[29] The Gras account goes on to state that Roudy's claims were sometimes excessive—for example, her request that 30 percent of the nominations to positions in radio and television be reserved for women: "Perhaps she wants to generalize the famous quota. She needs to be told, nicely, and as a preventative measure, that gender doesn't enter into the choice of university professors."[30] This narrative intends to deliver a lesson on the French refusal of affirmative action from what is presented as an objective, and normal perspective. It patronizes, even infantilizes the women's ministry whose representatives—described as out-of-date post-'68 feminists—do not conform to the norm of political actors. The minister's unrealistic demands for quotas seem to need to be corrected by paternalistic oversight. Roudy's claims are shown to be deviant, and this visualized deviance renders her ministry suspicious.

To complement her analysis of the published monographs on the Mitterrand era, Freedman concludes based on a study of ten newspapers that whenever the work of the Ministry of Women's Rights is mentioned, it is trivialized. Characterized as "feminist"—as being given money by the state to keep quiet (just as in popular culture men have always given women money to keep them quiet), as instigating a war of the sexes, as having an "old-fashioned charm" (*charme vieillot*) or overweening ambitions, as being "bitchy" (*une emmerdeuse*) and moralizing, as lacking ideas and enthusiasm, and, finally, as being useless—the Ministry is systematically devalued. Regardless of differences in the written materials analyzed, differences in the professional or political interest groups that supported or helped finance these materials, regardless of their left-wing or right-wing affiliations and readership, all of the representations of women that Freedman encountered in her study draw on the same devaluing tendency toward marginalization, deviance, and general illegitimacy of women's political power.

## *The Press and the Limited Legitimacy of the Female Political Body*

The belief in female deviance has become so normative that the press need only represent a woman in power to visualize this deviance. The pressure on Brunschvicg to adhere to public opinion, gender-norms, and the common knowledge of her time concerning legitimately constituted power is also evident from press reports. The press of the day expressed astonishment that suffragists like Brunschvicg can be "real women looking like everyone else" and not "a-sexual hybrid creatures in male garb." Other reactions confirm the normative masculine system in which Brunschvicg and other women in politics could only be aberrant.

The media representations of Brunschvicg range from the benevolent to the virulently racist and sexist. Most are based in some way on the "doxa" of the time and the received wisdom on feminine difference. Andrée Viollis in the newspaper *Vendredi* speaks of "her energy, her dignity, her clear voice imposing itself in all the congresses, her rigorous logic, the exactitude of her information, all of which makes her a good man of politics."[31] Henriette Sauret in *Dimanche-Illustré* offers a favorable view declaring that, like Brunschvicg, women must bring a "maternal" quality to meetings.[32] On the other hand, the nomination of three women in the Blum cabinet is described by the right-wing Action Française as "légèreté," as a replacement of political seriousness by a feminine "frivolity." In an article dated 1941, the male journalist Jean Théroigne used gender to make what is simultaneously an anti-Semitic, antifeminist, and anti-Popular Front attack on this "sub-ministeress."[33]

> But who can tell how many secrets of state were gathered and passed on by this Madam. The dying Republic appears to have wanted to give itself a female under-minister in its own image, softness, flabbiness, intrigues, affairs etc., ... a hundred kilos of fat.[34]

The metaphors in this right-wing diatribe from Vichy France aim at the parliamentary regime itself, personified by the female "sub-minister." The disqualification of Brunschvicg as a political representative is grounded in the illegitimacy of the female body. The disqualification of the Popular Front parliamentary system is effected by its feminization. Brunschvicg is attacked through her physical appearance, "her sizable person could not pass unnoticed" (*son importante personne ne pouvait pas passer inaperçue*), through her sexuality (portrayed as venal, and predatory), and through the concept of traditional feminine duplicity (as, Messalina-like, she extorts state secrets from men). The stereotyped assumptions about women, Jews, and the proper gender of power, which are appealed to in this discourse, are all the more insidious because of their covert appeal to the subconscious.

## *Edith Cresson as Deviant: A Victim of the Media*

It is paradoxical that the media image of Edith Cresson—her smile and "new look" consistently presented as her greatest asset, what *Le Figaro* saw as the feminine specialty of "the art of appearance" in contrast to "the art of government"[35]—was in the long run what condemned her. In her study of press coverage of French women in politics, Freedman presents two photographs of Cresson. In one, she sits, attractive and smiling, on a settee in a low-cut, sleeveless dress behind a huge bowl of roses. A reader of this sexualized image would not imagine he/she was looking at the new minister of European affairs notes Freedman. The small caption under the photo reads incongruously: "a huge task awaits our European parliamentarians."[36] A second photo, this time composed in the romantic rather than the sexualized tradition, shows an attractive Cresson about to embrace a smiling Rocard. Again visualizing deviance, it too is somewhat ironic in its caption "The Transfer of Power" (*La passation des pouvoirs*). The kiss comes to represent an aspect of a very particular transfer of power.[37] In printed texts, it is again Cresson's difference, her "feminine" qualities, that are stressed and not her policies.[38] Much of the subsequent journalism on Cresson, who dealt most unusually and courageously with the "masculine" portfolios of agriculture, trade and industry, and European affairs, would continue to insist on her smiles and seduction, her extreme *féminité*,[39] and the effect of stardom. These characteristics are opposed to competence: for example, to Pierre Bérégovoy's "quintessential professionalism" as minister of finance.[40]

Freedman observes that many political women are caught in a vicious circle, their appearance is focused on, praised or critiqued, so they must take care of their appearance. This in turn leads to accusations that they are too busy looking after their "look" and can only cope with "soft" ministries. Freedman illustrates this double-bind by quoting a journalistic description of the women Socialist ministers in the 1981 to 1986 government who had discovered Pierre Cardin and Yves Saint Laurent and master hairdressers for the televised Wednesday sessions; unfortunately, state the journalists, what the women politicians had to say was not at the same level as their appearance. For Freedman, a photo of Yvette Roudy published in *France Soir Magazine*, in a skimpy bikini by a pool on the Ivory Coast, captioned "One of the Rights of Women. Relaxation" (*Un des droits de la femme. Le repos*), illustrates, by its very excess, the absolute media obsession with the body of every female representative.[41] In the lineup, a few women are indirectly attacked, singled out for neglecting elegance, charm (the epithet "charming" is a constant), and seduction. Huguette Bouchardeau, for example, is described as "in a sweater and black pants" (*vêtue de pull et d'un pantalon noir*) and the French reader would be quick to understand the deviance and implied criticism that this image represents.[42] Most articles that present flattering detailed physical descriptions of elegant women politicians correspondingly relegate their political work to the background.

There is a difference between the reassuring and more maternal image of male-supported right-wing women and the image that tends to characterize the often more active and assertive women of the left. Qualities of stubbornness or combativeness (*battante, têtue*), ascribed particularly to Edith Cresson, Martine Aubry, Yvette Roudy, and Ségolène Royal, have given the press the leeway to characterize them as cold, or again, as furies. The different early images of Elizabeth Dole and Hillary Clinton come to mind in this respect—the former presented as the warm supportive wife of the senator and rarely as the Secretary of Transportation, and the latter as too assertive and frigid. Yet both right-wing and left-wing women are caught in the no-win situation of being deviant in politics, either as Queens of hearts (*dames de coeur*) or as masculine Iron ladies (*dames de fer*). Nicole Questiaux, described by the press as the "queen of hearts" in the ministry for National Solidarity, is said to have a heart that is bigger than her budget. She must therefore be watched closely by the tutelary office of the prime minister.[43] Certain set phrases circulate through the journalism of the late 1980s, one report influencing another. *Le Monde* also used *une dame de coeur* to describe Michèle Barzach only to be challenged by *Libération*'s question, *La dame de coeur cacherait-elle une dame de fer*?[44] (Could the lady of heart conceal an iron lady?).[45] Whatever the decision, the "woman of heart" running the Social Security office, for example, will necessarily "underestimate the financial constraints," as the iron (or stone or steel) ladies will conceal a vulnerable underbelly.[46]

Qualified and competent women still produce resistance even in an age of increasing awareness of the "politically correct" and EEO offices. This resistance is rarely directly misogynistic but often an unconscious displacement of disavowal—it takes the form, for example, of the right to censure the dress and (authoritarian) behavior of "unfeminine" women ministers. Such resistance is prevalent in the media. The general speculation on Edith Cresson's earlier "relationship" with Mitterrand could not feature in the same negative way in a male career. The photograph of Simone Veil's "shockingly" inelegant appearance (without her characteristic Dior suit and chignon) caught by a waiting photographer as she slipped out of her Paris apartment to go to the store would hardly be a scandal for a male minister. Women are accused either of seeking media attention (stardom) or of insufficiently attending to the media, of overconfidence or of icy distance; Michèle Barzach and Elisabeth Guigou have been constantly characterized as "icy" and Martine Aubry as *la dame de pierre* (the lady of stone). They are accused of too little or too much emotion, of being too political or too honest. They are either too manipulated by the prince or too independent. Ambitious or successful women who do not hide their talents still seem to pose a threat to established gender and power relations and are labeled both as "very feminine" or as "unfeminine" by journalists. Either way, this signifies illegitimacy. This has also been the case for Edith Cresson, Margaret Thatcher, Golda Meir, Indira Gandhi, and Helen Clark among others. There is a danger that the women themselves internalize such representations and come to see themselves as having some "deficit" as a female, as Indira Gandhi did, according to her female biographer.

## *The Press and Progress toward Legitimacy?*

In its constant recycling and reinforcement of ready-made notions on public women, the press has not been ahead of its time. In general, the question of women's legitimacy has been played out against the background of political movements toward the franchise, then representation, and later parity, but these movements do not constitute the simple linear progression their narrating might appear to give them. In countries outside France, too, the experiences of women have been mixed. On the one hand, in Ireland, Mary Robinson saw her 1991 election as president as the "psychic equivalent of the collapse of the Berlin Wall."[47] On the other hand, the economic liberalization in Russia and the former communist block has generally led to coalitions of new-style democrats and old-style conservatives that are dramatically reducing the gains made by women in child care and work and social protections under the communist regimes.[48] Kelber reports that in 1990, female representation in the Romanian parliament dropped from 34.3 percent to 3.5 percent; in Czechoslovakia, from 29.5 percent to 6 percent; in Hungary, from 20.9 percent to 7 percent; in Bulgaria from 21 percent to 8.5 percent; and in the German Democratic Republic, from 32.2 percent to 20.5 percent.[49] Despite the sense of the lack of legitimacy of the presence of the feminine in places of power that still apparently haunts the collective unconscious, and is reflected in the media, public opinion has in part adopted the new women's discourses. The absence of women in decision-making positions is today often viewed as illegitimate.

There have been a number of problematic female political careers in France—Georgina Dufoix, tried for complicity as a minister in office at the time of the drama of the Aids-contaminated blood scandal and pleading "responsible, but not guilty"; Edith Cresson particularly on the charge of nepotism, as European Commissioner; Michaux-Chevry under a cloud in Guadeloupe; the women of the right, including Yann Piat and Marie-France Stirbois, who stepped into the shoes of her dead husband for the Front national, or the excessive and crusading Christine Boutin and her campaign for censorship of "pornographic" and violent images. Generally, though, as high office holders, women have enjoyed an undeniable public popularity. In 1974, Simone Veil and Françoise Giroud were the most-liked persons in the government.[50] Twenty years later, Veil was still at the top of the popularity chart, although this did not save her from being dropped from government when Juppé replaced Balladur as prime minister. After the Socialists came back into office in 1997, the women ministers remained well ahead of their male colleagues in the opinion polls. Bouchardeau noted the encouraging recognition that accompanied her own presidential candidacy in 1981 as she spoke in over 150 towns, sleeping on friends' couches and continuing to meet the responsibilities of her university position in Lyon. Despite the mixed nature of women's success, Bouchardeau was sure that, given the positive electoral image of women candidates, the chances for this still rare species' success were probably better than men's.[51]

There is a gap between the opinions found in the French press and the public opinion garnered in polls. The press generally presented

Cresson's nomination to the office of prime minister as a publicity stunt on Mitterrand's part, a "rabbit pulled out of the hat," an ingenious new gadget to please women, and *Le Figaro* called it "the act of the prince."[52] A journalist from *Le Monde* stated that the centrists were hostile, whereas "women and feminist associations were delighted with the promotion of a woman to such a high office."[53] In fact, a May poll by the IFOP agency had shown that 28 percent of the general public questioned, men and women, was "very pleased" with the appointment and 49 percent was "quite pleased." As Freedman insists, this opinion was positive toward women representatives: according to a survey by the polling agency CSA in April 1987, 82 percent were favorable among the ecologists, 77 percent among the left, 72 percent among the center-right UDF (Union la démocratique française), 57 percent among the RPR (Rassemblement pour la République), and 50 percent among the FN (Front national). It may have been that public opinion was favorable precisely because the questions appeared to concern only hypothetical possibilities. Certainly public opinion was clear about a gendered separation of roles in a 1989 poll by the BVA institute. In this survey, 91 percent of those polled felt that a woman could hold a position as a minister of health, given that women were seen to be closer to daily life (according to 77 percent) and had greater intuition (according to 59 percent), whereas the Ministry of the Interior was considered to be less within their competence (according to 57 percent of those polled).

Contemporary history may be witnessing something of a turnaround with respect to the popularity of women in high positions around the world as well as in France. In 1999 Elisabeth Dole and Hillary Clinton were overshadowing their husbands in the press as potential political leaders, with Hillary planning to run for the Senate in New York. The moral fall of her husband, the first lady's wounding and her fidelity may paradoxically have helped permit the recognition of her competence, her acceptability in the collective consciousness, and her campaign victory in 2000. In the New Zealand election in 1999, two women, incumbent Prime Minister Jenny Shipley and incoming new Labor Prime Minister Helen Clark were the two favored candidates in prime ministerial public opinion polls.[54] Taria Halonen, former minister of foreign affairs became the first woman president of Finland in 2000. In the developing world, legitimated by caste and political dynasty in most cases, women are also emerging as preferred political candidates; in 1999, for example, the Bangladeshi prime minister was a woman.

## *Writing Legitimacy and Legitimate Difference as Progress*

While the new discourse being introduced by women creates a target for a certain humorous, or sometimes not so humorous, backlash, it at least creates a politics of presence. In its edition of 26 May 2000, for example, *Le Point* devoted a short and rather sarcastic article to the "feminine solutions" that Michèle Alliot-Marie claims to be seeking as the new president of the RPR in getting agreement on a candidate for Paris and ridding the party of its internal rivalries.[55] Although the arguments for the non-confrontational management style that "MAM" adopted are articulated in the article (those who elected her, from whom she draws her "legitimacy," she claims, do not want wars between chiefs and in-house struggles for power), the journalist nonetheless finds a ready-made target for humor in Alliot-Marie's attempt to impose "feminine solutions" and avoid conflict. But Fabien Roland-Lévy does also note Alliot-Marie's feat of "temerity" in sidelining the Parisian political heavyweight Tibéri in her own favor.

Considering the influence of the family on the motivations that lead women to enter politics, Janine Mossuz-Lavau argues that this influence is more significant for right-wing women for whom the cohesion of the family group is important. She admits, however, that the influence of the family has played a role in the choices of women leaders on the right and on the left, citing the father of Anne-Marie Idrac, Roselyne Bachelot, Françoise de Panafieu on the right, but also of Martine Aubry. The ideology of the mother, however, she adds, referring to the work on the leaders of the RPR party has also been shown to play a role.[56] Mossuz-Lavau concludes that "it does indeed seem that the time when women who entered politics followed fathers or husbands has past. Politics is no longer a family affair (except in the Front national)."[57] Mossuz-Lavau may well be underestimating the residual power and complexity of the family romance and the influence of the father. But she has identified progress.

This progress, we argue, goes hand in hand with the opening to conscious examination of discriminatory uses of language and of the competing arguments for women's political legitimacy (or illegitimacy). Progress lies in identifying the fixation on surrogacy and defining a context-specific and self-transforming feminine "difference" or legacy. Measured simply by the increase in the number and complexity of the analyses of legitimacy in political stories on and by women, and by the success of women who have reached and held positions of power, progress would seem considerable. Some commentators are impatient at the proliferation and generalizing of discourses that do not appear to lead to real, immediate, change for women. But if we accept, with Foucault, that discourse is power, and with Lacan, that knowledge of our language is the self-knowledge that alone leads to change, the proliferation of testimonial and analytical work on their legitimacy, predominantly produced by women themselves, is as sure a sign of progress as the success story of the parity movement, itself founded on a new discourse. As the critique of "sexist" language is disseminated by the women's texts, as the media becomes a little more self-conscious and the public more critical, it may be that the use of language such as "Blair's Babes" and "Juppé's Skirts" is beginning to create a public critical awareness and a general reaction in favor of political women.

## Notes

1. "Une femme politique est toujours sous la dépendance d'un homme... Il existe des femmes qui pénètrent dans les lieux du pouvoir et ne dérangent rien. Les hommes de pouvoir, quand ils mettent des femmes en place choisissent souvent des femmes aliénées. Elles ne font pas avancer les choses." Yvette Roudy in *Marie Claire,* no. 401, January 1986, quoted in Mariette Sineau, *Des Femmes en politique* (Paris: Economica, 1998), p. 143. All translations in this chapter are my own.
2. Interview with Yvette Roudy, 13 May 1992, in Laure Adler, *Les Femmes Politiques* (Paris: Seuil, 1993).
3. "Au début de mon mandat, on me disait, quand je défendais les droits des femmes: 'Oui, mais vous, vous êtes une exception car vous n'êtes pas vraiment une femme.' J'étais très bien accueillie par les hommes. J'étais la veuve de Pierre, ils avaient tous beaucoup de respect, ils projetaient sur moi l'affection, l'admiration qu'ils avaient pour Pierre. J'étais en quelque sorte l'émanation de Pierre Brossolette." Adler, *Les Femmes Politiques*, p. 138.
4. Aung San Suu Kyi, the daughter of Aung Sun, the founder of modern Myanmar (Burma), who won the 1990 national elections (and later, the 1991 Nobel Peace Prize for her non-violent resistance to the military takeover) has, for example, become a symbolically powerful figure of the nation's democratic resistance to the military regime in power. Magwati Sukarnoputri, who led the democratic opposition party to victory in Indonesia, and Corazon Aquino, leader of the opposition that toppled the dictatorship of Marcos in the Philippines, as well as a number of other women in the developing world. Sirimavo Bandaranike in Sri Lanka, the world's first woman prime minister in 1960, Chandrika Kumaratunga, also in Sri Lanka (president from 1994 and daughter of a prime minister who, along with Chandrika's husband, lost his life in the fighting against the Tamil guerillas), Indira Gandhi and Sonia Gandhi in India, Benazir Bhutto in Pakistan, have all carried on their fight in the name of assassinated husbands or fathers.
5. "Son père, l'avocat Jean-Denis Bredin, ancien associé de Robert Badinter, ayant été vice-président du mouvement de gauche, c'est tout naturellement qu'elle s'est intéressée à la politique." *Le Figaro*, 17 May 1991, quoted by Freedman, *La représentation journalistique des femmes politiques (vu à travers le bilan de "la décennie Mitterrand" depuis 1981), mémoire pour un DEA d'Etudes Politiques* (Diplôme d'études approfondies), Institut d'Etudes Politiques, Paris, September 1992, p. 36.
6. Personal interview, 1994.
7. The Bastid article is from the dossier on Cécile Brunschvicg held by the women's history library in Paris, the Bibliothèque Marguerite Durand.
8. The texts of the feminist theorist and philosopher Michèle le Doeuff argue that alone such mentoring relationships have permitted women to become philosophers, recalling Sartre's (in)famous remark to Simone de Beauvoir when he heard that she, too, had passed the *agrégation* exam in philosophy: "I will take you in hand."
9. "[I]l n'existe [sic] tant d'hommes qui puissent se vanter d'être le mari d'un ministre." Joy Cooper, *Cécile Brunschvicg: L'évolution de sa vision dans le cadre de l'histoire de la France et du féminisme français* (Ph.D. thesis, University of Sydney, 1996), p. 170.
10. Maurice Duverger is a well-known political scientist who has published a number of scholarly studies on political institutions in France.
11. In Adler, *Les Femmes politiques*, p. 151. Interviewing Marie-Madeleine Dienesch: "If she was eliminated from political life, it wasn't surprising. She didn't really have the knack of dealing with her male colleagues" (*Si elle a été éliminée de la vie politique, ce n'est pas étonnant. Elle n'avait pas trop la manière avec les collègues masculins*).
12. Thiery Fundéré, "La Chute de la dame de fer," *Le Point*, 26 May 2000, no. 1445, p. 14.
13. "Les femmes ministres avant 1981 ont été un alibi. J'ai moi-même été un alibi." *Le Matin*, 26 December 1986.

14. "L'organisation 'parti' est la plus misogyne, la plus allergique aux femmes qui soit. Aucune femme n'a réussi à faire une place dans un parti." Adler, *Les Femmes Politiques*, p. 168.
15. See also, Mattei Dogan et Jacques Narbonne, *Les Françaises face à la politique* (Paris: Armand Colin, 1955).
16. Adler cites René Rousseau's study, *Les Femmes rouges* (Paris: Stock, 1986).
17. The myth of a Madame de Maintenon who controlled the king as the power behind the throne was discredited by the historical research of Françoise de Chandernagore in her 1989 book, *L'Allée du roi.*
18. "Je n'ai jamais appartenu à aucun movement féministe, mais je leur rends hommage car ils m'ont ouvert les portes. J'arrive juste après. Avant, il y avait Yvette Roudy." Adler, *Les Femmes Politiques*, p. 192. Interview, 17 April 1992.
19. Ibid., p. 191.
20. "Je n'attendais pas plus des femmes que ce que j'attends des hommes, mais c'est différent. Ce sont des soucis, des expériences beaucoup plus proches de la réalité, du concret, des vraies souffrances, que ceux des hommes. C'est un apport indispensable pour que la politique soit traitée avec un regard très soucieux de la réalité et de la nature de la société, des misères qui la composent. Il y a une prédisposition des femmes plus évidente que celle des hommes à tout cela. J'aurais été elu en 1965 s'il n'y avait eu que des hommes. Les femmes ont élu le Général de Gaulle à cette époque." Adler, *Les Femmes Politiques*, p. 168.
21. Fouque studied under the literary critic Roland Barthes, and was psychoanalyzed by Lacan. She challenged the Lacanian tenet that there is only one libido, not two, and founded the women's publishing press, *Des Femmes*, to help make her point that "wherever the 'one' is set up as an absolute, the other side of the coin is totalitarianism."
22. Fouque has always been concerned with women's rights as well as women's difference. Despite the mysterious paralysis that has prevented her from walking, she traveled the world in support of her oppressed political sisters—Aung San Sun Kyi in Burma, the Bengali writer Taslima Nasreen, condemned to death by Muslim fundamentalists, the activist Kurd Leyla Zana, imprisoned for fifteen years, the Algerian Khalida Messaoudi, condemned to death for standing out against the dictates of the FIS (Front Islamic du Salut), the insurgent Islamic party. In parliament, she continues to denounce fundamentalism and its fear of the other (the woman, the foreigner), and to plead for freedom of intellectual and political expression.
23. Joy Cooper, *Cécile Brunschvicg.*
24. Ibid., p. 266.
25. Brunschvicg's words were part of a speech in 1912 to the Ecole Normale Supérieure, a select, higher-level educational training institution for women, quoted in Cooper, *Cécile Brunschvicg*, p. 52.
26. In Jane Freedman, *La représentation journalistique des femmes politiques,* p. 4. (Freedman quotes from Foucault's *L'ordre du discours*).
27. Ibid.
28. Solange et Christian Gras, *Histoire de la première République Mitterrandienne* (Paris: Robert Laffont, 1991).
29. Freedman draws on the sociological research of Ericson, Baranek, and Chan who argue that journalists systematically operate a visualizing of events that focuses on deviance in order to better establish the norm. Ericson, Baranek, and Chan, *Visualizing Deviance* (Toronto: Toronto University Press, 1989), quoted in Freedman, p. 8.
30. "Peut-être veut-elle généraliser le fameux quota. On doit lui signaler, gentillement, et à titre préventif, que le sexe n'entre pas en ligne de compte dans le choix des professeurs d'université." Solange et Christian Gras, *Histoire de la première République Mitterrandienne,* p. 78, quoted in Freedman, p. 64.
31. "Son énergie, sa dignité, sa voix nette qui s'impose dans tous les congrès, sa rigoureuse logique, la sûreté de sa documentation qui en font un bon homme poli-

tique... un heureux présage pour le droit de vote des femmes," quoted in Cooper, *Cécile Brunschvicg*, p. 170.

32. Ibid., p. 170.
33. In *Au Pilori*, 2 October 1941.
34. "Mais qui dira le nombre de secrets d'Etat que [*sic*] furent récoltés et passés par cette entremetteuse. ... Il semble que la République finissante ait voulu se donner une sous-ministresse à son image, mollesse, turpitude, intrigues, trafics etc. ... cent kilos de graisse." Cooper, *Cécile Brunschvicg*, p. 194. Cooper quotes Jean Théroigne in *Au Pilori*, 2 October 1941.
35. *Le Figaro*, 21 May 1991, quoted in Freedman, p. 88.
36. "Un énorme travail attend nos parlementaires européens." *Libération*, 25 May 1989, photo B in Freedman, following p. 41.
37. *Libération*, 17 May 1991, photo A in Freedman following p. 41.
38. In December 1997, Jenny Shipley, the daughter of a Presbyterian minister, became the first woman prime minister of New Zealand, representing the right-wing coalition government elected under the new proportional MMP electoral system. She was generally well received, despite reservations that her leadership was the result of a political coup against the prime minister in office during his absence in France. One small detail of the response, not perhaps without significance, was the remark made by one male member of Shipley's electorate, welcoming the new star home, a comment echoed through the New Zealand media: "I kissed Mrs. Shipley. She will be the first and last prime minister I get to kiss."
39. For example, in *Libération*, 17 May 1991, quoted in Freedman, p. 89 and *Le Quotidien de Paris*, 4 February 1992, quoted p. 52.
40. *Le Monde*, 3 April 1992, quoted in Freedman, p. 89.
41. *France Soir Magazine*, 29 May 1982, photograph C in Freedman, following p. 41.
42. *Le Monde*, 29 March 1983, quoted in Freedman, p. 24.
43. Solange and Christian Gras, *Histoire de la première République Mitterrandienne* (Paris: Robert Laffont, 1991), p. 140, quoted in Freedman, p. 29.
44. *Le Monde*, 25 June 1987, quoted in Freedman, p. 29.
45. *Libération*, 20 September 1987.
46. *Le Monde*, 1 July 1982, quoted in Freedman, p. 30.
47. Mim Kelber, ed.,*Women and Government: New Ways to Political Power* (Westport, Conn.: Praeger, 1994), p. xiv.
48. Abortion restrictions or prohibitions have since been legislated in Poland, Hungary, and the Czech and Slovak Republics.
49. Kelber, *Women and Government*, p. 20.
50. In a national survey, *L'Aurore*, 3 and 4 February 1975.
51. Personal interview, Paris, 1992.
52. *Le Figaro*, quoted in Freedman, p. 87.
53. *Le Monde*, 17 May 1991, quoted in Freedman, p. 86.
54. Jenny Shipley ran her November election campaign for the National party as a mother supporting and supported by a united family. Her labor rival, Helen Clark, ignoring the evident handicap of "not being a mother" and recognizing and avoiding the danger of a negative campaign being seen as a catfight, won the election. Shipley appointed two women to her Cabinet; Clark's first Cabinet contained eleven women out of twenty-six members.
55. "RPR Les secrets de la méthode MAM," *Le Point*, no. 1445, 26 May 2000, p. 11.
56. Pierre Brechon, Jacques Derville, Patrick Lecomte, *Les Cadres du RPR* (Paris: Economica, 1987).
57. "Il semble certes révolu le temps où la femme qui s'engageait en politique suivait le père ou le mari. La politique n'est plus une affaire de famille (hormis au Front national)." Janine Mosssuz-Lavau, in Michelle Perrot, ed., *An 2000: quel bilan pour les femmes?* p. 68.

# Part III

## Portraits of and Interviews with Political Women

# 5

# Interviews: From Assimilation to Non-Conformity

Women's political interviews are part of the body of texts creating forms of anti-power through the strengthening of the discourse of feminine political legitimacy. Interviewees use the medium for self-disclosure (or even self-discovery), self-justification, and to communicate information to their electorates indirectly. Political persuasion may also be on the agenda. An examination of two sets of interviews separated by ten years (1986 and 1996) demonstrates a change in the content and tone of women's interviews over the decade, supporting the hypothesis that the new ideas circulating on the airwaves and in the bookshops are having an influence.

## Changing Truths: From *Des Femmes en politique* (1986) to *Femmes et Citoyennes* (1996)

Much of the earlier social-science research on women in French politics derives from the interviews carried out by Mariette Sineau and her collaborators. These include forty interviews conducted between 1984 and 1985 with women senators, deputies, mayors of towns of more than 30,000 people, and party directors at the national level. The interviews were analyzed, synthesized and presented in a report to the Centre National de Recherches Scientifiques (CNRS) in 1986. Then, in 1988, they were published in a volume entitled *Des Femmes en politique*. Appointed ministers were excluded from Sineau's study, considered to be less able to respond independently of the system than elected representatives. Her interviews sought an answer to the question of whether change in the style of politics to incorporate other modes of decision making could come from inside the system.

The 1996 co-authored survey by Patricia Latour, Monique Houssin, and Madia Tovar, *Femmes et Citoyennes*, is made up of interviews with only twelve political women. The twelve women ranged from the Resistance fighter Lucie Aubrac, to the Communist *députées* Muguette Jacquaint and Hélène Luc, and the young president of the Conseil Régional du Nord-Pas de Calais, the ecologist Marie-Christine Blandin. The majority of the interviewees were chosen from the political left. While Sineau's work was informed by a rigorous social-science methodology, the 1996 text had a very different readership in mind. The ideological and pedagogical purpose of *Femmes et Citoyennes* is made clear by the division of the account of voting rights into easily studied sections and the limited set of interview questions. The approach to history of *Femmes et Citoyennes* is explicitly feminist. The tone of the historical summaries of women's actions to achieve political representation is celebratory. Interviewees are asked leading questions and their responses are then presented to the reader directly as primary data. The work includes women who were likely to have something new and progressive to say about women's roles in politics and omits conservative opinions. In this respect, it makes no attempt to reflect a cross-section of opinion. Women are asked to give their assessment of the traditional male power structures and their opinion on the recent campaign for parity.

On careful examination, despite its scholarly methodology, Sineau's carefully objective and more inclusive study also conceals a socialist and feminist focus. The premise of women's oppressed status and struggle for equal rights indirectly frames her investigation and exerts an influence on the questions articulated.

## *Misogyny and the Internalized Masculinity of Politics*

Sineau concludes that in 1986, despite changing public perceptions, increasing confidence in women politicians and even preference for (certain) women candidates, political women seem to have internalized the images of themselves constructed by men. The metaphors they use include "ugly duckling," "monster," and the "voice from space," and suggest the physical foreignness women feel that they embody in relation to the "masculine tide" in parliament. The perception is that misogyny, while neither willed nor conscious, nonetheless saturates interactions between men and women in positions of power. Feelings of solitude are common. Both locker-room humor (*grivoiserie*) and excessive courtesy (the very French mixture of *galanterie* and *gauloiserie*) are felt to be fences that set women apart. Women politicians interviewed by Sineau call politics the "last bastion."

Sineau claims that the media reinforces these feelings. As an example of the conception of the sovereign (state) as virile and of the fear of feminine (maternal) takeover, Sineau points to an opinion piece that appeared in the weekly entertainment guide, *Pariscope*. Expressing discontent at state intervention in his life in the anti-smoking campaign led by Simone Veil, the commentator writes: "It was a woman doing this, and women piss us off, they're always wanting what's good for us. They always want to play Mummy. Well, the state has become a woman, and this is intolerable."[1]

The image of the over-protective and authoritarian mother is part of a set of complex antifeminine images well known to feminist investigation. In a discussion of the virile mythology of totalitarian states, Sineau points out that in many pre-modern societies the symbolism of sovereignty was linked to male sexual potency, to power (*pouvoir*) as sexual potency or physical strength (*puissance*), and to animals such as the bull, the lion, or the ram. Sineau quotes Chirac on the military tactics of political campaigns: "Cities are like women, it's not enough to seduce them, you have to know how to take them."[2] The writer recalls Monique Pelletier's account of Giscard d'Estaing's astonishment when she attempted to talk to him, not of her work as *ministre déléguée* (junior minister) for women, but of political strategy.

Sineau also concludes that women have internalized the limits set to their territory by men. One of the charts that Bouchardeau presents in *Les Femmes et la politique* shows the commissions chosen by the deputies in 1986 revealing that the vast majority of women in politics themselves continued to elect health, education, and social services—all areas considered to be feminine. Many of Sineau's interviewees still consider that their function as wife and mother is the greatest asset to their political profile. On the other hand, the interviewees increasingly felt that an itinerary similar to that of their male counterparts, such as a diploma from Sciences-Politiques or from the ENA (National School of Administration), added to their legitimacy.

## *The Difficult Emergence of a Feminist Consciousness*

Three-quarters of the women interviewed by Sineau had a very negative view of feminism, and some rejected it outright. The term connoted a movement that was extremist, aggressive, ridiculous, and anti-male. Of the forty women interviewed, only Véronique Neiertz identified herself as a feminist. A mere fourteen of those women politicians interviewed saw reforms for changing the conditions of women's lives as important. The issues of parity and the value of female participation in government seriously concerned only the few activist women.

On the basis of her interviews, Sineau is pessimistic about what she calls "the difficult emergence of a feminist consciousness." The most common leitmotif throughout her interviews is the fear that a political role might create family problems and the desire for self-sacrifice, rather than a sense of legitimate pride in going beyond the traditional division of roles. Women as a group emerge from her study as having few possibilities of making gains against a form of masculine corporatism that is tinged with misogyny and resistant to outside competition.

The interviews in *Femmes et Citoyennes* suggest a partial modification of these attitudes. For example, Aline Pailler observes that she herself was not a feminist, her primary concern was the problem of social exclusion: "I have to confess that when I was a student, feminists were caricatures: they rejected their femininity."[3] Traditionally, the women in her family kept the house and took care of the details of daily living. But while making the television program "Regards de Femmes," she had discovered that the rights she had believed to be irreversible were not at all self-evident and this had sensitized her to the cause of women. Pailler's support for parity derives from personal characteristics that she finds in other women: the refusal of compromise and the need for independence.

Another example of changing attitudes over this period is provided by the interview in *Femmes et Citoyennes* with the historian Lucie Aubrac, who was nominated to the Provisional Consultative Committee as a member of the Resistance during the Second World War. Aubrac continues to assert her non-identification with feminism but again adds the significant theme of her newfound solidarity with women.[4] She remembers how her first priority had been the struggle against fascism and that she had felt no identification with the elegantly dressed suffragettes in hats who chained themselves to the railings of the Senate. But Aubrac goes on to recount a recent Congress in Tulle to commemorate the ninety-nine people hung and martyred in that town. The speech that honored the martyrs used the words of the poet-politician André Malraux, "Women in black, women of Corrèze" (*Femmes en noir, femmes de Corrèze*). Despite this statement, there were no women at all in the official delegation. Aubrac reacted violently and declared that she would return only when these "women in black" had been found.[5]

## *Region, Class, and Party as Predictors of Attitude*

Sineau considers class and party, not gender, to be the dominant predictors of political behavior among women politicians interviewed in the 1980s. Marie Jacq and Hélène Luc, like most other Communist women, for example, see their objectives as those of their party and deny any wish to participate in separate women's groups. Marie-Claude Beaudeau, a Communist senator, told Sineau that there was no solidarity between senatorial women and complained that the Socialist women did not vote for the amendments to allow a child to take the mother's name. Only two women, Christiane Papon and Florence d'Harcourt (from the right), expressed any desire to go beyond rigid party division and criticized the impossibility of a parliamentarian supporting an amendment put forward by the opposition. Hélène Missoffe expressed the feeling of most conservative women when she stated that things had changed enough for there to be no need for women's support groups. Edith Cresson was unwilling to be part of a women's group, or to address the woman question because of her mistrust of being labeled feminist or, indeed, different.

Sineau's earlier data also showed that region was an indicator of attitudes toward feminism, and that the feminization of elites was mainly an urban phenomenon. The degree of modernization in the sense of industrialization and development has an influence on the geographical representation of women. Regions have their distinctive and individualized features. Marie Jacq, for example, speaks to Sineau of her good fortune in living in the Finistère region in Brittany, with its strong Celtic tradition of the matriarchal home. Class, too, is a differentiating factor. In the mining towns of the north, as the Communist Denise Cacheux explains, men's lives were very difficult and it was seen as progress if their wives were able to stay home. How would they understand that women working could represent an improvement in their condition?

A change in discourse about feminism and a decline in the importance of party and class solidarity is detectable by the time Latour, Houssin, and Tovar carry out their interviews with women in politics. Their interview with the senator Hélène Luc for *Femmes et Citoyennes*, ten years after her interview for Sineau, for example, reveals significant changes in the Communist leader's attitude. Hélène Luc was now president of the Communist group, a member of the Senate, and elected representative in the Val-de-Marne. Luc still argues that right-wing women practice right-wing politics, but she adds that women of all parties bring something more concrete, authentic, and sensitive to politics. The politician expresses support for the resolutions of the charter drawn up at the 1992 Athens conference for increased female participation. The questions asked elicit the expression of her general admiration for women who fight for their rights, her heroines ranging from Louise Michel, Marie-Claude Vaillant-Couturier (a long-term deputy), Marie Curie, and the athlete Marie-José Perec, to the young women who took part in the recent protest march against cuts in the minimum wage. Hélène Luc's changed view in the 1990s reflects the major changes that have taken place in the Communist party over this period, but I would suggest that her belief that the increased presence of women can make a real difference in finding solutions to the current social problems has also been influenced by the one decade of women actually acting in politics and by the new discourse in circulation impacting on the political horizon.

Another Communist *députée*, Mugutte Jacquaint, made claims in her interview in 1996 for the existence of a particular feminine sensibility that identifies with the causes of solidarity and equality. She points out that women are being saddled with increasing burdens, including guilt for children's problems at school, for delinquency, and even for unemployment. Despite their often-privileged background and their lack of interest in social equality, Jacquaint finds heroines in the "middle-class" suffragists. Evidently well informed on the present debate around the rehabilitation of first-wave feminism, she insists on the need to recognize that the questions posed by the suffragists were necessarily framed in the terms of their own time. Women's rights, as she sees it from the left, are regressing in the face of encouragement to accept salaries for mothers who opt to stay home with children, increasing unemployment, the gender-gap in salaries, and the decreasing availability of day-care. Misogyny is still alive, even in the National Assembly where, Jacquaint observes from experience, it takes courage for women of any political color to express themselves differently from men—that is, she claims, more sincerely and more concretely. She recognizes that parity has a certain usefulness and considers the campaign to be an educative process.

The change in the discourse of these two Communist representatives is striking. Not only are both focused on the problems of their female constituents but both are speaking to the issues of feminine succession, parity, and the positive difference that women may bring to politics across party lines. A similar evolution in attitudes toward women's positive difference and parity can be found in the discourse of other Communist women.

## *From Assimilation (Sineau's Study) to Non-Conformity (Catherine Trautmann's Story)*

Sineau provides many examples of the over-compensating responses of the majority of elected women and their desire for assimilation. She reports their excessive conformity to social norms, their inferiority complexes, lack of autonomy, and fear of not being good enough. Examples include statements such as: "I always thought there was someone else more capable than I was"; "I find it very difficult to assert myself"; "I was very shocked by certain things that I would never accept to do myself"; "What would bother me would be to go and see people to ask them to vote for me"; "Speaking paralyzes me, it's terrible"; "You have to work really hard if you want to do things conscientiously"; I studied at the Institut des Hautes Etudes de Défense (Institute for Defense Studies) in order to be qualified; this way, they couldn't say that I wasn't competent." Sineau also points to the "queen bee syndrome"—a tendency in women who reach high positions in areas traditionally dominated by men to feel that they have done this on their own merits, quite independently of their gender, and to be unsympathetic to the efforts of other women. To the question, "You're a woman and a politician. Is it easy to live this double identity at this time and in this country?" two women simply answered that they didn't live their political identities as a woman.

In her interview for *Femmes et Citoyennes*, Catherine Trautmann speaks rather of the attraction of power—"politics is cannibalistic; it eats your life up, but also gets a hold of you."[6] The details given in a brief introduction to the interview construct a portrait of a modern political woman. A Protestant doctoral scholar of misogyny in the Bible, Trautmann discovered politics in May 1968 and joined the Socialist party in 1977. Trautmann claims she came into politics as all women come to power, by "breaking and entering." After time out to have a child, she became a candidate for the 1983 municipal elections as part of a required feminine quota and was elected as a municipal councilor. Trautmann says she was placed first on the Socialist list because no one really believed the slot was winnable. In 1986, she was elected deputy for the Bas Rhin and in 1988 became *secrétaire d'Etat* for the elderly and handicapped. Trautmann remained there until the dissolution of the government and her own defeat in an electoral district of Strasbourg. Refusing to give up, she fought a winning campaign for the position of mayor of Strasbourg in 1989 (a seat believed unwinnable, she notes, and that no one wanted). Trautmann acknowledges a debt to the Saturday morning training program organized by Yvette Roudy and attended by fifteen women that she claims prepared her to handle budgets and administrative government. After the June 1997 election, Catherine Trautmann became the spokesperson for the new Socialist government and minister for communication, giving up her office as mayor of Strasbourg in the interests of Prime Minister Jospin's reformist project limiting the simultaneous holding of multiple political offices. Trautmann agreed that parity legislation needed to be put in place, particularly given that the quota system had allowed her own initial access to politics, but she admitted that being the recipient of "discrimination positive" (affirmative action) had left a bitter taste.

This interview reveals Trautmann's strong awareness of the political system as an obstacle for her as a woman, but also as an adversary to be outwitted and outmaneuvered; assimilation is to be resisted. The time is ripe, she declares, for women to express themselves autonomously and energetically as she herself did, and continues to do, to prove that her responsibilities were not due to chance or the special protection of women. Very conscious of the way difference between the sexes can be rendered negative, Trautmann tells Elisabeth Weissman in another interview that if you make decisions, you're considered to be authoritarian, and if you're attractive, there are no doubts about how you got where you did.[7] The difficulty is proving one's ability to exercise authority without losing oneself. You have to come to terms with your femininity and experience it neither as a handicap nor as a seductive asset. Trautmann speaks differently from her male counterparts but is no longer making any apologies for where she has come from.

## Speaking Out about Difference

Sineau had already observed that certain women were beginning to argue for their right to be different from the feminine myths. Marie Noëlle Lienemann for instance, refused Yvette Roudy's advice that she change her high-pitched manner of speaking and wondered whether being a woman, once the handicap of feeling inferior is overcome, was not, after all, an advantage. Some years later, interviewed by Adler on 17 November 1992 for *Les Femmes Politiques*, Edith Cresson, too, expressed her pleasure in exercising what she felt was her very real power at Matignon: to influence industrial politics and the development of the nation's infrastructure, and to carry through a number of social projects. But quoting Jacques Chirac's "We will judge Edith Cresson by her actions. Madame Cresson is credited with having a strong personality" (*Nous jugerons Edith Cresson sur ses actes. On prête à Mme Cresson une forte personnalité*), Adler notes the continuing contradictions. The first woman prime minister was still trapped in the myths of the feminine and, in particular, was caught between the strong action required and the hostility this would arouse.

Sineau also notes an almost general attack from the women interviewed on the technocratic and incomprehensible character of political and administrative language, presented as a hollow discourse without feeling or true meaning, often oversimplifying and reductive. Seeking what they call direct and truthful speech, the interviewed women declare their frustration at being obliged to participate in time-wasting and boring ceremonials rather than direct action. Rule-bound debate and meaningless amendments, game playing and one-upmanship, opponent bashing, and a lack of respect for the other are deplored. Women seem generally to feel no desire to master the abstract language that establishes the identity of the group through repetition and through a liturgy disconnected from reality. This emphasis on women's different language grows in strength over the decade.

## *Balancing Work and Family*

The division between the world of politics and the everyday world has come increasingly under attack by political women since Sineau's survey. A further major survey of political attitudes carried out from 1992 to 1993 by Janine Mossuz-Lavau shows that the general public shares this critique. Women, who often regretted their sacrificed leisure or who were anxious to complete the tasks at hand and end unproductive meetings in order to return to their families, had the feeling that in contrast, their male counterparts accepted total commitment readily and even gladly. Many of the women interviewed expressed the view that it would be desirable for men to better balance work and family commitments and argued for a new balance in gender roles.

One question remains central in both studies. As women insist on their right to a life outside the family, is living simply being made more difficult? A poignant footnote is added to these reflections by Monique Pelletier's 1995 autobiographical work, *La Ligne brisée* (The Broken Line). In this work Pelletier, a trained lawyer, recounts the accident, just after her appointment as minister in 1978, which caused her brilliant husband to become a paraplegic without understanding or speech. She talks about the subsequent terrible struggle to balance his needs for care, the needs of a large family, and her own career. In *Femmes et Citoyennes*, most of the women interviewed considered a redistribution of gender roles to be necessary to enable women to function fully in the public arena. Marie-Christine Blandin, *conseillère régionale*, with children to raise, notes that the issues of guilt, of fatigue, or of the organization and reconciliation of responsibilities are very real, even though her partner shares many of the duties of child-rearing. Blandin observes that women are still "profoundly attached to the umbilical cord" and that this attachment is still deeply embedded in culture. She points out that the questions debated in political assemblies are not domestic, do not concern the problems of the everyday, and therefore are seen by women as less relevant to their lives.

The admission in the interviews of the difficulties of balancing work and family and the apparent irrelevance of politics to a basic life, anecdotal in many of these interviews, finds confirmation in a number of other academic studies of women in decision-making positions. A 1993 study of managerial women in France (and similar studies in North America) showed that women were somewhat less available in terms of hours per work week, less ambitious, more willing to play modest roles in the firm but also more able to live with others and to function on more than one level. Women generally reported less pleasure in long work hours and in climbing the ladder than did their male colleagues; their priorities remained different. However, the women recognized that this difference might be due to the complex of circumstances in which they find themselves, as much as to a "nature." According to the statistics, the four-day week is an ideal for the majority of young managerial women (most of whom have young children) but not for managerial men.

## *Toward a Critique of Sineau's Binary Masculine/Feminine Logic*

The implicit binary logic of Sineau's central question—do women reproduce male norms or do they innovate?—appears to be over-simplistic when the change in discourse is highlighted. One of Sineau's interviewees considers that successful political women reason and behave like men. Another asserts that (masculine) style must be seen as more important than equality. Behind these statements, Sineau finds the assumption that hard work and technical competence are a primary condition for entry into the political scene. It is also assumed that men will be competent in a field seen as natural to them. For many women already successful in politics, this equates with their rejection of any singularity in being a woman and their self-identification as a universal (male) politician.

In contrast, Trautmann's interview in *Femmes et Citoyennes* argues that from her own experience, both the prevalent masculine behavior of many female representatives and feminine sensibility ("being oneself") can achieve positive results. Women's greater scrupulousness and doubting of their absolute self-worth, their more hesitant speech, even their failures, as Trautmann claims, are not flaws or impediments after all. Simone Veil's response to Jacques Chancel in a radio interview for the series *Radioscopie* is a well-known illustration of how modesty balanced by considerable competence worked to enhance the minister's popularity: "As far as occupying this imaginary function that is being a prime minister, let me say right away that no, I don't feel at all capable" (*Quant à occuper cette fonction imaginaire de Premier Ministre, je vous dis tout de suite, non, je ne m'en sens pas du tout capable*). In contrast with the pretense of most male politicians that they know all there is to know about everything and are sure of their competence, Veil's self-doubt was seen as refreshingly honest and innovative. On the other hand, as the veteran lawyer and experienced public speaker Monique Pelletier[8] put the problem:

> They doubt their capacity, they read their papers, they think they have to use ready-made phrases, they don't innovate, and in this respect they have to be taught, taught, taught. I do not believe that without the ability to speak convincingly in public, to get one's message across, you can succeed in politics.[9]

Nonetheless, almost all of the twelve interviewees in *Femmes et Citoyennes* nuanced Sineau's questions by identifying a "feminine sensibility" and expressing respect for this alternative way of being.

## *The Interview as Part of the Body of Political Women's Self-Writing*

In their published form, the interviews in *Des femmes en politique* (1986) and *Femmes et Citoyennes* (1996) mirror women's changing view of the world of power. We have argued that influencing one another, these texts not only refract but also construct a feminine political vision. But the somewhat pessimistic image of women in politics that Sineau pieces together corresponds to some extent to her own gendered political experience, to her own hopes and disappointments, and to her particular critical agenda.

In a telephone interview with me on 19 December 1996, Mariette Sineau expressed her personal pessimism with respect to women's future in the party system, and repeated her conviction of an opportunity badly missed by the Mitterrand governments. She added that the lack of any real progress for women in France was paralleled in the United States, given what she saw as the disappointments of the first Clinton government. Only in relation to the parity movement did Sineau express cautious optimism. She acknowledged that parity had brought the first cross-party cooperation among women and the manifesto had made a public impact.

Françoise Gaspard indirectly supported Sineau's belief that her own academic career had not at all been helped by her specialization in women in politics. In a later interview with me, Gaspard observed that women's studies still had little academic credibility, pointing out that Jenson and Sineau's substantial *Mitterrand et les Françaises*, the only major French publication on Mitterrand's policies for women, had quite simply been omitted from a current social-science bibliography of work on the Mitterrandian era. With respect to the new history that tells the stories of women and political power, Sineau's studies are pioneering and central. Fragments of her studies echo through Bouchardeau's writing and influence much of the later work by political women. The "truths" of *Femmes et Citoyennes* are less about misogyny and barriers to women than about the positive aspects of women's resistance and heroism, pioneering feminist activism and progress. The voices we hear are personal, even intimate. The cues given by the two sets of interviews reflect the interviewer. They are also a product of the changes in the discourses circulating among the group of politically active women between the 1980s and the 1990s, carried by the new writing.[10]

## A Selection of Personal Interviews: June 1994–January 1996

A study of similar scope to Sineau's 1986 work or Mossuz-Lavau's 1993/94 interviews carried out in the new millennium would be very useful to gage how much the debate on women in politics has changed. While waiting for such a major study, which goes far beyond the scope of the present book, I effected a small number of interviews that provide a limited sampling of women's voices. The women included are selected to represent a cross-section of the political spectrum and of the political hierarchy: a *deputée* from an overseas *Département*, Christine Taubira-Delannon, who is *députée* for French Guyana; a well-known left-wing feminist, Véronique Neiertz, who is a Socialist Party *députée* and former minister; a right-wing parity leader, Roselyne Bachelot, who is an RPR *députée* and Head of the Observatoire pour la parité (Office for the Promotion of Parity); and finally an "ordinary" right-wing *députée*, Odile Moirin, with the RPR. (Interviews with an academic feminist and former mayor, and with three former ministers that focus particularly on their autobiographical writing are presented in later chapters.)

The first group of interviews focuses on a set of common questions on women's conception of their (changing) role in the political world. The questions woven into the interviews on the experience of political power are the following: On what terms are individual women accepted in the political world? Do women have a different conception and practice of power? Are the differences in class, ethnicity, and party between political women more significant than any sense of their common identity as women? What influence has the new discourse on women's representation had on their own careers? (The translation of these interviews into English is my own.)

## *Christine Taubira-Delannon, Independent Deputy for French Guyana*

(Interviewed in French in her office in the Annex of the Assemblée building in June 1994. Shortly after this interview, Christine Taubira-Delannon won a seat in the European Parliament on Bernard Tapie's list.)

**R.R.** What is power for you?

**Taubira-Delannon**. A way of acting, of helping others, relieving distress... a deputy has little power to change anything beyond voting for laws.

**R.R.** Does the fact of being a woman change anything?

**Taubira-Delannon**. I am not a feminist... I'm convinced there is a different relationship, with maternity, solidarity between generations, with the concrete and the everyday. I still look after my children's education—they are six, eight, twelve, and fourteen years of age—give free English lessons, and pursue my interest in art. That's essential. My political presence is all the more intense... Women have a different relationship to power.

**R.R.** Is the political universe masculine?

**Taubira-Delannon**. Yes, but it's subtle, underground, because of the emergence of women. Those women who succeed have to be determined. The presence of women is disruptive. Women work together to help one another... in Algeria, Mauritania and Senegal... two women from different camps can prevent an armed conflict by crossing the border. Women follow a different logic. They are transforming agents.

**R.R.** And parity?

**Taubira-Delannon**. A dual approach is needed... a mechanical and coercive one can only be temporary. The obstacles are in the minds of women. The problems for me come from the gap between a northern culture and a society with a third-world infrastructure. I have difficulty orchestrating the two. I speak. I explain... the 130,000 inhabitants in a territory that is 80 percent uninhabited... the matrifocal family, the number of children... the 30 percent unemployment that makes it impossible for women to have the choice of staying home with their children or working. Yes, the market alone is insufficient... the state must have a regulatory role to create equality of opportunity.

**R.R.** What is your feeling about obliging the high percentage of absent fathers in your part of the world to assume some parental responsibility for support of their children?

**Taubira-Delannon**. I'm absolutely against... against the destruction of the relationship between men and women. What creates perverse effects is when the social worker insists the partner leave the beneficiary... turns up to make sure they're not living together... The conditions attached to single-parent benefits disturb the relations of solidarity... The solidarity of the group and family relations would be sustained better without benefits... The state is interfering in the survival of the family unit... I'm lucky to have an intelligent husband who takes over the family responsibilities and gives support, is a haven of rest in moments of difficulty... He's not the boss...

**R.R.** And political parties in Guyana?

**Taubira-Delannon.** The traditionalist parties are completely macho. Our party puts forward 65 percent of women candidates. In Guyana, there's resistance but it is not manifested outwardly... that's rare. Female citizens don't have the same opportunities. It's very difficult for women. You carry the name of your children, their honor... the campaign trail is intolerably awful. I work against the corruption of power through the influence of local barons... against the exclusion of minorities... by means of feminine (not feminist) networks.

**R.R.** Do you have the enthusiasm, the energy to continue?

**Taubira-Delannon.** I have my children, I have many obligations, but I will continue the fight.

## *Interview with Véronique Neiertz, Socialist Deputy and Former Minister*

(In the Annex of the Assemblée Nationale, 1994.)

**R.R.** Can you tell me something about your political itinerary?

**Véronique Neiertz.** I lived through the late 1960s and early 1970s with the feminists of 1968, married, had children without access to contraception, came to politics through the struggle for women at a time when the right was in power... I learned at the bottom of the pyramid. François Mitterrand gave me some responsibilities in the opposition in the 1970s. In 1981 I was elected deputy and later given the portfolio of minister of consumer affairs (I've been re-elected as deputy since 1988). When Rocard left in 1991, Edith Cresson asked me to take on the Women's Rights Ministry. I was against a ghetto for women, a special ministry. I believed the time had come for mixed politics, representative for women's interests in every Ministry. The law on sexual harassment was being called for by the unions. I wasn't really in favor. I had worked in a firm in the United States and American legislation had given me cause for reflection. I passed legislation against the anti-abortion commandos. In 1992 their attacks still remained unpunished. This law was applied for the first time a month ago. My Ministry was blocked by the other Ministries. In five years in government my action was, like most women's, above all concrete action... the law on debt, on displaying prices, domestic accidents.

**R.R.** What has become of the ministry now?

**Véronique Neiertz**. There's no one. Simone Veil has social security and health.

**R.R.** And is there solidarity between women?

**Véronique Neiertz**. That doesn't exist. Parity is the discourse of a minority manifesting its existence... we are in competition... you have to defend your place or you're eliminated.

**R.R.** Who helped you?

**Véronique Neiertz.** The Socialists from my electorate, men and women... in France the associations are divided and there are no strong lobbies as there are in the United States.

**R.R.** What is your response to the parity movement promoted by Halimi?

**Véronique Neiertz**. It's not Gisèle Halimi's idea... it's Françoise Gaspard's. And she's suffered a lot in politics. She knows what she's talking about.

**R.R**. What did you think of Hillary Clinton's visit and her meeting with Simone Veil and Ségolène Royal?

**Véronique Neiertz**. A media affair... I have a lot of respect for Simone Veil even though I'm not always in agreement with her.

**R.R**. Can women represent as well as govern?

**Véronique Neiertz**. Attitudes die hard... Women in politics are a transgression. I'm addressed as *Monsieur le député*, *Monsieur le ministre*... all the mail with "sir" on it now goes into the wastebasket. The reality is that when you feminize the title, you devalue it... I was *secrétaire d'Etat* and kept the masculine title, *un secrétaire*, not *une secrétaire*. In the case of *la première ministre*, the words don't have the same content as *le premier ministre*, even if women are as competent as men. Men's language is now more discreet. Their behavior remains the same. There are no political mothers... we have had to invent, looking at what men do. I was helped in particular by François Mitterrand, who gave me responsibilities, accepted my appointment as minister. You have to belong to a group... I refused the *courants* as I didn't want to be in a women's ghetto.

**R.R**. Are you still politically committed?

**Véronique Neiertz**. You don't give up. There's a debate coming up on the family, a bill to send women home to their families... I said no. But everyone is in favor of this measure for a salary for working mothers to stay at home... less delinquency and less unemployment, they say. Under pressure, Simone Veil has changed the name from mother's allowance to a "parental allowance for raising children." Ségolène Royal is in favor, as it's another parental benefit. But what happens to the woman at the end of three years of child care? She's missed out on promotion... her retirement benefit is awful... she may not find work... one couple in two divorce. I've been in politics for twenty-five years, but it's not a political career... that wasn't ever our understanding of our commitment... I've fought for women... The discourse of the new generation is that everything is possible. It's not possible for all women.

## *Interview with Roselyne Bachelot, RPR Deputy and Head of the Observatoire Pour la Parité*

(Annex of Assemblée Nationale, June 1995.)

**Roselyne Bachelot.** My father was a *député.* We talked politics at home.
**R.R.** Is this paternal figure a necessary one in politics?
**Roselyne Bachelot.** You need a guide, a godfather in this Mafia, a protector. The role of the father, biological or political is important... as a spiritual advisor. Women don't have the same taste for politics.
**R.R.** What are your political motivations, goals?
**Roselyne Bachelot.** Love, a physical love for France, "Mother, here we are, as we are!"... the conscience of the nation, rally for the Republic, support for the government, service to the party.
**R.R.** Do you retain a certain freedom?
**Roselyne Bachelot.** Of course, if there were any question of an alliance with the National Front I would resign immediately. I try to bring together two things that are contradictory... working in the field and in Paris... my electorate is quite small and 80 percent urban, which allows me to concentrate on my work. I prefer the concrete tasks—family, health, the elderly, social problems. Perhaps I disarm people because I'm a woman. I've analyzed my electoral results from 1993. I lose votes on the right, in the bourgeois areas of Angers, and gain a popular vote on the left. In the second round, I win back the right vote. But what was placed in the voting boxes were 23,000 love letters.
**R.R.** What power do you have?
**Roselyne Bachelot.** The power to pass laws, to mediate.
**R.R.** It has been claimed that women have no power to represent.
**Roselyne Bachelot.** Representing can take absurd proportions but people are proud when I'm elegantly dressed and well presented... you need to remember that you come under an affectionately critical scrutiny... it's difficult... people have to see you as smiling and agreeable.

## *Interview with Odile Moirin, RPR Deputy*

(In the Annex of the Assemblée Nationale, June 1994.)

**Odile Moirin.** In 1991 François Mitterrand was elected. My ideas had been defeated. I decided to fight for my ideas. I hadn't been a militant until then and had no preparation.
**R.R.** What does political power represent for you?
**Odile Moirin.** I don't have the impression that I hold power. If I was elected, it was to be of service.
**R.R.** Does being a woman help?
**Odile Moirin.** It was a plus for the election... against one of the Socialist "elephants" (the party heavyweights). I campaigned at the grass

roots. I'm a woman, I played the woman card. Men are vain and ready to do anything to keep their seats. Women are candid, honest.

**R.R.** Has election involved choices?

**Odile Moirin.** Less space for private life... I wouldn't have made this choice at a younger age. I wouldn't have been mature enough. With young children, you would have to be terribly well organized.

**R.R.** Are women accepted?

**Odile Moirin.** Tolerated... being president of a regional council is not a woman's job. Not in any *département*.

**R.R.** Is there solidarity among women?

**Odile Moirin.** There are three women elected from the left... we don't see them... we support each other but we're not against men. Women don't stray far from the day-to-day... if you ask a man how to live on the SMIC (the minimum wage), he doesn't know.

**R.R.** Do you have political role models?

**Odile Moirin.** Bonaparte, De Gaulle, Golda Meir.

**R.R.** What do you think of the parity movement?

**Odile Moirin.** I'm enraged. I don't like quotas. Rocard's parity list didn't bring him much luck.

**R.R.** Are there differences between men and women's votes?

**Odile Moirin.** I've never tried to seduce the female electorate more than the masculine one.

**R.R.** In ways of representing the electorate?

**Odile Moirin.** A wardrobe is indispensable. People like crowned heads. Jeans pose a problem. You have to know how to dress. In the evening, I put on jeans and a T-shirt.

## *Telling a Similar Story across the Spectrum*

These four interviews reveal the very real experiential and contextual differences of the speakers and demonstrate a range of opinion on most questions. Still, many of the reference points are shared and the interviews show a remarkable general coherence—they are idiolects of a single language. The recognition of the male domination of the political world and the transgression represented by female presence was shared across the spectrum even though each of the women spoke of different responses to this domination. Moirin responded by "playing the woman card" to political advantage. The answer to masculine domination in politics for Taubira-Delannon was to assert women's solidarity and lead a party that fields 65 percent of female candidates. Neiertz responded to her feelings of male dominance by commitment to vigilance on legislation for women, arguing for a representative for women's interests in every ministry and refusing to respond to mail addressed to *Monsieur le ministre*. Bachelot's response was found in her championing of parity democracy. The tacit admission of the masculine domination of the political world can also be found in the statement by some of the women that they relied on patronage from a "father" figure. Roselyne Bachelot and Véronique Neiertz both note the importance of the godfather—De Gaulle and Mitterrand respectively—in their political career and Moirin cites Bonaparte, De Gaulle, and Golda Meir as her role models.

On women's difference, there was again a range of opinions, even though there are common parameters to the debate. Delannon believes women have a different relation with the concrete—the everyday—and show solidarity. Neiertz notes that competition rather than cooperation in politics is still the norm. Bachelot sees her emotional success with her electorate in the recent election as a function of her concern as a woman for family, health, and social problems. Moirin believes that women are candid and honest and know what it means to live on the minimum wage. Both right-wing women believe in the importance of the representational function and of dressing elegantly.

There was some evident dissent among the women on the issue of political parity. Moirin on the right is outraged, whereas Neiertz supports this "minority" movement as an expression of confidence in Françoise Gaspard's manifesto and left-wing radical positions. But overall, the common responses regarding the position of women in politics can be held up to highlight a growing influence of earlier feminist opinions on women and politics.

## *The Limitations of the Interview*

Certain limitations and repeated themes in the information obtained by interviews can be seen as a function of the genre. The writer Danièle Sallenave provides a negative analysis of the recent volumes of interviews such as the 1998 publication *Femmes en tête*.[11] For Sallenave, such interviews were taking advantage of the new popular interest in "women at the top" to trace conventional lives of good middle-class mothers who identify with a maternal function and have great children and no problems. Legitimacy comes through family and professional activity. There are relatively few failures and few uncertainties. Most women still feel they have been lucky. Few women are sure of being deserving. Many are still helped by fathers. The texts thus reflect the persistence of an internalized norm and rarely demonstrate a strong critical sense. The complexities of women's situation, the paradoxes of the constraints of freedom, of the right to both work and be a mother that brings often impossible or conflicting responsibilities are seldom fully opened up in these interviews. With their focus on success and progress, many of the women's accounts are too idyllic. Sallenave herself is not convinced that political women do much for the cause of women.

Another limitation of the interview genre is to be found in the motives and actions of interviewees. The interviewees' responses do not escape aspects of the "sound bite." Nor are the performance aspect and the competitiveness of the often antler-crashing masculine political media interview entirely absent. The political women interviewed were not unhappy about telling their story and giving their political opinions a hearing, eventually to reach a wider audience (or electorate) through publication. Like the political autobiography, the interview engages the public or the electorate as implied reader. It is evident that the interviewee expects the interviewer to serve his or her public image in some fashion. For her part, Huguette Bouchardeau was anxious that if I were to transcribe, translate, and publish my oral interviews with her, I would respect the requirements of written style and of good writing and not damage aspects of her image that were important to her. Responses to the interview questions take into account the "horizons of expectation" of the readers/the electorate.

The conventional autobiographical "pact" of truth and sincerity does operate in the interview at some level. Yet both the political interviewer and the interviewee recognize that personally/politically sensitive or damaging truths will not be divulged. Truth will be confined to particular levels of experience and, in some cases, filtered through a party censor for the consumption of the party followers. My own questions, like my use of language, also partially framed the responses I received. The language of my questions inevitably influenced the personal/political truths I was collecting. This is the case, at least in part, for all interviewers, whose own actions leave a mark on the process.

## *The Effects of the Interview as Women's Political Self-Writing*

Keeping the shortcomings of the interview in mind, it is still clear that there has been considerable change in the content of interviews with political women over a decade. The early staging of such themes as the masculine over-determination of the political has led to subsequent modifications in the public discourse. The modifications have meant a turning toward greater female autonomy and a valuing of feminine difference in the political arena. These changes are in part due to material transformations in women's political condition but also to the new texts by political women. If aspects of the more recent political women's interviews often sounded familiar, this was due to the recycling of the new understandings and of the language I had already heard in interviews with other would-be autonomous and legitimate political women.

Despite the element of performance and self-dramatization—and sometimes the staging of a "trial" and the need for self-justification and self-vindication as in much literary self-writing—the interviews reveal a degree of self-exploration and an importance given to analytical self-knowledge. After my interview with Christine Taubira-Delannon, who declared that my questions had given her the opportunity to think through and articulate her attitudes, she asked me to send her a copy of my tape upon my return to Boston, for her to use subsequently in her writing. Women speak/write in interviews perhaps in part to know what and why they need or want to write.

What becomes apparent is the need for each woman politician to construct her own narrative of "what women want" out of the set of political texts available. It can be argued that despite the specificity of the unwritten conventions of the interview, both the interview (which elicits responses by questions from the outside) and political autobiography (which speaks out from the inside somewhat more in the style of the undirected interview) are grounded both in prefabricated discourses and in a personal rewriting of these discourses to produce a hybrid new text of individuated personal story and collective public history.

## Notes

1. "C'était une femme, et les femmes nous emmerdent, car elles veulent toujours notre bien. Elles veulent toujours être la Maman. Eh bien, l'Etat est devenu une femme, et c'est insupportable." Mariette Sineau, *Des Femmes en politique* (Paris: Economica, 1988), p. 23. Sineau quotes Jean Dutourd.
2. "Les villes, c'est comme les femmes, il ne suffit pas de les séduire, il faut savoir les prendre." Serge July, "Les municipales, ça va faire mal," *Libération*, 24 January 1983, quoted in Sineau, *Des femmes en politique*, p. 25.
3. In Patricia Latour, Monique Houssin and Madia Tovar, *Femmes et citoyennes. Du droit de vote à l'exercice du pouvoir* (Paris: Les Editions de l'atelier/Editions Ouvrières, 1995), p. 118.
4. In 1998, a feature film, *Lucie Aubrac*, was made in Auvergne based on Aubrac's 1995 autobiography. This film helped alter the perception of women's roles in the Resistance as passive. Lucie Aubrac herself published a book early in 2000 explaining the Resistance to her French "granddaughters."
5. In *Femmes et Citoyennes*, interview with Nadia Tovar, pp. 74–75.
6. Elisabeth Weissman, *Les Filles, on n'attend plus que vous! Témoignages de Martine Aubry à Simone Veil* (Paris: Textuel, 1995). Interview, pp. 78–82.
7. Ibid., p. 80.
8. Raymond Barre's associate minister for the family and the feminine condition later nominated by Chirac to the *Conseil constitutionnel*.
9. "Elles doutent d'elles-mêmes, elles lisent des papiers, elles se croient obligées de recourir à des phrases toutes faites, elles n'innovent pas, et là il faut les former, former, former. Car, je ne crois pas que, sans prise de parole convaincante, enfin qui passe la rampe, je crois qu'on ne peut pas réussir en politique." Quoted in Sineau, *Des Femmes en politique*, p. 21.
10. Other sets of interviews with high-placed women have since been published, notably *Femmes en tête* by Evelyne Pisier and Françoise Barret-Ducroq (Paris: Flammarion, 1997).
11. Danièle Sallenave, "Les femmes de pouvoir ne font rien pour la cause des femmes," *Marianne*, 17 November 1997.

6

# Autobiographical Writing: From Left, Right, and Center

The attempt to share the reality of a woman's political life and the plight of feminine political difference with other women has led women politicians to write their stories.[1] This chapter offers a glimpse of the shared preoccupations present in the recent wave of published autobiographies by women in politics, all of which point to the existence of a distinctively feminine form of political autobiography.

Autobiography as a genre traces the origins of the writer's personality in childhood. Political writers seek the origins of their political vocation in these formative early years. In particular, the sources of one's political career are traced back to the (Freudian) family romance. In the recent women's autobiographies, this most often takes the form of the implicit or explicit discovery of the need for paternal legitimization (or the protection of the prince) and sometimes of an increasing interest in maternal legacy. Such a turn to the maternal legacy is then transformed into the project of introducing feminine difference in politics.

From Saint Augustin to Rousseau and through to Michel Leiris in the twentieth century, autobiography has also been characterized as a confessional genre. This involves the implicit staging of a trial of the self and attention to the injunction to tell "the whole truth and nothing but the truth" to judge and jury in the attempt to prove one's merit or to justify one's actions. In recent women's political autobiography, the imaginary "judicial" or courtroom scene plays a central role and assumes distinctive configurations. Women writers confess feelings of being under attack for their difference. They admit to being challenged to prove both their political competence and their femininity. They tell stories of how they felt like victims, and recount blows that often fall below the belt. Their self-defense takes a number of forms—the affirmation of legitimacy (as a political daughter, as a graduate of ENA) or of "being as good as a man," the assertion that it is possible to harmonize work and family life and reconcile public glory and personal happiness.

A remarkably consistent case for the participation of women in the political realm is made in almost all the recent autobiographies. This case most often includes the critique of the masculine politics in place, arguments in favor of parity, and the discussion of the implications for policy of a new feminine politics.

## The Literary Construction of a Political Life

Autobiography is conventionally a first-person narrative told in the present about one's origins and the development of one's personality in the past. Yet, as contemporary autobiography theory observes, this work of memory on life is also a work of the imagination. It is self-creation through writing as much as it is remembering. The writer selects a small number of "significant" moments among a myriad of possible past events and these events are organized into a narrative as a function of his/her present position. A political autobiography, for example, tends to construct the story of "how I fought my way to become a successful politician." Women's political autobiographies tend to construct a story along the lines of how she came to find the authorization to enter the political arena and the difficulties experienced, as a woman, in finding the strength, motivation, and justifications to survive in an unfamiliar world. This narrative is often accompanied by the creation of a feminine genealogy, incorporating the history of other political women, often as paragons of virtue, as in the left-wing autobiographies of Gisèle Halimi, Elisabeth Guigou, Ségolène Royal, and Françoise Gaspard, but also present in the work of the centrist Michèle Barzach, and to a lesser degree in the writing of right-wing women.

In all of the self-writing genres, as in life writing or biography, there is no single, unmediated truth of a life. The autobiographical "pact" of sincerity and truth, and of identity between author, narrator, and character, as developed by the theoretician of autobiography Phillip Lejeune, is common to both masculine and feminine autobiographies. In political autobiography, this "pact" is most often doubled by a public manifesto and is sometimes shaped by less than disinterested political goals. The more "feminine" a political autobiography, the more personal it is in voice and the more it includes intimate levels of recollection, reflection, and confession as women incorporate or address the formative discourses of the fathers/mentors and the mothers that are, in a sense, themselves taking shape, or being formed. The autobiographical pact of sincerity and truth is most often taken seriously as women transmit the legacy of their political experience to their political daughters.

Like men's political interviews and autobiographies, women's texts are grounded in the personal and the political, to varying degrees, producing both a personal story and a political history. The mix of private and public can vary greatly according to whether the writer positions herself closer to the traditional masculine story or to the newer feminine version. In some cases, this corresponds to a generational difference or to a right-left difference, as in the case of the less personal accounts of Michèle Alliot-Marie and Alice Saunier-Seïté. In other cases, with the left-wing Martine Aubry, for example, the mix of public and private can be a question of personality or style. Even where women's narratives borrow and identify with accepted "masculine" or traditional conventions of autobiographical writing, they tend to change the relation between public and private. This hybridization, or mix of the private and the political in the work, is increasingly evident in the recent autobiographies by French political women, which also appear to be predominantly addressed to women.

## *Gisèle Halimi: Writing toward a Feminist Social Consciousness*

The autobiographical texts published by Gisèle Halimi provide good examples of the characteristics of political texts enumerated above. Her autobiographies reconstitute the itinerary of the publicly recognized militant lawyer and politician, and committed feminist as something of a model for women.[2] Halimi begins her autobiographical accounts conventionally with her childhood. Born poor and Jewish in a traditional milieu and in a colonized country, Tunisia, she was also born a woman.[3] Halimi chooses to tell the story of her grandfather who prayed each day to thank God that he had not been born the (impure) woman who served him as his wife. Halimi claims that she became a lawyer in the establishment to work against its injustices, defending Tunisian independence fighters, unionists, and in the (in)famous case of Djamila Boupacha, the adolescent militant of the Front de Libération Nationale (FLN, or Algerian independence movement), tortured by the French army to extract a confession. This struggle against injustice led her to the feminist causes of women, founding the association Choisir-la cause des femmes with Simone de Beauvoir. Halimi was a pioneer activist in the fight to overturn the archaic 1920 law criminalizing abortion and contraception information. She recounts the now well-known tale of how she gained widespread publicity for her cause by orchestrating the trial in the Paris working-class suburb of Bobigny of the mother of a young adolescent who had helped her daughter obtain an abortion after a rape.[4] The public trial succeeded in publicly highlighting the social injustice and particularly the un-workability of French abortion law, which was what Halimi had aimed for.

### Political Power as Vindication of the Father (and Homage to the Mother)

Why did this founder of Choisir desire to win a seat in the political establishment and become a deputy despite her declaration in her autobiographical writings that she wanted to keep practicing law, to keep writing and that she had no intention of climbing the political ladder? She presents her electoral victory as both a political and a personal triumph, a form of revenge on the straight jacket of her early education and on poverty. That a Tunisian (that is, naturalized) form of Frenchness and a hybrid cultural product should be elected was, she claimed, theoretically the triumph of the ideal of a certain France. This ideal was centered on a France of justice and equality and not the France of privilege and colonizing expeditions she prosecuted. Similar sentiments on justice and political service are found at the other end of the political spectrum within the interviews of Simone Veil, although Veil has always remained very discreet about the injustice and exclusion (as a *déportée* and survivor of Auschwitz) at the origin of her motivation to succeed in the public world. Veil and Halimi share other themes in their writing. Both right- and left-wing women explore the awareness that their success is a vindication of their fathers' expectations, but claim that their achievements, their search for justice owe something to their mothers. Halimi and Veil both weigh the seduction of success against an expressed nostalgia for a return to a certain marginality and to "difference."

## A Feminist on the Campaign Trial

Along with themes of difference and exclusion, Halimi uses a writing style that mixes the public and private. In *Une Embellie perdue* (A Lost Patch of Blue Sky), the personal and political accounts of Halimi's disappointing experience under Mitterrand are closely interwoven in a characteristic "feminine" mix. The focus of the story is on the euphoric hope for change when Mitterrand's new Socialist government was elected on 10 May 1981, and for feminist change through her own action in her electorate and in parliament. It is a story of the "clearing in the sky", or *embellie*, and its subsequent loss or disappearance.

*Une Embellie perdue* tells a detailed story of what it meant to be a feminist on the campaign trail. Although she was not a member of the PS (Parti Socialiste), Halimi was offered the single candidacy for her group Choisir in 1981. Halimi claims to have refused to run the risk of diminishing the already minimal female representation in the French legislative body by running against another woman, Hélène Missoffe of the RPR party (Rassemblement Pour la République). Sent off to Blois as a candidate, she recounts the discovery that the Socialists there were supporters of Rocard and extremely hostile to her nomination. After other fruitless attempts by Pierre Bérégovoy to find her an acceptable electoral home, Halimi settled for a candidacy at Voiron in the mountain region of L'Isère. Supported by her husband, Claude Faux, himself an experienced politician, she set out on a grassroots campaign among the country folk and the misogynists. She was "a feminist in the fields" as the newspapers put it. Joined by colleagues from Choisir, Halimi's *parachutage*, or imposition from the outside, by the will of the National

Secretariat of the Parti Socialiste and against the local Socialist candidate, set off a fratricidal war. At the funeral of the former deputy-mayor and deputy, Jacques-Antoine Gau, the newcomer Halimi described how daunted she became by the manifest hostility around her. Feminism did not seem to fit as well with socialism as she had expected. She writes how the battle raged between the "macho" local militants and the supporters of Choisir. On the campaign posters, the closed fist and the rose overrode the feminist flag. Her *suppléant* (the deputy who would replace her should she be obliged to leave her office) told one of her helpers from Choisir, "You see, my dear, you musn't frighten them off. People here have outdated country ideas... And Women's Lib. scares them." The explanation that Choisir was not the MLF but a movement seeking change for men and for women made little difference. Nonetheless, writes Halimi, support was forthcoming from a number of the wives of local farmers.

## Feminist Disillusion with Life in Politics

Halimi had considered the National Assembly to be a sacred place of national reflection. Her disillusionment with its functioning was not long in coming. The patch of blue sky (*embellie*)—for which the newspaper that Halimi circulated in her constituency had been named—did not live up to its promise. Back in Paris, there was little government support for the independent Halimi or for her movement, Choisir. Halimi recounts how she felt like a foreign body in parliament because she did not have party affiliation. Like Bouchardeau and Giroud, she concludes that a deputy has no power. Proposals put forward by individual deputies become bills only if the executive is interested. She observes that of the eight major bills for women's rights that she introduced, none were supported.[5] On the other hand, her initiatives (in favor of abortion rights and equal employment opportunities) provoked attempts to exclude this "undisciplined intellectual."

Halimi's critique of the Socialist party executive and the undemocratic workings of the party led to what she presents as a Stalinesque and burlesque "trial" for lack of discipline by the powerful in the government. Deprived of support, and of any subsequent responsibilities, silenced in the critical debate on the sanctioning of three opposition deputies who were daring to question Mitterrand's past, Halimi recounts that she was finally forced out of the Assemblée. Halimi was given a six-month appointment on government business by UNESCO, then, in 1994, appointed as French Ambassador to that international organization. In fact, after her departure from government, Halimi renews her commitment to Choisir, to eradicating oppression through the transformation of society, as she puts it, by picking up the cause of parity democracy and, more particularly, by returning to writing and speaking.

Gisèle Halimi's autobiographical narrative is a retrospective self-construction, a search for legitimacy and an attempt to justify her loss of power. In this respect, it is not so very dissimilar from *Entre Nous* (Between Us) written by former conservative Prime Minister Alain Juppé in 1996. *Entre Nous* is an attempt to rehabilitate Juppé's image as a human and caring person. Halimi's lived experience is also transformed into a heroic journey; or *parcours du combattant*, a pioneering model or lesson for other women. In fact, Françoise Gaspard critiques Halimi's autobiographical writing as *angélisme*, an overly idealistic self-vindication that stresses public commitment and leaves out the less noble motivations and the more self-serving actions.

Notwithstanding the possible criticism of her confessional or "judicial" scene as too self-congratulatory, and despite Halimi's present need to stress the success of her political action, her work does make a contribution to the new body of feminine autobiographical writing. It does this most particularly in its reflection on the relation of a woman's political life to masculine politics, on the reconciling of work and family life, of public glory and personal happiness, and on the uses of feminine difference.

## Writing over the Public-Private Divide

Halimi's account of her electoral campaign and her subsequent pastoral work with her constituents in the region of L'Isère is juxtaposed with very personal reflections on what it has meant for her to be a wife and mother: "I often felt how much being a mother had limited my choices, narrowed the range of new interests, arrested my taste for adventure, in short had obliged me, by the very nature of things, to make my life more ordinary."[6] This had included limiting love affairs in order "not to destroy the image of the Father in her sons' unconscious."[7] The family has devoured her time, eaten her up with guilt, and led to difficult choices. On the other hand, her three sons and the granddaughter who at the end of the book Halimi presents as her hope for the future, have brought her emotional fulfillment. As a *députée* in the countryside and a trained lawyer, Halimi listens to the litany of disappointments of women seeking her advice as a lawyer on divorce and child-support payments. Despite her own thirty-year marriage, she concludes, disconcertingly, that a woman who wants to succeed in the public world with the same chances as a man has nothing to gain from marriage.

## The Difficulties of Feminist Freedom

The personal continues to be deeply interwoven with the public in this feminist political autobiography as Halimi dedicates a chapter to looking with open eyes at the alternatives Choisir is seeking for women. Focusing on the difficulties of freedom, she shares with her readers four stories of particularly incurable wounds deriving from the contradictions in women's situation. These are very intimate accounts of the lives of feminist friends from the 1970s beginning with the beautiful Shelia, who regresses to become the decorative, financially protected possession of a very rich industrialist thirty years her senior. There is Jacqueline, who is seen to resolve the contradictions of her need for freedom of choice and her desire to be loved and to be irreplaceable along with the contradictions inherent in her mixed Antillean-French, Black-White culture, by taking her own life. The personal drama of Annie, a doctor and psychiatrist, and the psychological fragility resulting from Marina's difficult past, also result in suicides.

These failures raise issues for Halimi of an inadequacy of feminine solidarity on her part. Her belief in liberty of choice for every individual, she writes, had prevented her from taking necessary action. Halimi concludes that feminism is not just a call for justice; it is often a total personal revolution, involving both head and heart and making changes that can be dangerous. (All revolutions devour some of their children.) Halimi speaks also of the companionship, the solidarity, the joys of Choisir, of different ways of speaking, of milk and tenderness. In this chapter of existential reflection on life and love by a publicly strong and militant feminist, what is striking is the uncertainty about global solutions, or any single path or truth, and the readiness to confide this intimate thinking about personal life and its failures as well as successes in her public writing.

## *Françoise Gaspard: Political Writer*

In Françoise Gaspard's autobiographical writing, the personal *is* the political. In one of the earliest women's autobiographical accounts of life in politics, *Madame le...* , Gaspard talks of the attraction of power, the pleasure of addressing the crowd, and why, as a woman, she disturbed people. In *Madame le...* Gaspard demonstrates that in politics more than anywhere else, when a woman disturbs, she is reduced to her sex.[8] As mayor of Dreux from 1977 to 1983, she was both admired and rejected. Her opponents accused her of lesbianism or intimated that she was Mitterrand's mistress. They even spread a particularly strange rumor about her involvement with an Arab lover, a story degenerating into a kind of collective delirium of rape and murder. Gaspard observes that the men around her felt threatened in their virility by the fact that a young woman would not observe the rituals of seduction that regulate the "normal" relations between the sexes, such as not allowing men to pay the bill or order the wine.

Gaspard had made her way into a man's world. From the account of her first work experience, sent on an internship from ENA with a *préfet* who was most unhappy to be assigned one of the rare political women, Gaspard deconstructs the universe she has entered. Her irreverent humor plays over institutions and attitudes from the inside. This deconstruction then creates the space for her own feminine political manifesto. She confesses that she did not like women and believes it took her more than thirty years to admit she was one. Yet, it did disturb her that women who succeeded in the public world of business and politics were often a caricature of men. The dilemma, for Gaspard, was being caught between the fear of power as denial of oneself as a woman and the fear of being a woman existing only by one's sexuality.

The stories that Gaspard tells journalist Elisabeth Weissman are as full of militant verve and as focused on gender issues as her autobiography—from the speeches of the Director at the ENA, which always began with *jeunes messieurs* ("Young men"), to her first impossible campaign in 1973 at Dreux and in its surrounding conservative villages, with a platform of legalizing contraception and abortion.[9] Miraculously, this won her 33 percent of the vote, a score she is convinced she owed to women. After her unexpected election in 1977, she claims, she cried, and not with joy, at the task before her.

As member of the executive committee of the Parti socialiste (beginning in 1977), Gaspard worked for the abolition of the death penalty, women's rights, and parity. She served as deputy from 1979 to 1981 for the European Community, and deputy for the Eure et Loir district from 1981 to 1988. I met her in her office as a member of the faculty of the Graduate School of Social Sciences (Ecole des Hautes Etudes en Sciences Sociales) in 1997. Our discussion left me with the impression of an intellectually rigorous, confident, and generously attentive interlocutor. The following is a translation of the parts of our conversation most relevant to the focus on writing by political women. It attempts to sound Gaspard's own views on the importance of the new texts, their relation to the French "exception," and their role in enhancing prospects for parity.

## Interview with Françoise Gaspard

(Ecole des Hautes Etudes en Sciences Sociales, 14 January 1997.)

**Françoise Gaspard**: Today the Senatorial Committee is hearing the "experts" on parity and taking depositions from women's associations.

**R.R.** On whose initiative?

**Françoise Gaspard**: Madame Demissine, a Communist senator for the North—I've worked with her and like her. She was already a feminist and then she went to the Beijing Women's Convention.

**R.R.** (…) Have you read any of the books on the list I sent you? Some are university studies, some autobiographies—they are very different. Which give the most truthful accounts, those that most resemble what you yourself have experienced as a woman in politics?

**Françoise Gaspard**: I'm interested in these texts for what I can learn or what they tell me about myself, in relation to my experience. I like Huguette Bouchardeau's writing—she's delightful and very intelligent—both *Choses dites de profil* (Speaking Indirectly) and *Un Coin dans leur monde* (A Corner in Their World). I'm very critical of books by journalists but Schemla's *La Femme piègée* (Woman in a Trap) is

*François Mitterrand with Françoise Gaspard, mayor of Dreux, celebrating the new generation of Socialists in office at the municipal level.*

good… Yes, her thesis on the press is valid and it is very well documented. Sineau and Jenson's book, *Mitterrand et les Françaises* (Mitterrand and French Women), yes—it's not on your list, is it?—that is quite a remarkable book. Can you believe that it was not included on a recently published list of major books on the Mitterrand era?

**R.R.** It's an illuminating omission… But, hasn't the attitude toward studies on women in the academic world been changing? I found a *mémoire* by Jane Freedman on the role of the media played in the difficulties experienced by Edith Cresson supervised by René Rémond, among the DEA theses completed at the Institut d'Etudes Politiques.

**Françoise Gaspard**: I co-supervise twenty or so theses. I'm completely overwhelmed. I can't say no to these young people. There are so few places and so few people in France working in these areas… but the situation is changing.

**R.R.** In political science, are there still only Mariette Sineau and Janine Mossuz-Lavau?… and the new women historians?

**Françoise Gaspard**: Yes… but young people are arriving on the job market…

**R.R.** Will you be standing again for political office?

**Françoise Gaspard**: I had said no. Next week, I will probably become a candidate in Dreux for the legislative elections. I've been urged to stand… the situation there is regressing all the time.

**R.R.** Do you want to?

**Françoise Gaspard**: No, I had made other choices for my life... I did my bit.

**R.R.** Do you think you will have the same impact in the field as you have in the academic world?

**Françoise Gaspard**: The movement for parity was developed and promoted out of my university work... in collaboration with others here.

**R.R.** Do you think that along with the parity manifesto, *Au Pouvoir, Citoyennes*, your autobiographical writing has also had some influence?

**Françoise Gaspard**: Yes, it's astonishing. Very young women have told me that *Madame le...* authorized them to continue their studies and enter politics.

**R.R.** Was it difficult to stage your life so publicly?

**Françoise Gaspard**: I didn't take up my pen spontaneously. I was having lunch with the American cultural attaché, talking about politics... someone tapped me on the shoulder—"I'm Françoise Verny"—and told me she wanted me to write a book. She is one of France's well-known woman editors.

**R.R.** You wouldn't have written it otherwise?

**Françoise Gaspard**: No.

**R.R.** Simone Veil said in her seminar on parity the other day that she believed that the concept of parity had not been well understood. If it had been, it would have been less well accepted.

**Françoise Gaspard**: I don't agree. When I speak of parity, I'm understood. Elisabeth Badinter and her elitist universalist group believe parity is essentialist... the merit of the idea of parity is to show the disparity that exists and to make people think about it. What is interesting is that it has pushed the Socialist party to adopt a parity platform for the elections and I have just heard that there are several women candidates in all the electoral districts. All that was needed to give women legitimacy was to remove competition... that has made everything possible.

**R.R.** When there's no competition women feel legitimate?

**Françoise Gaspard**: Yes, I'm sending out my students to do a study in ten days or so to ask these women why they have agreed to become candidates. The study should take two months.

**R.R.** Would you have any more or less difficulty with the legitimacy of another woman versus a man if you were working for them in politics—a woman prime minister, for example?

**Françoise Gaspard**: It would depend on the person, but a priori, no... I think that on the whole it would be easier.

**R.R.** (...) Are there any works missing from my list that are significant?

**Françoise Gaspard**: All the work of Geneviève Fraisse, including *Muse de la Raison*... the work by Eliane Viennot for which I wrote the preface, all of her work is very interesting...

**R.R.** Do you have a vision of the future for women in politics in France?

**Françoise Gaspard**: I'm an historian and a sociologist and I work on real life. What I can say is that France is behind; it has entered a period where it is catching up, but culturally, institutionally, and politically, unless there is a revolution, this will take longer than other countries [Discussion on the case of Sweden].

**R.R.** The U.S. has had difficulty accepting Hillary Clinton...

**Françoise Gaspard**: The four countries that have had the most difficulty accepting women in politics are the oldest democracies, those where democracy took form without women—Greece, France, the U.S., and Britain.

**R.R.** It is astonishing in a country of strong feminist movements like the U.S. to encounter such resistance to a woman accused of "wearing the pants."

**Françoise Gaspard**: American and French machismo are worlds apart. The French version is different—slyer, softer, coarser. Look at what happened last week in the Assemblée Nationale.

**R.R.** The protest by a woman representative at the rape of the policewoman... ?

**Françoise Gaspard**: (...) Yes, the comment by [the right-wing deputy] Cathala... "There's no fear of that happening to you."

**R.R.** (...) Do you find it possible to work with people as different as Gisèle Halimi and Roselyne Bachelot?

**Françoise Gaspard**: What a curious question. Gisèle Halimi is as impossible as she is talented (...); with Roselyne, there's no problem.

**R.R.** Isn't that paradoxical given that one is from the left, and the other from the right? Is Bachelot's cross-party Observatoire de la parité really operational or is it a cover?

**Françoise Gaspard**: It's a front.

## Being a Woman in Left-wing Politics in the 1990s

The women who formed Pierre Bérégovoy's new Socialist government in 1992 have been called "the younger generation." A number of them were former Mitterrandian advisors from the Elysée, for example Frédérique Bredin, and more notably, Ségolène Royal and Elisabeth Guigou. These three women, well endowed by birth, intelligence, education at an elite institution (the ENA), helped by an understanding husband or father, and mentored by a "prince" (François Mitterrand, Jacques Delors, or Lionel Jospin), all produced autobiographical texts and/or political manifestos in the Spring of 1997.

Youth and sports minister, former deputy, European deputy, and mayor of Fécamp, Frédérique Bredin found legitimacy as a graduate of Sciences Politiques and the prestigious ENA institute. In 1997, to disseminate her thesis of a practical politics, Bredin published a "Logbook"

(*Députée. Journal de bord*) of the daily joys and difficulties as an elected representative in Fécamp. Frédérique Bredin presented herself as a field worker, interested in finding ways of better combining work and personal life for herself and for her constituents. Speaking in an interview with Elisabeth Weissman, Bredin concedes that even though women are judged differently and are often set up as tokens, the political universe is no more difficult for women than for men. But women are concerned, she observes, that the balance in their personal relationships could be disturbed by the responsibilities of office.[10] Bredin concludes that there is difference between the sexes and women must not imitate the vanity and intolerance of men, or the masculine distance from reality.

## *Ségolène Royal and "The Truth of a Woman"*

For her part, Ségolène Royal entered politics as an advocate for a need for women's difference in political life. "I was unsinkable on women's questions, as I myself had experienced a long and painful emancipation," she states in *La Vérité d'une femme.* After seven years at the Elysée (1981 to 1988), as adviser to Mitterrand, Ségolène Royal decided to confront the risks of popular election and in June 1988, she defeated the vice-president of the Regional Council to become deputy for the Deux-Sèvres district, a rural area near Poitiers. Royal recounts how the *préfet* had called her the evening before the election results were due out to say "Dear Madame, I regret to inform you that your challenge has not been successful." His wishful thinking did not prevail. As the results from the last villages trickled in, she found herself ahead by 552 votes. In 1992, Royal became environment minister. In March of 1993, despite the Socialist *débâcle,* Ségolène Royal, who had protected and restored the local wetlands and helped give the goat cheese of the region, the *chabichou*, a national and international reputation, was re-elected with 53.4 percent of the vote. In the Jospin government of 1997, Royal became minister in charge of primary and secondary education.

"She's a Marie-Antoinette looking after her sheep" (*C'est Marie-Antoinette qui élève ses moutons*), interjected a deputy after one of Royal's speeches on agricultural questions. This analogy challenged her competence and her political legitimacy. Yet Ségolène Royal writes that the scorn and condescension shown her by the political insiders was in contrast to the attitudes of the straightforward country people she represented, who accorded legitimacy to her feminine values.

### Questions of Paternal and Maternal Influence

Royal's autobiography, *La Vérité d'une femme*, constructs her entry into the political world in terms of paternal and maternal influences. The daughter of a career army officer, brought up in a small village in the Vosges, Ségolène Royal describes herself as the fourth in a conservative family of eight children. She was raised in a town where the men and women sat on opposite sides of the church for a mass said in Latin and where the sons became soldiers and the daughters married. It was a community in which the women voted for right-wing candidates, as did their husbands. Recalling how she was exposed from an early age to remarks that put down the weaker sex, Ségolène Royal pays homage to the influence of her mother, who had studied agricultural science, was an anti-conformist, and inculcated a great love of nature in her children. It was the mixture of paternal military authority and maternal difference that formed her, claims Royal. As early as her first year at high school, Royal knew she did not want to share the destiny of the women around her, who were wholly dependent on their husbands. In her fourth year at high school she was passionately interested in the political debates led by one of the very few female role models, Françoise Giroud. By chance, there was a class in Nancy that prepared good students for the Institut d'Etudes Politiques (IEP). Successful in the competitive entry exam, Ségolène Royal went on to discover the existence of the elitist Ecole Nationale d'Administration (ENA) alongside the IEP in the Rue Saint-Guillaume in Paris. Royal was admitted to that prestigious male-dominated institution on her second try.

Political life is brutal, even cruel, writes Ségolène, and even more so for women. Those who declare themselves to be against the parity principle do not know what it can be like to be the object of the kind of attacks she confronted during her municipal campaign in 1995 at Niort. Her party headquarters was smeared with excrement; she was blamed for Nazi swastikas on the election posters of a rival party themselves responsible for the defacement in order to claim victimization; one of her children received an anonymous phone call threatening their "bitch of a mother." Repeating a claim made by the other Parity Ten women, Royal concludes that most woman in politics have experienced this kind of aggression, from Simone Veil to Martine Aubry, including Michèle Barzach and Edith Cresson.

Ségolène Royal also narrates the slap that every woman on the campaign trail receives when she is told by men to go home and look after her children. This is an attack that puts her off balance because it "denies the very legitimacy of her work."[11] Royal's reflections on the difficulties experienced more particularly by women in public office are embedded in her own life experience. Wednesdays, a key work day for government, are also half days at school, and like evenings and late afternoon, these are precisely the times that women would like to spend with their children. Yet, leaving a long-winded, ineffective discussion in parliament to spend time with children can harm a woman's reputation as a serious politician. Where male politicians invariably have a woman in the background to take care of their psychological and practical needs, most women in politics need to take care of everything themselves unless they too have the good fortune to have "a woman in the house." For Royal, this conflict of roles is the main reason why there are so few women in power. When she became assistant minister responsible for schools in 1997, one of Royal's proposed measures was to change the dates of the school holidays in February from Wednesday, a mid-week beginning that caused problems for working parents, to Friday.

In the light of her own different experience and values, but also drawing on economic theory, Ségolène Royal uses her autobiography to outline an alternative political philosophy and set of projects. Royal sets out to critique the adoption of Malthus's economic theory in practice. She wants to prevent social activity from being reduced to what has been called "productivity" and wealth from being expressed as exchange-value. Royal argues that in his *Principles of Political Economy*, Malthus accepts that it is human beings in good health with all of their talents that constitute wealth. However, only the increase in value from one year to another of exchangeable material objects could be given a measurable price and counted. Unfortunately, what was originally only a methodological exclusion of human value for Malthus was then taken for a fundamental exclusion. What constitutes the true wealth of the individual and binds a society, what is good for it—the quality of the air, the absence of violence, a high level of education, peace and the capacity to promote peace—"does not, Royal concludes, come from economic exchange."[12]

In the present system, Ségolène Royal claims, each business acts as if it is alone, forgetting it exists in a world of customers and a world of dangerous inequalities. What Ségolène Royal sees as a feminine concern with the fate of future generations and the strength of women's instinct to ensure the survival of their children is presented as a force for change. She argues that until there are more women at the head of governments, the dominance of commercial interests as revealed, for example, in the sexual exploitation of women or children documented at the Stockholm Conference in August 1996, will continue.

*La Vérité d'une femme* thus presents feminine priorities alongside a whole left-wing political and ecological program including taxes on capital and on the use of natural resources to lesson the burden of taxes on salaries. In the public health and environment sectors, Royal argues, profits should be invested only in the improvement of the public service, to be run by an eminent civil servant with a background in ethical service to the state, not by a clique of overpaid executives. Royal's text critiques the present state of French politics, the exclusion of women from government, unemployment, violence, problems with the environment and with food production. This means a critique also of the French failures to support human rights, including those of women, and calls for greater courage in European politics. Implicitly, the proposed ecological reform and rights activism are gendered feminine in a political world that is masculine.

## The Battle for Feminization of Names

The feminist academic Benoîte Groult demonstrated that language is never innocent and reflects the prejudices and unconscious desires of a society.[13] Groult identified with some humor the contradictions and incongruities in which French journalists are caught in regard to female political office. Groult uses an extract from a newspaper to highlight the absurd mix of masculine and feminine nouns and adjectives used around women in politics.

> "Frédérique Bredin est le plus jeune ministre," ... "cet inspecteur des finances, élue députê en 1988, puis chargée de mission à l'Elysée." "Martine Aubry est le nouveau ministre du travail"... "directeur du cabinet" de Jean Auroux et "directrice des relations au ministère de travail."

Minister, inspector of taxes, parliamentary deputy, cabinet director remain masculine nouns, whereas a director of public relations or deputy advisor to the president (*chargée* and *directrice*) can apparently take a feminine form. The unconscious logic at work here is that the feminine form of a profession is invariably the lower prestige form and a high prestige office must continue to be gendered masculine.

Royal had pointed out in *Le Monde* as early as 1990 that the vocabulary we use is implicated in the progress of ideas and noted the continuing use of "Madame *le* premier ministre" in every French newspaper.[14] This anachronistic masculine article before the noun "minister" revealed the extent to which the position remained connoted masculine, even for the women ministers themselves. In 1993, Ségolène Royal wanted to be called "*la* ministre de l'environnement" and asked for the 1986 circular on the feminization of names of professions to be put into practice. She was met with laughter and acerbic comments. This derision came even though UNESCO had just published a guide suggesting rules for those words in French that did not already figure in the circular. Again in 1996 in *Le Monde*, Royal asked why the official documents of the National Assembly continued to deprive *députée* of its feminine "e" while in other professions feminine forms had been introduced into the language.[15] There was even a feminine form for "bull-fighter" (une "torrera").

In *La Vérité d'une femme*, Ségolène Royal justifies her championing of the feminization of titles on the grounds that the structures of language influence forms of thought. She recounts the response from the right-wing politician, Philippe Séguin who said: "I am not personally convinced that this is the best battle for women."[16] As Royal responds acerbically to this indirect opposition, a man is of course not "personally convinced" of something that does not concern him directly and intimately. Moreover, she adds, "the best women's battle" is always another one—that is, for men, no battle at all.

As minister in the Jospin government, Ségolène Royal will witness the acceptance of the feminine form thanks, in part, to her own campaign supported by the other Socialist women ministers.[17] The subsequent public commitment by the leading newspaper, *Le Monde*, to a systematic and linguistically principled feminization of titles backed up the action of the women ministers. The war of the words may not be over but institutional resistance to the feminization of names of professions suddenly and unexpectedly folded in the late 1990s. The "Immortals" of the Académie Française continued to claim that feminization did not respect the time-honored rules of French grammar, but met an intellectually sophisticated response by a group of women, including grammarians, who proved their arguments to be disingenuous.

Ségolène Royal was not available to be interviewed and lacked the time to answer my written questionnaire, referring me instead to her book. The journalist Maurice Maschino also notes in the preface to his book of interviews conducted with political women, that Royal's response to his request for an interview was negative and somewhat impatient. Parenting four young children with her partner, François Hollande, himself a *député* since the 1997 election and more recently Socialist party spokesperson and then leader, Royal confronts issues of organization in her life in personally accommodating the public and the private. That she has chosen to publish several books is evidence of the importance she attributes to writing. Royal has written books on political policy, environmental concerns, on the interaction of senior citizens in community life, on the need to construct a place for young people in society, and a further book-length study arguing for the reduction of violence on television. The title of Ségolène Royal's political autobiography has two possible readings—The Truth of a Woman/One Woman's Truth. Her truth, then, is presented as the parity truth of the political potential of one half of humanity, with distinctive feminine concerns and interests, mostly still waiting in the wings, as she has personally experienced this situation.

## *Elisabeth Guigou and "Being a Woman in Politics" in 1997*

The title of Elisabeth Guigou's first political autobiography, *Etre femme en politique* (Being a Woman in Politics), also lays claim to an experience that has both a public and a personal interest. Like Ségolène Royal and Martine Aubry, Guigou is a graduate of the ENA. Like Royal, she was first part of the Mitterrand team, a presidential adviser, before she became a minister—in her case, minister of European affairs in 1992. *Etre femme en politique* appeared just before Chirac unwisely called early elections. In June 1997 Guigou returned to the Cabinet, the first woman to head the Ministry of Justice as *Garde des Sceaux*. Guigou was very much solicited in the televised media throughout 2000 as a spokesperson for the government and at the end of that year, she replaced Martine Aubry, when that minister retired, as number two in the French government. Just prior to this promotion by Jospin, Guigou had published a second political autobiography, *Une Femme au coeur de l'Etat* (A Woman at the Heart of the State). This work is predominantly a discussion of Socialist policies and is much less concerned with personal issues of legitimacy and difference.

In *Etre femme en politique*, comparing the mistakes of Edith Cresson and of Alain Juppé, Guigou concludes that what Prime Minister Edith

Cresson lacked above all was the legitimacy bestowed by the technocratic preparation in the traditional mold at the ENA. In Guigou's analysis, the conclusions drawn by the public on the two cases are very different. Despite Cresson's intuition, solidity, closeness to people, and dislike of technocrats, the fact that she did not belong to this elite made her appear incompetent; she was judged incapable of governing. In contrast, Juppé, who shared the background, language, and behavior of the elite, was considered to be capable of governing, and had simply governed badly. The second conclusion drawn by the public was that Juppé's failure was an individual one, whereas Cresson's bespoke the failure of all women, compromising their accession to the positions of high power for a long time to come.

Despite the conclusion that Cresson was disadvantaged by not graduating from the National School of Administration, Elisabeth Guigou, like Françoise Gaspard, begins to demystify ENA by writing critically about her own experience of the education it provides. Gaspard's book, *Madame le...*, claims that little of significance is taught at this place of predominantly elitist, masculinist, and traditionalist thinking. She advises young women to work hard to get into and take advantage of ENA, as she herself did from 1975 to 1977, if only to de-mythify this elite experience (you don't learn much there but value is added to your image) and to use ENA as a political springboard. Guigou's work, too, describes the prevailing snobbery of a privileged caste. While maintaining the critical distance of outsiders, both indirectly acknowledge how much their own destinies were affected by simply having a place

*Transfer of power: Elisabeth Guigou and Martine Aubry, October 19, 2000.*

in this concentration of young intelligence and future influence disseminated throughout the highest levels of French financial and administrative institutions.

Guigou recounts her growing up in Morocco, disgusted by a certain heavy stupidity among the "machos" but with no sense of any gender discrimination. If she felt different during her studies at ENA where twenty of the one hundred and fifty students were women, Guigou writes, this feeling of difference was less a consequence of her gender than of the difference between her origins as the daughter of a small farming couple and a world inhabited by an elite from the snobbish middle-class sixième, septième, and seixième *arrondissements* of Paris. Guigou presents her marriage at twenty to Jean-Louis as happy. Jean Louis has been supportive of her work and the raising of their son. She recounts how Jacques Delors, then Minister of Finance, took her under his wing in 1982, and offered her help in case of difficulty. But in the world of finance, Guigou argues, it was competence and work that guaranteed her legitimacy and authority, not "paternal" protection. She recalls the eight years spent at the Elysée from 1982, "taking the temperature" of the French franc and synthesizing information on the currency and external trade, as years of professional happiness.

Despite Mitterrand's expressed skepticism about an attractive woman's real interest in the world of finance—"Are you really in love with finance?"—Guigou does not share Jenson and Sineau's conclusions about Mitterrand. In her experience, Mitterrand liked the company of women and never underestimated them. She claims this was a consequence of his relationship with his generous and affectionate mother, Yvonne Lorrain. In Guigou's positive assessment, Mitterrand had not only made ministers of Bredin, Royal, and herself, but also encouraged them to stand for popular election. His actions were due to his visceral anti-conformism, his independent mindedness, his curiosity about difference, and his recognition of the advantage Giscard d'Estaing had drawn from the action of Simone Veil, Françoise Giroud, and Monique Pelletier.

Guigou writes that it was not until she accompanied the president on his visits to European capitals after 1985 and saw him every day, that the first difficulties in being a woman arose. This intimacy with Mitterrand aroused the envious and malicious rumor that her influence could not be explained only by professional competence.

> That was the first blow below the belt. There would be others, even more violent, beginning in October 1990 when I became part of the government. And especially when I decided that, as a minister, it was my duty to enter the electoral fray to win democratic legitimacy. It was then that I was to really find out what politics reserves for women.[18]

The difficulties Guigou encountered in the electoral campaign in the Vaucluse region, and the rebuffs she suffered once in power, reawakened what she calls her "feminist fiber" lulled by the years of professional success and personal happiness.

Guigou points out that women in powerful positions are always suspected of being abnormal and are always the object of curiosity. Ségolène Royal and François Hollande, for example, live under a public spotlight that sees the couple as rivals, in competition for the highest position. In Guigou's analysis, it is single women at the top who often suffer the worst from stereotypes—of lesbianism, careerism, hardness. After she lost her position in Juppé's cabinet, Elisabeth Hubert, advisor to Chirac, was told she should marry before the elections. Nicole Notat was obliged to combat gossip by declaring that single did not necessarily mean solitary. The deviance of their physical appearance among the dark suits and ties is often the subject of discussion.

## Visualizing Deviance: "A Fragile Amazon in a Red Blouse with Black Dots"

Commenting on Guigou's campaign in 1992, the journalist Hervé Algarrondo pokes fun at the battle between the "grouchy" Maastricht opponent, Philippe Séguin, and the pro-Maastricht "amazon," Elisabeth Guigou.[19] The word "amazon" functions here ironically to connote the non-feminine qualities of the female warrior, and contrast these with a set of eminently "feminine" epithets. The journalist insists on the calm self-assurance of Séguin, his straightforward and massive "No" to Europe and on Guigou's elegant "fragility" with her fair plait, red blouse with black dots, red jacket, and "her firm but graceful 'Yes.'"

Under Jacques Toubon, the affairs of the judiciary had become somewhat murky. When a rigid and visibly furious Toubon handed over power to the very cool and attractive Guigou before the TV cameras, he also attempted to gain a critical advantage by communicating the "deviance" of the situation. Feminine image or appearance was replacing masculine competence, claimed Toubon: "I cannot attempt to compete with the image. When it comes to action, that is another matter. We'll see." Guigou did not react to the attempt to undermine her legitimacy by reference to her physical appearance. She simply proceeded to outline in a clear and convincing voice the nature of the political project she considered had been entrusted to her—the separating of the judiciary from the executive branch of government to give justice a new autonomy and make it more accessible to ordinary people.

Guigou has neither disavowed nor foregrounded her difference—she has acknowledged and discussed it: "Public glory for a woman could only mean a terrible loss of personal happiness" (*La gloire ne saurait être pour une femme qu'un deuil éclatant de bonheur*). This quote from Germaine de Staël begins a very personal chapter in Guigou's book entitled "Public Life and Private Life." Guigou echoes Catherine Trautmann in arguing that women are less prepared to invest their whole life in politics or to put their political life before their family. This means women are correspondingly more able to accept and use failure. On the other hand Guigou uses the thesis of Jacques Baguenard, Jean Maisondieu, and Léon Metayer in *Political Men Do Not Have Children*, to highlight that male politicians are the opposite.[20] They are like Chronos, devouring the children he procreates because the excessiveness of power leads to the illusion of immortality and the desire to kill any potential competition, thereby sterilizing its holder.

Guigou writes of the constant guilt she felt at having to spend so much time away from her son Edouard, despite the continual presence of one of his two grandmothers and the fact that he did grow up to become a well-balanced young man. She is preoccupied by the tragedy of the suicide of the twenty-four year old son of Norway's popular labor prime minister, Gro Harlem Brundtland, presented as possibly influencing the successful politician's decision to withdraw from politics.

The husband problem also comes under scrutiny. As Simone Veil had put it, it is difficult for the husband not to be the center of attention in the couple. Men in less powerful positions than their wives are pitied. When Jean-Louis was asked if it was strange to be married to a minister, recounts Guigou, he had the personal confidence to put his interlocutors off-balance by replying that "he would happily be Elisabeth's driver."

## Difference, Change, and Writing

Guigou shares the position of Antoinette Fouque on the difference between the sexes:

> If equality is sacrificed to difference, the reactionary position of traditional societies who cloistered their women in domestic tasks denying them access to abstraction or the management of public space is reinforced; and if one sacrifices the difference between the sexes with the richness of life that this implies, to equality, women are neutered and the whole of humanity impoverished. The principle of equality must incorporate irreducible difference between the sexes, linked to procreation, the founding act of sexual species; and to bring about real equality, it must accept affirmative action.[21]

The woman politician argues that as long as this difference is recognized, women can bring change. The courage, tenacity, and devotion of the women militants who worked with her across France in the Maastricht campaign, in the party, or in women's groups, she claimed, made her aware of the "inestimable value" of solidarity among women.[22] Guigou's thinking is evidently influenced by the current parity discourse and this first autobiography, which speaks particularly to women and in a very personal manner, is now, in its turn, influencing the writing and speaking of other political women.

Once out of power, it was the need to reflect on her own experience and turn this to a more general intellectual and political purpose that led Guigou to exchange views with or interview a number of other political women in European politics and to write *Etre Femme en Poli-*

*tique*. This incorporates her own story and political agenda. It also provides a full history of other prominent contemporary political women. Guigou's book thus effects a synthesis of many of the new histories of political women, interviews, and academic debates. For example, it is evident that she has read Viennot's histories. Her book discusses the power of the five women regents between the fifteenth and the eighteenth centuries and the significant roles played by women in the Revolution. Quoting from Nicole and Albert Roy's recent political history of women, she also tells the story of Louise Weiss and the 18,000 votes by women placed in her illegal ballot boxes in 1935. The suffrage activists threw boxes of powder at the police when the police attempted to disperse the protesting women.

Guigou's work also sketches portraits of courageous political women throughout the world and contains references to her own interviews with more than thirty political personalities. They include Gro Harlem Brundtland, Margaret Thatcher, Mary Robinson, Vigdis Finnbogadottir, Kalida Messaoudi, Rita Süssmuth, Edith Cresson, Simone Veil, and Françoise Giroud. The claims for women are resolutely positive. From her own interviews with political women, Guigou observes their desire to change things by action, attention to everyday problems, and general independence. She notes the militant work for humanitarian causes of Emma Bonino, an Italian commissioner for Europe; the press conference called by RPR transportation minister (*secrétaire d'Etat aux Transports*) Anne-Marie Idrac, and Corinne Lepage, environment minister, to criticize the grandiose and environmentally unsound Rhine-Rhone canal project. The general conclusion of Guigou's rhetoric is that women's often-untapped creative power must be allowed to form a new critical mass that will humanize the old political world and its systems.

## A Woman in Trade Union Politics: The New Figure of Nicole Notat

One of the portraits of women that Guigou focuses on is that of union reformer Nicole Notat. As the head of the group within the CFDT Union seeking to introduce a new politics of cooperative management of work between labor and employer, Notat's case marks a spectacular female breakthrough. Notat has provoked strong reactions by showing the courage required to innovate, and by going against traditions. Guigou quotes Notat's response to the deep anti-woman sentiments embedded in the language used against her during demonstrations in 1995 and 1996. In an interview with *L'Express*, Notat had stated: "You don't use slogans like 'Notat, collabo' or 'rasez-là'" [Notat, collaborator, shave her hair off!] by chance. You already have to be impregnated with them. The words, the insults, and the way of looking sought to wound the woman. Racism and sexism have a common origin."[23] In late 1997, Nicole Notat, too, published her own autobiographical story entitled *Je voudrais vous dire. Nicole Notat avec Hervé Hamon*. Guigou re-presents the arguments of the parity discourse, re-cycling and strengthening that story. *Etre femme en politique* is of value for its amalgam of an intelligent scholarly overview of women's political history and authentic lived experience. It is with this combination that this "feminine" text acquires its own persuasive and even authoritative quality.

## *Arlette Laguiller: "It's My Whole Life"*

### Class, Gender, and Loyalty to the Father

On the extreme left, in Arlette Laguiller's 1996 political autobiography *C'est toute ma vie* (It's My Whole Life), the women's issues that dominate Gaspard's tales appear to be very secondary to a central ready-made, militant and universalist political credo. Yet Laguiller devotes a separate chapter to the "Rights of Women." In fact, her autobiography struggles with the problem of affirming commonalties among working-class comrades of Trotskyite conviction, while at the same time recognizing the specific and urgent problems of working women. Arlette Laguiller was chosen to run for Lutte ouvrière (The Workers' Struggle), in the legislative elections of 1973. In 2001, she was still firmly at the head of that extreme left-wing party and still a powerbroker, often interviewed by the media on the burning political issues of the day. Her obvious commitment to social justice and her staying power has made this rather marginal but very visible intransigent political woman something of a legend in France.

Laguiller's autobiographical search for a source of legitimacy for her lifetime commitment to politics has its origins in both class and gender factors. Laguiller tells the story of a childhood in the working class suburbs of Paris in the early 1950s in a one-room apartment with a sink that also served as a washroom for the three children and their parents. She recalls the humiliation of having to ask the butcher and the grocer for credit and recalls her first job in 1956, at age sixteen and a half at the Crédit Lyonnais bank, to bring home another much-needed pay check.

Laguiller also evokes her continuing political commitment to the principles of justice embodied in the person and philosophy of the martyred hero and father figure, Leon Trotsky. Her political analysis, based on Trotsky's writings, not only transcends the fall of the "false communism" of the Soviet Block but it explains it. Her political autobiography does not need to seek knowledge and authority, rather it repossesses and dispenses the truths of Father Trotsky. Laguiller traces her political commitment through her discovery of the history of the Trotskyite left, a left betrayed and decimated by the Stalinist takeover and transformation of the revolutionary, international, collectivist movement. She then follows in detail what she sees as the more contemporary political betrayals of the causes of the working class peoples by the French Communist party and the Socialists from the early Socialist party (the SFIO) to the present Parti Socialiste (from Blum to Mitterrand).

Laguiller also sees the "false left" as having betrayed the feminist principles found in the Marxist Revolution of 1917. An academic study by Jenny Chapman on politics and feminism confirms Laguiller's understanding that Russia before and after 1917 provides one of the very few instances of a major change in the relations between the sexes, seen as an achievement of the revolution: "The recruitment of women to revolutionary elites and the apparent integration of feminism into the political programs of men reached levels which have yet to be surpassed."[24] Laguiller does not provide an analysis of the reasons for these unusual new possibilities for women and their ultimate failure. She continues her story in order to denounce "the false left": Stalin, and Thorez, the French Communist leader, who betrayed such feminist principles and went back to the drive for dominance and to encouraging natalist policies. Laguiller adds that the Socialists of 1936 for their part did not touch the obsolete 1920 abortion law or support votes for women. She places the Programme commun de la gauche in 1981, and the Socialist government that followed under a heading entitled "The Great Disillusion."[25]

Despite attacks on the politics of the left, there is little evidence that Laguiller saw herself as being treated differently because she was a woman. Laguiller claims that she was never any less appreciated within her family because she was a female. She also asserts that she was absolutely equal with her fellow-revolutionaries in the PSU, in union activity, or within the Trotskyite movement. Of course she helped more with the domestic chores than the boys did, she writes. Of course, as a woman, she would be chosen as the spokesperson of Lutte ouvrière, thus putting its principles of "equality" into action. But the solidarity of class and of revolutionary political ideology transcended any possibility of discrimination against women within the movement. Arlette Laguiller nonetheless observes the displeasure of many of the husbands of her fellow militants when they occupied the premises of the Crédit Lyonnais in 1974.

Discussion of the differential treatment of women is found elsewhere in Laguiller's text. In 1981 Laguiller was invited to take part in a political debate between presidential candidates with Huguette Bouchardeau and Marie-France Garaud. According to Laguiller's text, such a proposal, refused independently by all three women candidates for the presidency, says a lot about the way certain authorities think about the place of women in political life—as in the Tour de France, a main race for men, she claims, and a secondary race, less intensely covered by the media, for women.

Laguiller describes the provisions she made for a different kind of political structure in her organization where women make up 40 percent of the membership, such as meetings at midday rather than in the evening. The difficulties of the working women whom Laguiller encounters are described with real sympathy—the lack of money, the double working day (a particular cause for concern), child care responsibilities, and the common fear of the humiliation and injustice of unwanted pregnancy. Laguiller protests against the unjust criminalization of many of those women who aided in abortions—1,000 a day in 1973 by the admission of the then-minister of justice, Foyer. She recognized the feminine solidarity that often lay behind the actions of the so-called *faiseuses d'anges* (back-street abortionists) and her book recalls the fate of the laundress, Louise Giraud, guillotined in the early 1940s by Pétain's collaborationist government for performing abortions, a scapegoat for the French military humiliation.[26] It is of particular interest that Laguiller focuses this chapter addressing the "rights of women" on the politics of sexuality and on issues of control over procreation and protection against sexual violence, rather than on the differences in salary and inequalities in the workplace between men and women.

This political woman who generally argues that social inequality is the source of all other inequalities and attempts to identify rights for women with the far left, does not claim her first allegiance to feminism. Yet her gender has a major influence on her writing as is evident in her discussion of the legitimacy (family romance) question, the nature of the justifications of her action, her concern with the politics of sexuality and with women's working conditions. Her interview in Elisabeth Weissman's book is entitled: "To work up my courage, I tell myself, 'go for it, you're a woman!'"[27] Laguiller confesses that she does not want anyone to be able to say: "We shouldn't have sent a woman." In this respect, her 1996 autobiography, still centrally committed to Trotsky and the class struggle, also bears witness to changing attitudes on the far left toward women's distinctive position in politics and to an increasing sense of the possibility of a common women's cause.

## Being a Woman in Conservative Politics

### *Alice Saunier- Seïté and Michèle Alliot-Marie: Identification with the Masculine?*

Rightist political women can also tend to underplay or attempt to deny gender issues: "You have to fight" (*Il faut se battre*) writes Alice Saunier-Seïté in *En première ligne* (On the Front Line).[28] This statement highlights Saunier-Seïté's firm stand against "ideology" in the name of maintaining "standards" in higher education. Similar military metaphors are found in Saunier-Seïté's earlier writing on her political role: "my career is the life of a soldier in the service of education" (*ma carrière est une vie de soldat au service de l'école*). Like these earlier technocratic accounts of the work of her ministries, her 1984 political manifesto, *Remettre l'état à sa place* (Putting the State Back in its Place), a call for less protection and intervention in individual lives and a deregulating move by a strong government away from the socialist ideology of 1981, makes absolutely no reference to her situation as a woman.[29] *Secrétaire d'Etat*, or assistant minister for universities, for five years, the first woman dean of a faculty (Brest), right-wing deputy and one of the earlier woman ministers, Alice Saunier-Seïté observes the conventions of the masculine world she has entered. Like many women in politics on the right of the political spectrum, Saunier-Seïté appears to seek legitimacy predominantly by using the language and operating within the conventions of the masculine world.

Michèle Alliot-Marie also seeks legitimacy through objective (masculine) writing. The daughter of a politician father, Alliot-Marie holds a doctorate in law and political sciences, served as *chargée de mission* in 1971 and 1978, and later as sports minister in Balladur's center-right government. In 1999, she was appointed the first woman leader of the right-wing RPR party and in 2001 found herself with the task of attempting to bring a fragmented party together in preparation for the upcoming legislative and presidential elections.

In an early 1983 book on the decision-making processes at the heart of the new technocratic Republic, *La Décision politique: Attention! Une République peut en cacher une autre* (Political Decision Making. Beware! One Republic may Conceal Another), the former minister argues that the republic of citizens hides a republic of civil servants who have legal and budgetary control of political acts.[29] The civil servants are part of an army of decision makers that include parliamentarians, directors or staffs of ministries, *préfets* (the administrative heads of the ninety-six départements in Metropolitan France), ambassadors, presidents of media corporations, journalists, trade-unionists, and financiers. In Alliot-Marie's analysis, the legitimacy of these elites, who are often a little less conservative than the masses, rests on the myths of nation, the social contract, the law, public service, the general interest, individual autonomy, and the state. Often, however, the action of these elites takes the form of an exhausting internecine struggle for influence so that, as she concludes, administrative mountains give birth to political mice.

Alliot-Marie argues that the French system of elites corresponds to a certain ideology of knowledge and democracy. The conclusion to her analysis is that the French should not stop at such an illusion of democracy, nor should they seek a government of the people by the people, for this can be tyrannical. She argues that since the Greeks, it has been the mechanisms of political decision making that constitute the touchstone of democracy. Alliot-Marie pleads for new and pluralistic criteria for entrance and promotion to the high civil service posts. She also seeks the renewal of the administrative bodies in a system fed by more and more open debate on decision making. Her analysis of the deficit of democracy occasioned by the power of the civil service is a reflection of, and an influence on, the critical discourse developing both on the left and on the right, which argues for the need for modernizing of government. It does not specifically mention the position of women.

Alliot-Marie's political treatise is influenced by her personal experience in government. Yet, in 1983 she appears to feel that her text has more weight written from a perspective of non-gendered (masculine) objectivity. Like Saunier-Séïté's work, this right-wing woman's text is a political analysis and critical manifesto that largely excludes the personal. Even to effect a radical critique of the system in place, a critique of the "deficit" of democracy in decision making, Alliot-Marie seeks legitimacy through a traditional univeralizing strategy, an objective (or "masculine") analysis, and an implicit affirmation of no gender difference. It is possible that this measured critique weighed in the later decision of the RPR party, seeking decorous unity in reforming modernity, to appoint Alliot-Marie as its first woman leader.

## *The Contradictions in the Discourse of Right-wing Women Politicians*

Although the discourse of right-wing women in power most often asserts "no-difference," as does the extreme left-wing discourse of Arlette Laguiller, this is invariably accompanied by evidence that gender does make a difference. Interviewed by Weissman in 1995, Elisabeth Hubert (deputy for the Loire-Atlantique area, vice-president for the RPR in the Assemblée from 1993, and a doctor fiercely opposed to socialized medicine) declared that if she had fought an electoral battle, it had nothing to do with being a woman.[31] Women simply have to fight as men do. As for misogyny in the RPR party, she claimed, older women who had to fight to get into high position were just as likely to block her path as men.

Yet feminine difference paradoxically underpins such commonplace assertions of equality (of no-difference). While declaring that she prefers a competent man to an incompetent woman, Hubert also asserts that she would choose any woman who was truly representative and determined. The problem, she adds, is that women have less thirst for power or they risk behaving like the "guys," the "trap into which fell Edith Cresson." In fact, Hubert finds misogyny deeply rooted at the level of local politics and wonders how women ever get elected to the Assemblée. Is thinking changing, she muses, or is it women's emerging reputation as hard workers that is responsible?

It is something of an irony that when she herself was appointed minister of public health in 1996, Elisabeth Hubert proved to be too outspoken and independent, and was accused of being insufficiently discreet. She very quickly lost her position along with the other "juppettes" through a decision by the "prince" and loss of paternal protection.

## *Michèle Barzach's* Truths and Taboos

The need for paternal protection is the principal subject of the centrist Michèle Barzach's 1994 autobiography, *Vérités et Tabous*, which tells the story of her exclusion in 1991 from the executive council of the right-wing Rassemblement Pour la République (RPR) party. Barzach held a ministerial appointment from 1986 to 1988, responsible for health and the family, was deputy for Paris for the XVième arrondissement from 1988 to 1991, and European deputy in 1989. Labeled a traitor for her independence and for what was seen as defection in her aspiration to join Michel Noir in the movement for the reform of an outdated neo-Gaullist party, her position as assistant mayor in the XVième arrondissement was taken from her, as a punishment. Chirac, she claims, told her that "the faithful do not say no to him" and "especially not a woman."[32] Later, in 1993 when the more center-right Union Démocratique française (UDF) party supported her renewed candidacy, RPR heavies exerted political pressure, writes Barzach, and this support was rapidly withdrawn.

Barzach's case has been characterized in some other women's writing as that of Pygmalion's Creation (legitimacy from the creator or the protector) but also as that of the *femme fatale*. In *Vérités et tabous,* Barzach reconstructs her story rather as that of a mother and a professional woman (a gynecologist with a thriving private practice), active in politics as *adjointe au maire* (assistant mayor), appointed minister in 1986 out of the blue, ten days after everyone else. Barzach labels herself a token woman, or "femme-alibi," perhaps with the bitterness of hindsight. She claims that she was a photogenic protégée, made and then broken by the "prince," Jacques Chirac. Recalling the blows that "aimed below the belt," Barzach observes that being a woman is a strength while one is in power and can take advantage of one's "femininity" but a notable weakness when one loses protection and thus legitimacy.

Françoise Giroud considers that, like Edith Cresson, Michèle Barzach had the image of a coquette, which is fatal in politics, for the coquette is seen as a seductive, devouring and dangerous woman: "The RPR never forgave her for being desirable. They made Barzach pay for her image. They all wanted her and didn't forgive her. Because of this, Barzach was massacred."[33] The "correct" image for a political woman is a maternal or non-sexual image. In an interview with me on 10 December 1996 in her office near the Invalides, Michèle Barzach reacted strongly to my recollection of Françoise Giroud's judgment. Barzach argued that if people had seen her as dangerous, this was not because she was too sexual or "midnight" but because she did not follow the rules. For her, it was the desire for independence that had particularly marked her struggle. Barzach claims that in government the notion of fidelity remains absolute both in the PC (Parti Communiste) and in the RPR where the least sign of dissidence is hunted out and eradicated. She concluded that women are thus not the only victims, as the same thing happened to the "Balladuriens," Balladur's supporters.

Cast out of parliament for her "unfaithfulness" to the prince after what she sees as years spent fighting for her political convictions to the detriment of her family life and the breakup of her marriage, Barzach is

*Michèle Barzach.*

using her autobiography to unburden her anger and resentment at felt injustice, to explain her positions and present her own particular political contributions. The hybridity of her desire to elaborate and communicate personal feelings on the impossibility of political life for a woman alongside ideas for better political organization and more effective social policies is increasingly a common aspect of women's political autobiographies, even on the right, along with the new solidarity with other political women.

Barzach's story illustrates the great power of appointment in the RPR vested in the national leadership, and of a construction by the Other that she finally rejected. "In any case, I made her," said Chirac.[34] "When I took her in hand, she was completely unknown… She owes her career to me."[35] The underlying story told by Barzach in her interviews and in her autobiography is both confession and renunciation of such a Pygmalion-Galatea relation. Redemption is seen to lie only in rejection of that powerful myth.

## The Case for the Defense: Feminine Difference

Having evoked the doubts arising from a legitimacy that could be given and then withdrawn by a prince, Barzach's autobiography follows the pattern we have detected of staging her defense in terms of the contribution made by her feminine difference. Michèle Barzach insists on the need to do politics differently, to fight against politicians' politics. She, too, echoes the common belief in the pragmatism, honesty, moral purpose, and lack of careerism that characterize the actions of political women.

Like Simone Veil, Barzach refused to vow unconditional loyalty to a party and its "apparatchiks." Self-vindication comes from staging the arbitrary and misogynist nature of the political taboos she had broken and bringing out what Barzach sees as the truths of her action. Her book is a didactic tracing of her own coming to knowledge as a means of raising political awareness amongst women in particular. When I asked Barzach whether *Vérités et Tabous* was symptomatic of a new feminine genre bringing together the private and the public, Barzach responded that she wrote her personal prologue to explain her disappearance from the public scene following the showdown with Chirac and her public humiliation on television. But what makes her political action different, she continued, is that it derives from life. Love and death become the motivation for her involvement in politics and her relation with the public is essentially affective.

## A Feminine Form of Autobiography

The new and typically feminine form of political autobiography corresponds particularly well to this affirmation of affectivity. Like Gisèle Halimi, Françoise Giroud, Huguette Bouchardeau, Elisabeth Guigou, and Ségolene Royal, Michèle Barzach interweaves personal memories (her prologue), a critique of the political system (her epilogue), and a policy manifesto (the body of her text). The second part of Barzach's book is devoted to seeking and proposing social and political changes for France and beyond. The final chapters situate Barzach's own itinerary within the emerging political history of women, from the false universalism of the 1789 Revolution through the century and a half of misogyny that left women passive citizens until 1944. Barzach notes with regret the disappearance of significant political women in 1993, Françoise Giroud, Monique Pelletier, Frédérique Bredin, Gisèle Halimi, and Yvette Roudy (even though they were women of the left). She retells the story of quotas and its transformation by the ongoing movement for parity. Barzach foregrounds parity as the new and central political cause.

Asked about the parity movement in her interview with me, Barzach spoke of the harmony of opinion and the very real warmth between the five women of the left and the five from the right in the parity manifesto group of which she was a member. Yet she considered that the government sponsored Observatoire pour la parité was "an absolute front." The left had made some moves toward parity, easier for them than for the right because they did not require removing politicians from presently occupied positions. The right, she stated, "hasn't moved and won't move."

In the *Encyclopedia of Political Women*, Barzach is portrayed with sympathy as a woman abused by the system. The presentation confirms Barzach's autobiographical self-portrait, and indeed the image created in my own interview: "She leaves many with the image of a sincere woman, treated unfairly, the impression of a missed rendezvous between the political world and a whole generation ready to identify with her spontaneity, her dynamism and her faith in the future."[36]

## *Yann Piat and the Godfather: "Alone, All the Way Up to the Back, on the Right"*

Further to the political right again, Yann Piat's text reveals a similar central theme despite the absence of any explicit identification with women.[37] She observes the problem of unequal power relations within marriage that led to her own divorce: "Michel can't bear any longer to be the husband of a 'public woman' or, after being Captain Piat, to have become the husband of Madame Piat."[38] Her analysis of the unequal gender relations within the Front national remains timid, masked by her own strong affective relation to the leader. Yet, although her story is a very traditionally organized account of a life and entry into the political world, it provides evidence of the kinds of non-rational, complex, emotional motivations or dependence that may lie behind women's reluctance to give up the protection of a political mentor. Issues of sexuality and gender are central in Yann Piat's work. Her political romance with her godfather, Le Pen, is not dissimilar to the symbolic relation of the extreme left-wing leader Arlette Laguiller with Trotsky. Asked to stand for legislative elections by the National Front leader, Jean-Marie Le Pen, and elected deputy for the Var region in 1986 at the age of thirty-six, Yann Piat was the only Front national woman in the Assemblée. Her book turns on her fascination with Le Pen as a father figure she must, in the final instance, resist and reject. Piat's work explores Le Pen's childhood as a ward of the state, which had left him with an enormous desire for revenge. This functions in many ways as form of self-deliverance from the spell he continued to cast on her. She finally brings herself to criticize the cult of the Front national leader, in a party where cohesion seems to be the central preoccupation and men are captives of their ambition. Piat admits that if she stayed for a time it was because of feelings of affection and her need for protection from "this guy who for a long time allowed me to believe that I was not alone in the world."[39] Excluded from the party by Le Pen in October 1988 for rebellion, her own isolation and nostalgia for paternal support after the break with the godfather are as evident in her autobiography as her revolt against Le Pen.

In *Seule, tout en haut, à droite*, Piat recounts her childhood as the daughter of unwed parents who were involved as journalists in defending French colonial power in Indochina and in Algeria. From this upbringing and her mother's friendship with Le Pen, who was Piat's godfather, she inherited many of the Front national tenets, which she enumerates in her autobiography as the need for more barriers to immigration, respect for France's traditional social structures, regret at the nation's diminished grandeur, and denunciation of socialist-Marxist aberrations. Piat's husband, a navy fighter pilot, was not very often at home. When Piat became involved in right-wing politics under the tyrannical paternal authority of Jean-Marie, she saw herself as bringing her femininity and her determination to "serve his cause." However, obliged to follow blindly the voice of her master, and more particularly perhaps, to give 9,000 francs of her salary a month to the Front national, she rebelled. Piat claimed that the party had not provided any of its promised administrative services. Refusing to vote against the RMI (a minimum living allowance paid to the unemployed over 25), Piat was subsequently excluded from the party by her mentor.

Yannick Piat, known as Yann, recognizes in her autobiography that she had been tricked ideologically and intellectually by Le Pen and warns of the need to look carefully at the credentials of the leaders of the future—to find men who will have the vocation of "shepherd" and not of charlatan, she writes. But she also registers the great emotional disappointment she experienced: "I loved Jean-Marie. I detested Le Pen. Farewell Godfather!" The metaphors are again revealing when Piat compares her lack of enthusiasm for the new center-right parties she tries to join, with her early intense commitment to Le Pen. There are, she writes, marriages of convenience that are more promising than marriages of passion. Piat became a member of the UDF, feeling nonetheless that she had betrayed her Front national electorate.

Yann Piat's autobiography also mentions her difficulties as the only woman on her floor in the National Assembly quarters. For example, there were the showers in groups of five in the middle of the corridor with no separate provision for women. She writes of her shock at finding a swastika painted on her garden gate, and the inner struggles whenever she left her two daughters to go to Paris. She too draws moral lessons from her experience of being a woman in politics: "To succeed in a career, a woman must look like a young girl, behave like a lady, think like a man, and work like a horse."[40]

In an interview with Michèle Barzach in December 1996, I asked the politician if she knew of the reasons behind the mysterious assassination of Yann Piat. The UDF *députée* was killed by two motorcyclists on a country road in the Var region in February 1994, while on her way home in her chauffeured car. Like many of the political women to whom I posed this question, Barzach answered that she had had no contact with Piat because she saw the Front national as a major enemy. But in her view, Yann Piat had reacted as any woman would have done in what was perhaps an overzealous moral fight against the drug mafia that had been implicated in making Piat's own daughter an addict. Although she was a controversial figure in her political family, Yann Piat, it would seem, was not a victim of her "friends" in the political world but rather of the bullets of mythomaniac gangsters.[41] The probable candidate for the mayor's office in Hyères paid dearly for her pretensions to power and it may not have been merely a coincidence that Yann Piat was a woman.

The first-person narrative used by Piat is based on the chronology, causality, and referential aesthetic that characterize conventional political memoirs. Her text holds a mirror to the political world in a very traditional form. It does not experiment with the radical alternation between the personal and the public that marks the autobiographical writing of Bouchardeau, Halimi, Royal, Guigou, Barzach, and even Laguiller. But in its staging of a battle with the domination of the strong prince and a confessional court scene, in its discussion of the particular situation of political women and their social and moral concerns, its moral lessons, including the eschewing of masculine forms of power, the content of Piat's extreme right-wing autobiography might well also be labeled "feminine."

## The Scissors Problem of Female Gender

The "scissors" problem of female gender—as old as gender itself and "more intractable than either conventional or feminist political analysis has fully recognized," in the words of the researcher, Jenny Chapman—is present directly or implicitly in almost all of the autobiographies examined in this chapter, from the extreme left to the far right.[42] Women are caught, claims Chapman, between their female gender and their aspirations in the world. The public sphere and its dominant values—a work world that demands availability and resistance to stress, a political world that requires material resources and public status, both marked by hierarchical relations—are not adapted to women's situations or to their other obvious (reproductive and caring) roles. Feminism remains controversial, perhaps because it has such profound implications for women's lives. The laws of recruitment that arise from this situation, as Chapman demonstrates, are that whatever resources are associated with success among men, women will have less of them, and whatever distinctive attributes women possess by virtue of their gender will be of little use to them when they compete on equal terms with men. The only "right" qualities, Chapman claims, are those possessed by winning men.[43] (Men, too, are submitted to this selection based on particular kinds of attributes and competitive performance to establish the winners and the losers.)

Most of the women's political autobiographies we have examined attempt to demonstrate that women too can desire to "win," but in their own manner, and that they are increasingly putting up a struggle both to escape allegiance to the father and to possess some "right" qualities that are not those of men. These "right" female qualities are shaped in rather different ways by the ideological contexts, right- or left-wing, from which political women emerge.

Nonetheless, it could be argued that much in the recycled or circulating material in these women's autobiographies remains idealized or incompletely analyzed, perhaps also touched by the *angélisme* of which Gaspard accuses Halimi. Like male political memoirs and autobiographies, these women's autobiographies could be accused of simplification, essentialism, naive optimism, or even self-interest. They have a new and significant message to tell—but perhaps also to sell. The economics of publishing, and in the French case, the politics of publishing, may have some influence on the truths told in these autobiographies by French political women about which the texts themselves remain silent. The pact of sincerity and truth covers truth only at certain superficial levels.

These women writers tend to adopt the discourse of empowerment and to eschew masculine forms of power. But power is not given up willingly and, as another theorist (Frey) suggests, if men who benefit from their power superiority have more access to structural power than women, and more of the resources that translate into power, there is no reason to expect them to give up their power. To get this power, or to hold it to redefine power, women do need to exercise "power over" or else, they must choose not to do so and to relinquish power. Thinking through empowerment, the feminist theorist Deutchman sees that "power to" pertains less to "feminist" than to "outsider" and wonders how long outsider status can remain uncorrupted, how long it takes for resistance to become collaboration, for "power to" to become "power over."

Deutchman critiques Flammang's assertion that women do not want power at someone else's expense (1983) as quite impractical in the oppositional win-lose fields of politics where others do not share the ideal of mutual support in realizing desired goals. She concludes that a feminist theory of power must be historical, structural, and non-essentialist. It must account for the evidence that argues for a convergence in men and women's behavior, delineate what is specifically feminist about "empowerment" and show how non-hierarchical behaviors can be politically effective. The autobiographies examined above have barely begun to engage with this challenge of defining the feminine empowerment they lay claim to.

The sociologist Bourdieu analyzes the field of power in terms of relations of strength and struggle and attempts to change the structures of power.[44] But these relations exist between equals, among peers, among "men." The political space is presented as one of a play, that is, to echo Derrida, as an infinite substitution of signs. In this context, Le Douré cites Hannah Arendt's characterization of Nixon's Vietnam politics as de-realizing and unreal to the point of being a product of the imagination, so great was the gap between the facts of the situation and the actions taken.[45] Mitterrand's decision to sink the very small and relatively harmless nuclear-protest yacht, *Rainbow Warrior*, in the port of Auckland, could similarly be seen as the result of the belief in a (non-existent) worldwide conspiracy or plot and a subsequent end-game set up against an imaginary enemy. Or again, the much more sinister fantasy of Hitler and Goebbels that Germany was the victim of an international Jewish conspiracy led to an unthinkably disordered end-game that presented itself as order, rationality, and strength. Opposed to this homogeneous, if hierarchical, masculine political space of power play, and enabling it to function, is the feminine domestic space, characterized not by game but by service.

For Freud, too, women are excluded from the process of civilization and from this masculine space of power play. This means, says Françoise Duroux, that Freud assigns women the role of sexual beings, the role of "nature" necessary for the production of its opposite, "civilization."[46] The late Petra Kelly of the German Green party argued, as do our feminine autobiographies, for an injection of community values into politics; one might say of feminine service into masculine game. However, Le Douré's argument is one of women's deliberate absence from a political space with which they are incompatible, rather than one of women's exclusion. Any change in reality or in people's perceptions of the conditions that make this gendered division and hierarchy necessary, according to Bourdieu, would indeed undermine domination, defined as the setting up of social identities as invariants, without leaving space for reciprocity and subjective choice. Many of our women's autobiographies are beginning to explore the question openly of where women should situate themselves in relation to the separate present spaces of "game" and of "service." In this respect, these texts are publicly undermining the invariable and eternal "masculine domination" that Bourdieu stages and analyzes.

## Notes

1. The political women's autobiographies discussed in this chapter include most of the major works (significant publications by publicly visible women) published before the end of the millennium. Some selection was necessary and this was based on the principle of including autobiographies across the political spectrum. None of these autobiographies have yet been commercially translated from French into English.
2. See Patricia Latour, Monique Houssin, and Madia Tovar, *Femmes et Citoyennes*, pp. 88–95 for a portrait of Halimi.
3. Gisèle Halimi, *Le lait de l'oranger* (Paris: Gallimard, 1998).
4. On the bench of the accused were the minor Marie-Claude Chevalier, raped by a classmate, Marie-Claude's mother, herself a victim of the shame and difficulty of being an unwed parent, and a work friend who had "helped out" with the abortion out of a sense of feminine solidarity.
5. These included her interventions in favor of introducing reimbursement of an abortion procedure (Interruption Volontaire de Grossesse), a "mixité" law to prevent part-time work from becoming wholly female (80 percent of part-time work was done by women in 1981; 83 percent in 1991), her non-support of a law giving police increased powers of checking identity papers, and her question to the government on the danger, high cost, and uselessness of the Superphenix nuclear reactor.
6. Gisèle Halimi, *Une embellie perdue* (Paris: Gallimard, 1995), p. 24.
7. Ibid.
8. Françoise Gaspard, *Madame le...* (Paris: Grasset, 1979), p. 213.
9. Elisabeth Weissman, *Les Filles, on n'attend plus que vous* (Paris: Textuel, 1996), pp. 51–53.
10. Ibid.

11. Ségolène Royal, *La Vérité d'une femme* (Paris: Stock, 1996), p. 80.
12. Ibid., p. 114
13. Benoîte Groult, "Cachez ce féminin," *Le Monde*, 11 June 1991.
14. Ségolène Royal, *Le Monde*, 9 March 1990.
15. Ségolène Royal, "Une torera, une deputée," *Le Monde*, 31 May 1996.
16. "Je ne suis pas intimement convaincu que ce soit le meilleur combat pour les femmes." In Ségolène Royal, *La Vérité d'une femme*, p. 84.
17. "la ministre déléguée à l'Enseignement scolaire" in *Le Point*, 20 September 1997, p. 18, for example. In the same issue of *Le Point*, a short news item announces that "la ministre de la Justice, Elisabeth Guigou" is unhappy at the small number of responsible positions held by women in the Justice Department and is requesting her ministry to give women candidates preference as often as possible.
18. Ségolène Royal, *La Vérité d'une femme*, p. 27.
19. Hervé Algarrondo, *Le Nouvel Observateur*, 30 July—5 August 1992, pp. 32–33.
20. Jacques Baguenard, Jean Maisondieu, and Léon Metayer, *Les Hommes politiques n'ont pas d'enfant* [Political men do not have children] (Paris: PUF, 1983).
21. Interview with Antoinette Fouque by Elizabeth Guigou, in *Etre femme en politique* (Paris: Plon 1997), pp. 234–235.
22. Elisabeth Guigou, *Etre femme en politique*, p. 28.
23. *L'Express*, 7 November 1996.
24. Jenny Chapman, *Politics, Feminism and the Reformation of Gender* (London: Routledge, 1993), p. xix.
25. Arlette Laguiller, *C'est toute ma vie: Une femme dans le camp des travailleurs* (Paris: Plon, 1996), pp. 169–192.
26. Claude Chabrol has made a film based on this story —*Une Affaire des femmes.*
27. "Pour me donner du courage, je me dis 'vas-y, t'es une femme!'" Elisabeth Weissman, *Les Filles, on n'attend plus que vous*, p. 70.
28. Alice Saunier-Seïté, *En première ligne* (Paris: Plon, 1982).
29. Alice Saunier-Seïté, *Remettre l'état à sa place* (Paris: Plon, 1984).
30. Michèle Alliot-Marie, *La Décision politique: Attention! Une Republique peut en cacher une autre* (Paris: PUF, 1983).
31. Elisabeth Weissman, *Les Filles, on n'attend plus que vous*, pp. 61–64. Weissman feminizes all forms except *député.*
32. Michèle Barzach, *Vérités et tabous* (Paris: Seuil, 1994), p. 14.
33. Françoise Giroud, "Le combat actuel est individuel," *Liberation*, 8 March 1993.
34. Mangin et Martichoux, *Ces femmes qui nous gouvernent* (Paris: Albin Michel, 1991), p. 252.
35. *Le Monde*, 20 February 1990.
36. "Elle laisse à beaucoup l'image d'une femme authentique, injustement traitée, l'impression d'un rendez-vous manqué entre le monde politique et toute une génération prête à se reconnaître dans sa spontanéité, son dynamisme et sa foi en l'avenir." Véronique Helft-Malz et Paule Levy, eds., *Encyclopédie des femmes politiques*, p. 41.
37. Yann Piat, *Seule, tout en haut, à droite* (Paris: Fixot, 1991).
38. Ibid., p. 117.
39. Ibid., p. 167.
40. Ibid., p. 125.
41. An article in *Le Point* (no. 1313, 15 November 1997, pp. 76–79) exploring the evidence to date on the implication of local career politicians in the decision by the drug underworld of the Provence-Alpes-Côte d'Azur region to rid themselves of this political woman, is inconclusive. The mafia boss, Jean-Louis Fargette, assassinated in 1993 in Italy, may have had dealings with local Union Démocratique Française leader, Maurice Arreckx. Yann Piat was blamed by some in the underworld as being somehow responsible for the death of Fargette. In any event, Fargette's language toward Yann Piat is documented as threatening and coarsely sexist: "We're blowing that broad away, that interfering female. She's had it" (*On est en train de l'assassiner,*

*l'autre, la femme. On lui a filé le coup de grâce*). Piat had sought financial aid for her campaign from Fargette's Marseille accomplice but this was refused by Fargette who did not want Piat to be elected. It seems that the meeting fuelled the myths that led a bar-gang of young out-of-work admirers of the drug-leader to accept the mission of "blowing away" Yann Piat. The apparent organizer of the crime, the "Macama Bar" owner, Gérard Finale, had wanted to prove himself as strong man and take over Fargette's place.

42. Jenny Chapman, *Politics, Feminism and the Reformation of Gender* (New York: Routledge, 1993).
43. Ibid.
44. Pierre Bourdieu, "La Représentation politique," *Actes de la recherche en Sciences sociales*, no. 36–37 (1981).
45. Hannah Arendt, "Du mensonge à la violence," *Essais de politique contemporaine* (Paris: Calman Lévy, 1992).
46. In "Pouvoirs pouvoir," *Futur antérieur* 5–6, no. 25–26 (1995), pp. 51–65.

# 7

# Biographical Writing: Simone Veil, Edith Cresson, and Martine Aubry

Three biographies of contemporary political women were in print by the end of the year 2000: Maurice Szafran's *Simone Veil. Destin* (Simone Veil: A Destiny, 1994), journalist Elisabeth Schemla's discussion of Edith Cresson in *La Femme piégée* (A Woman Trapped, 1993), and *Martine Aubry: enquête sur une énigme politique* (Martine Aubry: Inquiry into a Political Enigma, 1997) by Paul Burel, editorialist for *Ouest-France*, and Natacha Tatu, journalist at *Le Nouvel Observateur*. Not surprisingly, these texts present portraits of three women whose lives and careers have been the most dramatic or successful. The status and style of the biographies is quite similar; all three books could be labeled journalistic, destined for the wider reading public. However, the realities of these women's lives as they emerge in interviews or in their own writing often differ more than slightly from those the biographies would lead one to believe. These differences appear to depend less on the desire for sincerity and truth of detail than on the position and contexts of the biographer. His or her subjective reading at a greater or lesser distance from the object of observation, and the very nature of the project of recovery affect the story. One of the primary factors affecting the writing of a biography is, once again, gender.

## Maurice Szafran's *Simone Veil. Destin*

In the convention of biography, just as in that of autobiography, we find that personal history is essential to understanding the professional *parcours* of a woman politician. Maurice Szafran's 1994 *Simone Veil. Destin* recounts in detail the story of Simone's father, André Jacob, born in 1890 in Alsace. Szafran portrays André as a man who believed fervently in the secular, egalitarian principles of the French Republic. Szafran

*Simone Veil.*

also notes that André insisted that his wife give up her unsuitable studies in chemistry to be a full-time wife and mother. Milou, Denise, and a son, André were born in Nice, followed by Simone, who made her entrance into a materially comfortable world in 1927; the economic crisis of 1929 brought on considerable financial difficulties.

The biographer documents the paternal influence in Simone Veil's life and then focuses on the Holocaust history in a chronological, coherent, and dramatic narrative. Szafran describes how on 17 June 1940, the family listened with anguish to Pétain's widely acclaimed speech declaring that France must make peace with Germany and on 18 June, to De Gaulle's call for resistance from London. As in most French families of the period, the energies of all were deployed in feeding the family. These shared difficulties were compounded by fears of de-naturalization and deportation as the Vichy government promulgated anti-Jewish laws and the uncomprehending André lost his right to defend his country as well as his right to work as an architect under the quotas established for professions.

On 9 September 1943, the Germans replaced the uncooperative Italian army serving in Nice. The 30,000 Jews from Germany and the ghettoes of Eastern Europe taking refuge from fascism in the cosmopolitan city of Nice were trapped. The Jacob family dispersed, and Simone was sheltered by one of her teachers. In December the director of the school, fearing the consequences of a possible raid by the Gestapo, asked

Simone not to return. With the help of friends and teachers, Simone continued to prepare for her *baccalauréat* and sat the exam, advanced to May 1944 because of the imminent Allied invasion. Szafran recounts how at the end of May, imprudently out walking in the street with a friend, Simone was stopped by the Gestapo. Her identity papers were immediately recognized as false. She was followed and all of her family eventually arrested.

After transit in the French camp at Drancy, Simone, Milou and their mother Yvonne found themselves in a cattle car bound for Auschwitz-Birkenau, recounts Szafran. Her brother and father were part of another convoy from which no one returned. If Simone and her sister survived a camp programmed to degrade and exterminate human beings en masse and the absurd death march to Bergen-Belsen in northwestern Germany in February 1945, it was only because of the urgency to protect and support their beloved mother. Yvonne died in Bergen-Belsen of typhus and exhaustion.

## *Comparing Biographical and Veil's own Autobiographical Accounts*

Veil herself tells rather different stories. Whereas Szafran analyzes Veil's life from the perspective of his own desire to understand the Jewish experience, Veil has always been reticent to discuss her experience at Auschwitz. She is very critical of Szafran's choice of subtitle and explained to me that this title, "A Destiny," was proof that the book corresponded to her biographer's way of thinking and not her own. Veil's focus, I would argue, is more particularly on the maternal legacy than on her father's influence.

I asked Simone Veil explicitly about her reaction to the recently published biography of her life in her austerely elegant office near the Invalides on 13 December 1996. Veil responded by sharing that Szafran's mother had been deported but had never spoken of her deportation. In her opinion a kind of "transference" between Szafran's mother and herself had been effected. Veil was also critical of Szafran for focusing on certain aspects of her life and neglecting others. He did not understand, for example, that she might not share his socialism. Her Europeanism, on the other hand, either did not interest him, or was not understood sufficiently for him to speak of it. But for her, Maastricht was the logical consequence of her deportation, the only solution. In her mother's words: "If we get out of this one day, we will either have to kill all Germans or find reconciliation." According to Veil, her Jewish origins are not the whole truth of her personality. Perhaps a biographer needs to love and understand his/her character, conceded Veil, but this had not been completely the case for Szafran.

Of the 75,000 Jews sent from Drancy in France to Auschwitz, only 2,500 returned. Szafran's narrative, pieced together from the testimonies of friends and fellow survivors, and from his own interviews with Simone Veil, results in an apparently seamless story. This contrasts with Simone Veil's own discreet and incomplete tale. Szafran's biography centers on the Holocaust, Veil's Jewish background and how these factors influenced her later relationship to Israel and her defense of human rights. In her autobiographical work *Vivre l'Histoire*, a talking book published by Antoinette Fouque in the series, "Voix des Femmes," Veil's need to bear witness to the Holocaust in the name of its victims but the impossibility of doing so is sketched out only in fragmented personal anecdotes. *Vivre l'Histoire* (Living History) goes beyond the Jewish story and beyond the strangeness of a Liberation whose myths of Resistance left little place for those seen as unresisting "victims." Veil's text focuses on her life as a woman and as a politician—in France and in a Europe that includes Germany. Szafran, on the other hand, includes a chapter on disillusionment with the way the memory of the Holocaust has been reconstituted in recent films and literature that is clearly closer to his own preoccupations than to Veil's. Veil's reactions have been to affirm the courage of the many French people who did stand up against oppression, as well as to castigate the betrayal of Vichy and collaboration. She notes in particular those in Nice who made great personal sacrifices to help her family and to protect her and others in the Jewish population.

The determining image in *Vivre l'histoire* is Simone's fierce, rebellious, resistance to her father and allegiance to her gentle and beloved mother. Simone Veil deplores the financial dependency of her mother on her father, recalling her mother's injunction that women should have their own profession. The often absent father is both loved and contested for his tyrannical authority over his family and his domination of his wife. Simone Veil recognizes, however, that in her own marriage in 1946 to the orderly, serious, politically ambitious *énarque* (graduate of ENA) Antoine Veil, she sought a possessive family head, repeating the pattern of the Jacob family. Antoine Veil needed great persuasion before allowing his wife and the mother of his three children to "work." Simone tells a story in which she adopted the social conventions of their circle, but did quiet battle for the right to her own profession, if not as a lawyer then, in a compromise, as a magistrate.

Although Veil's life may be seen to be a universal destiny and a form of bearing witness as Szafran claims, Veil's own accounts allow an alternate reading that includes the difficult tracing of a new political path for women. A path constructed step-by-step through the labyrinth of the competing needs for paternal legitimization and for personal freedom. Szafran does preface his chapter on Veil's action for women (*Pour les femmes*) with an interesting quotation from Veil: "In the condition of the Jew and that of women, there is something similar. This conviction comes from my childhood, from my mother."[1]

## *From Justice to Politics: Not Left but Center*

Maurice Szafran presents Veil's defense of civil liberties under the cover of a perfect establishment identity as evidence of her complicity with the values of the left. Veil herself claims that she is seeking a new and difficult politics of the center. Veil joined a party, the UDF, only because it was necessary to be a party member to take her seat in the European Parliament. In her interview with me on 13 December 1997, she declared that Szafran was simply unable to understand many of her positions, including her self-distancing from the left. To some extent, this lack of understanding is also the case with respect to Veil's feeling for the significance of her position as a woman.

After the birth of a third son in 1954, Simone Veil began her studies to become a magistrate. In 1970, she was nominated general secretary of the Conseil Supérieur de la magistrature. Szafran quotes the portrait in *Le Monde* of 14 March 1970, enumerating the credentials that legitimated her position:

> Madame Veil is forty-two years of age. Deported very young, she holds a degree in law, studied at the Institute of Political Science, and has spent all of her career in the Justice Department. Married to an *inspecteur des finances*, mother of three grown children, she is a little woman, dark-haired and charming, reserved and discreet.

Szafran does not analyze this media presentation or its legitimization of the woman in politics by her recognizable family situation. We note that all the parameters are here for the standard description of a woman in high office—physical appearance, family status, husband's profession, and children. In this case, Veil's status as deportee, her educational background, and professional itinerary are also accorded some importance. A woman biographer, a Schemla for example, would have been more likely to have noticed and commented on this gender role stereotyping.

## *Minister of Health: The Difficult Legalizing of Abortion*

Veil's best-known political fight was for the abortion law. The story of the difficult reform of the repressive reproductive legislation of 1920, and of the new law to which Veil courageously put her name, has been told from a number of perspectives. From a feminist point of view, Gisèle Halimi, Françoise Gaspard, and Antoinette Fouque deplored the limitations of the 1974 Veil law legalizing medically supervised termination of pregnancy.[2] But all feminists applauded Veil's courage, her commitment to the goals of just and workable laws guaranteeing equality and dignity for all. In particular, the human emotion and experience she brought to her cause were recognized. The story told by women also makes it clear that the best hope for effective action was to work through influential men.[3] President Giscard wanted to move things forward for women according to Veil herself, who praises his will and political acumen. Prime Minister Chirac was not particularly in favor, considering it to be "women's business" (*un truc des femmes*). The center-right Giscard d'Estaing was elected president in 1974 with 54 percent of women voting for him. To pass his promised reform of the abortion legislation, he somewhat reluctantly decided to offer Veil the Ministry of Health.

Szafran noted that as a Jewish woman, less open to attack by Catholic opposition, Veil lent legitimacy to Giscard's attempt to pass this difficult government bill. Her moderation, record on human-rights issues, legal training, down-to-earth non-theoretical approach, and careful avoidance of any discourse of women's rights gave the proposed new law a chance of being accepted. Françoise Giroud, who had already declared herself in favor of legalized abortion in *L'Express* in 1972 would have been provocative to the right wing. Describing the debate herself, however, Veil writes that men would not have been submitted to the very personal attacks and to the "vulgarity" that she faced. Both Szafran and Veil herself observe that Veil felt deeply about attacks on her as a "Nazi" guilty of a crime against humanity "worse than Auschwitz," on her planned "genocide of babies," and on her assault on the integrity of the "race," and its "moral fiber."

It is an image from the exhausting and ferocious two-day televised parliamentary debate that figures emblematically on the front cover of Adler's *Les Femmes en politique*. Simone Veil appears in Adler's now well-known photograph, head bowed, weeping on the parliamentary benches. According to Adler's text, the image represents a courageous and sincere woman defending her abortion bill amendment by amendment before a pack of animals screaming for blood. But, as Adler points out, the public saw Veil's temporary moment of weakness as an indication of her humanity. Perhaps because, as Indira Gandhi's biographer suggests for Indira in a similar context, the public saw a woman hounded by predatory males and came to her protection, or perhaps because it recognized injustice.

Maurice Szafran does see that the IVG (abortion) debate was instrumental in modifying the public perception of both politics and women in politics. Simone Veil, he writes, did not produce the crisp, confident, polished pronouncements of her male colleagues but introduced her own more natural, less rigorously linear and logical discourse into politics. Szafran says her presentation was direct, but often hesitant and notes that the public perceived it as more real, spontaneous, and closer to their own experience.

Veil's own voice and in particular her down-to-earth anecdotes about the ambient misogyny in politics and her own responses to it pepper the new journalism on women in politics and other political women's texts. How could she fail to be irritated when an airline steward offered her *Elle* rather than the single remaining copy of *Le Monde* she had requested? Despite her new position as minister, notes Veil, she continued to accompany her husband to his political functions as supportive wife. At the same time, she asked that the two male police officers assigned to her protection be replaced by women. In her political battles, Veil's voice has been disconcertingly outspoken. She has consistently demonstrated that being "little" and "discreet" and "charming" were not the feminine qualities she was bringing to political life.

Veil considered Mitterrand to be devious. After you've shaken hands with Mitterrand, she said, you really have to count your fingers. Seeking an elusive centrist coalition, she was a supporter of the twelve *salopards* (bad guys) in 1989 who wanted to change the archaic structures of the right. Simone Veil has always been a personal friend of Jacques Chirac, whose warmth and open political ambition she appreciated. Yet, she stated openly that Chirac was not a political leader of the order to lead France.

Veil claims that it took the urging of her three sons and her husband for her to decide to take advantage of her great popularity among the electorate in 1993 and serve in the Balladur government. Here she stood out in her Chanel suits as a woman, but a woman of experience. Her portfolio of minister for associations, health and by her own insistence in 1993, urban affairs, was a massive one. In answer to my question on the significance of Veil's role in the reformist Balladur government, the director of the National Foundation for Political Science Alain Lancelot characterized her as a left-flank player, astutely placed by Balladur to be a brake on the hard-line right-wingers Pasqua and Séguin.[4] The language Lancelot used, loaded with gender-trait and gender-role stereotypes and the corresponding implicit judgments was instructive. Lancelot stated that the centrists in the "social" area and the right-wing in the "economic" arena would prevent Veil from "gushing feeling" (*dégouliner de sentiments*). The implication was that the feminine "heart" would be kept in check by the hard (masculine) world of realities and economics. This was not, in Lancelot's formulation, a tribute to Veil's new language or politics of justice and compassion.

One of the most popular ministers ever, Veil was not given any position in the Juppé government of 1995 and remains acrimoniously detested as difficult and authoritarian by many in the establishment. The Catholic magazine *La Vie*, however, classed this Jewish woman as second in the land for living Christian values. For some commentators, Veil's public popularity may have come partly from her maternal image, her image as a *femme de coeur*, and her courage as a survivor. Most women writers acknowledge that it also derives from her work as a politician, her competence, her lived defense of women's difference and role in government in a distinctive centrist feminine voice.

## *Veil on the Otherness Women Bring to Government*

Simone Veil herself has claimed that there are women in political life (among whom she would appear to place herself despite her own increasing taste for political power) whereas there are political men. In her intervention in 1993 at the Paris colloquium on parity, Veil was asked whether an equal number of women and men in parliament would change the situation. Approaching the question from a number of angles, and not without apparent contradictions, she mused that perhaps once they were present in equal numbers, women's behavior might become less specific. Women presently selected for office, she speculated, often possess a certain authoritarianism, and this is more particularly the case where they are a minority and have to defend themselves. The situations they experience are becoming closer to those lived by men but women, nonetheless, remain profoundly different. Their difference lies, according to Veil, not in their proverbial gentleness but rather in other aspirations, other needs, other ways of expressing themselves, necessary for balance in society.

> Men don't know what daily life is. They tell you they meet a host of people. It's not true. They meet activists and supporters. If you don't have something to tie you to reality, you lose your footing.[5]

Veil agrees with Halimi that the difference between the sexes could be the true driving force of equality.

In her interview with Elisabeth Weissman and speaking for the pedagogical feminist publication on women in politics *Les Filles, on n'attend plus que vous* (Young Women, We're Waiting Just for You), this political woman presents her own career as atypical. The choice of the prince in 1974, she is convinced that men, reluctant to give up their place, see women as rivals. They share a code of speaking, of living together as at hunting parties, says Veil, a way of creating a group of faithful and devoted supporters around them. Women in politics disturb the status quo and are too independent. They do not seek to create the same affective relationships to support their leadership as do men. For them, she says, politics is a commitment, not a game. Veil appreciates what she describes as women's closer connection to daily life, enjoys working with women for their authenticity, and wonders how young mothers manage to hold office. Noting that the European deputies, for example, are never at home, she remarks: "my husband would never have stood for it. But that was our generation."[6] Veil's own answers are very definite; her personal contexts, resolutely middle-class, based on family and a particular limited and privileged social circle emerge clearly as formative in her discourse.

## *Truths and Limitations of the Interview*

Both Veil's own text *Vivre l'histoire* and her interview with me tell a story that is different from Szafran's biographical tale. The interview, of course, also has its own agenda. Foregrounding the personal anecdote, the personal opinion, the individual voice and body language in a way that the biography or the autobiographical voice does not, my interview with Veil provided a sense of her down-to-earth and forceful manner of expression. Simone Veil's powerful physical presence and her gestures added meaning to her surprisingly unselfconscious words—conveying conviction, a certain warmth, and the impression of a determined personality. The content, however, was largely a repetition of ideas that I had encountered elsewhere, particularly in her other interviews and speeches. This interview reinforced my earlier conclusion on the limitations and often political nature of the content of interviews. Some of Veil's responses were defensive, self-justifying, or self-enhancing, sometimes at the expense of others, such as the women victims (Giroud, Cresson, Barzach) whom she identified as having less emotional independence than she herself had shown. Despite my resistance to the new popular myth of Veil as the forceful and popular political woman, which we were both bringing to our conversation, my overall sense was of a strong, confident, and very charismatic woman.

To my question on the influence of her father on her life decisions, Veil once again recalled the difficulty she had as a child accepting that her mother had to account for, or hide, the money she had spent on her children. She insisted that her own fierce determination to seek economic independence came from her profound admiration for her mother. Following through on this thought that women needed independence from men, Veil discussed the issue I had raised of "paternal" protection. She remarked that Françoise Giroud, who had always put forward the idea of sentimental independence in her editorials, had in fact attempted suicide when she was abandoned by her partner. Michèle Barzach, too, had believed that she was able to be independent of Chirac but she had not had the strength of position to do this. Despite her beliefs, this emotional relationship had invaded her life; she, too, had lost her gamble, claimed Veil. Veil observed that she herself did not feel as vulnerable to losing her independence through political dependence (on the prince) perhaps, she reflected, because of the events she had lived through. She had known the price of any measure of independence and been willing to pay for it, as in 1989 when she drew up her own list of candidates and lost the election. (Veil seemed to be unconcerned that she was setting up somewhat invidious comparisons with other women in politics. It is of significance that the ground she selected as the most significant for critique and ranking was the level of emotional autonomy.)

Veil recognized the sexism in French politics. She repeated two of the examples circulating at the time among women politicians of the unacceptable aspects of the "distinctiveness" of French traditions in this area. The first was the extraordinary spectacle of the two "wives" in church at the funeral of a president (Mitterrand) in a Catholic country. The second was the remark made the previous day by an apparently "perfectly decent" Socialist *député*, Cathala in response to an indignant speech by a middle-aged deputy, Suzanne Sauvaigo. Sauvaigo had been protesting about the rape of a young policewoman when Cathala quipped: "Well, that would hardly be likely to happen to you."[7] Veil is repeating an example that circulates through my interviews with many of the parity political women in that year.

### *Veil: The Private is the Public and My Major Work is for Women*

Responding to my questions on her public image, Veil believed that the image she projects is, above all, reassuring. Ordinary people, she said, identify with the fact that, for her, personal dramas and private life are more important than public events. Asked about her major contribution, Veil thought that this lay in her work for women. The mail she received showed that she had become a model, "a woman like us," as opposed to Françoise Giroud, for whom, she declared, she had great admiration but who was seen as an elitist journalist.

The curiously mitigated and non-left-wing character of Veil's feminism and the essentialist nature of her own understanding of (practical) women emerges in her interview responses. Although there was sincerity in her concern for women, and although she expressed a momentary regret for the more adventurous personal life her friends had been urging her to live, her own private life and family values have clearly remained conservative. Veil observed that she continued to make concessions to her own husband's career, such as agreeing to give up a dinner that interested her to accompany him. Veil recounted how she had advised her daughter-in-law to make more traditional concessions to her husband in the interests of keeping her marriage together.

Many of the themes that characterized the autobiographical writing by women were touched on in this interview, in part, of course, because of the nature of my questions. Veil's responses demonstrated the remarkable coincidence of women's concerns not made evident by Szafran. These concerns included the struggle with the need for legitimacy from the prince, the foregrounding of the maternal legacy and of women's potential political contribution through difference, the private as the political, and the obstacles such as sexism preventing women from achieving high political office.

In conclusion, the interview produced a rather different portrait than the biography, each one revealing specific strengths and limitations and the influence of gender (and political color). Maurice Szafran has written what the American literary critic Janet Beizer has labeled "bio(auto)graphy," that is, a biography exploring concerns that derive as much from the recovery of a past, from his own "autobiography" as from Veil's life. Biography, in any event, cannot do full justice to the speaking voice and the multiplicity of identities of any person. A fuller, albeit subjective, portrait emerges over time in Veil's own writing and speech, the portrait of a pioneer in a new political path for women working through the competing needs for paternal legitimization and for liberation.

## Elisabeth Schemla's Biography of Edith Cresson, *La Femme piégée*

There is no unmediated truth of a political life. I have suggested that Maurice Szafran's bio(auto)graphy reveals his history, personality, and preoccupations as much as it illuminates those of Simone Veil. This may be somewhat less true of the relationship between Edith Cresson and the teller of her story since both are women and share similar left-wing political convictions. Still, the never-neutral biographer, like the reader, necessarily brings her/his experiences and purposes to the reading.

The biographical study of Cresson by the well-respected journalist Elisabeth Schemla has its own political ends. Recently appointed editor-in-chief of *Le Nouvel Observateur*, Schemla is one of the few high ranking women journalists. Her text is partially a product of the rivalries and insider stories of political journalism. Schemla characterizes Edith Cresson as a woman politician trapped in an impossible situation, the sacrificial victim of dying socialism and living misogyny. Schemla argues that the media are unable to go beyond female appearance, presenting women as sexual animals out of place in politics. The sexism of the media world was something that Schemla would have known from intimate experience. Her story highlights the existence of archaic psychological fears that continue to make women in French politics appear illegitimate and are recycled by the media. In this respect, it is very similar to some of Françoise Gaspard's autobiographical revelations.

Born in 1934 in a middle class family, in Schemla's account, Edith Cresson had defiantly turned her back on a conservative, constricting mother, a strict Catholic education, and the hypocrisies of occupied France. Edith discovered her heroes in the male figures of the Resistance, the wartime family friend Marcel Lenz who was deported to Mauthausen and, later, François Mitterrand as founder of the Socialist party.

On 15 May 1991, Edith Cresson became the first woman prime minister of France. Edith appeared to have taken a last male bastion by storm with her charm and energy. Then, before the end of April 1992, as Schemla puts it, she had been abandoned by François Mitterrand, stoned by her Parti socialiste colleagues, lynched by the press, and disfigured by the *Bébête Show*. Schemla's metaphors of aggression on the female body are not innocent. Cresson was unwillingly forced to leave the government. Schemla's subtitle, *La Femme piégée* (A Woman Trapped) suggests that the female politician's fall from power was predetermined by her gender and the nature of her relationship to the political prince, not to mention the tradition of male politicians to "hunt in packs," as the influential right-wing *député* Philippe Séguin put it. In any event, the woman journalist cumulates metaphors that recreate the political world as masculine and feral.

## *The Man behind the Throne?*

Schemla notes that Edith Cresson was fifty-seven when she became prime minister. Her age and the presence of her husband and two daughters should have helped her image. Yet her relationship with her special advisor Abel Farnoux was immediately an object of speculation. Was he pulling the strings? Her portrait on the *Bébête Show* (a satirical evening television program that lampooned the ruling elites) was based quite shamelessly on sexual stereotypes, observes Schemla. Opposite Kermitt the frog (Mitterrand), Stephane Collaro and his two colleagues created a slinky and very sexualized panther, "Amabotte" (At Heel), to do the Frog President's every bidding.

Other women commentators, too, share the thesis that Cresson suffered from the protection of the prince. The head of the National Secretariat for Women's Rights of the Socialist party, Edwige Avice, claimed that the men of the party only tolerated women to the extent that they are their lovers or their invention. Edith was seen as the "favorite" of the men—a modern version of Madame de Maintenon, the mistress of Louis XIV. It was, paradoxically, Edith's reluctance to complicate her relationship with the party leaders by playing the rare woman card or indeed by working with Edwige Avice, that made her chances of success with Mitterrand and her male colleagues so much greater. At the congress in Rennes in 1989 her loyalty to Mitterrand, and her vote against Lionel Jospin, reinforced her status as the boss's favorite.

But, as Schemla insists, Cresson had as strong a political background as most of her peers. Responsible for the environment in the 1974 electoral campaign, she won political respect for a hard-fought grassroots campaign against the odds, in the conservative bastion of Châtellerault. Cresson finally became mayor of the farming district in 1983. Granted the third position on the list behind Mitterrand and Mauroy in 1979, and elected to the European Parliament after the 1981 Socialist victory, Edith Cresson was entrusted with the portfolio of agriculture minister in the new government. Operating in a very conservative rural environment traditionally hostile both to women and to the left, this provocative and free woman was accused of being a "stealer of husbands" and confronted by posters of the most sexist kind. "Let's hope you're better in bed than in the ministry" (*On t'espère meilleure au lit qu'au ministère*). Quickly embattled, she faced up to demonstrations and public protests and tackled the powerful agricultural union, the FNSEA, controlled by the Rassemblement pour la République (RPR). The more conciliatory and better-accepted Michel Rocard finally replaced her.

Edith Cresson was then given another masculine preserve, the Ministry of External Trade, at a time when the Socialists changed economic direction and were rapidly losing ground on all sides. In 1990, writes Schemla, unable to participate effectively in the preparation of the upcoming European Single Market (*Acte unique*) or to have any influence in a Rocardian government she considered to be too pro-market and pro-deregulation, Edith resigned. Like Martine Aubry, Edith Cresson had a sufficiently strong managerial background to begin a successful career in the private sector.

## *The Appointment of a Woman as Prime Minister: Mitterrand's Calculations*

Why did Mitterrand decide to appoint a woman as the new head of the government after the Gulf War in 1991 and, in particular, to recall Edith Cresson from her consulting firm? Schemla concludes that Mitterrand needed to appoint a non-careerist politician to attack the huge social-security deficit, to unify the industrial structures, and to stir up the set patterns of the political world. These reforms translated into the kamikaze appointment. The journalist bases this conclusion on an interview with the president on 13 November 1992. Mitterrand had calculated that a woman might be less contested by the opposition afraid of appearing sexist. He also felt that the appointment of a woman might woo back the increasingly disaffected female vote. Certainly Mitterrand's media and communications advisors were informing him that the current values were the "feminine" ones of humanitarianism, ecology, the search for harmony and connection. A woman prime minister might help restore general confidence in politics, and the bold anti-conformist move of appointing a woman might strengthen his own place in history. Despite these self-interested calculations, in Schemla's view, Mitterrand was nonetheless one of the few men in a closed and competitive political world to believe in the ability of women to exercise power.

Why Edith Cresson? There was only one woman with all the necessary qualities, Mitterrand told Schemla, and he had known that woman for more than a quarter century. In fact, as Giroud reiterates in her writing, Edith Cresson was one of the very few women to have followed the rules for entry, successively occupying positions of councilor, deputy, and mayor and fighting a battle for election at Châtellerault, where no man of the left wing had been willing to go.

Edith's relationship with Mitterrand was both her greatest strength and her major weakness. Schemla tells us that even when she was offered the position of prime minister, Cresson had doubts. Would Mitterrand give her the means to act, given that the other potential candidates would be hopping mad that a woman had snatched their due out of their grasp? Was she really the person for this high position? During the discussion with Mitterrand on 8 May, she put forward a comparison of her own and

Pierre Bérégovoy's qualifications. She considered she was less skilled in parliament than Bérégovoy and did not have the confidence of the business community he enjoyed. Cresson admitted that as an outsider to the party quarrels, she would be popular, but she felt the risk was that the mobilizing impact of surprise might be short-lived. Schemla indicates that, despite knowing that time was terribly short and her chances of success minimal, Edith Cresson accepted because she expected to have support from the party base. She felt she would be able to bring together the warring brothers since "the president would protect her."

The modern and dynamic image she sought, and that Mitterrand had asked of her, was in the end too non-traditional; free or blunt speech in the mouth of a woman offended. Her platform—pragmatic and moral—argues Schemla, was before its time.[8] Cresson's refusal to perfect and present a media image, and her often ill considered, off-the-cuff statements overshadowed most of her political messages. No one seemed to be listening to anything much other than the scandalous. No one was visualizing anything other than the deviant.

## *Scent of a Woman... The Pack Responds*

Seventy-three percent of the public polled approved of Cresson's prime ministerial appointment and French women were particularly appreciative. For Schemla, as for Sineau, Edith Cresson did not understand or exploit this affection or the responsibility she had as a woman toward women. It was not long before Edith's popularity polls went into rapid decline. As Schemla puts it, the "intruder" became a "rival" in the struggle for the best positions.[9] The party barons saw Mitterrand as a "grandfather," distributing largesse. In the press, difference manifested itself less in the reporting of any real change in government than in gendered ways of presenting the new prime minister. There was the interpretation given to Rocard's farewell kiss, for example. The departing Prime Minister Rocard kissed his rival and as Jean-Paul Huchon, the director of his cabinet interpreted this gesture for the *Journal du dimanche*: "A woman comes to Matignon. Everyone wants things to go well, so Rocard kisses the woman. That's what a woman is for, to be kissed."[10] The distance traversed since the suffrage debate during which one parliamentarian had stated "A woman's hand is to be kissed, not to hold voting papers" is not great. Yet Schemla suggests that it was specifically because Edith Cresson did not set out to charm the barons, because she turned her back on them in proud independence, that she lost the ensuing war.

On Anne Sinclair's popular current affairs television program *Le Point sur la table*, two evenings after the announcement of her appointment and before Edith had time to present her political plans, the nature of her illegitimacy and the backlash to her presence in power became evident. Edith was declared to be the publicity stunt and bluff of a president in political trouble, a puppet whose strings would be pulled by

Bérégovoy—a woman, in other words, without ideas or intelligence, a regrettable accident and an insult to political men. As Schemla puts it, the headlines of *Le Monde* the following day were already tolling her knell even before her baptism: "Cresson, for How Long?" A week earlier at her nomination, François d'Aubert had clamored: "He's giving us La Pompadour" (*On nous donne la Pompadour*). Jean-Marie Le Pen, for his part, had spoken of "the woman from the [Mitterrand] harem" (*la dame du sérail*).[11] The sexism Schemla analyzes is so stereotyped and so curiously unselfconscious that it speaks of the entrenched prejudices not only of the producers of the news but of the audience to which it is addressed.[12] In Schemla's analysis, the much-vaunted French femininity was manipulated to bring this woman in high office down to her proper (sexual) place and destroy her political credibility: "Edith Cresson is the mistress of the prince, his toy, a slut, an imbecile."[13] Edith Cresson would later describe the media representations as the sickening destruction of her image, and denounce in particular the suffering it imposed on her husband and daughters. Cresson, who had believed in the existence of virtual equality between the sexes, observed that photographers were always scandalously on the hunt for thighs and knees and the laddered stocking effect caused by an old scar. She claims the closeups continually taken of her rings and large earrings, as if these were signs of frivolity or incompetence finally led her to modify her normal physical appearance and tone down to severity and drabness.

Even some female journalists were less than understanding of Cresson's situation according to Schemla. For example, Claude Sarraute criticized Cresson's calling the humorists to order on the grounds of sexism. Sarraute claimed that Edith was asking for special consideration that men would not get. Interestingly, Sarraute's major criticism of Cresson was of what she saw as the latter's "aggressive lack of femininity!" confirming the too-much or too-little dilemma for political women required to remain "feminine."

The criticism of female politicians within the press as too feminine or too masculine is evident around the world. Even in a post-frontier, outdoors society like New Zealand where femininity is a less essential attribute in public women than in France, before Helen Clark broke through the barrier of unconscious public resistance to a woman in high office to be elected prime minister in 1999, the criticism of that leader of the Opposition was that she was "just like a man." Media reports said she should have her teeth and hair fixed, change her gravelly masculine way of speaking, smile more, dress differently, and be more "feminine." The campaign posters before the 1999 elections showed an air-brushed, attractive, smiling woman. The childless Helen had to simply refuse to enter into the "mothering" contest with her right-wing rival, Jenny Shipley to escape continuing criticism. Interestingly, once in power, Helen Clark appears to have won the sometimes grudging admiration of an electorate impressed precisely by her directness in speaking, her honesty, and her mountain-climbing temperament. Even the political media has shown some sympathy for this gender-bending image. Her predecessor and subsequent leader of the opposition, Jenny Shipley, on the other hand, had declared that she was foremost a wife and "Mum." Shipley had dressed a rounded and reassuringly feminine shape in discreet elegance, and purred her way softly if persuasively through media presentations and parliamentary speeches, always keeping any big stick well concealed. In mid 2001, the country was made aware of the complexity of issues around women in high public positions by a media fest when a very well-paid senior civil servant, Ms. Christine Rankin, took out a law suit against the government for unfair dismissal, alleging, much as Cresson had, that her distinctive style of dressing, short skirts and large earrings, had played a role in the non-renewal of her contract as the head of social services. Opinion was divided and Ms. Rankin was seen by some as provocative, by others as incompetent, but many women around the country including the leader of the opposition, Jenny Shipley, observed a short-skirt long-earring day in protest at what were perceived to be sexist attitudes at the heart of the government. Prime Minister Helen Clark refused to comment as her government defended itself against the charge of sexism by arguing that Ms. Rankin had not demonstrated the necessary competence. The allegations of overgenerous cleavage and "inappropriate" appearance and the counterclaims of the right of women to their personal style were left for the media to work with.

The media in France systematically criticized Edith's political action as well as the deviance of her physical appearance. The apprenticeship system was attacked as giving up on a traditional principle of the citizen's birthright to a general education (*devoir de culture*). The plans to repatriate illegal immigrants by air gave rise to a major outcry against these infamous "charter flights." After a virulent attack by her own party implicating Edith Cresson in the earlier scandal of the AIDS-contaminated blood in which she had had no part, Cresson had to withdraw the bill to indemnify the infected hemophiliac victims by a tax on insurance premiums. The creation of domestic positions with tax relief for families employing domestic help was less decried, but it was presented as the work of Martine Aubry, Cresson's labor minister.

Edith Cresson is, however, best remembered for the injudicious comments she was claimed to have made.[14] An overgeneralizing characterizing of the British as "25 percent homosexual" and not interested in women may not have merited quite the outcry from the British press that its republication occasioned in 1991, but it was unfortunate. The American television channel ABC used the remark for maximum media effect, calling in Flora Lewis of the *New York Times* to comment. The American journalist added her own observation that there had been rumors that Edith had been the mistress of Mitterrand, rumors that no one had ever denied. A further statement by Cresson was also making the rounds in the satirical political newspaper *Le Canard enchaîné* and echoed in the *Herald Tribune*, that the Japanese spend their nights thinking about ways "to get" the Americans and the Europeans. Cresson denied ever making this particular statement, although her outspoken opinions on the dangers of Japanese competition were well known.

In an earlier interview with Adler (28 November 1991), Cresson had declared that she did not speak the traditional political language, what she calls the hollow art of nineteenth-century oratory. Schemla judges this inability to speak the dominant discourse to be Edith's weakness. This is again the dilemma of too much or too little. If a woman on the benches of parliament shouts, she is a fury, a fishwife; a man who shouts is a great orator, protests a disillusioned Cresson.[15] She notes that "seventy-seven percent of French people said it was a very good thing to have a woman prime minister, but a lot of them didn't believe a word of it. Simply, they didn't dare to say the opposite."[16]

Perhaps misguidedly, notes Schemla, Cresson rejected the suggestion that she could improve her image by using the slogan *Edith Cresson, la dame du faire* (the action lady) in order to combat any image of *la dame de fer* (the iron lady). The latter appellation, bearing the stigma of virility, seems to have been applied to all mentally strong or determined women in power. Nicole Notat, reappointed at the head of one of the largest French unions, the CFDT, in 1996 and increasingly seen as a reformist figure after refusing to support the rigid interests of the railway workers in the fall strikes of 1995, has been labeled the "iron lady" and the "Czarina," despite her non-confrontational demeanor. Former New Zealand Prime Minister Jenny Shipley was most often characterized as "bossy" by those who disliked her.

The gap between the institutional status of the French prime minister—what was expected—and Cresson's speech and behavior was responsible for her rejection, concludes Schemla. The impression that Edith was under male influence—of Mitterrand, Farnoux, or Bérégovoy—along with the media scandals created by her less than careful or media-distorted personal comments were used against her. She was accused of lacking dignity. Schemla states that sure of her service to the president and the Republic, confident that she alone was exercising the power of her office, and immersed in what she saw as more serious political issues, Cresson did not appreciate the enormity of the gap between her own sense of herself and the media-driven public perception.

## *The Media: A Distorting Mirror on the Defensive*

In the weekly *L'Evènement du jeudi* in 1993, Stephane Collaro admits that the *Bébête Show* may have gone too far in its representations of Cresson, but argues that excess is a necessary risk to take for successful political farce.[17] She said some foolish things and "frankly," when the president chooses a physically attractive woman for prime minister there is some ambiguity, and comedians have the right to make jokes about this. The massacre was not her fault, but Mitterrand's, for sending the "poor girl" (*pauvre fille*) to the wolves without giving her time to study the issues—issues that she attacked with great energy but "with nothing in her head." Collaro added defensively that when Edith Cresson attacked the puppeteers, it was in the nature of things that they would respond aggressively.

In the same series, Jean-Marie Colombani, the chief editor of *Le Monde*, claims that Elisabeth Schemla's thesis that his newspaper had set out to destabilize this first woman prime minister was "incorrect." He declares that at the moment of Cresson's nomination, his paper alone had put forward the "analysis" that the president was making a huge mistake in flirting with populism and not remaining loyal to the then-prime minister, Michel Rocard: "Finally, those who knew the political players well had known for a long time that Edith Cresson did not have the ability to carry out these functions." By Colombani's own admission, then, Edith Cresson had been judged in advance and found wanting before she even took office. Behind the very defense offered by the press retroactively, in the choice of argument and language, the specters of women's illegitimacy are still clearly visible. Like Collaro, Colombani lays the blame on the "master" (*une erreur magistrale*), that is, on Mitterrand. But Colombani covers all bases, justifying *Le Monde's* reporting by claiming that Cresson was incompetent. There is no new evidence given for such a conclusion, just what is known by the initiated. Collaro and Colombani's self-defense is decidedly circular.

In his short interview with a journalist from *L'Evènement du jeudi*, Franz-Olivier Giesbert of *Le Figaro* also disavows any injustice on his part in relation to Edith Cresson. He admits that she had the courage to break "a number of taboos, initiating apprenticeships, within businesses, etc." The "etc." does limit the impact of his rare interest in the actual record of Cresson's government. This reticence is reiterated in Giesbert's central defense that a journalist's job is to "call a spade a spade" (*appeler un chat un chat*) when errors are made. This cliché of the "watchdog" function of the journalist hardly constitutes a sophisticated defense of the attacks made on female politicians like Cresson. Denying any media plot, Giesbert claims that Cresson's denunciation of the media is common to all failed politicians. He presents Cresson's subsequent rejection by the public as a function of her too-free speaking of her mind and argues that the public reacted violently and irrationally to this iconoclastic aspect of Cresson. Giesbert thus shifts responsibility from the press to its reader.[18] The associate director of *Le Nouvel Observateur*, Jacques Julliard, also speaks of an irrational public, but this time in its initial support for Cresson rather than its subsequent negative reaction. Julliard goes on to find Cresson was responsible for her own destruction.

> She arrived at Matignon with a huge capital of irrational support because she was a woman. She thought she could be Zazie at Matignon—that a change in

> style would help her to be accepted.[19] We can see with Balladur that France expects respectability, the respectability incarnated by Simone Veil at her level, and no one attacks her because she is a woman. Cresson, for her part, never understood the rules of the game. A prime minister has to be respectable, and the French people considered that she didn't represent them as she should.[20]

Julliard's analysis may be on target in the sense that respectability turns out to be particularly important for women even in a country where the public/private division has traditionally allowed the male heavyweights a measure of private freedom far greater than is found in Anglo-Saxon countries. Nonetheless, it is not totally convincing. Balladur, for all his respectability, failed in his bid for the presidency. And Veil may be respectable, but she has never been appointed prime minister. Once again, the choice of arguments and of language is revealing. Cresson did not meet the criteria or represent the French people as she should. She was somehow not legitimate and any pretext was a good one for proving her "incompetence" to govern or represent. The protection from which this attractive woman benefited was suspect.

In Schemla's reading the only things that kept Cresson from giving up the battle against the falling popularity polls, unemployment, the bullets of the opposition, and the media were her pride and fighting spirit, her determination to do her duty, and the conviction that her reforms were necessary to modernize the nation. She was supported by a few politicians only, including the competent and savvy, but in Cresson's case, somewhat impatient, Martine Aubry. Adler's conclusion from her interview with Cresson is that Cresson could not win against the weight of French institutions and the administration but that posterity would pay homage to her energy and to her belief in the Socialist program to change social conditions.

## *Two Paths Cross: Schemla's Biography Concurs with Cresson*

After her resignation, it was an embittered woman who met Mitterrand again on 4 May 1993 at the funeral of Pierre Bérégovoy. Cresson was convinced she was a victim of a Socialist plot and was angry with Mitterrand for not giving her the means to succeed and for abandoning her. In an interview for *Le Nouvel Observateur* in 1993, Cresson observed that she had believed that men and women had more or less equal opportunities in society until she became prime minister. She adds that she did not believe that the feminists understood the full extent of the misogynist functioning of the political class that treats women as competitors and outsiders. Mitterrand, too, protested his incomprehension of the resistance to Edith Cresson. He admitted that a certain antifeminism, much greater than he had suspected, permeated both the French public and the party.

Edith Cresson has internalized the metaphors used against her to claim a sense of having been thrown to the public like the "witch" in a witch-hunt. She concluded that the legitimacy accorded by the right to vote for women was insufficient for legitimate female representation. Legitimacy, Cresson claims, comes from the party apparatus and the media. Cresson states that there are a number of factors working against women in French politics. There is the *fait du prince*, the fact that the position of prime minister in France does not carry with it the full power to choose one's own ministers or to dissolve parliament, and the fact that women are still not considered acceptable for the presidency. In Cresson's embittered discourse, her greatest crime was to have demystified power. From a secret adventure of Titans reserved for the elect, she had brought it closer to the everyday world and revealed its machinations. On the personal level Cresson felt that she had made the wrong life choice.

Schemla's empathetic biography of Edith Cresson and her dissection of the linguistic mechanisms by which women are disqualified on the basis of their gender has been attacked as a feminist justification of the career of a less than competent politician. She has been criticized as appearing to want women to be given preferential treatment in a rough political world. Olivier Duhamel concedes that Cresson's errors might well have been a handicap, but he feels that being a woman in the circles of power was generally an advantage. In 1991, 49 percent of the French public polled approve of this new prime minister, almost the same number as those who had supported Laurent Fabius, who had also been nominated in the middle of a presidential term without elections. Only 31 percent consider being a woman a disadvantage. For Duhamel, this proves that Cresson had the benefit of the doubt and "contradicts the explanation given for her unpopularity later as being due to the machismo of the French."[21] Duhamel moves very quickly to this generalizing conclusion without analyzing the complexities that might lie behind the response to the ambiguous polling question. It did not ask "Do you want a woman as prime minister?" but rather "Do you think being a woman is an advantage?" The belief that women are favored and protected by positive action and by their rarity, coupled with the non-recognition of the kinds of obstacles women face, might well influence a "yes" that does not necessarily imply an endorsement of the action of a woman prime minister. Nor do such surveys reach the more deeply entrenched anxieties of identity and difference. In fact, following the televised debate in which Edith Cresson talked about sending undocumented aliens home by special flights, she initially obtained a 78 percent approval rating.[22] She was considered to be "likable" (79 percent) and easy to understand (85 percent) if the polls are to be given credence. Duhamel himself recognizes the passing effect of a warm welcome, the precariousness of the "woman-effect" and the findings registered by polls in general.

Hoping to win the people against the elites, Cresson lost both. By October, she had also lost the preference of women voters. Errors of political line, of style, of overconfidence, along with disappointed expectations, lead to the political accident according to Duhamel. Cresson's accidental unpopularity resulted in her dismissal but also made Mitterrand less popular and dragged Rocard down with the left in a general decline. The structural unpopularity of the regime, says Duhamel, due to the persistence of unemployment, the painful questions of immigration, and the financial scandals predated Cresson. Duhamel concludes that the change in prime minister could have helped lessen the problem, but the "accident" of Cresson's decline made it worse.

Reviewing *La Femme piégée*, the American academic George Ross also examines its thesis that the fate of Edith Cresson was in large part the responsibility of the misogyny of the Socialist elites and the French political class, along with her victimization by the press and the Bébête puppet.[23] Noting that as a journalist at *Le Nouvel Observateur*, Schemla may have had her own problems with her male competitors in journalism (Colombani, July, and Julliard), Ross nonetheless accepts her general argument. He adds that what is extraordinary about the situation is the degree to which the same elites have been able to stifle any debate about this issue since. Yet Ross also concludes that Schemla's own evidence shows Edith Cresson was "incompetent." The trail he follows leads to Erik Orsenna's political biography of Mitterrand, significantly entitled *Grand Amour*. In this work, Mitterrand's speechwriter critiques the Elysée under Mitterrand as the eroticized world of the Grand Séducteur and courtly/courtisanly love. This reading confirms the centrality of gender to the Cresson story.

## *Interview with Edith Cresson*

The centrality of gender was clearly evident in my interview with Cresson on 19 December 1996 at the Commission Européenne, 288 Boulevard Saint Germain, three years before Cresson was forced out of her position as European Commissioner for alleged nepotism. I have translated the major parts of this interview quite literally. Edith Cresson's words project a sense of her way of speaking that is very much part of her message.

**R.R.** How do you explain the gap between the public opinion that was so much in favor of a woman prime minister at the beginning of your term of office and the dramatic drop in popularity that appeared to show the superficiality of such an acceptance?

**Edith Cresson** [with some vehemence]. First of all, it is, in my opinion profoundly shocking to ask people whether they are in favor of a woman prime minister—the very idea of the poll—no one has ever asked if people were in favor of a male prime minister. Seventy percent said they were in favor, so a priori, except for those who lied, quite a few and 30 percent of those questioned were against, which is itself extraordinary, the question itself was shocking and the meaning lies in the 30 percent who considered it was not normal to have a woman in this position and dared to say so. The next issue is that the media and the polls work together in France. Journalists say something or other. Then they test the result of what they have said fifty times a day by opinion polls. In my case, this had nothing to do with my political action; only with my private person. Men are judged for their politics. Was Juppé's action in Corsica, his reform of taxes on wealth good or bad, for example? I carried out a political action over a wide spectrum and what interested the journalists was that I wore a chain around my neck with my name on it that my husband had given me and that I refused to stop wearing because I believe that symbols are very important, even if I'm considered old-fashioned. You have to fight for them [Edith Cresson pointed to the chain she was wearing].

**R.R.** Given the even greater unpopularity of the present prime minister, Alain Juppé, his difficulty in governing, do you see a real difference?

**Edith Cresson**. Yes, a fundamental difference. The first day of my job as prime minister, that very evening on the television, all of the journalists came together. Colombani... those who say "we're the elite," an extraordinary language, said it was a real catastrophe, not because I was a woman—they weren't stupid enough to say that—but because I didn't have the necessary qualities. I had been, in succession, agriculture, industry, external trade, and European affairs ministers. I had been elected as a local representative, mayor, deputy, *conseillère générale*, as a European deputy, a spectrum that relatively few men encompass, but despite all that, I could not be prime minister—you tell me why.

**R.R.** Did you understand what was happening to you?

*Edith Cresson.*

**Edith Cresson**. No. I became politically active when I was young and had no ambition. I looked after the things no one else wanted to do, the agricultural sector, and then young people and students. Well, I knew that one day, if we got to win the elections, I would probably have some responsible position. When the president proposed the Agricultural Ministry, an important portfolio, I knew that it was a "deliberate challenge" and I quite like challenges, so I accepted. I faced terrible opposition but it came from the right. What I hadn't expected was the machismo, the underhanded tactics, the deviousness.

**R.R.** Do you share the thesis of Elisabeth Schemla that you were a victim of very old misogynist reactions by the media and certain of your colleagues?

**Edith Cresson**: Given that Elisabeth Schemla is a friend—became a friend after her book—I'd say that her analysis is less than the truth (you can't tell all of the truth in any case), but what I saw, what I heard is unimaginable, indescribable: the insults, the screaming, the cowardice, too, and the slyness of the attacks in the press. Every Tuesday—the *Canard Enchaîné* comes out every Tuesday—on page two in the new format there are tidbits of gossip and there were whole columns of incredible stories about me, both invented and not. The story would say, for example, that Edith Cresson doesn't know what a staff member is and serves the coffee herself—for once it was true—but I don't see what's so extraordinary about that. What it means is that she is so incompetent at governing that she serves the coffee. So, I've seen the Queen of England serve coffee on television and I've seen men do it, too. But it reaches a level of frustration in them, I think, of fury because at the end of their political path they know they'll never be prime minister or perhaps never even minister.

**R.R.** Certain journalists criticized your relationship with Abel Farnoux and with François Mitterrand, and it has been said that you needed heroes or mentors. Are there elements of truth in all that or are we talking about the same phenomenon that casts Vincent Foster (who committed suicide during the Whitewater scandal) as Hillary Clinton's lover or attributes an Arab lover to Françoise Gaspard?

**Edith Cresson**: I don't think that's the case...

**R. R.** In Dreux. Gaspard recounts this in *Madame le ...*

**Edith Cresson**: Dreux is a racist city. At Chatêllerault, they didn't say that to me—they say that I give preference to the Arab population, that I allow them into the swimming pool free—a whole set of fantasies—that I gave Arab adolescents free scooters, only Arabs. Well, you know that France is very misogynist, fifteenth out of fifteen in Europe for the place of women. I'm not telling you anything you don't know. As for the fantasies about women, they're either too old or too young, too ugly or too beautiful, too much something or too little something else, and if she succeeds in something, it's because she has slept with a man who is the key—it's quite simple. And as for women in politics, some are needed, there's no way out of that. They're chosen the way you choose female poodles or mares—they take women because they are women. But, we on the left have had some remarkable women. As ministers, they were accepted. When I tried to set up a business training school for telephone operators, truck drivers, shop assistants, the money was refused. The model for a school has to be ENA. So you see the problem of women in France is not just a feminine problem but a problem of the selection of elites and of the way power is seen. Power is sacred and the key to the sacred is held by men, by definition. The simulacrum of the appearances of power is extraordinarily important for men and less for women. For women, to hold power is to have some active influence over events in society.

**R.R.** Where did you find the energy to stand up to all that, to continue; it must have been a heavy responsibility. Did you enjoy it?

**Edith Cresson:** Yes, a lot. I created things that appeared to me to be indispensable. I set up a system of apprenticeships that hardly existed in France. One hundred thousand young people were failing at school and leaving without training, with nothing. There were protests because I looked after these young people. The problem was one of what you might call ready-made ideas. That's the way French society is. French society needs to move forward. Women's practical and concrete competence are both all the more needed, and all the more contested because of this.

**R.R.** Certain initiatives weren't particularly successful politically—the journey to Clermont-Ferrand, for example.

**Edith Cresson**: What journey?

**R.R.** Wasn't there a train that went to Clermont-Ferrand to investigate unemployment... ?

**Edith Cresson**: That worked very well. We put all the government administrators who normally travel in chauffeured cars in a train and took them to Clermont-Ferrand to debate the unemployment question. There was no problem in taking a train. It worked very well.

**R.R.** I mention it because some political observers considered it to show a lack of political acumen.

**Edith Cresson**: Top government administrators taking the train—it was considered... it was practical and concrete. Everything one thinks is normal, if it is not pompous, empty of meaning, ineffective, is considered bad. The event was widely supported, and the debate was a consequential one. It's not a failure because it was criticized. Everything I did was criticized. It was a practical, concrete initiative.

**R.R.** What about your present job? Is it sufficient for you? Do you have possibilities for real action?

**Edith Cresson**: Yes, for example we set up a Second Chance School, which I opened in Marseilles with new pedagogical methods, with computers—we've brought in specialists from the American Accelerated School and from the Israeli School for Integration which has existed for fifty years and now helps Ethiopians and Ukrainians who don't speak the language—integration uses multi-media. In Marseilles alone, there are thousands of young people who drop out of the school with nothing—no one wants them—they're seen as socially disruptive. We're going to take five hundred, then a thousand volunteers, and different businesses have agreed to take them on. I couldn't ever have done that from Matignon. The new voluntary civic service will also train young people in the protection of the environment, care of the handicapped, work in disadvantaged neighborhoods. An apprenticeship system in the European Union will initially train 50,000. There's a number of such things I couldn't have done in power. I'm going around the monster instead of confronting it.

**R.R.** Do you plan on confronting the monster again?

**Edith Cresson**: Not under the same conditions.

**R.R.** Elisabeth Schemla called her book *La Femme piégée* (A Woman Trapped). In the *Encyclopedia of Political Women*, the title is given as *La Femme blessée* (A Woman Wounded). A Freudian slip or a misprint? Which of these two adjectives would you choose?

**Edith Cresson**: Neither of the two. I didn't like the title at all. And, if I was "trapped," I had my share of the responsibility. I wasn't tough enough with the president of the Republic over the composition of the government. I should have said no to a certain number of things. He was very much under the influence of Laurent Fabius, who had a list of people and... well... I considered it an honor, a mission, I was very enthusiastic, I wasn't sufficiently careful, I was too trusting.

**R.R.** Is the group for parity, of which you are a member, really effective?

**Edith Cresson**: Yes, we have been really effective. For example, the policies that the Socialist party have just adopted. When they insult us in parliament, as they have recently, when a woman deputy from the RPR was speaking about the rape of a young policewoman, Monsieur Cathala got up and said to this woman, who was older and not a pinup: "That couldn't happen to you." It's quite unthinkable. So Frédérique Bredin who is a deputy and a member of the Parity Ten asked for a public apology from her colleague in the name of the group. We are attempting to identify sexism with racism because when an Arab or a Jew is insulted, human rights can be invoked, but no one defends an insulted woman. People argue that we'll become like America. Someone who says that a woman has a lovely smile will finish up in court for sexual harassment, and doctors and lawyers can't discuss things with their clients without having to leave the door open, etc. If there are excesses of this kind, I don't think that this is a danger for us in France. Elisabeth Badinter's position is to say that in France, where men and women get along well and have relationships that are friendly, complementary, and emotionally significant, etc.—above all don't spoil all of that—in the name of some interest group (*communautariste*) policy for immigrants, young people, senior citizens, blacks, and women. Well, women are young people, blacks, immigrants, and half of humanity. I'm against segregation of categories, but women aren't a category.

**R.R.** The polls show that 86 percent of the public approves of parity. These are astonishing statistics. Do you think the public understands?

**Edith Cresson**: Yes. Our electors appreciate us exactly as they would appreciate men. I would even say that being a woman adds something extra, competence being equal. The electorate has more confidence in us and sees us as solid, hardworking and, again, there is less parading and concern for appearances.

Edith Cresson answered some further questions, such as those relating to the list of books on power by women in politics that I had sent to her earlier. Asked which of these books got the closest to the experience she had lived personally, after some hesitation, Cresson opted for the works of Roudy and Gaspard because, to use her words, they were "militant."

## *The Biography Versus the Interview*

The impression I gained of Edith Cresson through the interview was not the same as that transmitted by Elisabeth Schemla's biography. Although the positive energy and determination that marked Edith Cresson's passage in the political world was manifested in the interview with her insistence on her continuing social and political projects, Edith Cresson's somewhat authoritarian manner with the staff of the commission and a certain quality of voice in an interview that had aspects of a public performance made my own lines of communication strained. I had felt more in harmony with the bio(auto)graphical creation, with Schemla's search for the abstract and intellectual truths of Cresson's failure.

But the distinctively individual tone is the only new area found in Cresson's responses in this interview, which focused mainly on her fall from political grace. What she spoke of, the sexism among the media elites, the lack of support of a woman prime minister by government ministers, the critique of political popularity ratings, and support for the campaign for parity can be found in other interviews and is largely recycled. Cresson's comments include examples of the way the new discourse on political women is being constituted by the circulating and repetition of shared stories (Cathala's public expression of a rape myth/rape joke, for example), the French exception (Mitterrand's two partners), and certain repeated arguments (women are not a category or an interest group but half of humanity).

Cresson rejected the term "trapped" used to designate her situation by Schemla and the term "wounded" used in the printing error or *lapsus* in the *Encyclopédie*, yet both terms do appear appropriate to describe her situation. My own impression was that the woman speaking to me was still angry and embittered. Her response to this "wounding" was both defensive and combative. Cresson used and went beyond Schemla's analysis in the fierceness toward the anti-woman feeling in the French public and the level of misogyny in politics working against her.

As with past comparisons of biographical and autobiographical texts, there are differences between the biography and the interview. Schemla's empathetic biography of Edith Cresson, like Szafran's biography of Veil, is a "bio(auto)graphy." Like Szafran's text, Schemla's own contexts and experience, including her gender, influence the tale. But in this case, Cresson has not only approved of Schemla's thesis, she has espoused it for herself, and expanded on its discourses.

In 1999, Edith Cresson was implicated in a political scandal and was finally obliged to resign as European Commissioner after accusations of nepotism, inefficiency, and misused influence were levied at the Commission, and particularly at Cresson. This woman politician was accused, among other things, of having given undue influence (a consultancy position of some significance) to her dentist from Blois. Like the truths staged in the women's political autobiographies of the previous chapter, or those of Veil and Szafran's versions of Veil's life, neither Schemla's biography nor Edith Cresson's own readings of her political life (in interviews) partially inspired by Schemla's readings, provide the whole truth or the deeper realities of a woman's political life.

## Martine Aubry: l'énigme d'une femme politique

### *"Her Father's Daughter"?*

Like the biographies on Veil and Cresson, Aubry's biography is readable and fascinating for the inside stories. Like the previous two, the biography of Aubry's life is ultimately disappointing in the subjective nature and the limitations of the truths it reveals. Aubry herself has generally had little public interaction with those biographers, journalists, and academic critics, who would write her politics and her life. Described by all as a major and popular political leader, she is presented as that rare woman who has kept a place at the top—in Cresson's government, in the opposition as second to Jospin, and since June 1997 up until she resigned to seek election at the end of 2000, as second in the new Socialist government. Along with Elisabeth Guigou, Aubry has become a pivotal figure of the new deal politics. The Juppé government had been dismantling state enterprises and reducing certain traditional social protections while cooperating in the creation of new European institutions. With her inside knowledge of the workings of major corporations, Aubry was called upon to make vital decisions with respect to the new Socialist definitions and the directions toward modernization.

The 1997 biographical study of Martine Aubry by Paul Burel, editorialist at *Ouest-France*, and Natacha Tatu, journalist at *Le Nouvel Observateur*, is a narrative of anecdotal insider stories told for a curious and generally politically informed readership, but also for those interested in the itinerary of powerful women. It constructs a childhood dominated by the watchful eye of the father, Jacques Delors, demanding work, success, and service to others from his children. It presents a daughter who wants above all to please a father grudging of his praise. The biography also shows a daughter whose political commitment is not spontaneous but develops in the shadow of and is legitimized by this famous political father of French socialism. Following the parental commitment to social action, and civic service, Martine (Delors) Aubry chose to work in the masculine but less desirable or prestigious sector of labor where she remained in one way or the other starting in 1975, through a period of major economic transition in France.

In the biographical account, Aubry encountered misogyny as a staff member of Jean Auroux's ministry and at the Péchiney factory. Aubry is remembered for her reaction to the physical descriptions of women. Exasperated by business reports that opened with a mention of "the attractive little blond" or "the brunette in the charming pink suit," she began one of her own *compte-rendu* to the executive council with: "I met Mr. so and so, a handsome tanned young man, with a wonderful yellow tie." Martine's leadership, recount her biographers, was often considered to be too "authoritative"—a word we have encountered before, and have learned to read between the lines as a de-legitimating reaction to strong political women. According to her biographers' overview, Martine's legislative achievements to the date of their work in 1997—her earlier organization of public relation services at the Péchiney factory, and the success of the Foundation (FACE) she set up with major corporations in narrowing the social gaps and helping disadvantaged communities — remain local and limited.

It was inevitable that the press, too, would formulate reserves—predominantly with respect to Aubry's different political style. Her biographers note that she was generally presented in the mode of tart schoolmarm. Françoise Giroud may have been right when she claimed that Edith Cresson and Michelle Barzach did not survive because they were too seductive, too sexual, but Aubry's refusal to play the game of seduction was also criticized. For example one critic sniped that she was "a monk in skirts." Austerity seems to have appeared to Aubry to be the safer track: "What interests me is action, not appearance" (*Ce qui m'intéresse, c'est de faire, pas de paraître*) she declared in an interview. The interviewer-journalist on this occasion goes on to give details of her physical appearance that in French cultural contexts are somewhat disparaging: tailored business suit, scarf, flat shoes, at forty-three, Martine Aubry is what is called a down-to-earth woman (*Tailleur BCBG, foulard, escarpins. Martine Aubry, 43 ans, est ce qu'on appelle*

*Martine Aubry.*

*une femme carrée*). Other such descriptive media epithets from the period of her entry into government generally attribute masculine qualities to this political woman called a "superwoman" and seen to possess "authority," "moral intransigence," "frankness," "acerbic humor," and the "determination of a bulldozer."

An article in *Le Point* in 1996 presents a synthesis of readings of the "Aubry case."[24] Here Aubry is again seen as her father's daughter and as a top-down appointment in Edith Cresson's 1991 cabinet. She is presented as a protected woman, offered a job at the Elysée by Mitterrand when the government changed in 1993. In the biography, however, Aubry is also seen to have created her own independent network of intellectuals and trade unionists, technocrats, and social activists. The biographers highlight the fact that Aubry was pro-Maastricht, whereas the party has not always been convinced of pro-voting rights for non-French immigrants in local elections, although this was definitely not party policy.

The political scientist Alain Duhamel, co-author with Aubry of the *Petit Dictionnaire pour lutter contre l'extrême droite* (Little Dictionary to Combat the Far Right), echoes the biographical verdict of the "paradox" or enigma of Aubry in a thoughtful and sympathetic characterization. In *Le Point* in 1994, he portrayed this new star in the Socialist sky as combining both masculine and feminine character traits: "No one is less inclined than she is to the politics of seduction. Not that she's without personal charm: she brings together quite successfully a dominating energy and an interesting intellectual approach with a certain hypersensitivity. Direct and attractive when she feels confident, recalcitrant and with hackles up when something attacks her, her rare honesty is undeniable."[25] Duhamel describes an almost "bellicose sincerity," and adds a comment on Aubry's "taste for making decisions and effectiveness." The political scientist concludes that much as she is clearly the daughter of Jacques Delors, Martine also owes her success to herself.

In *Le Point* of 25 June 1999, a long feature article, entitled "The Fiasco of the 35-hour Working Week" by Jean-François Jacquier and Marc Nexon is quite unlike Duhamel's sympathetic portrait as it attempts to demolish Aubry's profile and her political record.[26] The vocabulary used to do this begins to sound familiar. Aubry is described as the "daughter of Jacques Delors." She is initially endowed with serious and reassuring qualities in the eyes of the CEOs by the presence of this left-wing Christian father for whom the economic realm is more important than the political. As a "woman who understands business," *énarque* and technocrat, she is the favorite (*la coqueluche*) in the 1990s of the most significant French bosses (Péchiney, Moulinex, Crédit Lyonnais, BSN, etc.). To this point, the overview is somewhat inspired by the 1997 biography which it cites. Ten years later, the authors continue, the bosses are now all complaining about the "authoritarianism" of Aubry.[27] The emotional investments of this "pasionaria" are showcased. Why so much stubbornness? ask the authors. The answer given is "the obsession with power" of this woman who "demanded" the Ministry of Finance when first invited to join the government and "held out" for the position of second in the government with a say in all major decisions. Since then, she has "invaded" the maximum amount of "territory" and everything "serves her ambition." As she contradicts her earlier positions, hers is an "intransigent politics of appearances." She is "cunning" and draws the great of the political world into her net by her "undeniable charm" and her "fascination." Aubry is "mad," unable to separate the trivial from the significant, her life absorbed totally by hard work with only a few hours out for a daughter, Clémentine (studying in the leading graduate School of Commerce, HEC), and surrounded by "slaves who adore her." If her foundation FACE in fact found jobs for 3,000 young people in 1998 (from 400 four years earlier) and had forty-six corporations supporting it instead of thirteen and over 600 businesses involved, this success came after Martine had handed over power. In her determination to get the 35-hour week accepted, her "will to power," it is claimed that she has neglected the major issues of health insurance and retirement benefits.

The authors of the article are clearly not in favor of the major changes necessitated by the 35-hour week and are politically motivated in their criticisms that contest the high figures of new jobs created by the measure and exhort Aubry to greater consultation and compromise (except, of course, with the "copines" or "girlfriends" with whom, it is claimed, she already meets once a month). Their portrait mounts an attack on Martine for both feminine seduction and emotionality and for unfeminine authoritarianism and will to power. It is constructed from gender-trait stereotypes as much as from her political actions. The article does concede that Aubry has major popular support and support among the rank and file of the Socialist party, which makes her "untouchable" and notes that the next stage in her ascending career as mayor of Lille by democratic election seems inevitable.

Martine Aubry is labeled by the opposition journalists as the daughter of a prestigious Socialist father, Jacques Delors, and as somewhat androgynous much as Helen Clark is labeled as lesbian or asexual. In this political woman near the top, both masculine and feminine qualities are necessarily flaws. The truths of Aubry's life and action, too, as they are presented both in 'her' biography and in critical articles are again influenced by the biographer or journalist's goals and contexts and framed by gender.

## *Martine Aubry: Masculine Approaches to Feminine Action?*

Insisting on protecting her accountant husband and her teenage daughter from media attention, Aubry has generally attempted to eliminate the personal from her discourse, although she did allow *Paris Match* to publish a personal profile when she left the government. This is generally dissimilar to the tack taken by Aubry's political contemporaries, Guigou and Royal, with whom she shares an education at the Ecole Nationale d'Administration. In public life, Aubry prefers to present an image of the non-seductive, competent technocrat, close to the masculine/universalist pole, and generally eschewing the feminine.

Aubry's writing, *Le Choix d'agir* (The Choice for Action, 1994) and *L'Urgence du social* (The Urgency of Social Questions) has made a contribution to a technocratic and economically based vision of the problems of unemployment.[28] This writing, nonetheless, might be qualified as feminine to the extent that like Ségolène Royal, Martine Aubry seeks a social policy that would guarantee quality of life as well as free circulation of people, goods, and services. Aubry's texts on policy directions for France, like her treatise on the dangerous and deceptive discourses of the National Front written with Duhamel, have had some political impact. Her persistent presence at this high level of power and her media visibility as a self-possessed and competent political figure committed to the general good have had a major impact. What the writing on Aubry shows, however, is that the traditional underlying misogyny of political journalism in France and the power of the "French exception" in terms of the valuing of feminine women and visualizing deviance remains close to the surface

In 1999, this strong and successful woman, who had attempted to stand outside the masculine-feminine distinctions, finally took up a position in favor of political parity for women and women's difference. Talking to Elizabeth Weissman on being a woman in politics, Aubry recounts that in the housing projects she visited it was the women who organize solidarity, have the courage to protect their youngsters from drug dealers, and keep their feet firmly on the ground. The women in the North she met during her first electoral campaign had rejected politics as it was practiced by men, and told her it was women's turn. "If our daughters go into politics one day," she adds, "this will be without apologizing for being there the way I had to during my studies."[29] Aubry's policy texts and manifesto, occasional interviews, and media appearances, her many less than smiling photographs, do impart a sense of the new politician and give an occasional glimpse of the woman through her own discourse and body language. The public appears to have taken this new model largely to its heart, although the enigma or contradiction apparent in the media representations of this political woman at the top have not all been resolved.

Comparing the three political biographies, Veil's case best reveals the gaps between the autobiographical and the biographical account of a life, but also the importance the gender of the biographer may have in these different representations. Veil's self-writing constructs the portrait of a pioneer breaking in a new political path for women while confronting the competing needs for paternal legitimization and for liberation, issues that Szafran's biography does not touch on. Cresson's case shows the mutual influence that can be exerted by the discourses of biographer and subject of similar gender and similar political perspectives dissecting a particular political experience. Aubry's case in particular, but really all three of the political biographies examined here, brings to light the difficulties in extracting the "real" or totalizing (vertical) truth about hybrid and changing political figures. They highlight the premise that a biography (or piece of political writing) has a horizontal rather than a vertical focus and tells as much about the author and his/her position, or about the moment, as about the subject. In the interviews most particularly and in the autobiographies—but also in the biographies—the common themes of women's difference, media prejudice, obstacles to women's advancement, need for the support of the prince continue to emerge and circulate, demonstrating effects of intertextuality. The interview, as we noted in an earlier chapter, reflects the shared and often limited knowledge of both the interviewer and interviewed and may elicit certain truths of the body. In the case of the biographical writing of the lives of Veil, Cresson, and Aubry, what becomes apparent is that even the very personal explorations of the other leave the "truth" hidden, the enigma unresolved.

## Notes

1. "Dans la condition du Juif et dans celle de la femme, il y a quelque chose de semblable. Cette conviction remonte à mon enfance, à ma mère." Maurice Szafran, Simone Veil. Destin (Paris: Flammarion, 1994), p. 183.

2. Abortion required parental permission in the case of a minor. The law allowed freedom of conscience for all medical practitioners not to perform abortions and incorporated an amendment giving directors of medical establishments (hospitals run by religious orders, for example) the right to decide whether their establishment would accept the procedure or not. It excluded reimbursement by social security.
3. In her interview with me, Veil completely rejected the claim made in Béatrice d'Intignano's recent major documentary work on French women, *Femmes si vous saviez*, that the abortion law was not the law that she, Veil, had wanted, insisting that she had completely accepted responsibility for this law as it was voted.
4. Lancelot has often served as consultant to the government and has been a member, for example, of the committee for constitutional reform.
5. Quoted in Maurice Maschino, *Après vous, messieurs. Les Femmes et le pouvoir* (Paris: Calmann-Lévy, 1996). Repeated in Elisabeth Guigou, *Etre Femme en politique* (Paris: Plon, 1997), p. 157.
6. "mon mari n'aurait jamais accepté. C'était notre génération." Elisabeth Weissman, *Les filles, on n'attend plus que vous. Témoignages de Martine Aubry à Simone Veil* (Paris: Textuel, 1995), interview, p. 86.
7. "Cela ne risquerait pas de vous arriver." A few days after my interview with Veil, the evening news of 20 December reported the angry response of Spanish women deputies to a similar, unthinking reduction of women to the physical and the sexual, and revelation of deeply rooted antifeminism on the part of the vice-president of the parliament in Madrid. He had stated publicly that women had been at the service of men for millennia and there was no good reason for this to change.
8. Cresson wanted to reduce the overweening power of the administration and the obstacles it put in the way of action, to limit the simultaneous holding of multiple public offices and require public officials to disclose their wealth, to cut waste and to decentralize (the ENA was to be moved to Strasbourg, for instance, and was not happy about that proposition). Cresson attempted to intervene strategically to bring industry and commerce together and to protect small businesses.
9. In *La Femme piégée* (Paris: Flammarion, 1993), Elisabeth Schemla writes of the humiliating "scent of a woman and of the end of an era" (*parfum de femme et de fin de règne*, p. 97).
10. Ibid., p. 105.
11. Ibid., p. 118.
12. Edith's inaugural speech was disappointing; the microphones were set for the male voice so her voice sounded high. Her delivery in such a formal setting was unconvincing. Yann Piat (formerly of the Front national but representing the UDF) made the comment that "We expected a woman's speech and what we got was a sexless discourse." At the last moment, the comics, Amadou, Roucas, and Collaro, decided to change the name of the puppet they were preparing for their *Bébête Show* from Didi-la-Teigne (Didi the Tear-away) to Amabotte (To Heel). They presented the French public with a certain hidden idea of women and a figure of Edith Cresson that was disfiguring rather than simply caricaturistic, claims Schemla. The female and feline Amabotte rubs herself up against the frog (President Mitterrand) Kermitt, cooing, while Rocard-Rocroa growls "Usurper" (*Bébête Show*, 29 May). The hysterical, sexualized panther-woman whispers: "My little low-life love. That means I don't give a jerk about it" (*Mon canaillou d'amour. Ça veut dire que j'en ai rien à branler*). The colloquial expression that is satirized and sexualized here is the response by Cresson that had created a scandal —"I don't give a dam about it" (*J'en ai rien à cirer*). Cresson had used this expression, perhaps injudiciously, to describe her feelings about the stock exchange. The panther figure later becomes beseeching and pathetic, calling Kermitt for help: "Help, my little goat-cheese, my love, they're all after me" (*Au secours, mon chabichou d'amour, ils sont tous après moi*). Cresson was presented as a seductive and sexual—an infantilized—animal in

heat. Summing up the nature and effects of this nightly media program that she describes in detail, Schemla comments that this trial by political satire, which should play a cathartic function, became a witch hunt as expressions like "vampire" and "she-devil" (*Vampire Diablesse*!) made an appearance.

13. In Schemla, *La Femme piégée*, p. 126.
14. In 1991 the *Observer* published an interview on love, sexuality, power, men, and misogyny given with her usual frankness by Edith Cresson in 1987, well before she became a central public figure. At the end, the interviewer observed that "In Anglo-Saxon countries, most men prefer the company of other males." Cresson agreed but added that "most of these men are homosexuals—perhaps not the majority but in the United States 25 percent are already, and in England and in Germany, it's much the same. In London, the men in the street don't look at you. Anglo-Saxon men aren't interested in women as women."
15. Schemla, *La Femme piégée*, p. 216.
16. Ibid., p. 217.
17. *L'Evènement du jeudi*, 7 to 13 October 1993.
18. There is no recognition that journalists might be caught up in, indeed feeding on, such an irrational public appetite. These journalists denied the need for a proposed referendum to demonstrate public support. They later recognized that they had been manipulated by the same irrational forces as the public.
19. Zazie was the young non-conformist heroine of Raymond Queneau's popular novel (and subsequent film) *Zazie dans le métro.*
20. Julliard quoted in Schemla, *La Femme piégée*, p. 41.
21. Olivier Duhamel and Jérôme Jaffré, "Edith Cresson à Matignon ou la confection d'une impopularité" (*SOFRES L'Etat de l'Opinion*, Paris: Seuil), 1993, pp. 109–123.
22. *Le Petit Dictionnaire pour lutter contre l'extrême-droite* (The Little Dictionary to Combat the Far Right), written by Martine Aubry and Olivier Duhamel some years later contained an entry on "charters" that caused a rift between the two women and the threat of a lawsuit by Cresson despite the fact that Duhamel withdrew his reference to Cresson's involvement in a politics of returning illegal aliens to their homeland in the second edition.
23. George Ross, review of *La Femme piégée*, in *French Politics and Society* 12, no. 4 (Fall 1994), pp. 91–93.
24. François Bazin and Joseph Macé-Scaron, "Femmes Politiques," *Le Point* 1236, 25 May 1996, pp. 62–66.
25. *Le Point*, no. 1119, 26 February 1994.
26. Jean-François Jacquier and Marc Nexon, "Le fiasco des 35 heures," *Le Point*, no. 1397, 25 June 1999, pp. 5–62.
27. Ibid. For example, "the ferocity with which the Minister of Labor and Social Solidarity is fighting to impose the 35-hour week on businesses that don't want it… " (p. 54).
28. Martine Aubry, "L'urgence du social," *Etudes*, April 1993, pp. 471–476 and *Le Choix d'agir* (Paris: Albin Michel, 1994).
29. Elisabeth Weissman, *Les Filles, on n'attend plus que vous*, p. 39.

# Part IV

## The Pioneers

# 8

# Huguette Bouchardeau and Political (Auto)Fiction: Power and the Unconscious

The apparent transparency and objectivity of such texts as the survey, the sociopolitical interview, and autobiographical or biographical history often conceal a more complex discourse. At some level, the implicit claims of the texts to "mirror" a shared and pre-existing reality directly or to provide some singular political truth falter, and fissures appear. As the voice of the teller emerges, and in some cases, consciously recognizes its own non-neutrality and distinctive origins, the boundaries between history and story, between grand-sweep objective third-person narratives and contextualized first-person experience, become less certain.

The new body of feminine political writing, and indeed also the biographical texts, bring a set of preoccupations to the fore that concern in particular women's political legitimacy and the value of their contribution to politics. Over the last decade there has been a shift toward greater awareness of the issues around women's political illegitimacy and an affirming of the positive value of feminine difference. As it investigates power, this writing tends to create new mixed genres that do not respect the conventions of traditional political memoirs. The texts bring the personal and the political more intimately together. The political autobiographies of Gisèle Halimi, Ségolène Royal, Elisabeth Guigou, and Michèle Barzac, examined in chapter six, for example, all share this genre-bending pattern.

Chapters eight and nine explore the work of two of the contemporary political women who have pioneered writing on power and have made the greatest impact on the public and the publishing worlds in France, Huguette Bouchardeau and Françoise Giroud. Their work is prolific across a number of different genres and the bodies of work both women writers create are experimental and innovative. I argue that the genre of "autofiction" in particular attempts to get close to an understanding of the influence of the unconscious on what it means to hold power.

*Huguette Bouchardeau.*

In the texts of both Bouchardeau and Giroud, women's self-analysis and the program for action that this initiates are contextualized within the wider arena of political meetings, political discourses, and the struggle for power. Despite the gendered character of this political field and the conflictual nature of power, in both Bouchardeau's and Giroud's texts, the affective and survival value elements in the relations between men and women are considered too great to be reduced simply to a battle of the sexes over the gender of power (or gender-power). The question that haunts the work of both women, then, is never couched in terms of aspirations to capture and hold personal or feminine power. Rather, the question, as Bouchardeau puts it, is that given her position as an outsider—a renegade not devoting her time to care of husband and children or love—can a woman in this male world really change political practice and not simply serve as a token, a pretext or excuse for her own absence?

## Huguette Bouchardeau's Journey: From Autobiography to (Auto)fiction

The political autobiography, *Un Coin dans leur monde* (A Corner in Their World), is the story of Bouchardeau's life in her chosen party. The (auto)fiction *Choses dites de profil* (Things Said Indirectly), is the story of a later specific cabinet appointment. The level and locus of Bouchardeau's discomfort with her role in the established political structures change from her first work to her later writing. The multilayered fiction, where analytic and imaginative, conscious and unconscious systems (as manifested in metaphor and forms of narrative) meet and clash, conceals/reveals a more subtle and complex understanding of the political experience than the political autobiography.

In the (auto)fiction, *Choses dites de profil*, the satisfactions of certain accomplishments do not counterbalance the deep sense of personal betrayal of political ideals, the sense of sickness without and within, or the fear of being a token and a decoy. Nor does the project of self-knowledge, the searching for a personal (left-wing) ethics of choice, resolve the simultaneous sense of the contradictory deep needs and impulses that derive from the relations between the sexes. As in Giroud's work, what is again at play is the unconscious fascination with (and conscious resistance to) self-loss and dissolution in the powerful masculine other.

In a series of interviews with me that present a more public view of the nature of political power and women's relation to power, Bouchardeau repeats her belief that women have most often reached positions of power through some form of recognition by men. Her analysis of this phenomenon in the interviews and in her various academic manifestos is developed at a less intimate level.[1] What is at issue in political parties, which are at the heart of democratic functioning in France, she argues, is not competence but the ability to take power, and this is foreign to women's culture. Where certain men see power as domination before they see it as action; women have difficulty coming to terms with the former. Men consider it their right to be designated for key positions. Bouchardeau's credo at this public level concludes with a form of the "difference" argument: progress in democracy would come only through women who are concerned with not sacrificing the multiple aspects of their lives to the power to dominate.

Bouchardeau's biographies seek to elucidate this difference further through historical studies of women's lives. These biographical studies investigate the pioneering role of the trade-unionist and secretary of the federation of unions of teachers Hélène Brion (*Hélène Brion: La Voie féministe*, 1978), the limitations and strengths of the life of Huguette Bouchardeau's own working-class mother, *Rose-Noël* (1990), and the grounded earthiness yet idealism of the nineteenth-century writer and politician Georges Sand (*La Lune et les sabots*, 1990).[2] Attempting recovery and analysis of the power and limitations in the balance of the private and public lives of Bouchardeau's various "mothers," these biographies are also "bio(auto)graphies," revealing much about the writer's own choices and preoccupations and softening generic boundaries.

## "A Corner in Their World"

This pioneer women's political autobiography, published in 1979, is presented explicitly as a first-person narrative.[3] The text is composed of chapters alternating between a reflection on Bouchardeau's own personal experience as national secretary of the left-wing Parti socialiste unifié (PSU) and a study of the experience of women in political parties in general. The structure of this work suggests that any understanding of the phenomenon of political power derives from the interchange between private and public.

Bouchardeau claims that it was in the women's section of the PSU that she and others learned to speak for themselves. Women needed to analyze together the manner in which their image had been fabricated in their own heads as in the heads of men. Women also needed to discover the familial and social mechanisms of the distribution of roles that drove their ways of thinking, acting, and living. Men in politics, states Bouchardeau, analyze only what is exterior—that is, the economic and political situations behind power relations.

Huguette Bouchardeau was born in 1935 into a working-class family of six children. Bouchardeau's personal story begins with a description of the monotony and insignificance of repeated household chores and the restrictive expectations that were the birthright of this working-class daughter. Her childhood serves as a counterpoint to the adult political analysis of gendered spheres. Examples of gender divisions include Bouchardeau's descriptions of the Thursday holiday from school spent darning the pile of family socks while her brothers watch a soccer game, or helping her mother with the younger children, tasks considered more necessary for the daughter than schoolwork. Huguette's childhood as a bright scholarship student in a private institution is formative in terms of the consciousness of class struggle. This is both an ideology shared with her father and a reaction against her mother's bounded role.

The university years that followed and her activity within a major student union group (L'Association Générale des Etudiants), brought an awakening consciousness of sexism and an escape from the obligations of being a second "mother" in a family of six children. In 1954, Huguette Bouchardeau was nominated for the position of general secretary of the student union in Lyon, at that time a union composed exclusively of males. Bouchardeau explains how she was asked to reconsider her candidacy on the grounds that women cannot hold up under debate, that the jokes of her male comrades would not be fit for her ears, that she would, in short, be out of (her) place.

"I believed I had only to show that I was good enough and that their arguments were ill-founded," relates Bouchardeau in her political autobiography. "I made the mistake, which we have since learned to recognize, of hoping to be recognized for merit without questioning the masculine norms of the game." The criticism of her candidacy, although presented as pragmatic, was based on opposition to competition from a woman. In the autobiography, Bouchardeau reflects on how the real nature of this opposition had remained hidden, perhaps even to her political comrades. She maintained her candidacy.

As an active member of the Union de la Gauche Socialiste beginning in 1958, Bouchardeau was invited to take on the post of national secretary for the PSU in 1979. A lucid Bouchardeau understood the enthusiastic party reaction of "You're a woman. That's great" to mean "You're a woman. That will look great." She found this more indirect way of denying female competence to be no less humiliating. In 1979 she headed the least "electoralist" of all parties because of the imminent presidential elections where a woman candidate was seen to present as an electoral advantage. She was told that a woman at the top of the party was to be merely its mouthpiece. Bouchardeau reiterates in a number of her writings the conviction that she would not have been selected for many positions if there had been any real possibility of power or political influence in the position. However, after running for the presidency, she subsequently found herself appointed by the admired François Mitterrand as environment minister. In her ministry, Bouchardeau claims, she had the same power as a man.

*Un Coin dans leur monde* gives a brief summary of Bouchardeau's public life: ten years teaching at a high school after university, passing the difficult *agrégation* in philosophy,[4] a position in the Department of Educational Sciences at the University of Lyon, activism in the Union de la Gauche Socialiste, then in the PSU, a party of the left, militancy in the teacher's union, action for Family Planning and the discovery of the women's movements through her work for the pro-choice organization, Movement pour la Libération de l'Avortement et de la Contraception (MLAC).

Yet Bouchardeau declares that she feels much more tempted to organize her story around the dates that mark the beginning of her married life and other domestic events rather than around these public events. The birth of her children and the twenty years of difficult compromises and practical questions, housework, children, meals, and buttons to sew on, leave their mark on her way of being. Loss of confidence, hypersensitivity to "his" judgments, fear of being incompetent, of being incapable of taking part in political jousting, are, for Bouchardeau, inevitable results of this narrowing of vision imposed by domestic roles.

## "A Few Words on Power"

In the second chapter, Bouchardeau describes the shock of finding herself in a central position inside a political organization after four years of working within its women's sector. Bouchardeau says the women's group provided its members with solidarity, reassurance, preparation for public debate and, indeed, with pleasure. Women's solidarity was important in her view.

> It has always been the male gaze that evaluates us, appreciates us, gives us the right to exist. To be able to stand up against sarcastic masculine judgments, we need to feel supported by others; otherwise, all that remains is the play of rivalries.[5]

There was no distinct line between the subjective sources of opinions and these positions themselves within the women's section. Language was concrete, references were to daily life, to children, to people's character and to time. Action was preferably local, in a factory or neighborhood.

Male political discourse, she argues, starts from theoretical and global positions. Bouchardeau explains how a woman singled out and invited into the male group is asked to sacrifice her "aggressive" feminist convictions to "serious analysis." In other words, women must adopt a male political discourse. The need for autonomous women's groups does not derive from any "difference" in the manner of understanding or reasoning of a man or a woman. Quite simply, she observes, it is the daily wielding of pots and pans that makes women more practical, more modest, less willing to generalize or theorize. At the same time, men's mastery of an abstruse political and economic discourse makes women believe that politics is a domain of male competence and leads them to keep quiet. The female politician states that when women do find the courage or urge to speak, their speech often appears too tense or emotional and this puts them at a disadvantage.

In any case, within the political parties, women's questions are inevitably marginalized according to Bouchardeau. For example, the existence of women's unpaid work, which has no place in classical Marxism, is not recognized as a serious theoretical question within her own party until it is posed by a man. Women's groups and individual women are caught between a need to hold positions of power and an awareness of the "traps of power." These traps begin with the father's oppressive control of his family and proceed to the politician's need to crush the other with his rhetoric.

> Because we had been sensitized to the relations of dependency on others manifest in daily life, family or love life, we attached more importance to the relations of power at work in all interpersonal relations. And we wanted to go beyond this kind of relation.[6]

Women do need to confront and contest men's power, claims Bouchardeau, quoting Susan Sontag: "Women cannot be liberated unless men's power diminishes."[7] They must fight not to be relegated to secondary support positions: "our struggle is itself based on the attack on that division of roles on which all power is based."[8]

Men consider themselves to be in politics by right while women tend to see themselves as without the appropriate lineage. For Bouchardeau dominant groups do not suffer from this kind of hypersensitivity that characterizes victims of both racism and sexism. Her personal difficulties with being a "displaced woman" or a woman "out of (her) place" are discussed in her following chapter entitled *Femmes déplacées.*

## *Displaced Women: Women's Spaces*

In order to fit in to the "masculine" political world, Bouchardeau describes how she conformed: "I liked jeans and bright dresses, I wore beige and a suit."[9] She attempts to avoid any behavior that might resemble the caricatures of sexually or emotionally frustrated, or unfulfilled "females," motivated by irrational and excessive responses of harpies or passionarias. Bouchardeau also demurs, sensing that these outer signs of the attempt to find approval in conformity to the inculcated feminine roles indicated self-censure.

The struggle in these early years in politics with a young family was both an inner and an outer one. Bouchardeau recounts the discouragement she experienced when faced with fierce disapproval from other women when, in 1968, she campaigned in the local market. Her children were twelve, seven, and two years old: "She should be ashamed not to be home with her family; what was her husband thinking of?"

Bouchardeau writes of how women in political office aroused fear, not only among men but also among women who seemed to be afraid of losing the male protection provided by the status quo and the loss of what they had taken to be their power as good wives. Afraid of being seen as "bad" women, or as harpies, they remained in the secondary role that nonetheless gave them value and security—the family. Duty, family, dignity, and femininity were synonymous. Conservatives of all persuasions have argued that women would lose by exchanging their occult power of the pillow and their intimate power over the family for more fragile institutional powers. Bouchardeau looks at Freud's explanation that women fulfill their desires for power and immortality in motherhood. While she is not at all persuaded that this is the case, and suspects that occult power is much overrated, Bouchardeau does ask whether women will learn to find pleasure in a political life dominated by the vocabulary of the hunt or of war. Pascal, Adler, and Sineau and the women politicians of the 1990s pose a similar question in their works on women and politics. Is this embattled life able to compensate women for the sacrifice of their traditional security or the pleasure brought by small day-to-day domestic joys? Do women indeed take pleasure in having power over others, or in making their mark in discourse or in thought? Will they come to experience the same health risks and lower life expectation as men under stress?

Bouchardeau's subsequent reflections on the limitations imposed by the traditional life of a woman provide a partial answer to some of these questions as she describes having to control her panic at being imprisoned in the demands of a growing family. She writes of her envy of the generation that came after hers, helped by birth control and increased technology to integrate one or two pregnancies into an accepted and acceptable professional life. This allowed the younger generation of women to continue to exist as people, even if it entailed juggling two lives in a very busy coexistence. Underlying her narrative is the implication that caring for others in a selfless and nurturing fashion was not in any way "natural" for her—this should not be the only way of being a woman. One of the metaphors that reinforces this conclusion is Virginia Woolf's *A Room of One's Own* figuring in pride of place on Bouchardeau's mantelpiece. Woolf's text represented the politician's delight in her tiny apartment in Lyon, where she stayed alone for the three days a week for her university teaching.[10] Bouchardeau is searching for a definition of her identity as independent of men and family, an identity of woman as more than the "other" of man and not coterminous with "mother."

The inequality inherent in the division of men's and women's roles is spelled out as Bouchardeau recalls the experience of her own professional and family life. Women feel guilty about deserting their family posts when they have to be absent for professional reasons. They feel responsible for the smooth functioning of the household even in their absence; no one else will keep the refrigerator filled, dinners prepared, clothes washed and ironed.

## *"Pyramids Are Tombs": Political Parties*

In her fourth chapter, Bouchardeau counterbalances her account of the limitations of the wife-mother with a return to her critique of life in a political party. She points out the danger a party faces of being controlled by a dogmatic caste of leaders, sure of their right to govern and cut off from the party base by their means or leisure pursuits. Leaders nominate candidates who then are dependent on these leaders. Such a system creates bureaucracy, inertia, and self-reassuring games of influence and preeminence, even in parties like her own where the possibilities of ever taking power are very limited.

In 1974, with the departure of Michel Rocard for a more visible career through the PS, the PSU attempted to depersonalize, decentralize, and de-hierarchize its structures and to change the division of labor. But Bouchardeau notes that attempts at collective self-governance and equality are fraught with difficulties. Such difficulties include the strong (unconscious) reasons left-wing male militants had for not insisting on change, for keeping their own wives at home, waiting for their husbands' return from long political meetings. The PSU is the laboratory party for ideas on health, public transport, immigration, and social questions. Yet a 1978 poster in favor of "the thirty-five hour week: time to live and to share household tasks" (*trente-cinq heures: du temps pour vivre et pour partager les tâches ménagères*) was a source of quite some irritation for her male colleagues. Bouchardeau also observes that women who accept working in a group often feel incompetent to take on higher, more solitary responsibilities. Women are unwilling to compete against men. Her text points out that if the PSU is not a useful instrument for women's political aspirations, if procedural questions and processes of nomination and attitudes toward gender-roles pose a problem even here, how much more would this be the case within the PS back in power in 1981 after a long exile?

Bouchardeau joined the PSU in 1960, became its *Secrétaire général* in 1979, its candidate in the presidential elections of 1981, and resigned from the party in 1985. In 1983 she was appointed junior minister and then full minister of the environment from 1984 to 1986. As president of the European Council of Environment Ministers, she was involved in measures against atmospheric pollution, acid rain, protection of forests, limitation of lead in gasoline, and transportation of toxic waste. Elected deputy for the Doubs in 1986 representing the Socialist grouping, she was re-elected in 1988 as the candidate of the Majorité Présidentielle pour la France Unie and remained in the *Palais Bourbon* (the Assemblée Nationale) until 1993.

## A Political (Auto)fiction: "Things Said Indirectly"

In her 1988 book, *Choses dites de profil* (Things Said Indirectly), this former minister for the environment introduces the reader to the routines, protocols, encounters, and structures of high political power in contemporary France.[11] The story of ten days in the life of an ostensibly fictional politician begins on 22 September 1985. In the opening pages, a narrator, in her fifties, sits at the table of an official reception in Ajaccio. She is ministerially attentive to questions and information, while silently recalling the recent events of her tour of the national parks in Corsica in her function as environment minister in Mitterrand's Socialist government. She tells her tale predominantly in the first person, but the conventional boundaries between narrative codes of confessional first-person autobiography and objective third-person fiction slip and mutate. That morning, the third-person commentary informs us, before her official visits to local sites of natural beauty, the minister, disturbingly, had begun to hemorrhage.

That morning, too, the helicopter had flown her within sight of the French military base at Aspretto. This was the very base that the world was just beginning to associate with the training of French frogmen responsible for blowing up a Greenpeace protest yacht in the small, friendly, and nuclear-free country of New Zealand in the distant South Pacific. The minister's personal understanding of the *Rainbow Warrior*[12] affair begins in the secrecy arising from France's long-standing and surprisingly cross-party pursuit of defensive autonomy through nuclear offensive power.[13] Yet the minister must remain publicly discreet, loyal to the French Socialist party in power and to Mitterrand as its leader and president, politically beyond reproach. The hidden truths of the *Rainbow Warrior* affair, the politician's repression of a personal reaction to protect her party is emblematic of the cancers that she will discover working insidiously at the heart of both the body politic and of her own body.

Over the following days, the reader accompanies the minister to a council of ministers in Paris where the *Rainbow Warrior* is disconcertingly not open to discussion even though two months have passed since the sinking and a number of discredited government accounts have been offered. The reader then follows the minister to an important EEC meeting of environmental ministers in Brussels, and watches her hammer out a compromise on automobile and air pollution legislation. The minister's small ecological victory is won by not quite playing the game, by "non-gentlemanly" behavior, and at the expense of the marginalization and disapproval of the intruder.

The intimacy of private life is juxtaposed with these political events. After a short weekend spent with her husband in the region of the Gard, the minister travels south to a *palombière*, a sportsmen's forest hut for shooting wood pigeons. The issue of hunting is sufficiently serious in France, as it is in the United States, to have given rise to a new political group, *Hunting and Fishing*. This pressure group is dedicated to the defense of so-called individual rights for hunters. For Bouchardeau, the political duty is to understand the hunters' case and their opposition to recent European legislation banning the use of nets.

On this visit, the heroine is subject to a sharp recurrence of the malaise that has been dully with her throughout these political events. Her emerging awareness breaks the surface only in the final pages. The silence on the sinking of the *Rainbow Warrior* was symptomatic of disease. The minister's triumph of Brussels was bounded by an established, unhealthy political system of compromise with manufacturing and national interests. The automobile in European cities is a "cancer," and the *palombières* of long tradition, male camaraderie, and excellent game have the "smell of death." These political ills are all paralleled by physical symptoms and culminate in the diagnosis of malignancy in the narrator's body. The "autofictional" journey through the "cancers" of the existing political orders seems to imply the need for a new political morality, less isolating and more concerned with human needs and relationships than with perpetuating the defensive structures of its power.

## *Ten Days in the Life of a Woman Environment Minister*

*Choses dites de profil* is called "a novel." Its overt content is given added meanings through its narrative forms, a combination of third-person and first person voices, and its metaphors, metaphors of imprisonment, cancer, and death.

In both first and third-person narrative modes, this woman's history/story takes its shape through the standard literary and narrative conventions of description, dialogue, character, plot and linear development, and verisimilitude ("trueness" to the ready-made idea we have of "real" or realistic life). As the narrative voice shifts from "I" to "she," the novel slips between life history and life story, between real and plot-text, posing the postmodern question on the (im)possibility of communicating new and individual experience.

Raised explicitly within the text is the particular "double bind" that so troubles a postmodern consciousness—that is, the question of our ability to know or invent, or even tell, the story of ourselves and our lives outside our existing texts and their narrative conventions: "What do we know of love outside the paths traced by our books and songs?"[14] Can we talk about our need for permanence and preference in relationships, our jealousies, or indeed our more recently discovered and contradictory desire for a room of our own, without using "the words of comedies, of tragic passions"—the words, in short, of others?[15] Do we, like the characters of the Harlequin romances on which our heroine's feminist friend is writing a thesis, construct our feelings and our lives according to a limited, repetitive set of ready-made words and situations? Perhaps we are not "living our own destinies," but move instead through the collective forest of symbols, selecting that word-world bubble (affection, friendship, love) into whose conventions we will then enter.[16] Or is there a correspondence in a real world (that is, not a constructed, textual, ideological world) for these names, these categories that we use to recognize, to set limits to, and to master our own lives, some necessary (essential and non-contingent) origin? Personal life is inseparable from the texts that surround and constitute us, according to Derrida, Foucault, and others in the French philosophical tradition. Yet Bouchardeau's writing also seems to situate itself close to the positive intuition that there is a correspondence between language and the real. Her texts include the hope of discovering new aspects of the real beyond the discourses in power.

Arnaud, her heroine's secret love, on the contrary, understands life through the language and literature in place. For this scientific journalist, knowledge is textual authority, experience is a repetition of classical situations and the world is a place in which all will always remain same, knowable, and therefore controllable. For Bouchardeau, Arnaud is the seduction of the impossible "right-wing" and "masculine" Other. He is her opposite in his conviction that the known is natural, transparent, and eternal, in his strongman taxonomies of control, and perhaps also in his "rapid and brutal" way of making love, his "smell of male solidity," and "strong moods"[17] or states of being. The "left-wing" and "feminine" narrator is fascinated by Arnaud's control of language, the ease with which he is able to find the suitable framework and the appropriate explanation of himself. She finds the courage to break off her problematic relationship with this Other only when her suspected cancer is medically confirmed.

The opposition that the writing of this dangerous liaison sets up cannot be reduced simply to male against female. Jean, the narrator's husband of more than twenty years, is not like Arnaud. A psychologist living alone in Saint-Etienne and seeing his working wife occasionally, Jean is characterized by his awareness of the difficulty of authentic verbal communication. Like his wife, he is presented as "left-wing," a term defined idiosyncratically in the course of the novel as believing that all is not known. Life and people can be changed and new worlds can be invented in Jean's eyes.

Jean proposes two images of man that point to the novel's core philosophical and political conviction, quoting a text by Cortázar. This text derives most probably from Freud's well-known biological metaphor modeling the human psyche as an amoeba. The first image in the tissue of quotations is that of a man amoeba who stretches out his pseudopodia to catch food in varying long and short movements until, finally, he reaches maturity, which Jean sees as "the worst of deaths" in the definitive "fixing" of these limited utilitarian patterns. The second is the man who thinks that nothing of interest is escaping him until some slight slippage momentarily reveals his fragmented being, his irregular pseudopodia, the intuition that "further on, where I see only limpid air, or else in this indecision, at the crossroads of choice, in the rest of reality that I do not know, I am waiting for myself in vain."[18] These are the problems of determinism and power that derive from a strong philosophical tradition in France. They are the questions surrounding the possibility of identity (political or personal) outside the (badly) prescripted one. Such questions also lie at the center of the French texts of *modernité* (Beckett, Robbe-Grillet, Duras, Simon, Sarraute, Barthes, among others) and also frame much contemporary feminist theory. In its philosophical themes and its concern with the abstract, theoretical truths of existence, in its interest in the meanings carried by form, Bouchardeau's political "autofiction," to use the term coined by the literary critic Serge Doubrovsky, a new sub-genre, somewhere between autobiography and fiction, places her clearly within a national (French) intellectual tradition.

## *The Body as Power*

The body as first authenticity, amoeba-like, and often beyond conscious control, is both a significant modern/postmodern and feminist issue. "Feminine" theories of writing from the body (Duras, Irigaray, Hyvrard, among others) have been exploring the possibility that it is in this pre-Oedipal and prelinguistic domain of non-separation, of symbiosis with the "mother" in the fluidity of the Kristevan primitive semiotic/maternal, outside the "father's" law and the language of the tribe, that the beginnings of an alternative to traditional politics might be found. If new desires, needs, emotions, relationships cannot be expressed exactly by existing words or divisions of the world, or the permanent "fixing" in place that these namings effect, perhaps an attentive listening to the "primitive" reactions of the body might provide a more unmediated knowledge. The minister's cancer, then, is a form of revelation.

The narrator of *Choses dites de profil* scorns primitive emotions. Intellectually and ideologically, she has theorized emotional reactions such as jealousy as a "cultural condition" arising out of the waiting that women do within the confines of the domestic for the man to return from his contacts with the wider public world and with younger, freer women. Yet when she finds her lover, Arnaud, sitting close beside her young press attaché and friend Isabelle, she feels an involuntary physical reaction. Fists clench, nails bite into her palms, a mass settles hard in the pit of her stomach. This violent primary reaction is only calmed by the subsequent reason and control of the "new" brain, or cerebral cortex. Significantly, positive power can be derived from these feelings only when the narrator subsequently takes up her pen and attempts to write them.

Bouchardeau suggests that the wellsprings of such "jealousy" seem to lie much deeper than anger at male-female inequalities or the unconscious desire for the kind of contact with Elke (or Isabelle) that men enjoy. In the novel it is the more immediate skin contact, the tone of voice, the touch of the narrator's hand on Isabelle's arm, for example, which best transmit tenderness, fear, or understanding. These elemental gestures may be "redirected" at a higher level by a social construction and become part of a learned or inherited body "language," itself reinforcing preconceived ideas of gender, class, and appropriate interaction with others, very much as verbal language does.[19] Like the stand for her ostrich egg that the narrator feels impelled to ask Arnaud to buy for her as a gift (an implicitly compulsive demand for some sign of commitment or exchange that Arnaud resists), or the white roses (not red) that he offers her when she cuts short her tour of Corsica to return to Paris for medical tests, these symbolic gestures originate at a very deep level before they are redirected or shaped by specific social codes and ends. For our philosophically trained and questing writer-protagonist, the biological or material or physical base does seem to have input into our other discourses and relevance for the questions of freedom and power she is posing in her work.

In this woman politician's tale, then, there is an attempt to re-write the body/mind dichotomy suggested by the Cartesian "cogito, ergo sum" (I think, therefore I am) as something closer to Merleau-Ponty's formulation, "I feel, therefore I am." Bouchardeau seeks to rewrite the separation of the private and the public and of the feminine and masculine at a deeper level and to give a voice to this level, which functions beyond verbal expression. The contradictory needs that the text insists on, for sophisticated city and for simple country, for public and private life, for affinities of mind and of body, for emotional commitment over time and for openness to new relationships and freedom, like the desire to know and understand the experience of others, and the exigencies of her own truths, cannot be neatly fitted into bipolar, mutually exclusive, and logical frames.

This intelligent, analytical *agrégée de philosophie* and hardworking, efficient minister, a logical and reasonable "self," then, is also portrayed as a person with irrational fears and doubts, loves and sexual jealousies, contradictions and desire for an absent absolute. Moved by a hidden unconscious that may manifest its concerns in the reactions of her body, she is also a product of her history, the social texts of her upbringing and education that her writing traces in reflections and flashbacks. The multiple and constantly moving character of identity and its corporeally and institutionally constructed nature bring Bouchardeau's ideas close to the thought of Foucault. Nonetheless, her emphasis on the subconscious, which Foucault eschewed, widens the scope of her reflection.

In the novel, these questions of power and the more abstract concerns of imprisonment within established sociocultural and political texts are grounded in the fragmented, complex, and incompletely "knowable" events of the body and personal experience. They are also formulated in response to very specific local, socioeconomic and political contexts and have a genealogy—the places and the history from which the narrator speaks. Bouchardeau summarizes the narrator's desire to "succeed" and her Socialist commitment as deriving from her reaction against the humiliation and disempowerment of the economic situation of the large family of limited means she was born into in working-class Saint-Etienne in the 1930s. Her feminist interests and her political career could stem from her need to reject her mother's condition of inequality. Daily preparing the "patriarchal" suits and shirts, welcoming home the "master" in a nightly family ritual, this mother who trembled like her children at the slightest raising of "his" voice, is described in retrospect and unequivocally as a "consenting slave."

Yet the influence of the family is more complex and indirect, and not amenable to complete capture by such labels. In spite of family difficulties and the unequal family hierarchy of power, the character of Jean points out that there is still love, life, and warmth of spontaneous feeling in this large urban family. This is lacking in his own suburban, middle class, ordered, and attentive upbringing. His parents may have been more educated and more equal but they are repressed and silent and unable to communicate emotion in any meaningful way. Jean's parents created unhappiness and a strong sense of confinement in their child.

Huguette Bouchardeau's text turns on the interrogative "writing" of the power she held with determination. It investigates critically and explores imaginatively a quest for legitimacy in the public arena. Her writing, like Giroud's, is a complex probing of her relation to maternal legacies and paternal legitimization. Refusing for women the single role of "frustrated satisfier," the female minister in the novel attempts to raise the question of the complex dialectics of power and powerlessness in the closets of our fantasies and in intimate relationships.[20]

## *A Woman Trapped?*

This political novel is thus made of the disparate fragments that constitute the story of a life and the history of a time. For Bouchardeau it was a combination of the Socialist political victory and the March of Women that catapulted her as a front-runner (or female token or figurehead?) into the political arena. Her position in public life was not due to an obvious political prominence or personal desire. Is there indeed in all this, her text seems to ask, a serious "taking control" of her life? During the numbingly busy years of childbearing, child raising, and university teaching, there had been little room for her own desires. Reflecting on these frames of economic necessity, family obligations, and her job, the narrator wonders retrospectively whether her own choice had in fact ever been a significant factor in any aspect of her life.

In full possession of the powers and privileges of government minister, surrounded by attention and sensitive to the beauty of the Corsican landscapes she is visiting, the narrator concludes that "all the elements of an agreeable cocktail had been brought together; everything except her own health, her own friends, her own desires."[21] Is this in fact empowerment, "power to change" or even "power over"? Is politics simply performing—playing one's role adequately in a preset scenario? "Did I say my lines well? Did people like my dress? Did I mime with exactness the feelings and convictions they expected?"[22] Perhaps these constraints of the political scene, the melding of the private person with a politically acceptable persona, are not so very different from the mother's persona of caring keeper of the immaculate shirts and polished floors.

The work ends with this suspicion of entrapment, staged indirectly through narrative device. Walking home from the frightening hospital verdict of cancer without, for once, the protective bubbles provided by priority ministerial transport, the protagonist is recognized and greeted by a group of women. Warmly and directly admiring of her political role, these women ask questions about the chances for the future of women in the political world. Why, the narrator asks, returning us to an image of her visit to the *palombière*, do I suddenly think of the blinded decoy wood pigeon, perched at the top of the pines, manipulated by the inexorable strings of the hunter, yet attracting lost migrations by the mad beating of her wings?[23] In a personal and non-universalizing voice, there is recognition that her search for self-realization and political change within the existing power structures is a compromised one. The road to power has blinded and prevented free flight. Like Françoise Giroud before her,[24] she must assume the shame of compromise, of speaking obliquely, or in the words of Saint-John Perse, which give the novel its title, "the shame that trembles on the lips of things said indirectly":

> la honte
> qui tremble sur les lèvres
> des choses dites de profil.

The questions raised in this novel by women's difference and difficult entry into ready-made ("masculine") structures of power cannot be answered definitively or from any absolute position. It is probable that the necessary solidarity with the (male) leaders/cult figures of the party (Prime Minister Laurent Fabius and President François Mitterrand) and the compromises of one's own convictions necessary to retain power limit political women's input into a new order.[25] Or a worse scenario, still: her political "success" may make her a decoy, like the wood pigeon, a distraction for other women seeking these new freedoms in other directions.

Huguette Bouchardeau's autofictional writing was an early expression of the new thinking evolving from the discourse of the major women's movements and of parity. The consequences of identification with male rules of conduct, notions of value, and political laws are not, however, those of negative self-doubt or traditional female self-reproach. The woman politician, caught in a web of texts she has not written, possessing power and responsibility but unwilling to internalize the alien forms of that power, decides to write to explore the imprisonments of language in language. Only words can break the spell of words.

Huguette Bouchardeau had not given up political power or the political frontline at the time of writing. In 1988, she was one of only thirty-three women among the 577 elected representatives to the French Assemblée Nationale. She was one of a new generation of women seeking a succession to the strength of those such as Golda Meir, Indira Gandhi, and Margaret Thatcher, who dared to challenge male politicians at their own game. The question was "what power"? The answer, her text seems to suggest is: not that power in place that is a product of "masculine" psychosexual development, as shaped by sociopolitical contexts. Not complicity with the lobby of those whose self-interests are served by nuclear armaments and the destruction of protest ships, or with the ecological degradation of the planet for immediate self-aggrandizement, or with the violence perpetuated in shooting/killing metaphorically feminized wildlife in spite of "a rough affection" for the birds shot. Not the compromises with the institutions of this power but rather a refusal to internalize their structures. A striving first for a greater degree of awareness at all levels of the texts that imprison and the continued hope for a trembling on the lips, the speaking of something less mediated, the writing power that might arrive at something new and more direct.

## Writing as Anti-Knowledge and Anti-Power

### *Carnets de Prague*

There are differences in the nature of the knowledge explored in Bouchardeau's interviews, party programs, political autobiography, and autofiction. Her three other (auto)fictions continue the investigation of women's emotional needs and psychological reactions to modes of power.

In the novel, *Carnets de Prague* (Prague Notebooks), Bouchardeau again reflects on the gap between conscious goals and the unconscious stirrings of desires and jealousies beneath the control and order of political and social institutions.[26] The three notebooks explore the relationship of the narrator with three different men against the backdrop of the history, architecture, and changing political faces of Prague.

The first story is the first-person narration of a university teacher from Lyon, like Bouchardeau herself. This narrator travels to Prague for a conference on Kafka with a friend, Serge, leaving behind her husband and daughter. Against the backdrop of the liberation of Prague and the "Spring" of July 1968, and the luminous discovery of the grandiose and extravagantly splendid disorder of the gilded baroque face of that city, the narrator lives a passionate three-day adventure with a hunter and conqueror. Serge orchestrates both the visit of the city and the relationship, reserving a dinner table without asking the advice of his companion, making love with a violence that takes no account of her pleasure. What is the female narrator seeking from the relationship? Perhaps, indeed, to make love, but also to be recognized and to share tenderness. The female narrator accuses Serge of being afraid of being taken over, eaten alive by hungry ogresses. There is no clear correspondence between the exterior political events of the liberation of Prague from oppression and the intense interior experience that also contains aspects of oppression.

In the second notebook, the narrator returns to Prague in June 1974 with her husband. This time she finds the poverty of the villages, the limitless and dehumanized fields of grain, crumbling roads and pollution, the sadness of a grotesque bureaucracy. The pronoun "we" replaces the familiar "you" (*tu*) and this time, the couple stays not in the golden and ochre town but in a grey area of the old town where soldiers are everywhere. Life with Pierre's gentleness and calm, his almost "feminine" side, creates a protective shell of shared tastes, concerns, and much affection. Yet the banality of conjugality is evident. This relationship is in sharp contrast with the tyranny and fragility of masterful love shared fleetingly with Serge.

The third male figure, the Jewish university professor, Karel, a specialist in Kafka studies, turns up on the Charles Bridge to meet Pierre. He tells his own story of being demoted to a trash-collector, replaced at the university by an expert in dialectical materialism. Karel represents the different and contradictory faces of the 1974 city. He signifies the

Prague of Mozart and Rilke but also of the political police constantly following them. A Prague where ordinary people live, but where there exists a more sordid underground city of political repression. There is no authority claimed in these stories, no general theory of the feminine or any single solution offered to the complex issues of political (and sexual) freedom and oppression.

## *Living in Community*

Bouchardeau's second novel, *La Grande Verrière* (The Glass-House Community) continues the reflection on the complex nature of desire in its relation to subjection and freedom.[27] The novel examines an experiment in the early 1970s of a community model that sought to alter the traditional relations of power at both the individual level and the level of the social group. The post-1968 experiment in reinventing the family unit is examined through a cast of disparate characters linked by their quest for something different. It is not without significance that the binoculars watching the "glass house" from the outside are focused most insistently on the sexual relations within the community. In the final instance, the weight of the structures outside and the jealousies inside overwhelm the fragile structure. This happens in 1973, just as Allende's fledgling, showcase, socialist state in Chile is overwhelmed by the weight of the army, the middle-class, and powerful North American interests—that is, the established structures.

The rhetoric and ideas at play in *La Grande Verrière* are those of the late 1960s and 1970s—third world, feminist, unionist, left-wing. Most of the women in the group have become active in the militant Mouvement pour la Libération de l'Avortement et la Contraception (MLAC), seeking legal access to abortion and participating in support for illegal abortion clinics. But the male members of the group are basically unsympathetic toward this women's cause. Didier argues that such militancy is folly in a region like Franche-Comté where strong traditional morality will provoke a backlash. Eric claims that abortion is destruction; Le Filou is ironic about such "women's problems." The narrator comments on the gender differences in opinions on how to change the world. Action, rallies, a strict separation between public and private life characterize the male world. Open discussion predominates among females for whom feelings and bodily experiences are central.

The debate about the viability of a community as a model for living and social organization is an intellectual and rational one. The narrator thinks through the relative importance of goals and organizational models. But the force that appears to motivate and preserve the community arises at an unconscious and emotional level. This is expressed by the metaphors of warmth and togetherness around a fire, or of a "bubble" that is a haven of protection, or by the age-old metaphor of family. Commitment to social, union, and political action, outside, is not sufficient.

There are autobiographical elements in this fiction. The arrival of the married couple, Jane and Bernard, in Besançon may well repeat a chapter in the life of the author and her husband. One of Bouchardeau's children is a member of an ecological community. The assiduous reader of Bouchardeau's work also recognizes elements from the biographical *Rose-Noël* (1990), the biography of Huguette Bouchardeau's mother, adapted in this fiction in the story of the divorce of Jane's parents.[28] Jane is forced to admit the deep divisions between her parents that she had always minimized. Although Jane had accepted the term "conjugal rape" in the women's groups, it seemed quite unacceptable to designate the relations of her parents in this manner. Jane is unable to come to terms with her parents' divorce. She situated herself in her father's camp on the grounds that her mother was no longer at all interested in sex.

*La Grande Verrière* adds a scene not present in *Rose-Noël*, in which the father meets with the daughter. He seeks her help to effect reconciliation with his wife, and awkwardly attempts to justify his mistress in terms of his wife's lack of desire and his unwillingness to frequent prostitutes. This admission of guilt causes Jane distress as the heroic image of her father is altered by his self-humiliation. The narrator concludes that "as a good feminist," Jane should be happy to witness her mother's "model rebellion." But after the divorce and the mother's distress at losing the family home, Jane begins to develop the intolerable and debilitating headaches that are apparently a psychosomatic manifestation of her refusal of her parents' divorce at some deeper level. Ideology, will, and choice are once again obliged to come to terms with the existence of the unconscious.

On the one hand there is the confinement imposed by the nuclear family and inhibiting taboos, on the other hand there is the recognition of the egoism of love and the rage to possess and the ultimate failure of the wider community sought. Between the two, Bouchardeau seeks understanding of women's unconscious desires and the implication of such desires for political structures. In Bouchardeau's writing, then, knowledge and power derive also from sentiment, relationships, and the unconscious, often as a kind of anti-knowledge or anti-power.

The new autobiographical fictions explore what the political memoir and the manifesto cannot: the complex—even contradictory—relations between rational and unconscious structures, creating a relation of "complementarity" in the Heisenberg sense (contradictory but not mutually exclusive truths). The writings of Bouchardeau constitute a call to women to engage in the present political contexts, while retaining an awareness of the compromises this implies and maintaining a search for a different and less compromised political existence. This will involve taking some account of the gap between rational goals and unconscious impulse.

There are gaps between the call to women to enter politics in the political autobiography *Un Coin dans leur monde* (1979), and the limitations, hypocrisies, and cancers unveiled in the participation in established political orders in the autofictions *Choses dites de profil* (1988) or *Le Déjeuner* (1992). The portrait of the failure of a community based on alternative lifestyle and power relations (*La Grande Verrière*) and the stories of intimate relationships (*Carnets de Prague*) suggest the complex relations of domination and submission, and the need for control that emerge in relations of personal commitment or jealousy (a form of competition) much as they do in the political arena. The gaps between these truths of conscious commitment and unconscious impulse cannot be filled in.

In 1978 Bouchardeau had already established a book series entitled "Mémoire de femmes" with the Syros publishing company. Since leaving politics in 1995, she has devoted herself to literature, setting up her own publishing house, HB Editions in Aigues-Vives, a small town where she also serves as mayor.

## Notes

1. Huguette Bouchardeau answered my questions in a long interview in 1993, in 1994, and again in January 1997. Along with the talk entitled "Un parcours politique" (A Political Journey) published in *Femmes Pouvoirs* (Women Powers) in Michèle Riot-Sarcey, *Femmes Pouvoirs* (Paris: Kime, 1993), pp. 51–58, papers read at a conference in Albi on 19 and 20 March 1992, these interviews articulate an explicit public political credo deriving from Bouchardeau's long experience in public life.
2. Huguette Bouchardeau, *Hélène Brion: La Voie féministe* (Paris: Syros, 1978). Brion's work for pacifism saw her on trial before the War Council for defeatist propaganda in 1917. In 1920, Brion argued that excluded from night work and from male professions and with no protection against male violence, women were in fact more exploited as women than as workers. Bouchardeau observes that Brion's male socialist comrades were unable to integrate the objectives of women's struggle and radically transform social relations.
3. Huguette Bouchardeau, *Choses dites de profil* (Paris: Ramsay, 1988).
4. The *agrégation* is the competitive, elitist national examination that gives access to teaching positions in tertiary education and higher level secondary education in France.
5. "Depuis toujours, c'est le regard des hommes qui nous évalue, qui nous apprécie, qui nous donne droit à exister. Pour être capable d'encourir les jugements et les sarcasmes masculins, il faut se sentir soutenues par d'autres, sinon, il n'existe plus que le jeu des rivalités." Huguette Bourchardeau, *Un Coin dans leur monde* (Paris: Syros, 1979), p. 34.
6. "Enfin, parce que nous nous trouvions sensibilisées aux rapports de dépendance à autrui qui se manifestent dans la vie quotidienne, familiale ou amoureuse, nous attachions plus d'importance à ce qui se jouent de rapports de pouvoir dans toutes les relations inter-individuelles. Et nous désirions dépasser ce type de rapports." *Un Coin dans leur monde*, p. 42.
7. *Temps modernes*, no. 317 (December 1972), p. 43.
8. Huguette Bourchardeau, *Un Coin dans leur monde*, p. 43.
9. "J'aimais les jeans et les robes gaies, j'ai mis du beige et un tailleur." Ibid., p. 56.
10. Traditionally, many tenured professors in France commute from their hometowns to the university where they teach two or three days a week.
11. Huguette Bouchardeau, *Choses dites de profil* (Paris: Ramsay, 1988).

12. *Rainbow Warrior* was the protest yacht of the international ecological organization Greenpeace, which was blown up in the harbor of Auckland, from where it planned to sail on a mission to protest the imminent series of French nuclear tests in the Pacific.
13. In 1993, nuclear testing was suspended in the wake of the Clinton administration's moratorium. A final series of tests in 1995 programmed by the new president, Chirac, aroused intense worldwide protest. In 1996, most of the world's countries, including France, finally agreed on a test ban.
14. Huguette Bourchardeau, *Choses dites de profil*, p. 136.
15. Ibid., p. 197.
16. Ibid., p. 131.
17. Ibid., p. 62.
18. Ibid., p. 81.
19. The notion of "redirection" is used in the sense that the ethnologist Konrad Lorenz gives it in his work. Lorenz postulates a "redirection" of primitive and general intra-species aggression in social ceremonies and rituals. In Greylag geese, for example, a complex greeting ceremony that is essential for sexual bonding derives from gestures of aggressive territorial defense. These ceremonies thus have their origin in instinctive drives initiated by brain-stem mechanisms that are much the same in all Mammalian species (aggression, appeasement/escape, and bonding). Yet even at the lower levels of the animal world, the arousal they provoke is subsequently "redirected" for more subtle social purposes.
20. This term is used to describe the masochistic, passive, security seeking (at the expense of pleasure) pole of what is seen as a universal, bipolar, and interdependent structure of the psyche in the study of sadomasochism by Marie Gear and Melvyn Hill, *Working Through Narcissism. Treating its Masochistic Structure* (Jason Aronson, Inc., 1982). The "bad satisfied frustrator" in fact believes that he is the "good frustrated satisfier"—and vice versa—in this narcissistic relationship.
21. Huguette Bourchardeau, *Choses dites de profil*, p. 11.
22. Ibid., p. 11.
23. Ibid., p. 282.
24. Françoise Giroud was the first *secrétaire d'Etat* for women's status in Giscard d'Estaing's first cabinet (1974–1976), and for cultural affairs during the period that saw the realization of the Centre Pompidou (1976–1977).
25. The writer, Marguerite Duras, angry former member of the French Communist party, also defended the government's action on the somewhat tenuous grounds of worldwide communist conspiracy, and a freedom-eating monster called Gorbachev! (Interview in *L'Autre Journal*). Duras remained a personal friend and admirer of François Mitterrand with whom she published a series of interviews in the same magazine. Duras was often as misguided in her political pronouncements as she was original and powerful in her creative writing.
26. Huguette Bouchardeau, *Carnets de Prague* (Paris: Seghers, 1992).
27. Huguette Bouchardeau, *La Grande Verrière* (Paris: Payot, 1991).
28. Huguette Bouchardeau, *Rose-Noël* (Paris: Seghers, 1990).

# 9

# Françoise Giroud: Rewriting Maternal Legacies and Paternal Authority

In *La Comédie du pouvoir* (The Comedy of Power, 1997), the journalist Françoise Giroud writes an account of her three years as a minister under the presidency of Valéry Giscard d'Estaing, first in Chirac's government (1974–1976) and later in Raymond Barre's cabinet in the Ministry of Culture (1976–1977). In 1978, Giroud resigned her political office in disillusionment and returned to writing. Her purpose in returning to writing was to demystify the political world she had just abandoned while her knowledge was still alive, not "reconstructed by memory" or "watered down by time," as in traditional political memoirs. Like Bouchardeau's writing, her project is to discover, within the well springs of power, the hidden mechanisms of high political office that might constitute a form of counter-power.

Giroud's account of her sojourn in the land of government concludes that the sooner people know that "the king is naked and his court with him" (in other words, that democracies do not have all-powerful fathers but only appointed clerks and servants), the better the chances that the relation between the individual and the state will change. The journalist and former politician feels that despite nostalgia for the great leader, citizens would then stop expecting everything from the government and cease rising up against the state as one does against a bad master.

Although Giroud finds corruption to be rare among an administration characterized by a strong sense of the state, in her estimation its capacity for change or reform is limited. Choosing government by election is fine, says Giroud, but do not count on governments to change life. She shares with Huguette Bouchardeau the conviction that local associations and citizens' action are more likely to solve problems of everyday organization.

*Françoise Giroud.*

## Giroud: The Outsider

Giroud's story of the elites of power and the structures of decision making is told from the perspective of an outsider, "surprising men at their games of power." She is particularly fascinated by the nature of the battles of strength between Giscard's refined and intellectual approach, and Chirac's cunning as a politician, what she sees as his instinct to kill and to win. Giroud says the president was neither the typical pater familias nor master, but rather the top of the class, shocked by the irrational and by passion, lacking the killer's instinct. It may be for these reasons that he was genuinely concerned with the advancement of women, however little, as his own memoirs show, he understood them. Chirac was in Giroud's eyes closer to the more rustic, timeless French traditions (*la France des profondeurs*), proud of his past, self-possessed, with good reflexes, and not eaten up by scruples: "He wants power, all the power. There are few known cases where such a combination does not bear fruit."[1]

Giroud found herself in the invidious and difficult situation of entering politics in 1974 "under the protection of a man"—"as if Valéry Giscard d'Estaing had offered me a gift of jewelry to satisfy some whim."[2] Giscard's Gaullist sense of France and his own historic mission as repository of the past and of the state, for Giroud, replaces any sense of ownership. Giroud sees the French system as perilous precisely because the president is at once head of a coalition that can be contested and the immovable father of the nation for a term of seven years. In Giroud's analysis, given the tendency of power to absolutism, to spread itself ever wider, the divorce between politics and real life is perhaps the biggest danger threatening those who govern and their advisors who know only the statistics.

Alongside Giroud's plea for a more grassroots and creative sharing in government, for the knowing and eschewing of an absolute or paternal authority, there is a story about women. Giroud shares with Giscard the conviction that women's history is central in contemporary societies, although she considers that Giscard missed the real point of women's desire for autonomy: "Do you think, he asked me, that women are going to want to live like men?"[3] For Giroud, it is the relatively harmonious evolution of men and women toward equivalence, not sameness, that constitutes the distinctively French experience.

## *A Separate Ministry for Women*

Giroud accepts the role of first *secrétaire d'Etat* for the status of women as a challenge. But it is not without significance that she quotes the dismissive comment made by Madame Rocard, the wife of the Socialist leader Michel Rocard: "Personally, I'm against the idea of a Ministry for Women; it makes me feel like a chimpanzee."[4]

Mariette Sineau's interviews with women politicians have shown the persistent resistance in France toward separate institutional offices for women. Elisabeth Badinter and Michèle Sarde have theorized the rejection of any kind of war of the sexes and the sense that women's identity in France derives more from their relationship with the opposite sex than from any group or "minority" status. Giroud's life and writing presents an example of the belief in the importance of maintaining a quality of seduction, an elegance defined in terms of femininity, and an interest in male company, while still maintaining independence, intelligence, and wit.

Giroud invests fully in her political mission, but never identifies fully with the women's movement. A certain realism with respect to the masculine structures of the political world in which she herself is implicated as a career woman does not prevent her from praising the solidarity of the women with whom she works. She claims to be able to empathize with women, even those with conservative positions she does not share.

> Women are dear to me, including the most dangerous: those for whom any woman who has escaped the ancient servitude in a number of aspects of her life is a living insult to their own mutilation, which is all the more painful because it is secret.[5]

At the end of the Ministry for Women experiment, Giroud seeks to resign after finding herself with no budget and no means for action. Giroud writes that she does not regret the two years where she "literally cloistered" herself in the company of women "in obsession and asphyxiation absorbed by the specific problems of their condition." There is a strong sense, however, that in the choice of the non-inclusive pronoun "their," although she identifies herself as "feminine," Giroud's first impulse is to situate herself outside, not inside, the community of women. She situates herself in the masculine world of decision making where she has been able to function professionally.

Jacques Chirac presented the new Ministry for Women as the expression of a vaguely perverse Parisian intellectualism. Giroud responded: "Within a fortnight, he'll have me setting up my office in the kitchen at Matignon making the coffee for the gentlemen of the UDF."[6] Journalists wanted to photograph Giroud with the grandchildren, the political woman's proof of being a "real" woman. They asked her to talk about her cooking. Giroud refused. She was working precisely to impose other criteria by which women could be judged, working to "invent" an as-yet non-existent new Ministry for Women.[7] Her recognition that all the parameters of modern societies meet in women's changing roles was an indication of the nature of the challenge Giroud found in the "woman question." Further evidence of this challenge was her interest in the factors that were, for example, making the divorce rate climb in the United States and the Soviet Union and the birthrate decline in both Germanies. At the same time, there remained and remains a strong humanistic element in Giroud's commitment, a clear awareness of the obstacles and inequities faced by many women within the present structures of authority. Giroud's acceptance of the challenge stemmed perhaps less from desire than from the feeling that even as a "token" woman, and despite her personal ambivalence, she had no right to refuse out of an obligation to other women.

Giroud's action was pragmatic and non-theoretical. She warns that while we seek answers to the questions of women's rights and the relations between the sexes, or attempt to alter the patriarchal structures of the family, the children and young people of industrial societies are becoming increasingly fragile. Anything that can be done to protect them is worthwhile even if, for the most part, family policy continues to seek to preserve patriarchy—what Giroud calls "domestic monarchy."

## *The Achievement of the First Ministry for Women*

Ministerial life was a tight network of conventions and politeness, with a script known by all the players, observes Giroud. The organization of the Ministry for the Status of Women (*Condition Féminine*) was not vertical, as in most ministries, but inter-ministerial. Giroud claims that nothing was impossible, except getting ministries to cooperate. In the name of their image and prerogatives, ministers tended to resist any kind of interference.

Despite difficulties with the institutional aspects of decision making, Giroud has much to her credit, including an extraordinary session of the Council of Ministers in 1976 where a large number of the "100 measures for women" elaborated in her ministry were accepted.[8] Each of the measures was worked out separately with the ministries concerned backed by the support of the president. Giroud says the measures were then presented to the ministers in a package whose magnitude, she notes, the individual ministries could never have guessed at. Giroud notes with humor the ambiguity of the response to what could not be directly contested in a modern "equal" world. Beneath the goodwill and understanding, she observes, surprise, concern, reservations, resistance, and finally resignation could turn by turn be detected. For, in their heart of hearts, she concludes, these men had never believed that measures so far from their real desires would actually be put in place. Giroud's tone is similar to that of Michèle Barzach—that is, the tone of someone who is very much an outsider. Giroud's "Program for Women, 1976–1981," took a long time to become reality and its impact was somewhat diminished by these delays, but it did bring about some reforms.

## *Personal Conclusions on Power*

Giroud's personal conclusions on the experience of being "in power" are not positive. She resents the necessity to give up her life to members of the public showing up at half-hourly intervals to solicit her aid. She dislikes the inaugurations, the visits to buildings and factories, the breakfasts at the Prefecture, the dinners at the Town Hall, large meals, too much wine, the endless files to study and assimilate. Giroud is irritated by the cordon of official cars, the sea of dignitaries between her and reality. Like most women who will write about their political experience, she expresses discomfort with the protective, isolating bubble created by the old-fashioned luxury of second-empire chandeliers, doormen, and police officers clearing the road for their chauffeured cars. Giroud remembers being called to order by the minister of the interior when she tried to escape the bodyguards and the escorts. The minister was told she was putting the dignity of France at risk by trying to make direct contact with the electorate. Giroud concludes that even if women keep their feet on the ground more readily than men, this life "inevitably corrupts you."[9] Once caught up in the mechanism, she confesses, it is difficult to stay indifferent to the popularity polls.

Seeking to understand what it was that made ministers so happy to be in this position despite their claims to the contrary and the limits to their power, Giroud offers an explanation in terms of sexualized ego satisfaction. The position creates a dilation of the ego, she claims in a striking piece of writing: "The self inflates, swells up, spreads out, caressed, courted, solicited, photographed, insulted, turned into a comic cartoon figure, the feeling of importance and uniqueness maintained by the whole apparatus that surrounds it. For the self no longer does anything like the common mortal."[10] In the final instance, in Giroud's analysis, women appear less overwhelmed by the "pleasure of the dilation of the ego" (*la jouissance dilatoire*) than men. This is not from superior wisdom but because, generally, power adds to male seduction while it detracts from female attraction.[11]

The rituals of the Council of Ministers encapsulate the "comedy" of power every Wednesday morning at the palace of the Elysée. The comedy is that ministers are cloaked in false mystery in the eyes of their staff and the preeminence of the president further excessively highlighted. This preeminence would later be diminished in the periods of coalition government (1986 to 1988, 1993 to 1995, and again beginning in 1997), in the duel between President Giscard d'Estaing and Prime Minister Chirac, for example, or between President Mitterrand and Alain Juppé, or again, the more recent struggle for preeminence between Chirac as president and Jospin as prime minister. Giroud describes the stilted accounts of ministerial activities and remembers a note she passed on to Alice Saunier-Seïté: "Dear Alice, did you have any idea that a Council of Ministers could be so boring?" (*Chère Alice, vous doutiez-vous qu'un Conseil des ministres peut être aussi ennuyeux*?) and the education minister's reply: "Dear Françoise, yes, for I have always been aware of the unfathomable childishness of the masculine sex" (*Chère Françoise, oui, car j'ai toujours constaté l'insondable puérilité du sexe masculin*). This note was certainly just one example of the general circulation of such personal missives in the guise of exchange of political information.

The critical humor of Giroud's pen attacks the attention paid to an atrophied and protocol-ruled male hierarchy, shrouded in small mysteries and focused on the heads of state. The civil servants that run the administration from one government to the next are a ball and chain around new ministerial initiatives and are implicated in the monarchical character of the government, writes Giroud. The public service sector in France absorbs 15 percent of the active population, and it is considered suicide for a government to touch this iron grid of salaries and indemnities.

## *Electoral Disappointments and the Return to Writing*

Giroud accepted with real pleasure an offer to work with Raymond Barre in the Ministry of Culture, where despite a very low budget, she felt that things were on the right path. Although anxious about her responsibilities as one of the first women in political power, she was "happy." Then Giroud found herself pushed into standing for election as a *députée* in a difficult seat, was attacked for misrepresentation of her war medals, lost the election, and left the government. She does not conceal her anger toward Chirac's entourage, who, she claimed, were unhappy at her success and had plotted her downfall.

After her defeat in the municipal elections in Paris, Giroud was anxious to recover her independence and return to writing. Although she felt that her decision to withdraw from politics was less than courageous, the belief that it was not moral to do a job badly and that, as a solitary hunter, she was not really suited for active political life, pushed her to resign. In writing, as Giroud recognized, she could transmit her knowledge of life, love, men and women, grandchildren, and her moral understanding (similar to Simone Veil) that what the world needs is not intelligent people, but people of courage and honor.

In turning back to the pen, Giroud renounced any further active role in national politics. Beginning in 1983, she was an editorialist for *Le Nouvel Observateur* and a literary critic for the *Journal du Dimanche* (1990 to 1994) and for *Le Figaro*. Starting in 1992, Giroud was a member of the jury for the *Prix Fémina,* a literary prize set up to give women a greater chance of winning than the traditional literary prizes that are largely in the hands of male juries. In 1996, in an interview with Elisabeth Guigou, Giroud again observed that she was simply not interested in political life given the mediocrity of political debate, although she agreed it could be challenging for other women.

Giroud's reflection on political principles and her personal feelings, and their convergence, appear as editorials, articles, daily diary entries, memoirs, autobiographies, biographies, and fictions, and along the way create distinctively new and mixed literary forms. Like the content, the form could be said to be feminine in terms of that fluidity that deconstructs genre and the traditional boundaries, and breaks down the dichotomy between the personal and the political to seek new forms of knowledge/power. The message that Giroud transmits is a desire to share with others the knowledge inherent in these "private lessons" in order to produce political lessons of resistance.

## Journalistic Writing on Women

### *Editorials in L'Express Magazine*

Throughout the late 1960s, Giroud had written influential articles for *L'Express*, collected in *Une poignée d'eau* (1992), on divorce and the protection of children, and against the view that women were taking jobs from men. She lauded the success of "Mlle. Chopinet" as *Major* (valedictorian) of the first graduating class that had accepted women in the prestigious *Ecole Polytechnique* and wrote against those who supported the 1920 law forbidding discussion of contraception. She encouraged women not to wait for Prince Charming and marriage in order to find themselves, since "it is in creating oneself that one finds oneself." In 1967, her advice to young women was to "do as you please. But please, in order to protect your own future, do it well" (*faites ce que vous voulez. Mais de grâce, pour votre sauvegarde, faites-le bien*). Giroud argued for the need for a woman to pass from the sometimes-agreeable situation of being a "colonized body" to autonomy and self-reliance. In another editorial for *L'Express*, entitled "Unmentionable Subjects" (*Ces choses-là*), she discussed the need to know and talk about female sexuality. In "Fairy Fingers" (*Les doigts de fée*), Giroud questioned the technical education system that still taught the dying art of sewing to large numbers of young girls. She also gently mocked Lionel Tiger's thesis of the future decline in the potency of American men if men are not permitted to remain dominant.

The collection in *Une Poignée d'eau* shows the wide-ranging character of her portraits of women. Giroud discusses the fragility and strength of Jacqueline Kennedy and the error of Jacqueline's remarriage to Onassis. She looks at the remarkable itinerary of the stateswoman Golda Meir, the daughter of a tradesman, who helped raise her two children by taking in washing, and became the general secretary of the Women's Council in the Union of Jewish Workers of Palestine in 1928 against the will of her husband. In Giroud's opinion, this indomitable woman both cured a serious health problem and led the war cabinet "with that forbidden drug, power."[12] Another editorial describes the kind of woman the electorate expects the president's wife to be—a good housewife but not too extravagant, well-dressed, dignified, but not too striking or original, not too intelligent but not foolish, to be seen at church, or, better still, at the market. She should be pitied if her husband has affairs, but it would be quite out of the question for her to reciprocate. A grandmother? That's excellent.

The "battle of the bra" led Giroud to the observation that women remain prisoners of men's gaze. But in 1975, an early survey of the way women saw themselves indicated they were quietly involved in a revolution. Forty percent of women did not consider marriage to be necessary; 37 percent of women claimed they would prefer to be a man. The account of her co-direction with Jean-Jacques Servan-Schreiber of *L'Express* between 1953 and 1977 as the first woman editor of a magazine not designed specifically for a female readership reveals Giroud overcoming her own fears and the prejudices of the milieu to be, she writes, "as good as a man." Read in the 1990s, these editorials reveal Giroud to have been the intelligent and witty conscience for women over more than three decades. Her full survey of French women published in 1999 (*Les Françaises*) documents the continued and major revolution in women's changing demands for independence, a revolution that her own editorials and example played a major part in creating.

## *Walking a Tightrope:* Elle *Magazine*

Giroud's long career in journalism included a period of eight years, beginning in 1945, working with Pierre and Hélène Lazareff for *Elle* magazine. At that point, Giroud insisted she was not a "feminist" in the sense generally given to the term, and that she felt no antagonism toward men. Her message to the readers of *Elle* had consistently been that the only true independence was economic, and was to be won at all costs. Giroud and Simone de Beauvoir, however, were never kindred spirits. Giroud considered de Beauvoir's denigration of motherhood as naive and her analysis of the domination of women by men to be insufficiently subtle. Giroud did not feel that *The Second Sex* corresponded to her own sense of what made her a woman. The feminine part of herself, she argued, was not a superstructure, an imposed veneer, but the frame—the essential part on which the rest was hung.

## *Ce que je crois* and *Leçons particulières*

*Ce que je crois* (What I Believe), published in 1978, is a political and personal manifesto characterized by a mix of rational analysis and subjective response to experience, a dissection of the political world and a confession of personal feelings and beliefs.[13] In the name of that very judgment and reason that Bergson denies women, and that Giroud claims she cannot discard, the writer nonetheless discusses the need to talk about one's feelings, the thirst for meaning that has never proven the existence of meaning, the desire that has never demonstrated the existence of the object of desire, and the violent awareness of being unique but fleeting like her own son, who died in an avalanche, buried beneath the snow until the spring thaw. She believes that trees suffer when their trunk is cut, that her plants wilt when she forgets to talk to them. Giroud claims that one transmits, but does not give, life, that happiness exists—since we feel its absence when suddenly it is no longer there — and that people contribute to bringing about what they fear or desire. Giroud writes of her commitment to lessening the tension of a world based on personal ambition, expansionism, and feats of arms and violence.

What Giroud traces explicitly in her 1990 autobiography *Leçons particulières* (Private Lessons), is the deeply personal discovery of her own need for paternal legitimization.[14] For Giroud, the drive to know "what one really wants," with all "the force of one's unconscious mind," makes the symbols of power in general (presidents, bosses, fathers, leaders of all kind) rationally suspect. This leads to the corresponding recognition that all regimes are founded more or less on coercion or subjection to a master. Unless one believes, as women have for so long, that this submission is to God's will, to so submit is to allow oneself to be smothered. The message that Giroud transmits is the recognition that autonomy is not instinctive. It is more natural to place one's trust in someone who is higher placed, stronger, more combative, or more powerful than oneself, so one has to fight consciously for this autonomy. Authority should come not from the prince but from one's own agency.

## *Autobiography and Journalism*

If we accept Philippe Lejeune's definition of autobiography in *Le Pacte autobiographique* (The Autobiographical Pact), *Leçons Particulières* would be the retrospective prose narrative of the development of a personality, told in the first person.[15] But as in Bouchardeau's writing, Giroud's self-writing is characterized above all by a breaking down of traditional lines, between the personal and the political, for example. Pain is permitted to make an appearance, along with the re-emergence of the unspeakable. This intimate writing is also public writing and the short vignettes that make up the book are not so very different from the journalistic articles that follow their own generic laws, laws of concision, tension, distance, and consonance with the immediate event, a genre in which the entire writer is condensed in the smallest article. In *Leçons*, there is discontinuity in the snapshots not unlike that found in Giroud's journalism, a narrative sliding between first-person confession and opinion and third-person narrative, between story and political history, self and other.

Giroud's rational utopia is of a world without masters. As she attempts to analyze this in *Leçons*, Giroud situates the roots of her allergy to power in her own father's early death. No real or substitute father had inspired obedience, respect, or fear. No real or substitute father had provided real or illusory protection. The first and master lesson taught by her father was one that this second daughter received on her birthday. Giroud records how her father had wanted a son: "When he saw me, he said 'what a calamity' and legend has it that he dropped me." The writer was to spend her life proving that being a girl was also good. This provided the motivation for being first in her class, for jumping, climbing and taking risks like a boy, for excelling in gymnastics. She was a *garçon manqué*, or tomboy. The death of her father, himself a journalist, left her with the image of masculine bravery, audacity, and seduction. This image was created by the family stories of his talent as a journalist, gift for languages, and courage against the Germans. But it also left her with the realization that men were not trustworthy. Free and independent beings, men could simply disappear. In her experience fathers break up, are vulnerable, and they die. Her mother, on the other hand could be counted on. She fights to feed you, claws like a lion, to protect you and shows the tenderness and solidity of women. Unlike paternal authority, she concludes, maternal authority does not coerce.

Giroud's second major lesson on life came from the humiliation of her indigent mother, dependent on the charity of her family, especially her domineering Uncle. Uncle Adolphe had decreed that as long as he was alive, no woman in his family would ever work. Giroud's lesson concerned the importance of economic power and economic independence for relations of power. The moral that the weak get crushed by the strong was reinforced by a further early experience. At school, France Gourdji

(Françoise Giroud's birth-name), a scholarship student, was required to take the blame for an infraction against the rules by a full fee-paying classmate, the daughter of a wealthy American businessman. What, in fact, she learned from this incident, Giroud claims, was to never allow herself to be crushed by manipulation (and to never crush others).

Learning shorthand and typing to gain a professional qualification, leaving school early to help the family (like Arlette Laguiller and Yvette Roudy), Giroud worked in a bookstore on the Boulevard Raspail. She became a script-girl with the help of the director Marc Allégret, and worked on Pagnol's *Fanny* in 1932 and Renoir's *Grande Illusion* in 1936. Her experiences include the highs of working with René Clair and Jean Renoir, the lows of a milieu where the feudal *droit de cuissage* (the infamous rite of the casting couch) was rampant. Giroud described the feminine condition and passed on her own lessons to young women—flee married men; they are never free on Sundays and rarely in the evening and, among other things, they will steal your youth. Giroud also critiques the "lessons" on power given by other women, again painting these women's portraits standing outside looking in. She presents the accounts of actress Josette Day who talked about how to select men for their money and influence, to "catch" them, in order to reject such advice. Humiliation of the other, any kind of abuse of sexual power on either side is to be avoided.

After an apprenticeship in journalism in Lyon, the help of Marcelle Segal (the celebrity "Dear Abby" columnist) in finding work, and a change of name for the radio, Giroud returned to Paris where the film industry was being rebuilt during and after the war. There Giroud would write the scenarios of more than twenty films. The lesson of this period was an acute and bitter one on the constraints imposed by the fact of being a woman, constraints she had hitherto ignored or denied. Pregnant by a man from whom she had been separated at the beginning of the war in 1940, there was no chance of finding help from an abortionist in Clermond-Ferrand under the Vichy regime. Despite the support of her sister, Françoise feels her youth and freedom disappear as her body grew heavier. Her impression was one of being forced to join a world from which she had attempted to remain separate: "I had often judged women to be babbling and tearful, fussing busily over petty problems. I was in the process of joining the order, absorbed in problems of milk and baby clothes, impossible to find at that time."[16]

The intimate and searching confession seems to curiously repeat aspects of her relation with her own father: "That unwanted little boy undid me. I hated myself for not loving him and later, I loved him too greatly. I never loved him as I should. We were never happy together, and he was a stone around my neck." This confession leads to the courageous transmission of the statement that one should not bring a child into the world if this involves crying at his birth. A second and desired birth, this time of a daughter, produced a quite different and happy relationship. The painfully intimate story of her brilliant son's difficult path through life ended tragically. He had finished medical studies and almost buried the hatchet with his mother when he disappeared skiing outside the authorized ski runs in the Val d'Isère resort. It was two months before his body was recovered when the shroud of snow had melted.

The intolerable experience of powerlessness and loss of self-determination in unwanted motherhood was doubled by the discovery of the inhumanity of loss of freedom. Arrested in March 1944 by the Gestapo and held at the prison of Fresne for her activity in the Resistance, Giroud experienced the fear of torture. She also discovered strength—in the power of habit and in believing that the ignominious character of National Socialism would be the flaw in the apparently powerful system that would bring about its collapse. These very personal experiences are recounted with the talent for dramatic synthesis, concision, and narrative control that characterize Giroud's professional journalism.

## *Lacan: Paternal Legitimatization and the Importance of Language*

Had she met the psychoanalyst Jacques Lacan at the age of twenty-five instead of in her forties after an attempted suicide, Giroud realizes, she would have been less hard on herself for her inadequacies, she would have loved different men, she would not have helped shape *L'Express*. What she calls the banal breakup of a relationship, a breakup that she had not initiated—with Jean-Jacques Servan-Schreiber, it could reasonably be assumed—allowed the unconscious wound of her childhood sense of inadequacy (that of not being a boy) to destroy her self-image sufficiently to provoke a violent desire to put an end to her life. In Giroud's lessons, as in Antoinette Fouque's experience, psychoanalysis was a remedy against ignorance and provided a way forward. Her four hundred sessions with Lacan led to the realization that her unconscious had been marked by someone else's language. Her desire had been imposed on her by the rejection of her femininity by her father, even before her birth. A lesson of this magnitude provoked the recognition that she had been "walking around with the left shoe on the right foot." This led to a painful questioning of her choices, ideals, and values. Giroud's desire "to be as good as" the boy her father had desired without losing her femininity had had a determining influence in her relation to both men and women.

Reflecting on what she herself may have transmitted, Giroud situates this mainly in terms of her possible contribution as a role model for feminine authority. She sees herself presenting a certain way of being a woman in a predominantly male world, of managing relations with men while asserting one's difference, and showing exemplary competence in one's writing. A meeting with Indira Gandhi in India elicited just such a portrait of exemplary feminine authority that insisted on the Indian prime minister's profound femininity: the grace of her hands, her way of thinking, her pragmatism, her love for her two sons, and her role as mother of the nation.

## *Les Hommes et les Femmes* (Men and Women)

Giroud was sufficiently fascinated by the complexity of the power relations between the sexes to explore this question in a series of discussions with the traditionalist but flamboyant intellectual and media-star Bernard Henri-Lévy in *Les Hommes et les Femmes.*[17] Characterized as a distinctively French discussion of "the French exception," this book remained on the best-seller list for many months in 1993 and was translated into a number of languages. Giroud concedes in her conversation with Lévy that there is still, in most women, and to varying degrees, a skilled courtesan—a courtesan able to simulate pleasure in the clumsiest of sexual embrace, to express convincing admiration for a physical, intellectual, or commercial exploit, to detect wounds and apply balm. Women in love will do this effortlessly and spontaneously as long as they receive reward. Good courtesans, on the other hand, are more conscious of what they are doing, never critical of the fragile ego of their property of the moment, tigresses in defense of their territory, wounding only when they sense the presence of the masochist, or if they are denied their reward.[18] On the other hand, Giroud sees modern women as claiming a right to their own happiness and rejects the mysteriously seductive masochistic creatures, attached to their own suffering that Bernard Henri-Lévy presents and recommends as "the eternal feminine."

Giroud's reflection in *La Comédie* on traditional feminine ways of wielding influence had also found food for thought in the person of the power behind the throne, the adviser of Giscard and Chirac, Marie-France Garaud. From the duchesses of the Fronde to Mme. de Porte, says Giroud, the history of France is full of women of this sort. In Garaud's case, nothing is written. Everything happens by telephone. The background is a deferent husband (a lawyer at the Supreme Court), two children, two maids, a law degree, a country estate in the Poitou, and the authority of the well-off middle-class. If there is "straw in the steel," continues Giroud, it is invisible, but Marie-France Garaud only exercised authority in the shadow of a man and refused the ministerial portfolio that Giscard would have entrusted her with. Behind the scene, she was all the more powerful, giving orders to all the ministers at L'Elysée.

Garaud expressed the conviction that front-line positions were for men and described herself as a reactionary and not a feminist. Yet, says Giroud, she was in complicity with women to make fun of the childishness of men, who fear or are subjugated by her influence. There is something so classically literary, almost mythical about this feminine *éminence grise*, described by Giroud as an "intellectual courtesan" (*courtisane intellectuelle*), unwilling to waste time with useless, non-rewarding (non-powerful) men, that has a fascination for men and women alike.

In *Ce que je crois*, there are portraits of new women. They are those women who no longer have the patience or the talent to make-up their faces and bodies, those who abandon the eternal comedy of "being a woman" and the role of courtesan and seek to be themselves, despite the refined satisfactions procured by theater and manipulation. Using metaphors increasingly common in the French feminist vocabulary, Giroud offers the hope that beyond the figures of the virgin and the mother, a non-mutilated, non-circumcised woman can yet be discovered within the "dark continent." Yet here again Giroud is personally honest: unable to pledge allegiance to the myth of the male as God, modern women, she claims, are also unable to do without men.

## Biography as Self-Exploration

### *The Life Story of the Devil's Wife*

Giroud's biographies of women organize the historical documents, first-person accounts, and letters that her own patient research has uncovered. But these texts also continue her own particular interest in the relations between male and female that help determine women's relation with power. Jenny Marx could not know, observes Giroud, that her future husband's words and work put at the service of the proletariat, would become the object of a cult or, indeed, give rise to "barbaric" political systems of which he himself had no conception.

In *Jenny Marx ou la Femme du Diable* (Jenny Marx or the Devil's Wife) Giroud describes how the brilliant balls, garden parties and salons of the first meetings between Jenny von Westphalen and Karl Marx gave way to a six-month period of waiting for the "imperious Moor" to return to Trier from his studies in Bonn. A semi-secret engagement was followed by seven years of waiting through the period of Karl's studies in philosophy and history. The love offered him by this sought-after young aristocrat, the cream of Protestant Trier society, was a source of pride to the son of Heinrich Marx. Although the secret consummation of their love when Jenny was twenty-five was a source of joy, it was a source, too, of guilty torment to Jenny: "I am bad. There is nothing good left in me except my love for you."[19] The years of waiting for Karl to establish the situation necessary for marriage were accompanied by illness and by anguish that his love would not last. Jenny had heroic fantasies—that Karl would lose his right hand in a duel and she would become his scribe, indispensable to his work. Her jealous and exclusive passion could only take the form of traditional female masochism and sacrifice.

The couple finally married without a bridal trousseau or dowry but with sumptuous silverware inherited from the Counts of Argyle. This silverware was pawned, or sold piece by piece, to tide them over the years of material difficulty and instability. Without fixed income, Jenny would be the one to hold the family together, soliciting an advance on an inheritance, and accepting help from a relative or from her rival for Marx's affections, Friedrich Engels. Fiercely ambitious for her husband and the recognition of his genius, Jenny would serve as Marx's secretary in exile and participate actively in political discussion. Expelled with Marx from Paris, she gave birth to the second of six children in Belgium. Returning to France in 1848 to foment revolution in Germany, Karl (now thirty-one) and Jenny (thirty-four) were exiled to England. Jenny shared her husband's conviction that history is subject to economic laws and to the dialectics of class war rather than to the intervention of individuals.

Giroud observes that the birth of a son by Karl to their devoted servant Lenchen—a child for whom the wealthy Prussian, Engels, would assume paternity until his own deathbed—must have overwhelmed the puritan, jealous, and reserved Jenny. But despite her own internal wound, a tacit complicity with Lenchen appears to have been motivated by the need to protect the reputation and respectability of the great man. There had been no historical account of these domestic events to cast Marx's greatness in a somewhat different light until Giroud's biography of Jenny. It was in her fifties, after years of what Giroud describes as deliberate self-subjugation to Karl's cause, that Jenny discovered the pleasure of feminine friendship with Lizzie Burns and her passion for the theater. Jenny died, aged 67, in 1881.

Karl Marx believed that women play a crucial part in social transformations and that social progress can be measured by the social status of the fair sex. He was not unaware of the difficulty of Jenny's life. Described by Wilhelm Liebknecht as "the ideal of womanhood," it was Jenny's noble womanly role to "humanize and educate the barbarian." Engels eulogized her for "an intelligence so clear and so critical, an energy so impassioned, a power of devotion so great." If Jenny had any power, this lay in her love for, and devoted service to her husband and her belief in his greatness. Marx himself remained absorbed by her memory until his death in 1883.

Giroud provides the reader with an implicit interpretation of Jenny's story. After thirty-two years of marriage, she concludes, Jenny von Westphalen would be "the first and willing victim" both of scientific socialism and of the love story of the impecunious revolutionary and the beautiful aristocrat. Had it not been for Giroud's pen, Jenny would have remained, in death as in life, the shadow behind a male hero. Although Giroud does not tell her reader what lessons to draw from the life she reconstructs, this nineteenth-century consenting "victim" of love and devotion to a great man is clearly an anti-model for modern women.

## *"The Art of Being Loved"*

*Alma Mahler ou l'art d'être aimée* (1991) is a story of a very different kind of traditional feminine power.[20] Giroud traces Alma's conquests, from the smitten artist Klimt, to her music teacher Zemlinsky, her subsequent marriage to Gustav Mahler, her relationship with the painter Kokoschka, and marriages to Walter Gropius, the famous architect, and to the writer Franz Werfel. The context was Vienna at the turn of the century, the old capital of Europe with its cafés, opera, theater, salons, where culture transcended a miscellany of nationalities. Giroud points out this was also the city where Freud was treating hysteria and prudery in his women patients and postulating that Eros and Thanatos, not reason, govern human beings. The story begins close to its end, in 1934. Alma, aged fifty-four, was entering a new relationship with a theologian. The relationship as presented by Giroud repeats the pattern of her life to date as a battle of the sexes, a need to seduce, a need to be dominated: "Everything within me just wants to submit to him, but I must repress my own desires. He is the first man who has ever conquered me."[21]

Like Jenny, a woman limited by her time to certain roles, Alma oscillates between the role of the conquered and the role of the Muse whose energy and love inspire the creator, between the role of *femme fatale* and the conqueror whose charm draws life blood. Alma's power, as Giroud presents it, was drawn from the representations she made of herself as a precious object, a superior being nourished by Nietzche, Wagner, Plato and irradiating a sovereign light "rare in women."[22] As Giroud interprets Alma's story, this woman with the temperament of a director of the orchestra, and probably the talent, had little chance of leaving a mark except by seducing the exceptional men around her.

Alma, who was convinced that Mahler's genius could make her better, married a man tyrannically determined to make her his supreme and beloved possession. When Alma wrote to him that she needed to become herself, he replied that she was his wife, not his colleague. Forbidden to compose by Mahler—"From now on, your only profession is to make me happy" (*Tu n'as désormais qu'un métier, me rendre heureux*)—she promises to obey and attempts to repress her own ambitions. Alma, however, is soon writing: "I have everything a woman can desire and yet, I have never cried as much as at this moment." What Alma finds unbearable in Mahler, comments Giroud, is less his reading of Kant to calm her childbirth contractions than the prohibition of any personal work to be accomplished. *Alma Mahler,* then, is a further study of the limited and limiting modes of power that could be exerted by late nineteenth-century women on their world through their influence over men.

## Cosima la sublime: *Mrs. Richard Wagner*

In 1996, Giroud published a biography of Cosima, daughter of the adulterous and stormy relationship between Franz Listz and Marie de Flavigny, comtesse d'Agoult (a nineteenth-century writer who adopted the pen name Daniel Stern). What Cosima's story demonstrates for Giroud, is the power of passion: "there is no obstacle that a woman is not capable of overcoming to capture the man she wants."[23] Refused a divorce by her first husband, Cosima commits social suicide, breaks with her father, Liszt, and loses her two eldest children to move in with Wagner. Even in the isolated village refuge in exile in Switzerland at Tribschen, the village people turn their backs on her. For a period, the king of Bavaria, Louis II, the passionately protective patron of Wagner, no longer communicates with the couple.

Giroud traces a life begun in 1837 on Lake Como in Italy and ending in 1930 in the Germany where Cosima had followed her husband, fascinated once again by the power of the grand love story—the total abnegation of a strong personality simply to smooth the path of a man twenty-four years her senior and the belief in this mission: "He has only me to understand him and to share his isolation in the world. My duty is to make him happy." Wagner sees himself magnified and beautiful in the mirror Cosima holds up to him, the infallible messiah. Giroud concludes: "It must be admitted that the method succeeded and no woman will have been more loved longer than she..."[24] "She has transmitted across the ages the mirage of eternal lovers."[25] The choice of the word "mirage" is indicative of Giroud's deepest judgment of this life choice for women.

## *Biography and Knowledge*

These biographies that highlight the kinds of power or the lack of power women can exert in their lives bring us back to questions of writing. Recovering the lives of other women objectively, drawing on historical documents and witnesses, as we noted in the earlier chapter on biographies of political women, is a less transparent enterprise than it appears at first sight. Despite the net of traditional biography flung open wide to catch the dates and details of witnessed public moments, and the "realism" of including a certain number of letters by Alma, or Jenny, or Cosima, Françoise Giroud herself is making the choice of significant moments, sifting authenticity and individuality from the conventional forms and language of the period, and negotiating the gaps and the empty spaces in limited or contradictory versions of women's lives. Although the description of a childhood, of a personality taking form, can be similar for both men and women, women's lives are seldom as rich in the public traces, their name rarely as evidently worthy of figuring on the cover of a biography as those of men.

It is the "power" of the Muse, traditional women's role of ideal and inspiration for "their men" that stands at the center of the stories of Alma Mahler and Cosima Wagner. Similarly, Giroud weaves an empathetic but critical web to analyze the nature of the power of Jenny's self-sacrificing devotion to the great man of her life. Sacrifices are not without the nobility of the passion that inspired them but the masochism of these female figures is made visible. Giroud's own concern with the paternal legacy and with staging women's repressed need to please the loved figure of authority, father or husband, is at the heart of these portraits. So, too, perhaps is the need to stage and examine her own fascination with the transforming power for women in inspiring love and being the object of great passion. But, of all Giroud's biographical investigations of women's lives, only the life of Marie Curie has produced the visible public marks, the independent and creative activity that make Marie-Curie a woman after Giroud's own conscious mind and heart. For Marie-Curie is a woman of authority in her own right, and not through the fame or notoriety of her relationships with men.

## Une femme honorable *(An Honorable Woman) as Bio-auto-graphy*

There is once again a projection of Giroud's own desires, disavowals of desire, and intellectual discoveries in the writing of *Une femme honorable*, published in 1981.[26] Marie Curie is a heroine, presented as a woman whose courage and passion for her work enabled her to resist the pleasures of simply waiting for a man. Curie was the first woman to teach female science teachers at the Ecole Normale Supérieure de Sèvres (in 1906) and at the Sorbonne; and, in 1995, the first woman to enter the Panthéon of the "Great Men" of the nation along with her husband. A Nobel prize winner in 1911 for her discovery of radium, Marie Curie is still listed in most dictionary entries under the entry for Pierre her husband: nonetheless, she refused to be merely the companion of that great man. Transcending most barriers in a men's world of science, Marie Curie, in Giroud's account, never subordinated her own character and achievements. And yet, much as Jenny replaced her father with Karl, or Alma put her lover in the privileged position of her father, so too did Marie move in a world where males formed her identity to a great degree.

Giroud's series of vignettes on Marie's thirst for knowledge suggest that despite the probable temptations of an early and thwarted romance, the young woman was able to function like a man. Her materially and academically difficult road to a degree at the Sorbonne was further evidence of the firmness of her purpose. The relationship Marie developed with Pierre Curie in France was one of relative independence, mutual respect, and equality in their work, although it still went without saying that, in public, Marie would be sitting in the audience for the first shared Nobel prize award while her husband gave the speech. Through the birth of Eve (later a fighter in the Resistance, journalist and the wife of an American ambassador), of Irène (later the scientist Irène Joliot-Curie and one of the three women ministers appointed to Blum's cabinet in the 1930s), and the accidental death of her husband, Marie Curie continued to center her life around the laboratory she came to direct, producing work of considerable intellectual and public importance. In Giroud's account, Marie-Curie—for whom relationships are integral, not secondary, but not lived to the exclusion of focused and significant public work—is "a truly honorable woman." Huguette Bouchardeau expressed the opinion in her interview with me that "Giroud's Marie-Curie" was the best of her biographies to date, perhaps because Giroud is able to empathize with this woman without concession or condescension.

## *Baring the Secrets of a Father of the Nation*

Giroud's 1995 dramatic narrative of the life of Georges Clemenceau, *Coeur de Tigre* (Tiger Heart), is her only biography of a male figure.[27] It is dedicated, not incidentally, to Jean-Jacques Servan-Schreiber, close companion and Radical party leader. It seems on the surface that Giroud herself succumbed to a nostalgia for an extraordinary and inaccessible "father" in the description of Clemenceau, that father of the young and turbulent French Republic The portrait of this "father" of a nation is doubled by the portrait of Georges's own exceptional father, Benjamin Clemenceau, imprisoned under the Second Empire for his resistance to Napoleon and sentenced to deportation to Algeria. Until his father's death in 1887, writes Giroud, Georges himself will not manage "to kill the father." This Radical republican statesman and hero of the First World War will remain bound to the image of the father as a "martyr to his ideals" and will feel guilty for not being worthy of the persecuted hero.[28] However, despite his later status of a father of the nation, observes Giroud, and the fact that women loved him "to his last breath," Georges Clemenceau was a less than perfect human being.

It is his political sense, his convictions and actions for the common good, his integrity, and courage to stand alone that make Clemenceau the object of Giroud's writing desire. But these are counterweighted by her portrait of his overweening pride, inability to make concessions, and conviction of his own infallibility. In particular, Giroud investigates Clemenceau's marriage on the rebound to the beautiful eighteen-year-old American, Mary Plummer. This wife would wait with her children, while her husband entertained his various mistresses. Suspecting an attachment between the lonely Mary and the children's tutor, Georges insisted she accept divorce under threat of imprisonment for adultery and sent her packing back to America. Mary was separated from her children and left without resources. Georges was boastfully triumphant. In her need to demythify the heroic myth of the father, particularly in his unjustified domination of women, Giroud is here again writing bio-auto-graphy.

*Françoise Giroud publishes* Coeur de Tigre, *a biography of Clemenceau.*

## The Diaries of a *Parisienne*

In 1993, Giroud tried her hand at a new genre, spending three hours each day writing a diary, which the Editions du Seuil later published without corrections as *Journal d'une Parisienne* (Diary of a Parisienne).[29] In 1996, in *Chienne d'année, Journal d'une Parisienne 2* (A Difficult Year. Diary of a Parisian Woman 2), Giroud repeated her successful experiment.[30] Attempting to take hold of events as they happen by their "slippery skin," the writing reflects the movements of public and private life as they are experienced by an observer situated in contemporary Paris.[31] Contrary to the conventions of the genre, the political diary does not pretend to be for personal consumption only.

Intelligent personal analysis remains the hallmark of this writing, which makes no claim to be complete, definitive, or objective. The occasional errors of interpretation or judgment have not been eliminated. For example, Giroud was wrong in her assessment of the possibilities of a political career for the humanitarian Bernard Kouchner of "Doctors without Borders." Giroud observes that despite his friends, courage, compassion, and great popularity, Bernard Kouchner, as an Independent, would not be able to make a political career without a party and political support network. She advised that he should not in fact "roll in the dirt of politics." Kouchner did just that and was appointed minister in the 1997 Socialist government, becoming involved in peacemaking in Kosovo. Giroud notes in their order of occurrence in the political world: Juppé's food for thought comment that in politics "The main rule is to please" (*la grande règle est de plaire*), a rule this somewhat emotionless and authoritarian personality will himself have great difficulty in respecting, and the nomination of the former magistrate Simone Veil to the Ministry of Social Affairs in 1993, rather than to the more "masculine" Justice Department despite her legal background.[32] She describes her own attendance at the meeting on parity in the Assemblée Nationale. Noting the nomination of Kim Campbell as prime minister in Canada and of Tansu Ciller as prime minister in Turkey, Giroud observes that the right-wing women's presence, even as tokens, makes a difference. These apparently fragmented comments bring her to articulate the central question of our own study—why are there so scandalously few women in political office in France and why has the equality prescribed by legal texts not become equality in practice: "No careful analysis of the phenomenon has ever been carried out." What is specific about France? Is it the Latin part of the Gallic heart? Or is it the electoral modes—since a candidate has to be designated by the local branch of a party (*fédération*) and then has to compete with others for designation to an electoral district (*circonscription*)? In any case, concludes Giroud, the whole machinery of the political system, its plumbing and piping, "allows misogyny to prosper."[33]

The 1996 diary is as firmly anchored in the day-to-day cultural and material contexts and problems of Paris, as it is wide-ranging in spirit and intelligence over world events. A daily watch on the lead-up to the presidential elections includes comment on Chirac. Giroud describes his vitality, increased by his growing popularity, but his inability to do more than talk about the social division between those with work and opportunities and those without. The diarist also comments on a television interview with Martine Aubry whom she judges to be direct, precise, rigorous and likeable, with a true passion for public affairs and a love of others. The often deceptively modulated tone holds attention, as unexpected phrases make a lightning strike. If there is any law that women are prepared to defend, by marching in the street if necessary, writes Giroud, it is the law that released them from the condition of animals: "Only animals produce offspring without desiring them."[34] Giroud describes her own difficult visit to Bosnia and the terror on the faces of the women arriving from Zepa, the latest security zone seized by the Serbs, the account of widespread hunger while night life went on much as normal in neighboring Split.

Giroud notes the courageous victory of the female Algerian athlete, Hassiba Boulmerka in the 1,500-meter sprint at the European championships. For Giroud, Boulmerka is a symbol for women who refuse to submit and of an Algerian population that wants to live. Giroud opposes a boycott of the Women's Conference in Beijing on pragmatic grounds because, she says, despite China's human rights record, figures and truths will be revealed there: "Although women will not change the world, they can sometimes make it move forward." The entry for 6 September notes the courage of Hillary Clinton, speaking out at the Beijing conference on the female babies killed and the "enslavement" of women, obliged to have abortions or to be sterilized. She reads the O.J. Simpson case as a sad day for American justice, describes Elisabeth Hubert's announcement without consultation of the increase in the daily hospital co-payment as a "clumsy" move by the health minister. Giroud also pays a final homage to Mitterrand, who died a few days into 1996. She concludes that Mitterrand was ambitious, resolute, patient, strong in dissimulation and strategic intelligence, faithful in friendship if not in love, and worthy of her affection. Only very occasionally do her remarks strike a false note, but on 21 November, for instance, she writes that very few women were present at the book signing of *Coeur de Tigre*, her political study of Clemenceau: "Women are put off by everything that smacks of politics. They want to read about love, the dears... Well, not all of them. But still a considerable number."[35] Here again, Giroud situates herself apart from the mainstream or "a considerable number" of women.

Nonetheless, these private/political diaries construct a new journalistic genre with a wide circulation to inform and to influence—perhaps inspired by traditional women's self-writing (nineteenth-century private diaries) but adding a new public political component and functioning along the lines of Annales history writing with its emphasis on the details of everyday life.

## *A Novel,* Mon très cher amour

Giroud's 1994 novel, *Mon très cher amour* (My Dearest Love) tells a fictional tale this time.[36] It focuses on the importance of early childhood experiences, and of the negative power of jealousy that tears at and destroys love. Giroud's heroine, a woman in her forties, is described as "on her own" whereas, as the heroine is at pains to point out, a man in a similar position is seen as "free." The divorced, former trophy wife of a roving surgeon is finding independence and a sense of self through her work as a literary agent in Paris. She comes slowly to fall in love with a younger and still impecunious lawyer, Jerzy, who is working on the case of a young woman from a prominent family driven by jealousy to kill her deliberately cruel lover. This case is a kind of *mise en abyme* or interior duplication of the heroine's own jealousy. The heroine's jealousy turns out to be devastatingly destructive of her own self-image, the mortal blow to her love, and the negation of the autonomy of the self and the other in which she had believed.

The powerful irrational forces behind human relationships are the moral center of this story. Elements of Giroud's own life and wisdom (the lifelong impact of childhood events and importance of parental influence on later behavior and relationships) are present indirectly and transformed in this fiction, which puts human, and particularly sexual, relations at the heart of both private and public matters.

## On Writing

### Arthur ou le bonheur de vivre (*Arthur, or the Joy of Living*)

In 1998, Fayard published Giroud's twenty-second work since 1952, in the form of memoirs containing, once again, portraits of François Mitterrand and the writer François Mauriac, lessons for living, commentary on contemporary French society, on women, on Giroud's own life, losses, and loves, all brought together in a very personal yet public (journalistic) style. Giroud passes the torch of her wisdom to the next generation in a reaffirmation of the creative—even revelatory—power of a "word" that comes both from without and from deep within: "One does not write what one wants, she claims, one writes what is dictated by a force within. Or one constructs a text, and that is something quite different."

### *Power and Literary Form*

Power, in Giroud's writing, as in Bouchardeau's, lies in the unconscious and its motivations and drives. This is similar to the role that the unconscious or the need for legitimization plays in power. Power is also found in knowledge. Writing, defined as a struggle against oneself to serve ideas, causes, and people, becomes Giroud's own instrument of empowerment and a reason for her existence. It serves the recognition of old servitudes, such as the need for paternal legitimization, or jealousy, and plays a part in the fight against ignorance.

In the French literary tradition, the rhetorical aspects of a discourse have always had significance, and in modern literary theory, form is also meaning. To some extent, Giroud writes against and redefines the dominant discourses by means of new mixed forms—new journalistic texts that combine the philosophical, the socio-critical, and the personal. The linear plot with beginning, climax, and resolution creating continuity, causality and coherence becomes more episodic. The present writing/writer filters the meanings of the past. Giroud uses and sometimes transforms a number of traditional genres: the novel that explores the more intimate of her preoccupations with power relations between a man and a woman, the autobiography that authorizes a confession and a credo, the memoirs that transmit the decanted wisdom of a life, the biography that works through her own convictions on power through a study and understanding of its operation in the lives of others, the diary that provokes an immediate reflection on the significance of events as they happen, and the journalism that analyzes, extracts the kernel of meaning from events and understands and attempts to inflect their direction. Her relation to discourse appears to be governed by both choice and by chance, by a reaction against power and an exercise of power, as in a Foucauldian frame. It is both determined (by a past, a culture, a language and sets of literary and generic conventions) and produced by sudden and momentary irruption (*surgissement*) of thought and feeling as in Foucauldian "genealogy."[37]

What Foucault presents as the myriad forms of power—knowledge, family, kinship, technology—all play a role in Giroud's writing on power, as does the attempt to recover other, more "subjugated knowledge"—like that of maternal legacy. Giroud shows that the relation between paternal authority and maternal legacy can be explored in writing, and indeed be transmitted in new literary and political "lessons." It is the case for Giroud as for Foucault that power, everywhere and nowhere, attempts to grip us at the point where desires and possibilities for self-definition emerge. We are both agents and victims of a power that is constitutive as well as oppressive. Relaxing constraints (on sexuality, or women's participation, or on conventions of genre) is not therefore inherently liberating. For Giroud, bodies and minds, like literary conventions, are pre-shaped; however, they are never totally trapped in power. They can be investigated, understood, written differently—as a rejection of the need for paternal legitimization and the valuing of a rediscovered maternal legacy.

## Notes

1. "Il veut le pouvoir, tout le pouvoir. On connaît peu d'exemples où cette combinaison demeure stérile." Françoise Giroud, *La Comédie du pouvoir* (Paris: Fayard, 1977), p. 256.
2. "la protégée du patron... comme si Valéry Giscard d'Estaing m'avait offert un bijou pour satisfaire quelque caprice." Ibid., p. 229.
3. Giroud continues: "Diable! Même avec lui, il y a encore un fameux travail à faire pour que la nature de l'évolution féminine soit comprise. Au moins y met-il de la bonne volonté" ("Good Heavens! Even with him, there is an awful lot of work to be done to instill some understanding of the nature of the changes in women's situation. At least his intentions are good"). *La Comédie du pouvoir*, p. 147.
4. "Moi, je suis contre le principe de la Condition féminine, ça me donne l'impression d'être un chimpanzé." Ibid., p. 66.
5. "Les femmes me sont chères, y compris les plus dangereuses: celles pour qui, toute femme ayant, dans plusieurs aspects de sa vie, échappé à l'antique servitude est un insulte vivant à leur propre mutilation, d'autant plus douloureuse qu'elle est plus secrète." Ibid., p. 228.
6. "Dans quinze jours, il va me demander d'installer mon bureau dans la cuisine de Matignon et de faire le café pour les messieurs de l'UDF." Quoted in Helft-Malz, Véronique Helft-Malz and Paule Levy, eds., *Encyclopédie des femmes politiques*, p. 151.
7. Giroud refuses to conform to this traditional image: "Je travaillais précisément à ce que l'on jugeât une femme sur d'autres critères."*La Comédie du pouvoir*, p. 82.
8. Among the measures proposed by Giroud in 1974 were the requiring of the signature of both spouses on the tax return, the lowering of the retirement age for women to sixty, a family aid supplement for families with a child under three to be paid whether the mother works or not. A two-year leave of absence without pay after the legal period of maternity leave, which could be taken either by the father or the mother, was opposed by the president but was proposed one year later as an amendment and this measure, too, was passed.

9. "le sûr est qu'il corrompt." *La Comédie du pouvoir*, p. 119.
10. "C'est la dilatation du moi que la fonction provoque. JE se gonfle, s'enfle, s'étale, se dandine, caressé, courtisé, sollicité, photographié, insulté, caricaturé, entretenu par tout l'appareil qui l'entoure dans le sentiment de son importance et de sa singularité. Car JE ne fais plus rien comme tout le monde. JE arrête, décrète, tranche, favorise, nuit, nomme, déplace. JE traverse les villes en trombe, précédé de motards casqués qui font gicler de part et d'autre de leur sillon les automobilistes comme du gravier. JE ne circule qu'accompagné d'un garde de corps, c'est donc que son corps n'est pas n'importe quel corps." *La Comédie du pouvoir*, p. 231.
11. Ibid., p. 233.
12. Françoise Giroud, *Une Poignée d'eau* (Paris: Laffont, 1992), p. 272.
13. Françoise Giroud, *Ce que je crois* (Paris: Grasset, 1978).
14. Françoise Giroud, *Leçons particulières* (Paris: Fayard, 1990).
15. Philippe Lejeune, *Le pacte autobiographique* (Paris: Seuil, 1985).
16. "J'avais souvent jugé les femmes babilleuses et larmoyantes, agitées de préoccupations mesquines. J'étais en train de rejoindre la confrérie, absorbée dans des problèmes, inextricables à l'époque, de lait et de layette." *Leçons particulières*, p. 88.
17. Françoise Giroud, avec Bernard-Henri Lévy, *Les Hommes et les Femmes* (Paris: Orban, 1993).
18. *La Comédie du pouvoir*, p. 105.
19. "Je suis mauvaise. Il n'y a plus rien de bon en moi sauf mon amour pour toi." Françoise Giroud, *Jenny Marx ou La Femme du diable* (Paris: Laffont, 1992), p. 40.
20. Françoise Giroud, *Alma Mahler ou l'art d'être aimée* (Paris: Laffont, 1988).
21. "Tout en moi ne demande qu' à me soumettre à lui, mais il faut me repousser mes propres désirs. Il est le premier homme qui m'ait jamais conquise." Ibid., p. 11.
22. Ibid., p. 12.
23. *Cosima la sublime* (Paris: Fayard/Plon, 1996), p. 10.
24. Ibid., p. 77.
25. Ibid., p. 280 ("Aussi a-t-elle prolongé à travers les années le mirage des amants éternels").
26. Françoise Giroud, *Une femme honorable* (Paris: Fayard, 1981).
27. Françoise Giroud, *Coeur de Tigre* (Paris: Plon/Fayard, 1995).
28. Ibid., p. 18.
29. Françoise Giroud, *Journal d'une Parisienne* (Paris: Editions du Seuil, 1994).
30. Françoise Giroud, *Chienne d'année, Journal d'une Parisienne 2* (Paris: Editions du Seuil, 1996).
31. Entries on the international political events of 1993 include the war in Bosnia in which, for the first time in the century, observes Giroud, the Serbs use rape systematically as an instrument of power. The efforts of the humanitarian organization ACIF (International Action Against Hunger), of which Giroud is honorary president, are recounted. Giroud also analyzes the GATT agreement on international trade and its clause protecting French culture through the exclusion of the audio-visual sector, and Clinton's first electoral victory in the name of reinventing America. On the national scene, the morose economic situation figures along with the legislative elections in France that will result in a landslide for the right. She assesses such events as Bérégovoy's tragic suicide; stripped of his honor and his successes by the media, he could not accept the image of himself reflected by the public. The many scandals in France—in government, sport, and business—are discussed, including the end of innocence in sport with the rigged soccer match between Marseilles and Valenciennes and the downfall of the entrepreneurial opportunist and politician Bernard Tapie, who owned the Marseilles team. Minor personal activities are not separated in any way from these major political events. The reader follows the observations of a journalist and public personage in encounters with well-known writers and artists, but also follows a woman meeting with her family, a granddaughter, a great-granddaughter. Her stories include the gathering of the jury to decide the Fémina literary

prize, conversations with her butcher or taxi driver, a reception given by Pamela Harriman, the American Ambassador, or a trip to Madrid for a book signing of *Les Hommes et les femmes* and a quick visit to the feminist minister of social affairs, Cristina Alberti. Interspersed with intimate reflections on the difficulties of aging (Giroud was 77 in 1993), on the life-sustaining value of desire (*c'est le désir qui vous tient vivant*), the pleasure of music and painting, the reflections on political power become diffuse and non-synthetic.

32. Françoise Giroud, *Journal d'une Parisienne*, p. 56.
33. Ibid., pp. 110–111.
34. Françoise Giroud, *Chienne d'année, Journal d'une Parisienne 2*, p. 191.
35. "Les femmes sont très facilement rebutées par tout ce qui a une connotation politique. Elles veulent qu'on leur parle d'amour, ces chéries... Enfin, pas toutes! Mais bon nombre encore." Ibid., p. 269.
36. Françoise Giroud, *Mon très cher amour* (Paris: Grasset et Fasquelle, 1994).
37. In his essay on "Nietzsche, Genealogy, History," Foucault argues that in traditional history, events are given a false unity and coherence and are deprived of their singularity and immediacy, reduced to oversimplified configurations to accentuate their final meaning or value. Genealogy is the historical investigation into the conditions of emergence of a work that presents the self as a free subject responsible for action in the public sphere, but recognizes the possible irruption of the unconscious and the conditioning of the system and of language. Biology, language, the unconscious, and the economy, for Foucault, are all hidden determinations of our identity.

# Part V

## In Conclusion

# Afterword

This book has traced the major changes in women's political presence in France and the perceptions of that presence over more than half a century since women gained eligibility to vote and to stand for political office. Changes have not always been linear and progressive, and deeply internalized gender norms mean that backlash and regression to old norms of exclusion, separate spheres, and inequality continue to remain possible. Yet the substantially increased numbers and visibility of French women in politics in this millennium, and the quite singular parity legislation, have created an undeniable, if unexpected, new political phenomenon.

As we have seen, women's appearance in force on the political scene has been accompanied both by laws favoring women's interests and by a new body of texts in the form of histories, interviews, surveys, biographies, autobiographies, and fictions. In regrouping and analyzing these writings, I have attempted to offer an explanation of how a new exceptionalism, the principle of parity democracy, came to replace the older French "exception," defined as the masculine overdetermination of the symbols of the political world, the premium placed on a universal femininity identified with the intimate and the domestic, and the trailing position of France in Europe for female representation. The writing and the circulation of these stories have indeed "made a difference" in women's penetration into almost all of the sacred places of the political universe and it is precisely this "difference," sometimes strategic, sometimes deeply ideological, that has structured and continues to structure women's own claims to shared power or empowerment.

Although many of the women's political narratives (interview, political autobiography) adopt the standard conventions of the genre and perpetuate *lieux communs*, they also develop a new narrative, one that rises out of women's lived experiences and perspectives. This new narrative has become increasingly accepted as relevant and newsworthy. In recovering lost women's voices and acknowledging activist women as precursors, women's writing on power celebrates women's political action as empowerment and unsettles the old universalist (arguably masculinist) narratives. The biographies of women pioneers, like the texts on the lives of political women, create a female genealogy and set up political mothers as role models to compete with founding fathers.

While the media may still largely follow the tradition of "visualizing deviance" when it represents political women (in terms of appearance, dress, and gender traits rather than performance), women's texts have been increasingly promoting the counter-discourse that insists on the value of feminine difference in politics and the capacity of women to change the political world. Is this counter-power necessarily within traditional power, as Foucault would argue? Many women's texts have repeated Joan Scott' s analysis of the constructed nature of the standard political discourses around feminine difference, which inhibit women's desire for access to power. They argue for difference, but not that restricted domestic difference that led to women's exclusion at the Revolution!

Other women's texts have begun to tell political stories differently, layering the personal and the political in new ways and constructing non-conventional textual forms. As we have seen, this occurs differentially across genres and most intensively in Huguette Bouchardeau's "autofictions" (which lie somewhere between autobiography and fiction) and Françoise Giroud's experimental journalism (somewhere between the private diary, editorial writing, and political autobiography). These women explore the centrality of the Freudian "family romance" and the power of the unconscious in the shaping of preferences and desires. Both bring to the surface of their texts things that can be said only indirectly.

Giroud comes to some understanding of the deep need for paternal legitimization, the strength of her unconscious need to please the father. In the exceptional political contexts of the three cohabitation governments (1986/88, 1993/95, and 1997/2002), the appointment of women from outside the political parties, the *fait du prince*, was used by both prime minister and president as they competed with each other to be seen to be modernizing the French democratic system. With momentum for reform coming also from male political leaders, women have had additional incentives to come together across the political spectrum. But Giroud responds consciously, textually, to the need to be accorded legitimacy by the father, to be "as good as a man," that has dictated her choices by affirming the value of the rejected maternal legacy for life in politics. Bouchardeau, too, reveals the hidden "malignancy" at the heart of a masculine politics, the cancer that women in politics must take steps to avoid contracting.

In Bouchardeau's preface to this book, she warns against the "rather too vague expression of hope of seeing politics modified by women's presence" and against the failure of the judgments made on the vanity of certain forms of political power "to change the rules of the game from conquest of preeminence to quest for excellence." Throughout this study we have asked where knowledge/power should be located in these political women's writing projects. Even keeping in mind Julia Kristeva's claim that all texts absorb and transform other texts and that the subject itself is simply a site of intertextuality, our corpus seems to be saying: "in a certain subversion of knowledge/power." Knowledge—of the need for paternal legitimization, for example—need not simply serve to shore up the institutions it models, but can take the form of a conscious affirming of emotional, personal, maternal values. Although the language we have investigated still most commonly observes the conventions of Realism and is used "to reflect," as if transparently, the lived political world, it is also possible to detect a recognition that language constructs realities. Some of the writing we have followed also reflects, but rather less transparently, Julia Kristeva's concern with the need for paternal legitimization for the psychic survival of women, hints at the ideal "feminine writing" from a fluid and desiring body of the kind theorized by Luce Irigaray, or parallels aspects of Kristevan "polymorphous perversity." Both Elisabeth Badinter and Françoise Giroud, for example, argue at once for the importance of a femininity that is different and an essential part of being a woman and the need for women to develop and use aspects of their creative "virile" side in politics. Michelle Perrot identifies the changing symbolic and internalized representations of difference in a postmodern world as the capacity to change identities, the capacity to be at once same and other. Although the texts we have studied are largely about women's agency and are generally removed from the multiple, de-centered, and un-self-knowing subjects of postmodernism, a number of our writers eschew the old battle of the sexes for a politics of freedom and diversity.

In answer, then, to the central question posed in our study, as a body of texts with its own specificity, generating its own new and freer forms, and to the extent that this writing reaches a receptive reading public, women's political writing can break the frame and rewrite power.

# Appendix 1
# Comparative Perspectives

This study has assembled and critically examined the stories told by French women about their own lives in politics. It has argued that this women's writing has not only reflected but also altered the relationship between gendered identity and political leadership. This appendix aims to widen the focus by situating these French stories within the contexts of worldwide accounts of women's experience of political participation. These are the outside stories that have had some influence on the French discourses on power and gender. These stories also serve to highlight the "French exception"—to pinpoint, reaffirm, and critically examine the distinctive character of French contexts and discourses.

## Comparative Histories of the Suffrage

Historians have until recently neglected suffrage history because of its association with the narrow class, racial base, and liberal politics of first-wave feminism. The first states or self-governing countries to give women the suffrage, white colonial or pioneer farming societies with a predominance of males that displaced an indigenous population, were geographically marginal to the political centers of the women's movement. The states and countries that gave women the vote between 1890 and 1902 included self-governing New Zealand (which granted women the vote in 1893, but without the right to hold political office), two British colonies, Southern Australia and Western Australia, the state of New South Wales, and several states in the American heartland.[1] Wyoming entered the Union as a state in 1890 with women's suffrage already enshrined in its constitution (in 1869). According to historian Patricia Grimshaw, suffrage had been signed into law by a governor in a fluid political situation, somewhat to the surprise of everyone.[2] Colorado and Idaho, where statewide referenda on female suffrage had been approved by a majority of men, were admitted to the Union in 1877 and 1890.

The partially independent two-house colonial legislatures in Southern and Western Australia responded to the influence of the suffrage movement—bolstered by its alliance with the temperance reformers—because the premier of Western Australia hoped to adulterate the strength of the radical vote of groups of single men, particularly the militant miners in Western Australia.[3] The stories of the passing of the 1893 Electoral Act in New Zealand portray a premier, Richard Seddon, planning to foil passage of the bill, and two members of the Upper House upset at his antics voting for a bill they would otherwise have opposed. In New Zealand, the suffragists allied with the Women's Christian Temperance Union (WCTU) and worked closely with sympathetic males. This has made it possible for some feminist historians to argue that women's suffrage was a product of historical contingency and that suffrage was gifted by men, rather than being a result of women's active struggle.

A number of feminist suffrage histories have foregrounded the limits to women's agency or critiqued what they see as a dialectical relation between women's agency and patriarchy.[4] Women and their peaceable, nurturing qualities of domestic organization were seen as vital in tempering the violence of a frontier society of single males. Most historians consider the strength of support for the WCTU to be the greatest single contributing factor in the success of the early suffrage movements. Votes for women, it was argued, would give more weight to the voice of women (a minority and therefore less threatening than in France where they constituted the majority), for family and order against the social scourge of alcoholic fathers. In contrast, the temperance movement never succeeded in recruiting many women in France although the suffrage leaders signed on.

With respect to male support for the suffrage, there were significant factors that were peculiar to colonial countries; in particular, the proud affirmation of the democracy of the new world as against the class-ridden mother country, men's community with women in the search for a new and separate identity, and their common membership of the white race in the context of co-existence with indigenous races. Not to mention the Protestantism reinforced by the close cooperation between husband and wife in rural agricultural communities that was a factor of increased egalitarianism both in the colonies and in the Scandinavian countries.

The severe interrogation of the early suffragists' credentials is undergoing some revision. For example, there is Ellen Dubois's recent retelling of the American story, which insists on the clever adaptation by the reformers of their traditional gendered sources of power. Another example comes from Patricia Grimshaw, who develops a post-1980s reading of the Australian history. Such new readings are attempting to respect the way the reformers themselves perceived their specific situations and their relationship to men and to male politicians, and to look closely at the intersections of the problem of alcohol, anger at the maltreatment of women, and women's rights. The often-acute problem of male drinking on the frontiers could be seen to be linked closely to general problems of women's status and (lack of) power and with the present concern with countering the causes of violence against women. Like the French histories, these recent stories of the suffrage reconstruct the past as a function of present contexts. As the new narratives begin to circulate, they give birth to other complementary or competing stories.

The stories from pioneer or frontier communities reveal major differences in the character and circumstances of the suffrage debate in the old and new worlds. Richard Evan's comparative study, for example, locates the success of the early women's vote in the antipodes as a consequence of the immature state of political processes and parties. In contrast, he represents the older, more sophisticated French concept of citizenship (universalism) and electoral system as causes of late suffrage in France.

## France and Quebec: The Importance of Social Context

In a contemporary study of the differences and similarities in two French speaking countries, France and Quebec, *Droits des femmes en France et au Québec: 1940–1990: Eléments pour une histoire comparée* (The Rights of Women in France and in Quebec: 1940–1990: Elements of a Comparative History; Montreal: Editions du Remue-ménage, 1993), Mariette Sineau and Evelyne Tardy focus particularly on the extent to which the political situation is always intricately connected to the social. In 1918, Quebec granted women the right to vote and eligibility for political office. Women in France did not receive these rights until 1946. But in France, in 1949, 7 percent of elected representatives were women whereas there was only one woman in the Canadian House of Commons. Legal rights do not appear to translate directly into representation or to correspond necessarily to social practice.

Along with the Napoleonic code of laws, the province of Quebec shared much of the nineteenth-century French legislative heritage that defined married women as minors under the authority of a head of the family. But social contexts for women were different. Secularization came much later in Quebec than in France. In 1884, a restricted right to divorce existed in France and people could be married non-religiously. Divorce was not possible in Quebec until 1968. In Quebec, education for women was in the hands of nuns opposed to secondary classical education for women and in favor of teaching home economics. Public funds were refused for girls' schools until 1960, and not until 1962 could married women work as teachers. The number of women in the workforce and in the professions was considerably greater in France than in Quebec in the 1960s. Whereas the church in France needed women's support in its rivalry with the state and remained open and liberal, the conservative and interventionist church in Quebec, sufficiently strong not to need women, closed itself to women's emancipation.

After liberals replaced the Nationalist-Clerical Party of Duplessis in Quebec in 1960, there were dramatic changes in attitude toward married women working, women's education, and the birthrate. The Quebec Legislative Assembly had its first elected *députée* in 1961. Reproductive rights came quickly with contraception legalized in 1959 (1967 in France) and abortion in 1969 (1975 in France). Beginning in 1989 in Quebec, a child could take the name of either the father or mother. The reversals in women's positions after 1960 occurred less because of the changes in women's representation (although in 1990, 18.4 percent of Quebec's *députées* were women compared to France's 5.5 percent) than because of the replacement by the liberal state of the Catholic Church's hegemony over the family, education, and health.

Sineau and Tardy conclude that the three-and-a-half million Quebec women have an advantage over the twenty-five million French women in the vitality and importance of their women's movements, the legislation against sexism in advertising, and the feminization of language. Sineau compares the furor in the press after Yvette Roudy proposed Benoîte Groult's language reform report for feminizing names of professions in 1995, and the Quebec press in 1993, which almost unanimously referred to the Prime Minister Kim Campbell as *Madame la première Ministre*. In France, where the logic of the universalist case was argued by the Academy *immortels* as late as January 1999, it took until the new millennium for *Madame la Ministre* to become common usage.[5]

Along with the importance of social change in Quebec, and in the French case, with the weight of a tradition less affected by quiet or, indeed, noisy revolution, what these debates highlight once again is that the story told (or grammatical principle evoked) is dependent on the ideological positions and personal investments of the teller(s). Most feminist stories of women's suffrage in Europe seek and find heroines who change history/herstory. And indeed, the generally negative comparative picture of the effectiveness of the feminist groups in France by Sineau and Tardy is contradicted by other accounts—for example, by Gisèle Halimi's autobiographical accounts of the effective interaction from 1981 between her feminist group Choisir and the government. Strategy is as much at stake as truth (which is relative) in the telling of these comparative political stories. The critical perspective of the French feminist insider writer (Sineau) comparing Quebec favorably with France may have the pragmatic goal of moving things forward. Similarly, advocacy of parity or equality of representation within a new trinity (Liberté, égalité, parité) puts the wider political questions of equality, difference, and republicanism on the table, in a manner that foregrounds women's interests.[6]

## The European Perspective

French women now have a developing second identity as European women. This means French women have the advantage of the European Parliament, Commission, and Court directives to back up their claims and override national laws. Equality measures have developed out of the economic framework of integration and fair competition—in particular directives for equal pay, equal treatment at work, and equal treatment in social security.

British political scientist Catherine Hoskyns argues that the Action program on Equal Opportunities was furthered by the forceful presence of Yvette Roudy in 1982 at the meeting of the Council of Ministers in her capacity as French minister for women's rights.[7] This was the first time a committed woman had influenced the debate on policy at council level. Hoskyns' study concludes that although no women-centered measure tackling the overlap between paid and unpaid work survived through Commission and Court in this period, the strong policy on equality in employment did finally permit some spill-over into sexual politics (pregnancy, sexual harassment, and child-care recommendations) and into the political representation of women.[8] Women's organizations, the European Network of Women (ENOW) and the Center for Research on European Women (CREW), brought together in 1990 in the European Women's Lobby, have aided what has been called a "politics of presence" in the Commission and the Parliament.

Hoskyns' own feminist critical frame is evident from her language and objects of study, and notably in the observation that there is as yet no common understanding that the concept of equality needs to be applied in ways that take account of difference in women's situations (caring roles, pregnancy, maternity). But, she adds, women still means mainly "white women in paid employment." Little is being done for underrepresented women from the bottom up, and women's policy is not community-based but is constructed by elite groups with resources for networking.

The British academic's concern that the nation-states might lose their ability to deal adequately with social policy issues parallels the concern among many French women that mothers, for example, might lose some of their considerable existing benefits under the Equal Treatment Directives. (For example, the European Union currently stipulates fourteen weeks of maternity leave only. France allows sixteen weeks paid maternity leave.) National contexts, then, as well as particular social histories and contexts, determine stories on and from Europe. Women's thinking in France, nonetheless, would support Hoskyns' general conclusions. Europe is seen as having provided a remarkable training ground for women in politics and as constituting a significant factor in the support for and legitimization of their presence in places of power.

## The Progressive Scandinavian Models

### *Rethinking "Equality" in Finland*

The Scandinavian countries, with their early suffrage and high levels of female representation, have been held up as exemplary models in the writing of French women politicians and academics. The view from the inside is often more self-critical. The Finnish political scientist Marja Keränen claims that the politics of equality and the prevailing liturgy of gender neutrality ("we are all equal") in her country have not resulted in real "progress" for women. The gender "neutrality" of the 1960s had the negative effect of concealing the gendered differences in social position. A series of critical feminist papers edited by the political scientist argues for a necessary further step that would involve taking account of women's different lives.[9] Keränen writes that an emphasis on difference is not an attempt to return to the past but rather to initiate a new kind of progress.

In Finland, claims Keränen, the ideal civil servant does not mix work and family, the division of labor is still gender-based, thinking is binary, and the wage-gap is larger than in other Scandinavian countries. The male bonding traditionally effected by continuing parliamentary debate in the sauna is dying a more difficult death than expected. Women are being co-opted. Where women ministers, backed by women's organizations in the generations before the 1970s, saw themselves as representatives of women's voices, now women in high office are more likely to be chosen by male leaders of the parties, adds Jaana Kuusipalo.[10] The first generation of women cabinet ministers consisted typically of leading figures of the women's sections of their political parties. The second generation had participated in the activities of the women's sections but became involved in career tracks as non-university educated professionals of political or public organizations or as highly educated experts in the fields of social or health care, culture, or education. In the third generation in the 1970s and 1980s, education and political vocation become more important and links to women's groups infrequent. Possibilities for ministers to act "as women" were limited. That the 1950s conception of sexual difference was replaced by a conception of equality as similarity has for Tuija Parvikko, tragically eliminated attention to what (masculine) culture has suppressed. She quotes the American Carole Pateman to argue that women can become members of civil society only as individuals, not as women. Keränen, too, does not consider it sufficient to "add women and stir" but argues for a "staring at women as different," with a "difference" the depth of which has not yet been grasped.[11] These pro-difference arguments have evident links with the discourse developing around parity in France.

## *Gro Brundtland and Norway*

A close-up of the situation in Norway inevitably focuses on the success of Gro Brundtland, who became environment minister in 1974 at age thirty-five and prime minister in 1981. Brundtland headed three governments, and was head of the Labor party until 1992. She retained widespread popularity in and out of office, and became a model of success for women in politics. Her husband, a newspaper journalist and editor of conservative confession, helped at home with the parenting. The Norwegian parliament, the Storting, has a changing and nursing room for political mothers with infants. It was with some satisfaction that Brundtland told Gloria Steinem the story of a little Norwegian girl who couldn't understand that a man she saw on television was head of a country.[12]

Under Brundtland's 1986 government, the working week was reduced to 37.5 hours and paid maternity leave increased to 24 weeks. Two women led the other major parties: Anne Enger Lahnstein, the Center (farmers') party, with a platform that was anti-abortion and anti-Europe, and Kaci Kullman Five, the Conservative party. Although right-wing women and left-wing women did not share the same agendas, it has been claimed that the whole Norwegian political system has been permeated by the feminine values pursued in these years, particularly in the protection of peace and of the environment.

Despite Brundtland's success story,[13] and twenty years of women's representation, the argument has been made that rights regressed in the 1980s, in terms of the salary gap between men and women and the small number of women in the higher paying jobs in business, industry, and banking.[14] Some feminist political analysts tell the story that as women enter politics, men bail out for the greater power of the corporate world and international markets. As in Finland and other Scandinavian countries, the goal of the feminists is increasingly a post-equality "woman-friendly" society that "would enable women to have a more natural relation to their children, their work, and their public life."[15] Once again, this is a discourse that echoes across the discourses of both right-wing and left-wing women and in the French pro-parity stories.

## *A Swedish Heroine*

Like Norway, Sweden has its story of a founding woman pioneer. Alva Myrdal designed the blueprint for the welfare state to resolve the need for both labor and for babies. Alva encouraged women not to be tied to a housewifely existence that would center on a man, nor to be forced to remain celibate and childless in order to fight for equality. Leaving her teenage children to live what she saw as women's newly possible "second life," Alva worked for disarmament and the environment, chairing the Stockholm International Peace Research Institute she had helped plan through its first year in 1964. In 1967, she joined the Swedish cabinet as disarmament minister, twenty-five years after her husband—twenty years longer due to the handicap of being a woman, she noted with irony. In 1982, she was awarded the Nobel Peace Prize.

Sweden has legally abolished all formal barriers to women's full integration into public life and developed the most generous social policies in the world. The political gains made in the 1980s were made possible by the 1979 Equal Status Act and the dramatic introduction by all parties of the principle of nominating no fewer than 40 percent and no more than 60 percent of either sex to their slates of candidates at every level. The social policy gains concerning parenting are considered world-class. For example, either parent can remain home for up to twelve months after the birth of a child on almost full salary with a maternal month and a paternal month that must be taken by the respective parent so as not to be lost. Parents of infant children can also elect to work a six-hour day. Swedish fathers are allowed ten days at birth to care for their wife and child and either parent can take up to sixty days per child if the child or regular caretaker is ill.

The laws are advanced but, as in France, there is apparently an inevitable gap between law and practice. In Sweden, too, the inside stories are of men dominant in the boardrooms and in the powerful labor unions. Men still encounter resistance from employers and workmates when they attempt to stay home with their young children. Work statistics showed that 45 percent of women held part-time jobs compared with 5 percent of men in the early 1990s. Although 60 percent of first-year students in the tertiary area were girls, only one-third of postgraduate students were women in 1992. Despite the cautionary tales introduced by these inside stories, Swedish legislation is held up as a model and an inspiration by many French women who think and write about politics.

## *Iceland: A Women's Party*

In Iceland, Vigdis Finngogadottir won the presidency on a feminist, pacifist, and nationalist platform in 1980, encouraged by her father, and inspired by the 1975 women's strike in which she had taken part. There were still very few women in the sixty-three-seat multi-party Althing at the time. A grassroots, consciousness raising Women's Alliance group formed a Women's List Party (Kvennalistinn) and three surprised women won seats in the 1983 election. By 1991 there were fifteen women parliamentarians, five from the Kvennalistinn party.

Kvennalistinn is a party in which all decisions are made by consensus after consultation, and the leadership is rotated among their women members in parliament. The Women's Alliance wants work done within the home to be revalued and recognized. For example, they propose to have work at home counted as work experience when homemakers return to or enter the labor force. Evidently not all women in the other political parties supported the procedures and policies of this feminist, all-woman alliance, but its successful story has become food for political thought throughout Europe, including within France.

## Gender-Traits Difference versus Gender-as-Difference

Do women have a special aversion to war? Benazir Bhutto sought to ease tensions with India over Kashmir despite objections by the military. At the same time, she pursued nuclear weapons development. Other women leaders to develop nuclear weapons include Golda Meir, Margaret Thatcher, and Indira Gandhi. Violeta Chomorro oversaw the demilitarization of the Contras and put a politics of consensus and reconciliation in place with Humberto Ortega, a Sandinista, as her chief military officer. But Indira Gandhi sent troops to assist the Bengali rebels and to flush demonstrators out of a Sikh temple. Thatcher sent a military force to retake the Falkland Islands from Argentina in 1982 and troops to the Gulf War against Iraq in 1991. To register the surprisingly "masculine" intractability or impregnability shown by these women, Indira Gandhi (the war of 1971), Golda Meir (the war of 1967), and Margaret Thatcher (the Falklands affair in 1982) were labeled "Iron Ladies," making them, in one sense, honorary (but suspect) "men." From another perspective, they were simply flawed women.

Insofar as particular concern for women's issues is concerned, the histories of women leaders also diverge. Gro Harlem Brundtland appointed seven women cabinet ministers to her seventeen-minister cabinet. Mary Bourke Robinson as president of Ireland made a commitment to the advancement of women.[16] Helen Clark as first elected woman prime minister of New Zealand in 2000 appointed a very feminized cabinet; her predecessor, Jenny Shipley, did not. Margaret Thatcher's cabinet was composed solely of men, and she rejected any special attention to women. So did Chomorro, who eliminated most of the welfare programs to help women including nutrition and child care centers. Chomorro also suspended support for feminist groups who had mainly opposed her candidacy. As for leadership style, Brundtland addressed her colleagues by their first names and appeared to be people-oriented; Margaret Thatcher declared that she was a conviction and not a consensus politician, and Chomorro was considered to have a style with both participatory and authoritarian elements. In their book on women leaders worldwide, d'Amico and Beckman conclude that generalizing about the nature of women's leadership has proved frustrating and argue the need to move away from asserting gender-trait difference when what is in play is gender-as-power.[17] Many of the French texts have focused on gender-trait difference and there has been an increasing interest in heroines or strong female role models among the French women writers.

## *Women Leaders Worldwide: Surrogates for Men*

Our study of French women politicians noted that many women fit a new general feminine category of "surrogate," selected as substitutes for dead, assassinated or indisposed father or husband. Among those outside France who have taken this "widow's walk," expected to carry on the same policies and represent the same interests as the male they stand in for, we note Sirimavo Ratwatte Dias Bandaranaike whose husband was assassinated in 1959 in Sri Lanka; Khalida Zia, widow of the president of Bangladesh, Ziaur Rahman, assassinated in 1991; Indira Nehru Gandhi in India whose father was also assassinated; and Benazir Bhutto who took the place of her father, Zulfikar Bhutto, after he was hanged by General Zia's military government. Maria Peron in Argentina, Violeta Chamorro in Nicaragua, and Corazon Aquino in the Philippines were also surrogates. Most of the surrogate women from the developing world belong to a traditional elite with a family-based political tradition.[18] A version of surrogate power is also something found in the U.S. The traditional U.S. categories for political leaders (old wealth or traditional elite with a family-based political tradition, new wealth or commercial elite, European immigrant who rises through party politics, technocrat) do not appear to be particularly relevant to women's professional backgrounds, or their status and income, often derived through the husband.[19] As we noted in chapter 4, French surrogacy is strong and takes the particular forms of father-daughter political mentoring or power from the prince (*le fait du prince*).

## *Margaret Thatcher: Iron Maiden or Perverse Nanny?*

A chapter by the British journalist Kenneth Harris on Margaret Roberts Thatcher in *Women and World Politics*, once again tells us as much about the male journalist as it tells us about his object of study. Margaret idolized her father, gained a place at Oxford and, at twenty-six, married Denis Thatcher. Elected in 1959 as Member of Parliament for Finchley and the only woman in Edward Heath's cabinet in 1970, Thatcher's election as leader of the Conservative party in 1975 was "a bombshell." In 1979, she became prime minister, leading the Conservatives to victory again in 1983 and 1987. A party revolt against her stubborn resolve to introduce a poll tax in place of the existing system of local taxation removed her from office in 1990.

Harris produces an analysis of a prime minister who both lets herself be taken in by good-looking males to whom she gives preferment[20] and is herself a seductress.[21] She cajoled, she hectored, she manipulated, and she shed tears, writes Harris. The journalist does not attempt to come to terms with a certain inconsistency in his description—bullying behavior in an otherwise excessively feminine woman—implying that this is an inconsistency in the figure described. He quotes "Professor"

Anthony King "who as a Canadian brings a valuable objectivity to the subject" to the effect that men found it hard to stand up to Margaret Thatcher[22]: "Most well-brought up Englishmen have no idea what to do with a strong assertive woman... ": "Women to them are mothers or nannies to be feared or sisters to be bullied (or, alternatively, adored); they are not colleagues or fellow politicians, to be stood up to and shouted at when necessary."[23]

There is a formulation here of the problems Thatcher posed by confusing gender expectations. She is being reproached with an out-manning and an un-manning of the men who, faced with her unaccustomed behavior, are torn between "the desire to strike" and "the desire to sulk," according to King. This, then, is a story of the phallic mother and the "wimps" whose manhood she threatens. Thatcher's influence derives from the "formidable female personality" that both "enabled her to dominate her colleagues in the British Government" and constituted her power abroad.[24] Her casting as perverse nanny and as iron lady insists on the paradox that Margaret Thatcher represented. The larger-than-life portrait of a somewhat monstrous phallic mother may correspond to British mythologies of the feminine, but, in spite of the title's promise, "Prime Minister Margaret Thatcher: The Influence of her Gender on Her Foreign Policy," and in contrast to Elisabeth Schemla's biography of Cresson, the protrait is presented without any substantive analysis of these mythologies by the male journalist.

## *"A Man's Idea and Wrong": Golda Mabovitch Meir*

Women can also give accounts of their situation that, if not as unconsciously sexist as Harris's, are somewhat confused about the role of gender and playing/refusing the gender card. Golda Mabovitch Meir, like Thatcher, claims that being a woman never hindered her in any way at all: "I never knew a man who gave in to an argument of mine because I was a woman—except one, my husband—and they had the open-mindedness and the manliness to accept my idea if they thought it was right. I always tried to reciprocate—I didn't expect privileges because I was a woman, and if the majority was against me, I accepted it, even if I knew it was a man's idea—and wrong."[25] For a woman who went down in legend as tough and mannish, and who is putting forward a "no difference" claim, Golda Meir's words are surprisingly couched in terms of difference. In particular her reference to "men's ideas" shows the underlying tensions in her words. The greatest difficulty for Meir was precisely that "women who want and need a life outside as well as inside the home have a much, much harder time than men because they carry such a heavy double burden."[26] Meir, a figure of masculine power in the collective imaginary, the opposite of femininity, thus also contributes to the discourse on women's difference in politics.

## *Benazir Bhutto: Paternal Legitimization*

Benazir Bhutto's autobiography, *Daughter of Destiny*, provides a summary of her origins in a family where her father wished to give his daughters the same opportunities as their brothers.[27] Benazir's father was prime minister of Pakistan from 1971 until his imprisonment during a military coup in 1977. Benazir, then, was "her father's daughter," as the account of an elitist education in governance and law at Harvard's Radcliffe College and at Oxford University indicates. Bhutto stood for election against her brother in 1993 and explains that her brother did not think of her as a political leader who had waged a political battle and triumphed, but rather as a sister who should give him his rightful first place.

Like many contemporary Muslim women leaders and thinkers, Bhutto situates her arguments in favor of an improvement in women's status in history and in a return to an earlier purer Muslim tradition. For example, she highlighted Mohammed's interdiction of the practice of killing female infants and his calling for education and inheritance rights for women. Using history, was, Bhutto argues, the soundest position from which a woman could contest the religious right who opposed her own Pakistan Peoples' party.

When General Zia was killed in a plane crash in 1988, Benazir became prime minister. In 1990 she was charged with corruption and detained before being cleared of the charges. In 1996, Bhutto was again accused of corruption by the president and her government dissolved. In 1997, she went into exile, and her assets in Swiss bank accounts were frozen. In contrast to Bhutto's own characterization of her political career in terms of "destiny" (a term that Simone Veil rejects), the balance sheet of her work as a woman politician is mixed. During her presidency, Pakistan had fewer than 1 percent of female representatives and Bhutto showed an apparent lack of interest in extending the term of the twenty seats previously reserved for women in the National Assembly.[28] The shadow of the accusations of corruption still hangs over her. Benazir Bhutto fits both the patterns of dynastic inheritance distinctive to the developing world and the pattern of the father-daughter walk prevalent in Europe.

## *Indira Gandhi: Her Father's Daughter*

Despite differences occasioned by generation and culture, the biography of Indira Gandhi who carried much of the weight of governing 700 million people from 1966 to 1984, contains a strikingly similar story of the power of paternal and dynastic influence. Pupul Jayakar's intimate biography of the friend who came to be known as "Mother India,"[29] comments only discreetly on the nature of the strong grandfather-father-daughter connection.[30] Indira Nehru was raised in a family fervently politicized by the cause of Indian independence from Britain. Indira was little influenced by the domestic part of the house even though she grew up in a culture where women were secluded by the system of purdah and strict separation between the sexes. She was instead formed by travel through the towns and villages of traditional India with her father, studies in Europe, and later education in Indian culture, again authorized and organized by her father.

After she left her husband to work as her father's confidante and aide, Indira was elected prime minister in 1966. Indira's energy was drawn from the support of the ordinary people, the earth, and from service, claims her biographer, but also the imperative of the political perpetuation of the family dynasty. When the newly appointed prime minister showed she could not be manipulated, she became an obstacle. In 1969, excluded from the Congress Party for her "rebellion" against its decisions, she formed her own more radical group of the party (Congress I) that largely dominated the 1971 elections. In 1975, Indira Gandhi imposed a much-criticized state of emergency, arrested leaders of the opposition, and censured the press. Myths were emerging in the villages about forced sterilization leading to men fleeing into the sugar-cane fields to hide at first sight of any official vehicle. Indira had become a mythical form of feminine energy, a powerful and malevolent figure.

Imprisoned for "abuse of power" until the end of the session, and aware of personal danger, Indira decided to fight to remain in politics. Splitting the Congress party for a second time, she was swept triumphantly back to her former position as prime minister by the young guard in 1980, ruling until her assassination in 1984.

There are apparent contradictions in Indira Gandhi's conception of the future for women. She was critical of the West, claiming the emancipation of women in Western nations had meant the imitation of men. Liberation for women, in her opinion, should be the right to be "themselves." Her praise of the sustaining qualities inherent in women's traditional culture is closer to ideas and feelings that many women of the developing world have been formulating in the last decade than to a Western discourse of equality or rights. Women of the landed aristocracy and some women of the middle classes, treated as property, handed down from father to husband, she admits, live a very real servitude. Society has them in its grip. Nonetheless, they let themselves be carried by the current. Only education, economic autonomy, and their own energy will one day erase this conditioning and liberate them. Indira stated that women of the villages follow ancestral rhythms and, rooted in the earth with eternal dignity and an ageless strength, they are able to accept both joys and sorrows. Her biographer, Jayakar, who may well be inflecting the discussion, suggests in an interview with Indira that women have a creative energy, wellsprings of hidden power that they may or may not develop the aptitude to tap into. Indira concurs, adding that freedom should not require women to abandon this essence of their femininity.

Another assessment of Indira Gandhi's life, this time by a feminist and a non-Indian author, is based on very different assumptions. Mary

Carras, who also interviewed Indira Gandhi, writes the story of the daughter of an upper class, well-educated, politically important family. Carras points out that class enabled Indira to transcend gender. This is something that Benazir Bhutto stated for her own case. In the South or developing world, politically ambitious women from a liberal, progressive patrician family appear to have a reasonable chance of succeeding as surrogates. Carras insists on Indira's assertiveness, created by the need to play by the established masculine rules. Her leadership style, Carras observes, was universally described as confrontational. Carras concedes that Indira Gandhi made some positive moves for women. She appointed a Committee on the Status of Women in India in 1971 and took some measures on marriage, divorce, and dowry that helped middle-class women. The sixth five-year plan (1980–1985) did take modest initiatives toward improving the education, employment, and health of women. But Gandhi claimed to be a person with a job rather than a woman. She did not, argues Carras, carry her nurturing traits into her public policy and public life.

Indira admitted that her own upbringing was an exception, saw herself as her father's daughter, and defined herself as without feminine "seduction." She did not attribute the obstacles across her path, or indeed her success, to being a woman. Timid, reserved, less than articulate, she may initially have doubted her own competence but always appeared to be very sure of the legitimacy that gave her the strength, the motivation to continue. This, I would argue, derived from being her father's daughter, from the surrogacy that in its own very particular forms has also characterized French women's reflection on their political legitimacy.

*****

Non-Western women tell their political histories in terms of resistance to Western influence and attempt to situate their power within their own traditions rather than in a (sometimes-misrepresented) feminism of Western origin. The conclusion to the study of worldwide leaders by d'Amico and Beckman goes no further than the general (Western) questions: what kinds of gender perceptions are covered by labels like "Iron Lady"? How does fear of the authoritarian mother figure re-emerge in public life, or how does gender shape the policy choices of male leaders in their concern not to be seen as "Nervous Nellies" (as Lyndon Johnson characterized his critics during the Vietnam war)?

This brief excursion through comparative territories reinforces a number of our earlier conclusions, notably that differences in historical and social contexts do affect the points of view, forms, and the content of the tales told—whether these be tales of suffrage in the old and new worlds, of legal rights versus social practices in France and Quebec, of a new European-based politics of presence, France looking outward at Northern models or Scandinavia looking inwards. When considering the case of developing countries, it is of interest to note that the biographies on and autobiographies by political women reflect the national mythologies and gender norms of that writer's country. A Western feminist reads Indira Gandhi's contribution to politics quite differently from Gandhi's female Indian biographer. The understanding of "equality" or of "feminine difference" is therefore also culture and gender-specific. Still, it is also of interest to note that, across nationalities, the widow or father-daughter track continues to provide women with major political options. The recognition of the importance of paternal legitimization for the exercise of power and the affirmation of maternal legacies (of feminine difference) is common across cultures and ends up shaping the momentum that will produce a form of counter-power.

## Notes

1. Caroline Daley and Melanie Dolan, *Suffrage and Beyond: International Feminist Perspectives* (New York: New York University Press, 1994) argue that the significance of the peaceful and quiet achievement of suffrage in New Zealand and Australia, well before the militant mass movements that led to American women's enfranchisement in 1920 or universal suffrage in Britain in 1928, and without the media interest that accompanied mass rallies or hunger strikes has often been overlooked.
2. Patricia Grimshaw, "Women's Suffrage in New Zealand Revisited: Writing from the Margins," in *Suffrage and Beyond*, pp. 25–41.
3. Aware of the anomaly in the disparity between voting rights in the new nation between the states and the Commonwealth, the Commonwealth of Australia later conceded the vote to all Australian women, excluding Aboriginal women, in 1902. Aboriginals were not enfranchised until the post-world war era.
4. Karen Offen's paper, "Women, Citizenship and Suffrage with a French Twist" argues that the French concept of citizenship and the electoral system were the principal causes of late suffrage for women. In *Suffrage and Beyond*, pp. 151–170.
5. Geneviève Fraisse, feminist philosopher and *députée* in charge of an inter-ministerial office for women's rights helped this process along with Josette Rey-Debove, an executive editor of *Le Robert* dictionaries, who attacked the academicians in their own field of grammar. Rey-Debove argued that, in fact, in 95 percent of cases, French nouns in the singular may be adapted to accommodate either gender.
6. Emily Eakin, "Liberté, égalité, parité," *Lingua France* (April 1998), pp. 68–71.
7. Catherine Hoskyns, *Integrating Gender: Women, Law and Politics in the European Union* (London: Verso, 1996), p. 210.
8. The more conservative European Court of Justice resisted aspects of the Parliament's affirmative action. The Kalanke case condemned quotas in the public sector as detrimental to men and to equality of opportunity. In 1996, it handed down a second judgment of illegal discrimination against men. As a result, Britain agreed to offer men at 60 the free health care available to women of 60 and over (previously available only to men from 65). This tendency has now been reversed.
9. Marja Keränen, ed., *Gender and Politics in Finland* (Aldershot: Avebury, 1990).
10. Jaana Kuusipalo, "Finnish Women in Top-Level Politics," in *Gender and Politics in Finland*, pp. 13–36.
11. Marja Keränen, "Modernity, Modernism, Women," in *Gender and Politics in Finland*, pp. 112–127.
12. Gloria Steinem, "Norway's radical daughter." *Time*, 25 September 1989, pp. 42–44. Recounted in Kelber, *Women and Government*, p. 84.

13. A success story but with some very painful moments. In 1992, Gro Brundtland's eldest and adult son committed suicide and the prime minister resigned as head of the Labor party. In late 1996 she announced her retirement from national politics.
14. Surveys show that most women continue to gravitate to the lower-paying service, social, and public sectors, work thirty hours compared to men's thirty-nine hours, and earn 80 percent of men's average wage, calculated on a full-time basis. Almost 90 percent of caring, including care of the elderly, is done by women, and women spend twice as much time each day (more than four hours) on household tasks than men.
15. Stang Dahl, Tove and Helga Maria Hernes, "After Equality," *Scandinavian Review* (1988), pp. 2–7, quoted in Mim Kelber, ed., *Women and Government: New Ways to Political Power* (Praeger: Westport, Conn.; London, 1994), p. 88.
16. D'Amico and Beckman cite the work of Patricia Lee Sykes, "Women as National Leaders: Patterns and Prospects," in Michael Genovese, ed., *Women as National Leaders* (Newbury Park, Cal.: Sage, 1993), p. 226.
17. Comparing leadership styles in D'Amico and Beckman's book, Harvey Williams tells the story of Violetta Barrios de Chamorro who headed the UNO party in its unexpected victory in 1990. She was chosen largely for her symbolic surrogate value and her social position as a descendant of the traditional families. Subsequently, claims Williams, she governed independently, refusing to turn over power to the "rightful" holders in the UNO or to the vice-president and presenting a tenacity and political skill that surprised and perplexed her opponents. Corazon Aquino, however, quickly relinquished the goal of social reforms under pressure from established domestic and international interests, and moved back toward established political routines. Perhaps, her biographer Vincent Boudreau concludes, "one should not ask whether women bring new perspectives to politics, but if they can defend these against the established political order" and the return to routine. See "Gender, Class, and the People Power President," in *Women in World Politics*, p. 82.
18. Kenneth Harris, "Prime Minister Margaret Thatcher: The Influence of Her Gender on Her Foreign Policy," in *Women in World Politics* (Westport, Conn.: Bergin and Garvey, 1995).
19. Francine d'Amico and Peter Beckman, in *Women in World Politics*.
20. "She appreciated the presence of good-looking males who responded to her femininity. Some of these were granted preferment that they may not have had from a male prime minister." In fact this leader of a political party "never ceased to be aware of her femininity and of its effect on the powerful men around her," *Women in World Politics*, p. 62.
21. Ibid.
22. Ibid., p. 63.
23. Ibid.
24. Ibid., p. 68.
25. Ibid., p. 111.
26. Ibid., p. 110.
27. Benazir Bhutto, *Daughter of Destiny: An Autobiography* (New York: Simon and Schuster, 1989).
28. In India, for example, there were 14.1 percent of women in the Parliament's House of the People by the early 1990s and the constitution was being amended to reserve 30 percent of legislative seats at the grassroots level for women. In Mim Kelber, ed., *Women and Government: New Ways to Political Power*, pp. 27–28.
29. Pupul Jayakar, *Indira Gandhi* (New York: Pantheon Books, 1988) was re-edited in 1992 and translated into French in 1994 (Paris: Plon) by André Lewin, ambassador of France to India 1987–1991.
30. Indira Gandhi was assassinated by a Sikh from her personal guard in 1984.

# Appendix 2

## Overview of the French Political System

For those unfamiliar with the workings of the French political system, and for those looking for a kind of who's who list of French politicians, this appendix offers a general outline of the organizational structure of the semi-presidential French political system with its "two-headed executive," a list of major political parties and their leaders in 2001, political pressure groups, political party movement in 2001, and a list of women who have held ministerial and other political positions since 1959.[1]

### General Outline

In the Executive, the president appoints the prime minister and may dismiss him/her. Since the 1962 referendum, the French president is elected for a seven-year term with the role of arbitrating the constitution, while the government (prime minister, council of ministers) is responsible for the day-to-day running of the country. Nonetheless, successive presidents have intervened in policy-making and all four presidents of the present Fifth Republic, established in 1958, have taken on the roles of both head of state and chief of the executive.

The National Assembly is made up of 577 deputies elected by direct universal suffrage with a two-ballot uninominal (single candidate) majority (first-past-the-post) polling system. One-third of the Senate's 321 members is elected every three years for a nine-year term by electoral colleges in each of the ninety-six metropolitan departments made up of deputies, regional councilors, general councilors and municipal council representatives. The National Assembly (previously known as the Chamber of Deputies), which convenes at the Palais Bourbon, and the Senate, which meets in the Palais du Luxembourg, together constitute Parliament. The Senate has traditionally been mostly male-dominated.

Each parliament is elected for a period of five years. Since the adoption of the August 1995 Constitutional amendment, the National Assembly has had a single session each year, beginning on the first working day of October and ending on the last working day of June. Each deputy is also a member and participates in the work of one of the National Assembly's six standing committees. Article 34 of the Constitution defines their role, which includes passing annual finance bills (the budget). Statutes may be initiated by the government (in the form of *projets de loi* or government bills); after consultation with the *Conseil d'Etat*, and these are discussed by the Council of Ministers before heading to one of the two assemblies for debate. Bills may also be introduced by members of Parliament (in the form of *propositions de loi* or members' bills). In practice, during recent legislatures, fewer than one in five of the statutes passed started off as members' bills. Both government bills and members' bills are debated by the two assemblies, shuttling back and forth between them.

At the sub-national level, there are three tiers of local administration: the *commune*, the department, and the region, in addition to France's overseas territories and regional bodies (*collectivités territoriales*) with special status (Paris, Marseilles, Lyon, Corsica, Mayotte and Saint-Pierre-et-Miquelon).

These local bodies have increasing female representation. In 1986, the number of offices that could simultaneously be held was limited by the law to two, so that the offices of mayor, departmental councilor, and deputy can no longer be retained together. The tendency is to combine the functions of mayor and deputy, and this has provided more openings for women at the regional level. In 1999, the debate was still ongoing on whether office-holding should be restricted further, with many favoring the less restrictive option of permitting one local and one national mandate.

## Major Political Parties and Their Leaders in 2001

Citizens' Movement, or *Mouvement démocratique des Citoyens* [MdC] [Jean Pierre CHEVENEMENT];

French Communist Party, or *Parti communiste français* [PCF] [Robert HUE];

The Greens, or *Les Verts* [Dominique VOYNET];

Independant Ecological Movement, or *Mouvement écologique indépendent* [MEI] [Antoine WAECHTER];

Left Radical Party, or *Parti Radical de Gauche* [PRG] (previously Radical Socialist Party, or PRS and the Left Radical Movement, or *Mouvement Radical de Gauche* [MRG]) [Jean-Michel BAYLAND];

Liberal Democracy, or *Démocratie libérale* [DL] (originally Republican Party, or PR) [Alain MADELIN];

Movement for France, or *Mouvement pour la France* [MPF] [Philippe DE VILLIERS];
National Front, or *Front national* [FN] [Jean-Marie LE PEN];
Rally for the Republic, or *Rassemblement pour la République* [RPR] [Michelle ALLIOT-MARIE];
Socialist Party, or *Parti socialiste* [PS] [François HOLLANDE];
Union for French Democracy, or *Union pour la Démocratie française* [UDF] (coalition of UDC, *Force démocrate*, or FD, RRRS, PPD) [François BAYROU];
Union of the Centre, or *Union du Centre* [UDC] [leader NA]
Workers' Struggle, or *Lutte ouvrière* [Arlette Laguiller]

## Major Political Pressure Groups

Communist-controlled labor union (Confédération Générale du Travail), or CGT, nearly 2.4 million members (claimed);
Independent labor union (Workers Struggle), or Force ouvrière, 1 million members (est.);
Independent white-collar union, or Confédération Générale des Cadres, 340,000 members (claimed);
National Council of French Employers (Conseil National du Patronat Français), or CNPF;
Socialist-leaning labor union (Confédération Française Démocratique du Travail), or CFDT, about 800,000 members (est.)

## Political Party Movement in France in 2001

The victory of the left in the 1997 general election led to the Fifth Republic's third right/left cohabitation, following those between 1986 and 1988, and 1992 and 1995. This time the situation was reversed, with a right-wing president and a left-wing government. The defeat of the right in the general election, followed by losses in the 1998 regional elections, contributed to its fragmentation, with splits accentuated by the personal ambitions of a number of party leaders. Its two main components, the RPR (*Rassemblement pour la République*—Rally for the Republic) and the UDF (*Union pour la Démocratie française*—Union for French Democracy), are divided.

In 1998 a split occurred between free marketeers and other center-right politicians, who had waged common cause since 1978 under the banner of the UDF, founded by former President Valéry Giscard d'Estaing. Some free marketeers now belong to *Démocratie libérale*, which succeeded the former *Parti républicain* and is led by Alain Madelin. Others have remained in the UDF, aligning themselves with the Republican, independent and free-market wing of the movement. The center-right, now in the majority in the UDF, have regrouped around François Bayrou's *Force démocrate.* Since 1995, *Force démocrate* has combined the former CDS (*Centre des Démocrates-sociaux*) and PSD (*Parti social-démocrate*). Other parties established by former members of the UDF include Jean-Pierre Soisson's *Mouvement des Réformateurs,* Charles Millon's *La Droite,* and Philippe de Villiers' *Mouvement pour la France.* The divisions within the Republican right stem in large part from differing attitudes toward the *Front national* (FN). Some right-wing politicians have moved closer to the extreme right party, with whom they share the leadership of a number of regional councils; others are opposed to any concession to it. The FN has gained a foothold in several regions championing an anti-European form of nationalism. Although since May 1998 there has been a formal alliance of the elements that make up the "Republican opposition", i.e., the RPR, UDF, and *Démocratie libérale,* this has not eliminated the divisions between different groups on the right.

The left also has its internal conflicts, widely reported during the 1980s, but these have become less pronounced. The *Parti socialiste* remains the most powerful component in the ruling left-wing coalition known as the *gauche plurielle* (multi-party left). The recent *Mouvement des Citoyens* (Citizens' Movement) led by Jean-Pierre Chevènement is situated to the left of the *Parti socialiste.* After losing a large proportion of its activists and supporters, some of them to the *Parti socialiste* in the past two decades, the *Parti communiste* has succeeded in maintaining a 9–10 percent share of the electorate in the past few years, reworking its policy while continuing its "historic" function of representing the working classes.

The ecologists appeared on France's political scene in 1974 and are divided into rival factions. One of these, *Les Verts* (the Greens), was represented in the Jospin government. A second group, Brice Lalonde's *Génération Ecologie* has moved closer to the RPR and UDF.

The 1997 general election confirmed the rise of the extreme left. The most important group appears to be *Lutte ouvrière* (Workers' Struggle) led by Arlette Laguiller, followed by the *Ligue communiste révolutionnaire* (Alain Krivine). The extreme left is gaining support particularly amongst the unemployed, defenders of the rights of illegal immigrants, and opponents of government measures.

**Women Who Have Held Ministerial Positions (1959–2001)[2]**

| Position<br>Policy Field | Dates of Office<br>Name | Number of Women<br>Affiliation |
|---|---|---|
| **De GAULLE Presidency (1958–1969)** | | |
| **DEBRE Cabinet** | (8 January 1959 to 14 April 1962) | 1 woman appointed |
| Junior Minister Social Affairs in Algeria | (January 1959–April 1962)<br>Nafissa SID CARA | (Pour l'Algérie française) |
| **Fourth POMPIDOU Cabinet** | (6 April 1967 to 10 July 1968) | 1 woman |
| **COUVE de MURVILLE Cabinet** | (10 July 1968 to 20 June 1969) | 1 woman |
| **POMPIDOU Presidency (1969–1974)** | | |
| **CHABAN-DELMAS Cabinet** | (20 June 1969 to 5 July 1972) | 1 woman |
| Junior Minister Education; Social Security | (May 1968–June 1972)<br>Marie-Madeleine DIENESCH | (Mouvement républicain populaire, or MRP/RPR) |
| **First MESSMER Cabinet** | (5 July 1972 to 28 March 1973) | 1 woman |
| Junior Minister Public Health; Social Security | (July 1972–April 1973)<br>Marie-Madeleine DIENESCH | (MRP/RPR) |
| **Second MESSMER Cabinet** | (2 April 1973 to 27 February 1974) | 2 women |
| Junior Minister Education | (April 1973–February 1974)<br>Suzanne PLOUX | (Union des démocrates pour la République, or UDR) |
| Junior Minister Public Health and Social Security | (April 1973–February 1974)<br>Marie-Madeleine DIENESCH | (MRP/RPR) |

**Women Who Have Held Ministerial Positions (1959–2001)** (*continued*)

| Position<br>Policy Field | Dates of Office<br>Name | Number of Women<br>Affiliation |
|---|---|---|
| **Third MESSMER Cabinet** | (27 February 1974 to 27 May 1974) | 1 woman |
| Junior Minister Public Health and Social Security | (February 1974–May 1974)<br>Marie-Madeleine DIENESCH | (MRP/RPR) |
| **Giscard d'ESTAING Presidency (1974–1981)** | | |
| **First CHIRAC Cabinet** | (27 May 1974 to 25 August 1976) | 6 women |
| Junior Minister Justice (Garde des Sceaux) | (June 1974–1976)<br>Hélène DORLHAC | (Républicains Indépendants, or RI) |
| Junior Minister Women's Status (Condition féminine) | (July 1974–March 1977)<br>Françoise GIROUD | (Divers Gauche) |
| Junior Minister Preschool Education | (June 1974–January 1976)<br>Annie LESUR | (Centrist) |
| Junior Minister and Minister Universities | (May 1976–May 1981)<br>Alice SAUNIER-SEITE | (PR) |
| Junior Minister Consumer Affairs | (January 1976–1978)<br>Christiane SCRIVENER | (PR) |
| Minister Health; Health and Social Services; Health and Family | (May 1974–May 1981)<br>Simone VEIL | (UDF) |
| **First BARRE Cabinet** | (25 August 1976 to 29 March 1977) | 4 women |
| **Second BARRE Cabinet** | (29 March 1977 to 31 March 1978) | 7 women |

**Women Who Have Held Ministerial Positions (1959–2001)** (*continued*)

| **Position**<br>**Policy Field** | **Dates of Office**<br>**Name** | **Number of Women**<br>**Affiliation** |
|---|---|---|
| **Third BARRE Cabinet** | (3 April 1978 to 21 May 1981) | 5 women |
| Junior Minister Culture | (July 1974–March 1977)<br>Françoise GIROUD | (Divers Gauche) |
| Junior Minister Health and Social Security | (March 1977–April 1978)<br>Hélène MISSOFFE | (UDR) |
| Junior Minister Women's Employment | (January 1978–May 1981)<br>Nicole PASQUIER | (Parti Républicain, or PR) |
| Junior Minister Justice (Garde des Sceaux); Minister for Women's Status | (January 1978–May 1981)<br>Monique PELLETIER | |
| Junior Minister and Minister Universities | (May 194–May 1981)<br>Alice SAUNIER-SEITE (PR) | |
| Junior Minister Consumer Affairs | (January 1976–March 1978)<br>Christiane SCRIVENER | |
| Minister of Health Social Security; Health and Family | (May 1974–May 1981)<br>Simone VEIL | (UDF) |
| **MITTERRAND Presidency (1981–1988)** | | |
| **First MAUROY Cabinet** | (21 May to 23 June 1981) | 6 women |
| **Second MAUROY Cabinet** | (23 June 1981 to 22 March 1983) | 6 women |
| **Third MAUROY Cabinet** | (22 March 1983–19 July 1984) | 6 women |

**Women Who Have Held Ministerial Positions (1959–2001)** (*continued*)

| **Position**<br>**Policy Field** | **Dates of Office**<br>**Name** | **Number of Women**<br>**Affiliation** |
|---|---|---|
| **FABIUS Cabinet** | (19 July 1984–20 March 1986) | 6 women |
| Associate Minister Youth and Sport; Junior Minister Civil Service; Minister and Junior Minister Consumer Affairs | (May 1981–July 1984)<br>Edwige AVICE | (PS) |
| Minister Environment | (March 1983–March 1986)<br>Huguette BOUCHARDEAU | (PS) |
| Minister of Agriculture; Overseas Trade and Tourism | (May 1981–March 1986)<br>Edith CRESSON | (PS) |
| Junior Minister Family; Minister Social Affairs and National Solidarity | (May 1981–March 1986)<br>Georgina DUFOIX | (PS) |
| Junior Minister Public Service; Associate Minister and Junior Minister Consumer Affairs | (May 1981–March 1986)<br>Catherine LALUMIÈRE | (PS) |
| Minister National Solidarity | (May 1981–June 1982)<br>Nicole QUESTIAUX | (PS) |
| Associate Minister Rights of Woman (chargée des Droits de la Femme), Minister (Droits des Femmes) | (May 1981–March 1986)<br>Yvette ROUDY | (PS) |
| **Second Jacques CHIRAC Cabinet** | (20 March 1986 to 10 May 1988) | 4 women |
| Junior Minister Education | (20 March 1986–10 May 1988)<br>Michèle ALLIOT-MARIE | (RPR) |
| Associate Minister Health and Family | (March 1986–May 1998)<br>Michèle BARZACH | (RPR) |

**Women Who Have Held Ministerial Positions (1959–2001)** (*continued*)

| **Position**<br>**Policy Field** | **Dates of Office**<br>**Name** | **Number of Women**<br>**Affiliation** |
|---|---|---|
| Junior Minister Education (Teacher Training) | (March 1986–May 1998)<br>Nicole CATALA | (RPR) |
| Junior Minister French-Speaking World (la Francophonie) | (March 1986–May 1988)<br>Lucette MICHAUX-CHEVRY | (RPR) |
| **Second MITTERRAND Presidency (1988–1995)** | | |
| **First ROCARD Cabinet** | (10 May 1988–23 June 1988) | 6 women |
| **Second ROCARD Cabinet** | (23 June 1988–16 May 1991) | 6 women |
| **CRESSON Cabinet** | (16 May 1991–April 1992) | 7 women, including Cresson |
| **BEREGOVOY Cabinet** | (2 April 1992 to 29 March 1993) | 7 women |
| Junior Minister Women's Rights | (June 1988–May 1991)<br>Michèle ANDRE | (PS) |
| Associate Minister Foreign Affairs; Cooperation and Development | (May 1998–April 1992)<br>Edwige AVICE | (PS) |
| Minister European Affairs; Prime Minister | (May 1998–April 1992)<br>Edith CRESSON | (PS) |
| Associate Minister Family, Rights of Woman, Solidarity | (May-June 1988)<br>Georgina DUFOIX | |
| Junior Minister Consumer Affairs; Women's Rights (Droits des Femmes) | (May 1988–April 1992)<br>Véronique NEIERTZ | (PS) |

**Women Who Have Held Ministerial Positions (1959–2001)** *(continued)*

| Position<br>Policy Field | Dates of Office<br>Name | Number of Women<br>Affiliation |
|---|---|---|
| Associate Minister Communication; French-Speaking World | (May 1988–April 1992)<br>Catherine TASCA | (PS) |
| Junior Minister Social Affairs and Employment, responsible for Senior Citizens and the Handicapped | (May–June 1988)<br>Catherine TRAUTMANN | (PS) |
| Minister, Employment and Training | (May 1991–March 1993)<br>Martine AUBRY | (PS) |
| Minister Youth and Sport | (May 1991–March 1993)<br>Frédérique BREDIN | (PS) |
| Associate Minister for European Affairs | (May 1991–March 1993)<br>Elisabeth GUIGOU | (PS) |
| Minister Environment | (April 1992–March 1993)<br>Ségolène ROYAL | (PS) |
| Associate Minister Housing | (April 1992–March 1993)<br>Marie-Noëlle LIENEMANN | (PS) |
| **CHIRAC Presidency (1995– )** | | |
| **BALLADUR Cabinet** | (29 March 1993 to 18 May 1995) | 3 women |
| Minister Youth and Sport | (March 1993–May 1995)<br>Michèle ALLIOT-MARIE | (RPR) |
| Associate Minister Human Rights and Humanitarian Action | (March 1993–May 1995)<br>Lucette MICHAUX-CHEVRY | (RPR) |

**Women Who Have Held Ministerial Positions (1959–2001)** *(continued)*

| Position<br>Policy Field | Dates of Office<br>Name | Number of Women<br>Affiliation |
|---|---|---|
| Minister Social Affairs and Health | (March 1993–May 1995)<br>Simone VEIL | |
| **First JUPPE Cabinet** | (18 May 1995 to 7 November 1995) | 12 women |
| **Second JUPPE Cabinet** | (7 November 1995 to June 1997) | 4 women |
| Junior Minister Decentralization | (May–November 1995)<br>Nicole AMELINE | (UDF) |
| Junior Minister Foreign Trade | (May–November 1995)<br>Christine CHAUVET | (PR) |
| Minister of Solidarity between Generations | (May–November 1995)<br>Colette CODACCIONI | (RPR) |
| Junior Minister Education (Research) | (May–November 1995)<br>Elisabeth DUFOURCQ | (RPR) |
| Junior Minister Education (Schools) | (May–November 1995)<br>Françoise HOSTALIER | (UDF) |
| Minister Public Health | (May–November 1995)<br>Elisabeth HUBERT | (RPR) |
| Minister Tourism | (May–November 1995)<br>Françoise de PANAFIEU | (RPR) |
| Junior Minister Urban Problem Areas (quartiers difficiles) | (May–November 1995)<br>Françoise de VEYRINAS | (Centrist) |

**Women Who Have Held Ministerial Positions (1959–2001)** *(continued)*

| **Position**<br>**Policy Field** | **Dates of Office**<br>**Name** | **Number of Women**<br>**Affiliation** |
|---|---|---|
| Junior Minister Employment | (May 1995–June 1997)<br>Anne-Marie COUDERC | (RPR) |
| Junior Minister Transport | (May 1995–June 1997)<br>Anne-Marie IDRAC | (Centrist) |
| Minister Environment | (May 1995–June 1997)<br>Corinne LEPAGE | (Independent) |
| Junior Minister French-Speaking World | (May 1995–June 1997)<br>Margie SUDRE | (Centrist) |
| **JOSPIN Cabinet** | (4 June 1997–2001) | 10 women |
| Minister Employment and Solidarity | (June 1997–2001)<br>Martine AUBRY | (PS) |
| Minister Youth and Sport | (June 1997– )<br>Marie-George BUFFET | (PCF) |
| Junior Minister Tourism | (June 1997– )<br>Michelle DEMISSINE | (PCF) |
| Junior Minister Health and Social Action | (June 1997– )<br>Dominique GILLOT | (PS) |
| Minister Justice (Garde des Sceaux) | (June 1997–2001)<br>Elisabeth GUIGOU | (PS) |

**Women who have held Ministerial Positions (1959–2001)** *(continued)*

| Position<br>Policy Field | Dates of Office<br>Name | Number of Women<br>Affiliation |
|---|---|---|
| Junior Minister SMEs Trade and Crafts | (June 1997– )<br>Marylise LEBRANCHU | (PS) |
| Junior Minister Women's Rights and Professional Training | (June 1997– )<br>Nicole PERY | (PS) |
| Associate Minister Education (Schools) | (June 1997– )<br>Ségolène ROYAL | (PS) |
| Minister Culture and Communication | (June 1997–2001)<br>Catherine TRAUTMANN | (PS) |
| Minister Environment | (June 1997–2001)<br>Dominique VOYNET | (Les Verts) |
| **Women in Ministerial Positions (October 2001)** | 9 women | |
| Minister Youth and Sport | Marie-George BUFFET | (PCF) |
| Minister Employment, Solidarity | Elisabeth GUIGOU (PS) | |
| Junior Minister Solidarity (Senior Citizens) | Paulette GUINCHARD-KUNSTLER | (PS) |
| (Garde des Sceaux) Minister Justice | Marylise LEBRANCHU | (PS) |
| Junior Minister Housing | Marie-Noëlle LIENEMANN | (PS) |
| Junior Minister Budget | Florence PARLY | (PS) |
| Junior Minister Rights of Women and Training | Nicole PERY | (PS) |
| Associate Minister Family (Young People) | Ségolène ROYAL | (PS) |
| Minister Culture and Communication | Catherine TASCA | (PS) |

## Dates of Legislative Elections since the Fifth Republic

| | |
|---|---|
| 23 and 30 November | 1958 |
| 18 and 25 November | 1962 |
| 5 and 12 March | 1967 |
| 23 and 30 June | 1968 (dissolution after social unrest) |
| 4 and 11 June | 1973 |
| 12 and 19 June | 1978 |
| 14 and 21 June | 1981 |
| 16 March | (proportionnelles [proportional representation]) |
| 5 and 12 June | 1988 |
| 21 and 28 March | 1993 |
| | 1998 |

## List of Députées

| | |
|---|---|
| AILLAUD | Thérèse |
| ALQUIER | Jacqueline |
| ALLIOT-MARIE | Michèle |
| AMELINE | Nicole |
| ANDRIEUX-BACQUET | Sylvie |
| AUBERT | Marie-Hélène |
| AURILLAC | Martine |
| AVICE | Edwige |
| AYME de la CHEVRELIÈRE | Marie-Magdeleine |
| BACHELOT | Roselyne |
| BACLET | Albertine |
| BARBERA | Myriam |
| BARZACH | Michèle |
| BASSOT | Sylvie |
| BATIER | Aimée |
| BELLO | Huguette |
| BENAYOUN-NAKACHE | Yvette |
| BEUZELIN | Michèle |
| BOISSEAU | Marie-Thérèse |
| BONVOISIN | Jeanine |
| BOUABSA | Kheira |
| BOUCHARDEAU | Huguette |
| BOUSQUET | Danielle |
| BOUQUILLON | Emmanuelle |
| BOUTIN | Christine |
| BREDIN | Frédérique |
| BRICQ | Nicole |
| CACHEUX | Denise |
| CASANOVA | Odette |
| CATALA | Nicole |
| CHAIGNEAU | Colette |
| CHAPENTIER | Françoise |
| CHAVATTE | Angèle |
| CHEPY-LEGER | Annette |
| CHONAVEL | Jacqueline |
| CLERGEAU | Marie-Françoise |
| CODACCIONI | Colette |
| COLOT | Geneviève |
| COMMERGNAT | Nelly |
| CONSTANS | Hélène |
| COUDERC | Anne-Marie |
| CREPIN | Aliette |
| CRESSON | Edith |
| DAUGREILH | Martine |
| DAVID | Martine |
| DELABIE | Marcelle |
| DENISE | Monique |
| DEVAUD | Marcelle |
| DIENESCH | Marie-Madeleine |
| DIEULANGARD | Marie-Madeleine |
| DOUAY | Brigitte |
| DUFEU | Danielle |
| DUFOIX | Georgina |
| DUMONT | Laurence |
| DUPUY | Lydie |
| ECOCHARD | Janine |
| FIEVET | Berthe |
| FEIDT | Nicole |
| FOST | Paulette |
| FRACHON | Martine |
| FRAYSSE-CAZALIS | Jacqueline |
| FRITSCH | Anne-Marie |
| GASPARD | Françoise |
| GASTEBOIS | Françoise |
| GENISSON | Catherine |

**List of Députées** (*continued*)

| | | | |
|---|---|---|---|
| GOUTMANN | Marie-Thérèse | PAPON | Christiane |
| GOEURIOT | Colette | PAPON | Monique |
| GOURNAY | Marie-Fanny | PATRAT | Marie-Thérèse |
| GRZEGRZULKA | Odette | PEROL-DUMONT | Marie-Françoise |
| GUILHEM | Evelyne | PERRIN-GAILLARD | Geneviève |
| HALIMI | Gisèle | PEULVAST-BERGEAL | Annette |
| HARCOURT (d') | Florence | PIAT | Yann |
| HAUTECLOCQUE (d') | Nicole | PICARD | Catherine |
| HELLE | Cécile | PLOUX | Suzanne |
| HOFFMANN | Jacqueline | PORTE | Jeanine |
| HORVATH | Adrienne | PREMONT (de) | Brigitte |
| HOSTALIER | Françoise | PRIN | Jeannette |
| HUBERT | Elisabeth | PRIVAT | Colette |
| IDRAC | Anne-Marie | PROVOST | Eliane |
| IMBERT | Françoise | QUESTIAUX | Nicole |
| ISSAC-SIBILLE | Bernadette | REYNAUD | Maryline |
| JACQ | Marie | RIGNAULT | Simone |
| JACQUAINT | Muguette | RIVASI | Michèle |
| JAMBU | Jeanine | ROBERT | Dominique |
| KHEBTANI | Rebiha | ROBIN-RODRIGO | Chantal |
| LACUEY | Conchita | ROCA | Gilberte |
| LALUMIÈRE | Catherine | ROIG | Marie-Josée |
| LAUNAY | Odette | ROUDY | Yvette |
| LAZARD | Jacqueline | ROUSSEAU | Monique |
| LEBLANC | Chantal | ROYAL | Ségolène |
| LECUIR | Marie-France | SAUGES | Odile |
| LEPAGE | Corinne | SAUVAIGO | Suzanne |
| LEROUX | Ginette | SICARD | Odile |
| LIENEMANN | Marie-Noëlle | SID-CARA | Nefissa |
| LIGNIERE-CASSOU | Martine | SIGOURET | Marie-Magdeleine |
| MARRE | Béatrice | SOUM | Renée |
| MALAVAL | Marie-Claude | STEPHAN | Yvonne |
| MARIN-MOSKOVITZ | Gilberte | STIEVENARD | Gisèle |
| MARTINACHE | Madeleine | STIRBOIS | Marie-France |
| MARTINEZ | Henriette | SUBLET | Marie-Josèphe |
| MATHIEU-OBADIA | Jacqueline | TAUBIRA-DELANNON | Christiane |
| MICHAUX-CHEVRY | Lucette | TOUTAIN | Ghislaine |
| MIGNON | Hélène | THOME-PATENÔTRE | Jacqueline |
| MISSOFFE | Hélène | TISNE | Monique |
| MOIRIN | Odile | TOURAINE | Marisol |
| MORA | Christiane | TRAUTMANN | Catherine |
| MOREAU | Gisèle | TROISIER | Solange |
| MOREAU | Louise | TRUPIN | Odette |
| NEIERTZ | Véronique | VAILLANT-COUTURIER | Marie-Clothilde |
| NEVOUX | Paulette | | |
| NICOLAS | Catherine | VERGNAUD | Claire |
| OSSELIN | Jacqueline | VEYRINAS (de) | Françoise |
| PANAFIEU (de) | Françoise | ZIMMERMANN | Marie-Jo |

## Dates of General Senatorial Elections since 1959

| | | | | | | |
|---|---|---|---|---|---|---|
| 1962 | 1965 | 1968 | 1971 | 1974 | 1977 | 1980 |
| 1983 | 1986 | 1989 | 1992 | 1995 | 1998 | 2001 |

Note: In September 2001, the number of *sénatrices* increased from 20 to 33 representing 10 % of Senators, a proportion comparable to the proportion of women *députées*. The parity principle was imposed on senatorial candidates for the first time in the 17 *départements* (out of 31) where the election system was one of proportional representation.

## List of Sénatrices to 2001

| | | | |
|---|---|---|---|
| ALDUY | Jacqueline | FRAYSSE-CAZALIS | Jacqueline |
| ALEXANDRE-DEBRAY | Janine | GAUTIER | Gisèle |
| ANDRE | Michèle | GOUTMANN | Marie-Thérèse |
| ANGLADE | Magdeleine | GOLDET | Cécile |
| BARDOU | Janine | GOURAULT | Jacqueline |
| BEAUDEAU | Marie-Claude | GOURNAY | Marie-Fanny |
| BEAUFILS | Marie-France | GROS | Brigitte |
| BEN GUIGA | Monique | HAUTECLOCQUE (d') | Nicole |
| BERGE-LAVIGNE | Maryse | HEINIS | Anne |
| BIDARD-REYDET | Danielle | HENNERON | Françoise |
| BLANDIN | Marie-Christine | HERVIAUX | Odette |
| BOCANDE | Annick | LAGATU | Catherine |
| BORVO | Nicole | LEBELLEGOU-BEGUIN | Geneviève |
| BOYER | Yolande | LETARD | Valérie |
| BRISEPIERRE | Paulette | LUC | Hélène |
| CAMPION | Claire-Lise | MATHON | Josiane |
| CARDOT | Marie-Hélène | MICHAUX-CHEVRY | Lucette |
| CREMIEUX | Suzanne | MIDY | Monique |
| DAVID | Annie | MISSOFFE | Hélène |
| DELABIE | Marcelle | OLIN | Nelly |
| DEMESSINE | Michelle | PAGANI | Odette |
| DERYCKE | Dinah | PAPON | Monique |
| DESMARESCAUX | Sylvie | PERLICAN | Rolande |
| DEVAUD | Marcelle | POURTAUD | Danièle |
| DIDIER | Evelyne | PRINTZ | Gisèle |
| DIEULANGARD | Marie-Madeleine | RAPUZZI | Irma |
| DUMONT | Yvonne | RODI | Nelly |
| DURRIEU | Josette | ROZIER | Janine |
| DUSSEAU | Joëlle | SAN VICENTE | Michèle |
| EDELINE | Hélène | SCELLIER | Gabrielle |
| FÉRAT | Françoise | SELIGMANN | Françoise |
| FOST | Paulette | VERMEERSCH | Jeannette |

## Notes

1. Information for this appendix is taken from a number of sources, including the following Web-sites:

   http://www.adminet.com/poli/
   http://www.brook.edu/fp/cusf/analysis/women.htm
   http://education.guardian.co.uk/schools/french/story/0,7913,471902,00.html
   http://www.extense.com/bin/x2cgi_view.cgi?userID=64393794&view=on&query=chir
   http://www.france.diplomatie.fr/france/gb/instit/instit09.html
   http://www.ipu.org/english/issues/wmndocs/classif.htm (France is no. 59)
   http://www.ladocfrancaise.gouv.fr/cgi-bin/multitel/CATALDOC/
   http://www.quid.fr/web.php? web=/WEB/FEMMES/Q016270.HTM

   *List of deputies by gender*:
   http://www.assemblee-nat.fr/tribun/gs2.asp

   *Current Cabinet*:
   http://www.premier-ministre.gouv.fr/fr/p.cfm?ref=412

2. Information taken from the lists compiled by Helft-Malz and Lévy, *Encyclopédie des femmes politiques*, pp. 359–368 and from Gill Allwood and Khursheed Wadia, *Women and Politics in France 1958–2000* (London: Routledge), 2000, pp. 40–42 and from the above Websites.

# Appendix 3

## Parity in the Press: February–July 1996

The following brief chronological survey of the journalism on parity lists the articles that appeared between February and July 1996 in Paris in order to provide a sense of the actors, the nature of the debate, the variety of opinion, and the degree of public interest in the parity question over a limited period of time—the four-month period during which the debate was strengthening. In 1996, only 36 percent of journalists were women, often in junior positions, and the readership of daily papers was predominantly male (the readership of *Le Monde*, for example, was 57 percent male in 1999).

"Are women afraid of Politics?" (*La Politique fait-elle peur aux femmes*?), asks Michelle Demessine, a 48-year-old Communist senator (later Jospin's tourism minister) in the Communist paper, *L'Humanité*, on 13 February. She proceeds to attempt to "put the question of parity clearly." Six out of the fifteen people in her Communist Senate working group are women and, claims Demessine, their perception of life is different from that of men. According to her, "this does not necessarily mean that women are instruments of progress, but that their participation on the basis of parity is, for me, a form of real democracy" (*Cela ne veut pas dire pour autant que les femmes sont facteurs de progrès, mais leur participation à parité est pour moi, une forme de démocratie réelle*).

An article in the Catholic daily *La Croix* (2 April), also sympathetic to the parity cause, uses figures to remind its readers that France is still last in Europe for female representation, with 6 percent *deputés*, 5 percent *sénateurs*, 7 percent *maires*, 20 percent *conseillers municipaux*, 5 percent *conseillers généraux*, and 12 percent *conseillers régionaux*. The journalist notes that the world average for female representation dropped from 15 percent in 1988 to 11 percent in 1995 but on a more optimistic note, adds that currently 30 percent of women occupy the European Parliament. The positive change in attitude that showed 43 percent of the public in favor of a woman president in 1974 and 84 percent in 1996 is also noted.

The IFOP poll of 29 and 30 May showing 80 percent of the public in favor of parity is reported in a number of papers. In *Le Figaro* (7 June), a male, conservative journalist, Alain-Gérard Slama, pronounces against this verdict on parity and argues for equality before the law without consideration of sex, race, or religion. The enemy, he claims, is not the state but "tribalism." Yet also in the conservative *Le Figaro* (20 June), the woman journalist Nicole Barbin recalls the scandalous dismissal of Mitterrand's Prime Minister Edith Cresson and *les juppettes* (Juppé's skirts) and approves of the parity campaign to break down male chauvinism in the political world.

In a major article in *L'Express* (6 June), the eminent political analyst Olivier Duhamel notes that the scorn attached by the media label *juppettes* to political women as late as 1996 and the humiliation of their short five-and-a-half months in office has created a backlash against the male "capture" of political power. This has given support to the parity principle. Power, Duhamel argued, is quite well distributed across generations and regions but very poorly between the sexes—although it is also not particularly well distributed across classes (the latter are, however, becoming less distinct). But even if the equal rights guaranteed by the revolution acquired the force of law only in 1971, democracy, for Duhamel, "deserves better" than parity. The present Constitution appropriately did not recognize particular groups or particular origins. This argument that parity would, in fact, be a regression of principle, reducing human beings from citizens to their original specificity will recur in his later media articles. Sexual difference placed over and above shared humanity could open the way to other criteria for preference—color or ethnicity, for example. Olivier Duhamel appears to agree with Badinter and the feminists against parity on principle. Nonetheless, he concludes, with Halimi and the parity feminists, that evidently, nothing will change without a parity principle. Parity should therefore be admitted but as an exception—a parenthesis in democratic principles—a legally allowable temporary suspension of the Constitution in the light of the urgent need for change.

In *L'Express* (20 June), Michel Rocard, a Socialist deputy to the European Parliament, puts forward a concrete proposal to achieve parity by dividing electoral districts in two and presenting a male and a female candidate, using two sets of ballot boxes. Yvette Roudy, the former minister for the status of women and then for women's rights, and mayor of Lisieux, writes in *Vendredi* (21 June) that "Fifty Years is Long Enough," defending parity on the grounds that there is already a principle of quotas at work in the French system of representation. This is, she argues, a geographical quota fixed by division into districts and regions.

On the opposite side, in *Le Figaro* (26 June), a journalist who signs as F.T. argues vehemently that female quotas are anti-constitutional and contravene the principles of universality, equality, liberty, and the dignity of the human person. In *Le Figaro* of the following day, the indomitable Françoise Giroud argues against F.T. and in support of parity out of a deep sense of frustration with the present situation. Giroud, like Duhamel, nonetheless advocates caution. Her article on the trap that male-female parity may represent reflects her own experience and a certain skepticism toward the nature of political power. It is an illusion, she claims, to believe that a deputy has any real power. She/he is a social worker who must vote with his/her party and is seldom consulted. Giroud, then, is willing to support the cause but warns that parity is not the ultimate solution.

On the same day, in the left-wing paper *Rouge*, Josette Trat argues in "What's New on Parity?" that the need to change daily life and the division of labor between the sexes is just as pressing an issue as parity. In *L'Express* of 11 July, Olivier Duhamel critiques Rocard's suggestion of two sets of ballot boxes, closer, for Duhamel to an unacceptable separate development than to common humanity and equality of rights. In "Parity without Principles," Duhamel notes the bitter taste left by an argument for parity based on effectiveness alone and taking no account of the problem that distinguishing between sexes is anti-constitutional.

On the right, Jean-Marie Rouart, writing for *Le Figaro* (11 July), forwards arguments for the same case but less convincingly, claiming much as Jacques Chirac does that it is better to change social norms than to impose rigid and constraining legal solutions. His somewhat illogical conclusion is that women in Europe have won equality: "Let them use it."

*Le Figaro* published another article a week later on 19 July, "Why Women Shun Politics" (*Pourquoi les femmes boudent la politique*), along with a review of the comprehensive new study on women by Béatrice D'Intignano. In her book *Femmes si vous le saviez* (Women, If You Only Knew), D'Intignano makes a plea for greater political equality and for a list system for the 1998 elections, arguing that on most fronts, other than in politics, women are continuing to make advances. For example, one out of three businesses is created by a woman and 26 percent of heads of firms are women. Although women at the top are most often found outside of the big corporations, the small and medium-sized businesses they operate are succeeding better. French women also continue to live 8.2 more years than men. In many other respects, D'Intignano is generally critical of feminism and argues for the need for affirmative action for men. Her book is reviewed and discussed in a number of other newspapers and the facts it has assembled are thoroughly rehearsed in editorials and reviews.

Other books, including an academic study entitled *La Raison des Femmes* published in 1992 by Geneviève Fraisse, a philosopher and historian of women's movements at the CNRS (Centre National de la Recherche Scientifique) are reviewed in a number of newspapers in July. For Fraisse, equality under the law has proved insufficient, and parity as a figure of equality and freedom is the logical result of the nineteenth-century universalism and utopianism of Marx, Fourier, and Saint Simon. Fraisse concedes that universality, understood as neutral, is philosophically grounded whereas the idea of parity, proposing the association of the universal with duality and the recognition of difference, does pose a philosophical problem. She nonetheless supports parity for its usefulness as a weapon in a world where the 32 women out of the 577 members of the Assemblée help govern but, according to Fraisse's analysis, have no power to represent.

Michelle Coquillat argues that "we are born men and women." Simone Veil pleads for immediate action—"Don't leave things to time"—and sets a time frame for gradually increasing quotas to attain parity in 2010. A number of other articles evoke the United Nations objective of parity by corrective measures accepted at the Beijing conference in 1995. These press articles reveal both the complexities of the intellectual arguments and the essentially pragmatic defense of the parity cause. They also show the polemical and attention-catching potential of parity arguments and provide a glimpse of the role of the media in circulating ideas and responses on the parity question to the intellectual and to the wider public. There have been no major studies to date on the impact of the media on the issue of parity.

# Select Bibliography

## Women Politicians Writing on Power


Alliott-Marie, Michèle. *La Grande peur des classes moyennes.* Paris: Editions de la Table Ronde, 1996.

———, *La Décision politique: attention une République peut en cacher une autre.* Paris: PUF, 1983.

Aubry, Martine. *Il est grand temps...* Paris: Albin Michel, 1997.

———, *Le Choix d'agir.* Paris: Albin Michel, 1994.

Aubry, Martine, and Olivier Duhamel. *Petit Dictionnaire pour lutter contre l'extrême droite.* Paris: Seuil, 1995.

Aubry, Martine, and Pierre Rémy. "L'Urgence du social." *Etudes* (April 1993): 471–476.

Avice, Edwige. *Terre d'élection, voyage en parachuté dans le Dauphinois.* Paris: PUG, 1993.

Barzach, Michèle. *Vérités et tabous.* Paris: Seuil, 1994.

———, *Le Paravent des égoismes.* Paris: Odile Jacob, 1989.

———, "La place des femmes en politique." *Futur antérieur,* no. 19–20 (1993): 7–17.

Bouchardeau, Huguette. *Simone Weil.* Paris: Julliard, 1995.

———, *La Famille Renoir.* Paris: Calmann-Lévy, 1994.

———, *Le Déjeuner.* Paris: Editions François Bourin, 1993.

———, "Un parcours politique." In Riot-Sarcey, ed. *Femmes, pouvoirs.* Paris: Kimé, 1993.

———, *Carnets de Prague.* Paris: Seghers, 1992.

———, *La Grande Verrière.* Paris: Payot, 1991.

———, *Commission des communautés européennes, Femmes d'Europe,* no. 67 (December-January 1990–1991).

———, *George Sand. La Lune et les sabots.* Paris: Laffont, 1990.

———, *Rose Noël.* Paris: Seghers, 1990.

———, Communauté économique européenne. "La femme en chiffres" (décembre 1989).

———, *Choses dites de profil.* Paris: Editions Ramsay, 1988.

———, *Femmes d'Europe: 10 ans* (June 1988).

———, *Les Femmes et la politique.* Unpublished manuscript, 1987.

———, *Le Ministère du possible.* Paris: Alain Moreau, 1986.

———, *Un Coin dans leur monde.* Paris: Editions Syros, 1979.

———, *Hélène Brion; la voie féministe.* Paris: Editions Syros, 1978.
———, *Pas d'histoire, les femmes.* Paris: Editions Syros, 1977.
Boutin, Christine. *Pour la défense de la vie.* Paris: Tequi, 1993.
———, *Une Ethique sans citoyens.* Paris: Edition Universitaire, 1991.
Bredin, Frédérique. *Députée, journal de bord.* Paris: Fayard, 1997.
Catala, Nicole. *Droit social européen.* Paris: Litec, 1991.
Catala, Nicole, and Michel Aurillac. *Pour une société de progrès et de liberté.* Paris: Albatros, 1988.
Chauvet, Christine. *Les Femmes dans l'économie française.* Paris: Denoël, 1995.
Chauvet, Christine, and Marie Thérèse Bianchi. *Lettre Ouverte aux hommes qui ont peur des femmes en politique.* Chantilly: Olemans, 1990.
Cordon, Violaine de. *Vivement des femmes.* Paris: Balland, 1987.
Cresson, Edith. *Avec le soleil.* Paris: Lattès, 1976.
Demessine, Michelle. *Femmes d'ici, quatre générations de femmes dans le Nord-Pas-de-Calais.* Dunkerque: Westhoeck, 1985.
Devaud, Marcelle. *Itinéraire exceptionnel d'une femme politique française de l'après-guerre.* Paris: Editions Carvalho, 1997.
Dorlhac, Hélène. *Changer la prison.* Paris: Plon, 1984.
Gaspard, Françoise. "La parité entre égalité et indifférenciation: dialogue avec Françoise Gaspard." *Revue française des affaires sociales,* no. 4 (1998): 33–40.
———, *Les Femmes dans la prise de décision en France et en Europe.* Paris: l'Harmattan, 1997.
———, *Le Foulard et la République.* Paris: La Découverte, 1995.
———, "De la parité: genèse d'un concept, naissance d'un mouvement." *Nouvelles Questions féministes* 15, no. 4 (1994): 29–44.
———, *Une Petite Ville en France.* Paris: Gallimard, 1991.
———, *La Fin des immigrés.* Paris: Seuil, 1984.
———, *Madame le...* Paris: Grasset, 1979.
Gaspard, Françoise, and Philippe Bataille. *Comment les femmes changent la politique. Et pourquoi les hommes résistent.* La Découverte: Paris, 1998.
Gaspard, Françoise, Claude Servan-Schreiber and Anne Le Gall. *Au pouvoir, citoyennes! Liberté, Egalité, Parité.* Paris: Seuil, 1992.
Giroud, Françoise. *Les Françaises: de la Gauloise à la pilule.* Paris: Fayard, 1999.
———, *Arthur ou le bonheur de vivre.* Paris: Fayard, 1997.
———, *Cosima la sublime.* Paris: Plon/Fayard, 1996.
———, Radio France-Culture (Radio interviews), 9, 10, 11 December 1996.
———, *Coeur de tigre.* Paris: Plon/Fayard, 1995.
———, *Chienne d'année. Journal d'une Parisienne 2.* Paris: Seuil, 1995.
———, *Journal d'une Parisienne.* Paris: Seuil, 1994.
———, *Mon très cher amour.* Paris: Grasset, 1994.
———, *Jenny Marx ou la Femme du diable.* Paris: Laffont, 1992.
———, *Leçons particulières.* Paris: Fayard, 1990.
———, *Alma Mahler, ou l'Art d'être aimée.* Paris: Laffont, 1988.
———, *Le Bon plaisir.* Paris: Mazarine, 1983.
———, *Une Femme honorable.* Paris: Fayard, 1981.
———, *Ce que je crois.* Paris: Grasset, 1978.
———, *La Comédie du pouvoir.* Paris: Fayard, 1977.
———, Secrétariat d'Etat à la condition féminine. "Cent mesures pour les femmes." Paris: La Documentation française, 1976.

———, *Une Poignée d'eau*. Paris: Laffont, 1973.
———, *Si je mens*. Paris: Stock, 1972.
Giroud, Françoise, and Bernard-Henri Lévy. *Les Hommes et les femmes*. Paris: Orban, 1993.
Gros, Brigitte. *Presse: La Marée rose*. Paris: Albatros, 1984.
———, *Quatre heures de transports par jour*. Paris: Denoël, 1970.
———, *Une Maison pour chaque Français*. Paris: Denoël, 1976.
Guigou, Elisabeth. *Une Femme au coeur de l'état*. (Entretiens). Paris: Fayard, 2000.
———, *Etre Femme en politique*. Paris: Plon, 1997.
———, *Pour les Européens*. Paris: Flammarion, 1994.
Halimi, Gisèle. "La Parité entre égalité et indifférentiation." *Revue française des affaires sociales*, no. 4 (October-December 1998): 33–34.
———, *La Nouvelle Cause des femmes*. Paris: Seuil, 1997.
———, "Rapport de la Commission pour la parité entre les femmes et les hommes dans la vie politique." Observatoire de la parité, 1997.
———, *Droit des hommes et droits des femmes: Une autre Démocratie*. Ville Saint Laurent: Fides, 1995.
———, *Une Embellie perdue*. Paris: Gallimard, 1995.
———, *Femmes et citoyennes*. Paris: Editions de l'atelier, 1995.
———, "Pour un nouvel ordre démocratique, exposé de *Choisir-la-Cause des Femmes*," Beijing, Fourth World Conference of Women, 4–15 September, 1995. Strasbourg: Council of Europe publication, 1995.
———, "Egalité ou démocratie: utopie ou défi." Beijing colloquium, Fourth World Conference of Women, 4–15 September, 1995. Strasbourg: Council of Europe publication, 1995.
———, "Plaidoyer pour l'égalité." Preface by Halimi. Strasbourg: Council of Europe publication, 1995.
———, "Participation égale des individus et des groupes: le défi de la démocratie paritaire." Strasbourg: Council of Europe publication, 1995.
———, "Du particulier à l'Universel." Strasbourg: Council of Europe publication, 1995.
———, "Egalité = Parité," *Le Monde*, 22 April 1994.
———, *La Cause des femmes*. Paris: Gallimard Folio, 1992.
———, *Le Lait de l'oranger*. Paris: Gallimard Folio, 1990.
———, *Quel Président pour les femmes?* Paris: Gallimard, 1981.
———, *Le Programme commun des femmes*. Paris: Grasset, 1978.
———, ed. *Femmes: Moitié de la terre moitié du pouvoir*. Paris: Gallimard, 1994.
Halimi, Gisèle, and Eliane Vogel-Polsky, "Une Europe citoyenne sans les citoyennes?" *Le Monde*, 4 May 1996.
Harcourt, Florence. *La Loi du clan*. Paris: Plon, 1998.
Laguiller, Arlette. *C'est toute ma vie: Une femme dans le camp des travailleurs*. Paris: Plon, 1996.
Laôt, Jeannette. *Stratégie pour les femmes*. Paris: Stock, 1977.
Lepage, Corinne. *On ne peut rien faire Madame le ministre*. Paris: Albin Michel, 1999.
Lienemann, Marie-Noëlle. *Lettre au futur président de la République sociale*. Paris: Ramsay, 1995.
———, *Les Cannibales de l'Etat: Changeons les institutions. Coup de gueule contre la technocratie*. Paris: Ramsay, 1994.

———, *La Fracture*. Paris: Gallimard, 1991.

Ministère des Droits de la femme. *Les Femmes en France dans une société d'inégalités*. Paris: La Documentation française, 1992.

Moirin, Odile. *L'Enfance en détresse*. Paris: Patrick Banon. 1996.

Moreau, Gisèle. *Toujours, elles*. Paris: Editions Sociales, Messidor, 1989.

———, *Libres et egales*. Paris: Editions Sociales, Messidor, 1982.

———, *Aujourd'hui les Femmes*. Paris: Editions Sociales, S.E.P.C., 1981.

Neiertz, Véronique, and Claude Estier. *Véridique histoire d'un septennat peu ordinaire*. Paris: Grasset, 1987.

Papon, Christiane. *Femme avenir*. Paris: 1976.

Pelletier, Monique. *La Ligne brisée*. Paris: Flammarion, 1995.

———, *Nous sommes toutes responsables*. Paris: Stock, 1981.

Piat, Yann. *Seule, tout en haut, à droite*. Paris: Fixot, 1991.

Questiaux, Nicole. *Traité du social*. Paris: Dalloz, 1989.

Questiaux, Nicole, and Guy Braibant. *Le Contrôle de l'administration et la protection des citoyens*. Paris: Cujas, 1973.

Questiaux, Nicole, and Jacques Fournier. *Le Pouvoir du social*. Paris: PUF, 1979.

Roudy, Yvette. *Mais de quoi ont-ils peur? Un vent de misogynie souffle sur la politique*. Paris: Albin Michel, 1995.

———, "Rapport à l'Assemblé Nationale française. Rapport d'information sur l'Egalité professionnelle entre les femmmes et les hommes," no. 1161, 1989.

———, "Un Ministère pas comme les autres. Un projet, une stratégie pour les femmes." In FEN, *Le Féminisme et ses enjeux: Vingt-sept femmes parlent*. Paris: FEN-edilig, 1988.

———, *A Cause d'elles*. Paris: Albin Michel, 1985.

———, *La Femme en marge*. Paris: Flammarion, 1975.

Royal, Ségolène. *La Vérité d'une femme*. Paris: Stock, 1996.

———, *Pays, Paysans, Paysages*. Paris: Laffont, 1993.

———, *Le Ras-le-bol des bébés zappeurs, Téléviolence: L'Overdose*. Paris: Laffont, 1989.

———, *Le Printemps des grands-parents. La nouvelle alliance des âges*. Paris: Laffont, 1987.

Saunier-Seïté, Alice. *Remettre l'état à sa place*. Paris: Plon, 1984.

———, *En Première ligne*. Paris: Plon, 1982.

Secrétariat d'Etat aux Droits des femmes et à la vie quotidienne et l'Institut national de la statistique. *Les femmes: Contours et caractères des études économiques, France*. INSEE, 1991.

Scrivener, Christiane. *L'Europe, une bataille pour l'avenir*. Paris: Plon, 1984.

Stirbois, Marie-France. *La France des terroirs et des clochers 1989–1993: le bilan parlementaire du seul député Front National*. Paris: Editions Nationales, 1993.

Taubira-Delannon. *La Pêche en fiches*. Guyane: Cejup Graficentro, 1992.

———, *Cap sur l'horizon*. Guyane: Editions Cayenne, 1992.

Toutain, Ghislaine. Secrétaire d'état chargé des Droits des femmes, gouvernement de France. *L'emploi au féminin. Pour une méthode de la mixité profesionnelle*. Paris: La Documentation française, 1992.

Veil, Simone. *Vivre l'histoire*. Paris: Des Femmes. La bibliothèque des Voix, 1985. Interviews with Antoinette Fouque.

Veil, Simone, and Anne-Françoise Khanine. "Simone Veil face aux parlementaires: son témoignage sur le contexte et les enjeux de la loi sur l'avortement en France." *Lunes*, no. 1 (1997): 53–60.
Vermeersch-Thorez, Jeannette. *Vers quels lendemains*. Paris: Hachette, 1979.
Voynet, Dominique. *Oser l'écologie et la solidarité*. Paris: Editions de l'Aube, 1995.
Weiss, Louise. *Mémoires d'une Européenne: Combats pour les femmes 1934–39*. Paris: Albin Michel, 1980.

## Secondary Sources

Abensour, Miguel, ed. *Ontologie et politique: actes du Colloque Hannah Arendt*. Paris: Editions Tierce, 1989.
Abzug, Bella. *Gender Gap*. New York: Houghton, Mifflin, 1984.
*Actes du Colloque international du 12–14 avril, 1989. Les Femmes et la Révolution française*. Toulouse: Presses Universitaires de Toulouse, 1990.
Adler, Laure. *L'Année des adieux*. Paris: Flammarion, 1995.
———, *Les Femmes politiques*. Paris: Seuil, 1993.
Agacinski, Sylviane. *Politique des sexes*. Paris: Seuil, 1998.
Albistur Maïté, and Daniel Armogathe. *Histoire du féminisme français du Moyen Age à nos jours*. Paris: Editions des femmes, 1977.
Amar, Micheline, ed. *Le Piège de la parité. Arguments pour un débat*. Paris: Hachette Littératures, 1999.
D'Amico Francine and Peter Beckman, eds. *Women in World Politics*. Westport, Conn.: Bergin and Garvey, 1995.
Appleton, Andrew, and Amy Mazur. "Transformation or Modernization: The Rhetoric and Reality of Gender and Party Politics in France." In Joni Lovenduski and Vicky Randall. *Gender and Party Politics*. London: Sage Publications, 1993, pp. 87–112.
Arendt, Hannah."Du mensonge à la violence." French translation in *Essais de politique contemporaine*. Paris: Calman-Lévy, 1972.
Aubert, Nicole, Eugène Enriquez, and Vincent de Gaulejac, eds. *Le sexe du pouvoir. Femmes, hommes et pouvoirs dans les organisations*. Paris: Desclé de Brouwer, 1986.
Auclert, Hubertine. *La Citoyenne*. Paris: Syros, 1982.
———, *Le Vote des femmes*. Paris: Editions Giard et Briene, 1902.
Bachrach, Peter and Morton Baratz. "The Two Faces of Power." *American Political Science Review*, no. 56 (1962): 942–952.
Badinter, Elisabeth. "Tout pouvoir est viril." *L'Histoire*, no. 160 (November 1992): 14–15.
———, *Paroles d'homme*. Paris: P.O.L., 1989.
———, *L'Un est l'autre: Des relations entre hommes et femmes*. Paris: Odile Jacob, 1986.
———, *L'amour en plus: Histoire de l'amour maternel XVII–XXième siècle*, Paris: Flammarion, 1980.
———, ed. *Le XXe siècle des femmes*. Paris: Nathan, 1992.
Baguenard, Jacques, Jean Maisondieu, and Léon Métayer. *Les Hommes politiques n'ont pas d'enfant*. Paris: PUF, 1983.
Bakhtin, Mikhail. *Esthétique et théorie du roman*. Paris: Gallimard, 1978.

Balandier, Georges. *Le Détour. Pouvoir et modernité.* Paris: Fayard, 1985.
Bard, Christine, ed. *Un Siècle d'antiféminisme.* Paris: Fayard, 1999.
———, *Les Filles de Marianne, histoire des féminismes 1914–1940.* Paris: Fayard, 1995.
Bard, Christine, and Jean-Christophe Coffin. *Madeleine Pelletier: logique et infortunes d'un combat pour l'égalité.* Paris: Côté-femmes, 1992.
Barkman, Kerstin. "Politics and Gender: The Need for Electoral Reform." In *Politics* (Manchester) 15, no. 3 (1995): 14–146.
Barnes, Barry. *The Nature of Power.* Cambridge: Polity Press, 1988.
Barret-Ducrocq, Françoise, and Evelyne Pisier. *Femmes en tête.* Paris: Flammarion, 1997.
Bartolini, S. "The French Party System." *Western European Politics* 7, no. 4 (1984).
Bashevkin, Sylvia. "Changing Patterns of Politicization and Partisanship among Women in France." *British Journal of Political Science*, 15 (1985): 77–85.
———, ed. *Women and Politics in Western Europe.* London: Cass, 1985.
———, Baudelot, Christian and Roger Establet. *Allez les filles!* Paris: Seuil, 1992.
Baudoux, Claudine and Claude Zeidman. *Egalité entre les sexes: mixité et démocratie.* Paris: L'Harmattan, 1992.
Baxter, Sandra. *Women and Politics: The Visible Majority.* Ann Arbor: University of Michigan Press, 1983.
Beauvoir, Simone de. *Le Deuxième Sexe.* Paris: Gallimard, 1949.
Beckwith, Karen. "Comparative Research and Electoral Systems: Lessons from France and Italy." *Women and Politics* 12, no. 1 (1992): 33.
Bendix, John. "Women and Politics in Germany and Switzerland." *European Journal of Political Research*, no. 25 (1994): 413–438.
Benguigui, Yamina. *Femmes d'Islam.* Paris: Albin Michel, 1996.
Bennett, Linda, and Stephen Earl Bennett. "From Traditional to Modern Conceptions of Gender Equality in Politics: Gradual Change and Lingering Doubts." *The Western Political Quarterly* (March 1992): 92–111.
Benoit, Yvert. *Dictionnaire des ministres.* Paris: Perrin, 1990.
Béraud, J. *Désir et pouvoir.* Unpublished thesis, université de Rouen, 1980.
Bernstein, Robert. "Why are there so few women in the House?" *Western Political Quarterly* 39 (March 1986): 155–163.
Bhutto, Benazir. *Daughter of Destiny: An Autobiography.* New York: Simon and Schuster, 1989. Published in French as *Benazir Bhutto: Une Autobiographie.* Paris: Stock, 1989.
Birnbaum, Pierre. *Les Elites socialistes au pouvoir: 1981–1985.* Paris: PUF, 1986.
———, *La Classe dirigeante française.* Paris: PUF, 1978.
———, *Les Sommets de l'état. Essai sur l'élite au pouvoir en France.* Paris: Editions du Seuil, 1977.
Blanc, Olivier. *Itinéraire politique et bibliographique d'Olympe de Gouges.* Paris: Editions Côté Femmes, 1993.
Blanquart, Louise. *Femmes: l'âge politique.* Paris: Editions sociales, 1974.
Bolle de Bal, Marcel. "Démocratie paritaire: valeur humaniste ou utopie féministe?" *Revue Nouvelle*, no. 8 (1995): 74–81.
Borella, François. *Les Partis politiques dans la France d'aujourd'hui.* Paris: Seuil, 1990.

Bourdieu, Pierre. *La Domination masculine*. Paris: Seuil, 1998.
———, *Les Choses dites*. Paris: Minuit, 1987.
———, "La Représentation politique." *Actes de la recherche en sciences sociales*, no. 36–37 (1981).
Braud, Philippe. *Le Suffrage universel contre la démocratie*. Paris: PUF, 1980.
Brechon, Pierre, Jacques Derville, and Patrick Lecomte. *Les Cadres du RPR*. Paris: Economica, 1987.
Brimo, Albert. *Les Femmes françaises face au pouvoir politique*. Paris: Montchrestien, 1975.
Buckley, M., and M. Anderson, eds. *The Women Equality in Europe*. London: Macmillan, 1988.
Burke, Mike. *Valeurs féminines, le pouvoir demain*. Paris: Village mondial, 1998.
Burel, Paul, and Natacha Tatu. *Martine Aubry. Enquête sur une énigme politique*. Paris: Calmann-Lévy, 1997.
Bystdzienski, Jill M. *Women Transforming Politics*. Bloomington: Indiana University Press, 1992.
Carras, Mary C. *Indira Ghandi in the Crucible of Leadership*. Boston: Beacon, 1979.
Carrol, Susan J. *Women as Candidates in American Politics*. Bloomington: Indiana University Press, 1985.
Cattelin, Anne-Marie. *L'Europe au féminin. 172 millions d'Européennes au jour le jour*. Paris: Ramsay, 1992.
Cayrol, Roland. *Le Grand Malentendu*. Paris: Seuil, 1993.
Chandernagor, Françoise. *L'Allée du roi*. Paris: Pocket, 1989.
Chapman, Jenny. *Politics, Feminism and the Reformation of Gender*. London: Routledge, 1993.
Charzat, Gisèle. *Les Françaises, sont-elles des citoyennes?* Paris: Denoël Gonthier, 1972.
Chiche, René, and Bertrand Deveaud. *Vies privées: la face cachée des politiques*. Paris: Belfond, 1995.
Chodorow, Nancy. *The Reproduction of Mothering: Psychoanalysis and the Sociology of Gender*. Berkeley: University of California Press, 1978.
Chombeau, Christine. "Pour un principe de parité entre hommes et femmes dans les instances politiques." *Le Monde*, 6–7 June 1993.
Clark, Linda. *Schooling the Daughters of Marianne*. Albany: SUNY Press, 1984.
Cojean, Annick. "Le Parcours des combattantes." 3 January, 1999, 12.30. Televised interviews on Channel 5 (La Cinquième Chaîne).
Colombani, Jean-Marie. *De la France en général et de ses dirigeants en particulier*. Paris: Plon, 1996.
Commission européenne. *Les Femmes, actrices du développement régional*, 1996.
Commission of the European Communities. *Women in Power. Final Report. Athens Conference and Summit*. Brussels, Belgium, November 1992.
Condorcet. *Journal de la Société de 1789*. Fédération féministe du Sud-Est, 1913.
Connell, R.W. *Gender and Power*. Stanford, CA: Stanford University Press, 1987.
Conway, Jill, Susan Bourque, and Joan Scott, eds. *Learning about Women: Gender, Politics, and Power*. Ann Arbor: University of Michigan Press, 1989.

Cooper, Joy. "Cécile Brunschvicg; L'évolution de sa vision dans le cadre de l'histoire de la France et du féminisme français" Ph.D. Thesis: University of Sydney, 1996.
Coquillat, Michelle. *Qui sont-elles? Les Femmes d'influence et de pouvoir en France.* Paris: Mazarine, 1983.
Couderc, Anne-Marie (preface). *Encyclopédie des femmes politiques sous la Vième République.* Paris: Patrick Banon, 1996.
Couderc, Marie-Louise. *Elles, la Résistance.* Paris: Messidor, 1983.
Dahlerup, Drude. *The New Women's Movement: Feminism and Political Power in Europe and the USA.* London: Sage, 1986.
Daley, Caroline, and Melanie Nolan. *Suffrage and Beyond. International Feminist Perspectives.* New York: New York University Press, 1994.
Darcy, R., Susan Welch, and Janet Clark. *Women, Elections and Representation.* New York: Longman, 1987.
Dauphin, Cécile. "Culture et pouvoir des femmes." *Annales: Economies, Sociétés, Civilisations,* 2 March-April 1986; translated as "Women's Culture and Women's Power: Issues in French Women's History." In Karen Offen, Ruth Roach Pierson, and Jane Rendall, eds. *Writing Women's History: International Perspectives.* Houndmills, Basingstoke, Hampshire: Macmillan, 1991.
Debray, Régis, and Emmanuel Monnick. *Le Scribe.* Paris: Grasset, 1980.
———, *Refaire la France.* Paris: Plon, 1945.
Decaux, Alain. *Histoire des Françaises.* Paris: Perrin, 1972.
Delphy, Christine. *Nouvelles Questions Féministes,* no. 4 "La parité pour," Paris 1994; and no. 2 "La parité contre," Paris 1995.
———, *Sexe et genre. De la hiérarchie entre les sexes.* Paris: éditions du CNRS, 1991.
———, "Les femmes et l'Etat." In *Nouvelles Questions Féministes,* 6–7 (1984).
Delwasse, Liliane. "Les Femmes en politique." *Le Monde,* 7 March 1982.
Demangeat, Catherine, and Florence Muracciole. *Dieu et les siens.* Paris: Belfond, 1990.
Desanti, Dominique. "Des Garçonnes aux 'pros' d'aujourd'hui." *Le Monde,* 15 August 1984.
Deutchman, Ellen. "The Politics of Empowerment." *Women and Politics* 11, no. 2 (1991): 1–17.
*Dictionnaire de l'histoire des femmes du XXe siècle.* Paris: Nathan, 1995.
Dijkstra, Sandra. *Flora Tristan.* London: Pluto, 1992.
Dogan, Mattei, and Jacques Narbonne. *Les Françaises face à la politique, comportement politique et condition sociale.* Paris: Albin Colin, 1955.
Dottin-Orsini, Mireille. *Cette femme qu'ils disent fatale.* Paris: Grasset, 1993.
Doumic, François, and Pascal Perrineau, eds. *Le Guide du pouvoir.* Paris: 1973–1993.
Dreyfus, Hubert L., Paul Rabinow, and Michel Foucault. *Michel Foucault, un parcours philosophique: au-delà de l'objectivité et de la subjectivité.* Paris: Gallimard, 1984. Translation by Hubert L. Dreyfus and Paul Rabinow. *Michel Foucault, Beyond Structuralism and Hermeneutics.* Chicago: University of Chicago Press, 1983.
DuBois, Ellen. *Feminism and Suffrage: The Emergence of an Independent Women's Movement in America, 1848–1869.* Ithaca, N.Y.: Cornell University Press, 1978.

Duby, Georges, and Michelle Perrot, eds. *Histoire des femmes en Occident: XXe siècle.* 5 volumes. Paris: Plon, 1992.

Duchen, Claire.*Voices from the Women's Movement in France.* London: Hutchinson, 1987.

———, *Feminism in France. From May 68 to Mitterrand.* Boston: Routledge and Keagan Paul, 1986.

Duerst-Lhati, Georgia, and Rita Mae Kelly, eds. *Genderpower, Leadership, and Governance.* Ann Arbor: University of Michigan Press, 1995.

Duhamel, Olivier. *Portrait d'un artiste.* Paris: Flammarion, 1997.

———, *La Politique imaginaire.* Paris: Flammarion, 1995.

———, "President and Prime Minister." In Paul Godt, ed., *Policy Making in France.* London: Pinter Publishers, 1989.

Duke, Lois. *Women in Politics. Outsiders or Insiders.* Eaglewood Cliffs, N.J.: Prentice Hall, 1993.

Duroux, Françoise. "Constat polémique, fondements." *Futur antérieur*, volume 5–6, no. 25–26.

———, *Pouvoirs Pouvoir.* 1995, pp. 51–65.

Du Roy, Albert, and Nicole. *Citoyennes! Il y a cinquante ans, le vote des femmes.* Paris: Flammarion, 1994.

Duverger, Maurice. *Les Partis politiques.* Paris: Armand Colin, 1976.

———, "La participation des femmmes à la vie politique." Paris: Unesco, 1955.

Ehrmann, Henry, and Martin Schain. *Politics in France.* New York: Harper Collins, 5th edition, 1992.

Enriquez, Eugene. "Le Pouvoir et son ombre sexuelle." In Nicole Aubert, Eugene Enriquez, and Vincent de Gaulejac, eds. *Le Sexe du pouvoir: femmes, hommes et pouvoirs dans les organisations.* Paris: Desclée de Brouwer, 1986.

Ericson, Baranek, and Chan. *Visualizing Deviance.* Toronto: Toronto University Press, 1989.

Escoffier-Lambiotte, Claudine. "La Sirène du RPR." *Le Monde*, 25 March 1987.

Evans, Richard. *The Feminists: Women's Emancipation Movements in Europe, America and Australasia 1840–1920.* London: Croom-Helm, 1979.

Fabius, Laurent. *Les Blessures de la vérité.* Paris: Flammarion, 1995.

Fallot, Evelyne. "Michèle Barzach: Who's That Girl?" *Express*, 11–17 December 1987.

Fauré, Christine. *Encyclopédie politique et historique des femmes.* Paris: PUF, 1997.

———, *La Démocratie sans les femmes.* Paris: PUF, 1985. Translated as *Democracy without Women. Feminism and the Rise of Liberal Individualism in France.* Bloomington: Indiana University Press, 1991.

Favier, P., and M. Martin-Roland. *La Décennie Mitterrand.* 2 volumes. Paris: Seuil, 1990 and 1991.

FEN. *Le Féminisme et ses enjeux. Vingt-sept femmes parlent.* Paris: FEN-Edelig, 1988.

Finlay, Fergus. *Mary Robinson: A President with a Purpose.* Dublin: The O'Brien Press, 1990.

Flammang, Janet. "Feminist Theory: The Question of Power." In *Current Perspectives in Social Theory*, vol. 4, ed. S.G. McNall. Greenwich, Conn.: JAI Press, 1983.

Folbre, Nancy. *De la différence des sexes en économie politique.* Paris: Des Femmes-Antoinette Fouque, 1997.

Foucault, Michel. *Power/Knowledge. Selected Interviews and Other Writings 1972–1977.* Trans. Colin Gordon et al. New York: Pantheon Books, 1980.

———, *La Volonté de savoir*; *L'Usage des plaisirs*; and *Le Souci de soi.* 3 volumes. In *L'Histoire de la sexualité.* Paris: Gallimard, 1976. Trans. Richard Hurley as *The History of Sexuality.* New York: Pantheon Books, 1978.

———, *L'Ordre du discours.* Paris: Gallimard, 1970

Fouque, Antoinette. *Il y a deux sexes.* Paris: Gallimard, 1995.

Fraisse, Geneviève. *Les Femmes et leur histoire.* Paris: Gallimard, 1998.

———, "Où en sont les femmes en France?" *Lunes,* no. 6 (1999): 7–15.

———, "La souveraineté limitée des femmes." *Libération,* 14 June 1994.

———, "Quand gouverner n'est pas représenter." *Esprit* 3–4 (March-April 1994): 103–114.

———, *La Raison des Femmes.* Paris: Plon, 1992.

———, *Muse de la raison, la démocratie exclusive et la différence des sexes.* Aix-en-Provence: Alinéa, 1989.

Frappat, Bruno. "Sa Majesté très cathodique." *Le Monde,* 8–9 December 1985.

Freedman, Jane. "La représentation journalistique des femmes politiques (vu à travers le bilan de 'la décennie Mitterrand' depuis 1981)." Mémoire DEA d'Etudes Politiques. Paris: Institut d'Etudes Politiques. 1992.

French, Marilyn. *La Fascination du pouvoir.* Paris: Acropole, 1987.

Friedan, Betty. *The Second Stage.* London: Abacus, 1983.

Frischer, Dominique. *La Revanche des misogynes.* Albin Michel, 1997.

Furet, François. *Le Passé d'une illusion: essai sur l'idée communiste au XXe siècle.* Paris: Laffont/Calmann-Levy, 1995.

Garaudy, Roger. *Pour l'avènement de la femme.* Paris: Albin Michel, 1981.

Gautier, Arlette. *Le Sexe des politiques sociales.* Paris: Côté Femmes, 1993.

Gelb, Joyce. *Feminism and Politics: A Comparative Perspective.* Berkeley: University of California Press, 1989.

Genovese, Michael A., ed. *Women as National Leaders.* Newbury Park, Calif.: Sage, 1993.

Genette, Gérard. *Figures II.* Paris: Editions du Seuil, 1969.

Gertzog, Irwin. *Congressional Women: Their Recruitment, Treatment and Behavior.* New York: Praeger Publishers, 1984.

Giffard, Jacques. "Les Françaises et la politique." In *Revue juridique et politique. Indépendance et coopération,* 4 October-December 1974.

Gilligan, Carol. *In a Different Voice.* Cambridge: Harvard University Press, 1983.

Giscard d'Estaing, Valéry. *Deux Français sur trois.* Paris: Flammarion, 1984.

———, *Démocratie Française.* Paris: Fayard, 1977.

———, *Le Pouvoir et la vie.* Paris: Livre de Poche, volume 1 (1988); volume 2 (1991).

Godineau, Dominique. *Citoyennes tricoteuses: les femmes du peuple à Paris pendant la Révolution française.* Aix-en-Provence: Alinéa, 1988.

Godt, P., ed. *Policy Making in France.* London: Pinter, 1989.

Goldmann, Annie. *Les Combats des femmes.* Paris: Casterman-Guinti, 1996.

Gordon, Linda. *Heros of Their Own Lives.* New York: Viking, 1988.

Gouges, Olympe de. *Ecrits politiques 1788–1791.* Paris: Editions Côté-femmes, 1993.

———, *Oeuvres.* Presented by Benoîte Groult. Paris: Mercure de france, 1986.

Gourret, Laurence. *Benazir. L'Envers du voile*. Paris: Denoël, 1997.
Gras, Solange, and Christian Gras. *Histoire de la première République Mitterrandienne*. Paris: Robert Laffont, 1991.
Grimes, Alan P. *The Puritan Ethic and Woman Suffrage*. New York: Oxford University Press, 1967.
Groult, Benoîte. *Ainsi soit-elle*. Paris: Grasset, 1975.
Guibert-Sledziewski, Elisabeth. *Idéaux et conflits dans la Révolution française: études sur la fonction idéologique*. Paris: Meridiens Klinksieck, 1989.
Guéraiche, William. *Les Femmes et la politique*. Paris: Editions de l'atelier, 1999.
Guichard, Marie-Thérèse. *Le Président qui aimait les femmes*. Paris: Robert Laffont, 1993.
Guillaumin, Colette. *Sexe, race et pratique du pouvoir: l'idée de nature*. Paris: Côté femmes, 1992.
Gwilym, Lowri. *Women in Politics (Simone Veil)*. Women Make Movies: New York. Videocassette, 1989.
Haase-Dubosc, Danielle, and Eliane Viennot. *Femmes et pouvoirs sous l'Ancien Régime*. Paris: Rivages, 1991.
Harris, Kenneth. *Thatcher*. London: Weidenfeld & Nicolson, 1988.
Hartsock, Nancy. *Money, Sex and Power: Toward a Feminist Historical Materialism*. Boston: Northeastern University Press, 1983.
Hause, Steven. *Hubertine Auclert, the French Suffragette*. New Haven: Yale University Press, 1987.
Hause, Stephen, and Anne Kenney. *Women's Suffrage and Social Politics in the French Third Republic*. Princeton, N.J.: Princeton University Press, 1984.
Helft-Malz, Véronique and Paule Levy, eds. *Encyclopédie des femmes politiques sous la Vième République*. Paris: Editions Patrick Banon, 1996.
Henry, Natacha. "Gender Parity in French Politics." *The Political Quarterly* 66, no. 3 (July-September 1995): 177–180.
Héritier, Françoise. *Masculin-féminin. La pensée de la différence*. Paris: Odile Jacob, 1996.
Hirschmann, Nancy J., ed. *Revisioning the Political: Feminist Reconstructions of Traditional Concepts in Western Political Theory*. Boulder, Colo.: Westview, 1997
Hoffmann, Stanley, ed. *L'Expérience Mitterrand*. Paris: PUF, 1987.
Hollified, James, ed. *Searching for the New France*. New York: Routledge, 1991.
Hoskyns, Catherine. *Integrating Gender: Women, Law and Politics in the European Union*. London: Verso, 1996.
Huard, Raymond. *Le Suffrage universel en France, 1848–1946*. Paris: Aubier, 1991.
Hubert, Agnès. *L'Europe et les femmes*. Paris: Apogée, 1998.
Huddy, Leonie. "Gender Stereotypes and the Perception of Male and Female Candidates." American Journal of Political Science 37, no. 1 (February 1993), 119–147.
Ince, Kate, and Alex Hughes. *French Erotic Fiction: Women's Desiring Writing, 1880–1990*. Oxford and Washington: Berg, 1996.
Irigaray, Luce. *Le Souffle des femmes*. Paris: Editions ACGF, 1997.
———, *Le Temps de la différence*. Paris: Livre de poche, 1989.
———, *Ethique de la différence sexuelle*. Paris: Editions de Minuit, 1984.
Jenson, Jane. "Le féminisme en France depuis mai 1968." *Vingtième siècle* 24 (October-December 1989): 55–62.

———, "Representations of Difference. The Varieties of French Feminism." *New Left Review* 180 (1990).
Jenson, Jane et al., eds. *The Feminization of the Labor Force: Promises and Prospects.* London: Polity, 1988.
Jenson, Jane, and Mariette Sineau. *Mitterrand et les Françaises.* Paris: Presses de la Fondation Nationale des Sciences politiques, 1995.
———, "François Mitterrand and French Women: Un rendez-vous manqué?"*French Politics and Society* 12, no. 4 (Fall 1994): 35–52.
Jobert, Michel. *Lettre ouverte aux femmes politiques.* Paris: Albin Michel, 1976.
Juppé, Alain. *Entre nous.* Paris: Seuil, 1996.
Kadish, Doris. *Politicizing Gender. Narrative Strategies in the Aftermath of the French Revolution.* New Brunswick: Rutgers University Press, 1991.
Kahn, Kim Fridkin. "Does Gender Make a Difference? An Experimental Examination of Sex Stereotypes and Press Patterns in Statewide Campaigns." *American Journal of Political Science* 39, no. 1 (February 1994): 162–195.
Kaplan, Gisela. *Contemporary Western European Feminism.* New York: New York University Press, 1992.
Kaufmann, Jean-Claude. *Femme seule et le prince charmant.* Paris: Nathan, 1999.
Kelber, Mim, ed. *Women and Government: New Ways to Political Power.* Westport, Conn.: Praeger, 1994.
———, "Gender and Mangerial/Leadership Styles: A Comparison of Arizona Public Administrators." *Women and Politics* 11, no. 2 (1991): 19–39.
Kelly, Rita Mae, Mary M. Hale, Jane Burgess, and Barbara Burt-Way. "Gender and Sustaining Political Ambition." *The Western Political Quarterly* (March 1992): 10–25.
Keränen, Marja, ed. *Gender and Politics in Finland.* Aldershot: Avebury, 1990.
Kirkpatrick, Jeanne. *Political Women.* New York: Basic Books, 1974.
———, *The New Presidential Elite.* New York: Russell Sage, 1976.
Klejman, Laurence, and Florence Rochefort. *L'Egalité en marche: Le Féminisme sous la Troisième République.* Paris: Presses de la Fondation Nationale des Sciences Politiques, 1989.
Kriegel, Blandine. *Philosophie de la République.* Paris: Plon, 1998.
———, *La Cité républicaine*, volume 4 of *Chemins de l'Etat.* Paris: Galilée, 1998.
Landes, Joan B. *Women and the Public Sphere in the Age of the French Revolution.* Ithaca, N.Y.: Cornell University Press, 1988.
Lang, Jack. *Demain les femmes.* Paris: Grasset, 1995.
Latour, Patricia, Monique Houssin, and Madia Tovar. *Femmes et citoyennes. Du droit de vote à l'exercice du pouvoir.* Paris: Les Editions de l'atelier/ Editions Ouvrières, 1995.
Laubier, Claire, ed. *The Condition of Women in France, 1945 to the Present: A Documentary Anthology.* Routledge: London, 1990.
Lebigre, Arlette. "Le temps des régentes." *L'Histoire*, no. 160 (November 1992), 26–29.
Le Doeuff, Michèle. *Le Sexe du savoir.* Paris: Aubier, 1998.
———, "Des femmes, de la philosophie… ," in *L'Etude et le rouet.* Volume 1, Paris: Seuil, 1989.
Le Douré, Hélène. "Du pouvoir politique et poïetique. Schéma d'un raisonnement." *Futur antérieur* 5–6, no. 25–26. *Pouvoirs Pouvoir* (1995): 95–113.
Léger, D. *Le Féminisme en France.* Paris: Sycomore, 1982.

Lejeune, Philippe. *Le Pacte autobiographique.* Paris: Seuil, 1985
Lesselier, Claudie, and Fiammeta Venner. *L'Extrême Droite et les femmes.* Villeurbanne: Editions Golias. 1997.
Lévy, Deborah. "Women of the French National Front." *Parliament Affairs,* no. 42 (1989): 102–111.
Lévy, Paule, and Véronique Helft-Malz, eds. *Encyclopédie des femmes politiques sous la Vième Rébublique.* Paris: Patrick Banon, 1996.
Lipietz, Alain. "Parité au masculin." *Nouvelles Questions Féministes* 15, no. 4 (1994): 45–64.
Lipovetsky, Gilles. *La Troisième Femme: permanence et révolution du féminin.* Paris: Gallimard, 1997.
Lister, Ruth. *Citizenship: Feminist Perspectives.* Basingstoke: Macmillan, 1997.
Lovenduski, Joni. *Contemporary Feminist Politics: Women and Power in Britain.* Oxford: Oxford University Press, 1993.
Lovenduski, Joni, Marianne Githens, and Pippa Norris, eds. *Different Roles, Different Voices: Women and Politics in the United States and Europe.* New York: Harper Collins College, 1994.
Lovenduski, Joni, and Jill Hills, eds. *The Politics of the Second Electorate: Women and Public Participation.* London, Boston: Routledge and Kegan Paul, 1981.
Lovenduski, Joni, and Vicky Randall. *Gender and Party Politics.* London: Sage Publications, 1993.
Lukes, Steven. *Power: A Radical View.* London: Macmillan, 1974.
Majnoni D'Intignano, Beátrice. *Femmes, si vous saviez…* Paris: Editions de Fallois, 1996.
Mangin, Catherine, and Elisabeth Martichoux. *Ces Femmes qui nous gouvernent.* Paris: Albin Michel, 1991.
Marks, Elaine, and Isabelle de Courtivron. *New French Feminisms: An Anthology.* New York: Schocken Books, 1981.
Martin, Jacqueline, ed. *La Parité. Enjeux et mises en oeuvre.* Toulouse: Presses universitaires du Mirail, 1998.
Maschino, Maurice T. *Après vous, messieurs. Les Femmes et le pouvoir.* Paris: Calmann-Lévy, 1996.
Mathieu, Nicole-Claude. *L'Anatomie politique. Catégorisations et idéologie des sexes.* Paris: Côté femmes, 1991.
Mazeaneau, Lucienne. *Dictionnaire des femmes célèbres, tous temps, tous pays.* Paris: Robert Laffont, 1992.
Mazur, Amy G. "Symbolic Reform in France: *égalité professionelle* during the Mitterrand Years." *West European Politics* (October 1992).
Mazur, Amy G., and Andrew Appleton. "Transformation or Modernization: The Rhetoric and Reality of Gender and Party Politics in France." In Joni Lovenduski and Vicky Randall, *Gender and Party Politics.* London: Sage Publications, 1993, pp. 86–112.
McBride Stetson, Dorothy. *Women's Rights in France.* Westport, Conn.: Greenwood Press, 1987.
Mc Nay, Lois. *Foucault and Feminism: Power, Gender and the Self.* Cambridge: Polity Press, 1992.
Meehan, Elizabeth, and Selma Sevenhuijsen. *Equality Politics and Gender.* Newbury Park, Calif.: Sage, 1991.

Melzer, Sara E., and Leslie W. Rabine. *Rebel Daughters: Women and the French Revolution.* New York: Oxford University Press, 1992.
Meyer, Nonna, and Pascal Perrineau. *Les comportements politiques.* Paris: Armand Colin, 1994.
Ministère des Affaires sociales, de la Santé et de la Ville et ministère des Affaires étrangères. *Les Femmes en France 1985–1995.* Rapport établi par la France en vue de la quatrième conférence mondiale sur les femmes. Paris: Documentation Française, 1994.
Mitterrand, François. *Mémoires interrompus: entretiens avec Georges-Marc Benamou.* Paris: Odile Jacob, 1994.
Meyer-Stabley. *Les Dames de l'Elysée.* Paris: Perrin, 1995.
Moi, Toril. *French Feminist Thought: A Reader.* Oxford: Basil Blackwell, 1987.
Moinet, Jean-Philippe. *La Politique autrement.* Paris: Balland, 1994.
Montreynaud, Florence. *Le XXième siècle des femmes.* Paris: Nathan, 1992.
Moses, Claire G., and Leslie Rabine. *Feminism, Socialism, and French Romanticism.* Bloomington: Indiana University Press, 1993.
Mossuz-Lavau, Janine. *Hommes/Femmes. Pour la parité.* Paris: Presses des Sciences Politiques, 1998.
———, *Les Français et la politique: Enquête sur une crise.* Paris: Editions Odile Jacob, 1994.
———, "Le Vote des Françaises dans les années quatre-vingt-dix." *French Politics and Society* 12, no. 4 (Fall 1994): 64–76.
———, "Les Electrices françaises de 1945–1993." In *Le Vote des Françaises à 50 ans.Vingtième Siècle. Revue d'histoire* 42 (April-June, 1994). Paris: Presses de la Fondation Nationale des Sciences Politiques, 1994.
———, "Le vote des femmes: le pouvoir de dire non." In Michèle Riot-Sarcey, ed. *Femmes, Pouvoirs.* Paris: Kimé, 1993.
———, "Le Revirement des femmes." *Le Monde,* 18 August 1993, p. 7.
———, "Le Vote des femmes en France (1945–1993)." *Revue française de Science Politique* 43, no. 4 (August 1993): 673–691.
———, "Women and Politics in France." *French Politics and Society* 10, no. 1 (1992): 1–8.
———, *Les Lois de l'amour: Les politiques de la sexualité en France (1950–1990).* Paris: Payot, 1991.
———, "Femmes et hommes d'Europe aujourd'hui." Numéro spécial des *Cahiers de femmes d'Europe,* no. 35 (1991).
———, "La mutatation de l'électorat féminin." *Le Monde.* Dossiers et Documents. Mai 1988.
———, *Les Femmes dans le personnel politique en Europe. Rapport pour le Conseil de l'Europe* (Division des Droits de l'homme), Strasbourg, 1984.
———, "Le parcours électoral des Françaises." In *Choisir, La Cause des femmes,* 64 (August–September 1984).
Mossuz-Lavau, Janine, and Armelle le Bras-Choppard, eds. *Les Femmes et la politique.* Paris: l'Harmattan, 1997.
Mossuz-Lavau, Janine, and Mariette Sineau. *Enquête sur les femmes et la politique en France.* Paris: PUF, 1983.
Narbonne, Jacques, and Mattei Dogan. *Les Françaises façe à la politique.* Paris: Cahiers de la Fondation Nationale des Sciences Politiques, 1955.

Nelson, Barbara J., and Najma Chowdhury, eds. *Women and Politics Worldwide.* New Haven, Conn.: Yale University Press, 1994.
Norris, Pippa. *Politics and Sexual Equality. The Comparative Position of Women in Western Democracies.* Wheatsheaf: Brighton, 1987.
Northcutt, Wayne, and Jeffra Flaitz. "Women and Politics in Contemporary France: The Electoral Shift to the Left in the 1981 Presidential and Legislative Elections." *Contemporary French Civilization* 7, no. 2 (Winter 1983): 183–198.
Notat, Nicole. *Je voudrais vous dire. Nicole Notat avec Hervé Hamon.* Paris: Calmann-Levy, 1997.
Offen, Karen. "Women, Citizenship and Suffrage with a French Twist." In Caroline Daley and Melanie Dolan, *Suffrage and Beyond: International Feminist Perspectives.* New York: New York University Press, 1994, pp. 151–170.
Offen, Karen, Ruth Roach Pierson, and Jane Rendall, eds. *Writing Women's History: International Perspectives.* Houndmills, Basingstoke, Hampshire: Macmillan, 1991.
Orsenna, Erik. *Grand Amour.* Paris: Seuil, 1993.
Ouzouf, Mona. *Les Mots des femmes: essai sur la singularité française.* Paris: Fayard, 1995.
Parlement européen. *Les Organismes chargés de la promotion de l'égalité des chances entre les femmes et les hommes dans les Etats membres et les institutions de l'Union européenne.* Série droit des femmes, 1995.
Parodi, Jean-Luc. "Les femmes préfèrent les femmes." *Le Point,* 15 June 1987.
Pascal, Jean. *Les Femmes députées de 1944 à 1988.* Paris: Pascal, 1990.
Pégard, Catherine. "Michèle Barzach: le ministre nouvelle vague." *Le Point,* no. 769, 15 June 1987.
Perrineau, Pascal. *Le Guide du pouvoir.* Paris: Editions Doumic, 1991.
Perrot, Michelle. *Quel bilan pour les femmes?* Paris: La Documentation Française, 2000.
———, *Les Femmes ou les silences de l'histoire.* Paris: Flammarion, 1998.
———, *Les engagements du vingtième siècle.* Special issue of *Vingtième Siecle.* Paris: Presses des Sciences Politiques, 1998.
———, *Femmes publiques, entretiens avec Jean Lebrun.* Paris: Textuel, 1997.
———, "Le XIXe siècle était-il misogyne?" *L'Histoire,* no. 160 (November 1992): 32–37.
———, "Histoire et pouvoirs des femmes." In *Le sexe du pouvoir. Femmes, hommes et pouvoirs dans les organisations.* Paris: Desclé de Brouwer, 1986.
Perrot, Michelle, ed. *Une Histoire des femmes est-elle possible?* Paris: Rivages, 1984.
Perrot, Michelle, and Georges Duby, eds. *Histoire des femmes en occident: Le XXième siècle.* Paris: Plon, 1992.
Perrot, Michelle, Georges Duby, and Geneviève Fraisse. *A History of Women in the West.* Volume IV, *Emerging Feminism from Revolution to World War.* Cambridge, Mass.: Belknap Press of Harvard University, 1993. Includes the following translations: "Writing the History of Women," "Orders and Liberties," "Daughters of Liberty and Revolutionary Citizens."
Pfefferkorn, Roland, and Alain Bihr. *Hommes, femmes, l'introuvable inégalité.* Paris: Editions de l'Atelier, Syros, 1997.

Philippe, Annie, and Danielle Hubscher. *Enquête à l'intérieur du parti socialiste.* Paris: Albin Michel, 1991.
Phillips, Anne. *Feminism and Politics.* Oxford: Oxford University Press, 1998.
———, *The Politics of Presence.* Oxford: Clarendon Press, 1995.
———, *Engendering Democracy.* Oxford: Oxford Polity Press, 1991.
Piat, Colette. *La République des misogynes.* Paris: Plon, 1981.
Picq, Françoise, and Monique Cahen, eds. *Libération des femmes: les années mouvement.* Paris: Seuil, 1993.
Pisier, Evelyne, and Françoise Barret-Ducrocq. *Femmes en tête.* Paris: Flammarion, 1997.
Pons, Philippe. "Une Socialiste à l'assaut d'un monde politique masculin." *Le Monde*, 5 March 1987.
Proctor, Candice E. *Women, Equality, and the French Revolution.* Westport, Conn.: Greenwood Press, 1990.
Rabaut, Jean. *Histoire des féminismes français.* Paris: Stock, 1978.
Rabine, Leslie W. and Sara E. Melzer. *Rebel Daughters. Women and the French Revolution.* New York: Oxford University Press, 1992.
Rabinow, *Michel Foucault, un parcours philosophique: au delà de l'objectivité et la subjectivité.*" Paris: Gallimard. 1984. English translation: Michel Foucault : "Beyond Structuralism and Hermeneutics."
Randall, Vicky. *Gender, Politics, and the State.* London: Routledge, 1998.
———, *Women and Politics. An International Perspective.* London: Macmillan, 1987.
Randall, Vicky and Joni Lovenduski. *Contemporary Feminist Politics.* Oxford: Oxford University Press, 1993.
Rendall, Jane. "Citizenship, Culture and Civilization: The Languages of British Suffragists, 1866–1874." In Caroline Daley and Melanie Nolan. *Suffrage and Beyond. International Feminist Perspectives.* New York: New York University Press, 1994, pp. 127–150.
Rétif, Françoise. *L'Autre en miroir.* Paris: L'Harmattan, 1996.
Rey, Henri, and Françoise Subileau. *Les Militants socialistes à l'épreuve du pouvoir.* Paris: Presses de la FNSP, 1991.
Reynolds, Siân. *Alternative Politics: Women and Public Life in France between the Wars.* Stirling: Stirling French Publications, 1993.
———, *Women, State, and Revolution: Essays on Power and Gender in Europe since 1789.* Brighton, Sussex: Wheatsheaf Books, 1986.
———, "Marianne's Citizens? Women, the Republic and Universal Suffrage in France." In *Women, State, and Revolution: Essays on Power and Gender in Europe since 1789.* Brighton, Sussex : Wheatsheaf Books, 1986.
Rihoit, Catherine. "Elections: le complot contre les femmes." *Marie-Claire*, no. 401, January, 1986.
Riot-Sarcey, Michèle, *Histoire du féminisme.* Paris: La Découverte, 1998.
———, "Désassujettissement. Quelques réflexions sur la domination." *Futur antérieur* 5–6, no. 25–26. In *Pouvoirs pouvoir* (1995): 39–50.
———, *La Démocratie à l'épreuve des femmes.* Paris: Albin Michel, 1994.
Riot-Sarcey, Michèle ed., *Utopie et politique.* Paris: Albin Michel, 1998.
———, *Femmes, pouvoirs.* Paris: Kimé, 1993.
Ripa, Yannick. *Les Femmes, actrices de l'histoire, France, 1789–1945.* Paris: Sedes, 1999.

Rochefort, Florence. "La Citoyenneté interdite ou les enjeux du suffragisme." In *Le Vote des Françaises à 50 ans. Vingtième Siècle. Revue d'histoire* 42 (April-June 1994). Paris: Presses de la Fondation Nationale des Sciences Politiques.

Rolland, Gabrielle. *Seront-elles au rendez-vous? La nouvelle cause des femmes.* Paris: Flammarion, 1995.

Rosanvallon, Pierre. *Le Sacre du citoyen. Essai sur le suffrage universel en France.* Paris: Gallimard, 1992.

Roudinesco, Elisabeth. *Théroigne de Méricourt.* Paris: Seuil, 1989.

Rousseau, Renée. *Les Femmes rouges. Chronique des années Vermeesch.* Paris: Albin Michel, 1983.

Rudelle, Odile. "Le Vote des Femmes et la Fin de 'L'Exception Française'," pp. 52–65. In *Le Vote des Françaises à 50 ans. Vingtième Siècle Revue d'histoire* 42 (April-June, 1994). Paris: Presses de la Fondation Nationale des Sciences Politiques, 1994.

Saint-Criq, Régine. "Une autre place pour les femmes." (*Fédération Nationale des élus Socialistes et Républicains* (FNRSR). Study prepared for the Socialist and Republican representatives' Association.

Saint-Criq, Régine, and Nathalie Prévost. *Vol au-dessus d'un nid de machos.* Paris: Albin Michel, 1993.

Sarazin, Michel. *Simone Veil. Destin.* Paris: Robert Laffont, 1987.

Sarde, Michèle. *Regard sur les françaises: Xième-XXième siècle.* Paris: Stock, 1983.

———, "L'Action du ministère des droits de la femme, 1981–1986: un bilan." *French Review* 61, no. 6 (May 1988): 931–941.

Sawicki, Jana. *Disciplining Foucault: Feminism, Power and the Body.* New York, London: Routlege, 1991.

Schemla, Elisabeth. *Edith Cresson, la femme piégée.* Paris: Flammarion, 1993.

———, "Une nouvelle révolution française: la parité." *L'Express,* 6 June 1996, pp. 29–31.

Schneidermann, Daniel. "Michèle Barzach: la dame de coeur." *Le Monde*, 25 June 1987.

Scott, Joan Wallach. *La Citoyenne paradoxale. Les féministes françaises et les droits de l'homme.* Paris: Albin Michel, 1998. Translated by Marie Bouré and Colette Pratt from the English, *Only Paradoxes to Offer.*

———, *French Feminists Claim the Rights of "Man": Olympe de Gouges on the French Revolution.* St. Louis, Mo.: Washington University, 1991.

Scott, Joan Wallach, and Brian Tierney. *Western Societies: A Documentary History.* New York: Knopf, 1984.

Sellier, Michèle. "La Mairie dans le cursus politique." *Pouvoirs*, no. 24 (1983): 81–91.

Sineau, Mariette. "Les deux faces de la parité," *Le Monde Diplomatique*, Paris, December 1999.

———, "Les femmes politiques sous la 5ième République: à la recherche d'une légitimité électorale."*Pouvoirs*, no. 82 (1997): 45–57.

———, *Vingtième Siècle. Revue d'histoire*, no. 43 (July-December 1994): 72–78.

———, "Les Citoyennes n'ont pas pris la Bastille." *L'Histoire* 160 (November 1992): 8–11.

———, "Droit et Démocratie." In Françoise Thébaud, ed. *Histoire des femmes*, volume 5. Paris: Plon, 1992.

———, "Pouvoir, modernité et monopole masculin de la politique: le cas français." *Nouvelles Questions féministes* 13, no. 1 (1992): 39–61.
———, "D'une présidence à l'autre; La politique socialiste en direction des femmes (10 mai 1981–10 mai 1991)." *French Politics and Society* 9, nos. 3–4 (Summer-Fall 1991): 63–81.
———, *Des Femmes en politique.* Paris: Economica, 1988.
Sineau, Mariette, and Jane Jenson. *Mitterrand et les Françaises.* Paris: Presses de la Fondation Nationale des Sciences politiques, 1995.
Sineau, Mariette, and Janine Mossuz-Lavau. *Enquête sur les femmes et la politique en France.* Paris: P.U.F., 1983.
Sineau, Mariette, and Evelyne Tardy. *Droits des femmes en France et au Québec: 1940–1990: éléments pour une histoire comparée.* Montreal: Editions du Remue-ménage, 1993.
Sollers, Philippe. "L'Une et l'autre." *L'Express,* 11–17 December 1987.
Somerwine, Charles, and C. Maignien. *Madeleine Pelletier: une féministe dans l'arène politique.* Paris: Editions Oeuvriers, 1992.
Spencer, Samia, and Theresa McBride. "Women Cabinet Ministers: Ornament of Government?" *Proceedings of the Annual Meeting of the Western Society for French History* (1984): 243–256.
Summers, Anne. *Dammed Whores and God's Police: The Colonisation of Women in Australia.* Ringwood, Vic.: Penguin, 1975.
Szafran, Maurice. *Simone Veil. Destin.* Paris: Flammarion, 1994.
Tannen, Deborah. *You Just Don't Understand: Men and Women in Conversation.* New York: Ballantine, 1990.
Tatu, Natacha, and Paul Burel. *Martine Aubry. Enquête sur une énigme politique.* Paris: Calmann-Lévy, 1997.
Thatcher, Margaret. *10 Downing Street. Mémoires.* 2 volumes. Paris: Albin Michel, 1993.
Thébaud, Françoise, ed. *Histoire des femmes.* Paris: Plon, 1992.
Thévenin, Nicole. "Féminisme et PCF," *Politique Aujourd'hui,* nos. 3–4 (Summer 1981): 100–102.
Thompson, Joan Hulse. "Role Perceptions of Women in the Ninety-Fourth Congress (1975–1976)." *Political Science Quarterly* 95, no. 1 (Spring 1980): 71–81.
Touraine, Alain. *Qu'est-ce que la démocratie*? Paris: Fayard, 1994.
Tricot, Catherine, Françoise Gaspard, Michèle Riot-Sarcey, and Françoise Duroux. "A propos de la parité." *Futur antérieur* 28, no. 2 (1995): 131–145.
United Nations. Division for the Advancement of Women. *Women in Politics and Decision Making in the Late Twentieth Century.* A United Nations Survey. Dordrecht, Boston, London: Martinus Nijhoff Publishers, 1992.
United Nations. *The World's Women, Trends and Statistics 1970–1990.* New York: United Nations, 1991.
Varikas, Eleni. "Refonder ou raccommoder la démocratie? Réflexions critiques sur la demande de la parité des sexes." *French Society and Politics* 12, no. 4 (Fall 1994): 1–34.
Venner, Fiammeta, and Claudie Lesselier. *L'Extrême Droite et les femmes.* Villeurbanne: Editions Golias, 1997.
Véron, Jacques. *Le Monde des femmes.* Paris: Seuil, 1997.
Verney, Françoise. *Mais si, messieurs, les femmes ont une âme.* Paris: Grasset, 1995.

Viennot, Eliane. "L'Exception française: une très vieille histoire." *Après-demain,* no. 380–381 (January-February 1996): 5–8.
———, "Parité: les féministes entre défis politiques et révolution culturelle." *Nouvelles Questions Féministes* 15, no. 4 (1994): 65–89.
———, ed. *La Démocratie à la française ou les femmes indésirables.* Paris: Publications de L'Université Paris VII: Denis Diderot, 1997.
Waring, Marilyn. *Three Masquerades: Essays on Equality, Work and Hu(man) Rights.* Toronto: University of Toronto Press, 1997.
Weed, Elisabeth. *Coming to Terms: Feminism, Theory, Politics.* New York: Routledge, 1989.
Weissman, Elizabeth. *Les Filles, on n'attend plus que vous. Témoignages de Martine Aubry à Simone Veil.* Paris: Textuel, 1995.
Weitz, Margaret Collins. "La "Première" Femme de Strasbourg: entretien avec Catherine Trautmann." *French Review* 66, no. 5 (April 1993): 713–717.
Williams, Melissa. *Voice, Trust, and Memory: Marginalized Groups and the Failings of Liberal Representation.* Princeton N.J.: Princeton University Press, 1998.
Wilson, Frank. *French Political Parties under the Fifth Republic.* New York: Preager, 1982.
———, "Evolution of the French Party System." In P. Godt, ed. *Policy Making in France.* London: Pinter, 1989.
Witt, Linda. *Running as a Woman: Gender and Power in American Politics.* New York: Macmillan, 1994.
*Who's Who in France.* Paris: Editions Lafitte.
Young, Hugo. *The Iron Lady: A Biography of Margaret Thatcher.* New York: Farrar, Straus, Giroux, 1989.
Zaidman, Claude. "Les acquis des femmes en France dans une perspective européenne." *L'Homme et la société* 25 (1991): 147–157.
Zylberberg-Hocquard, Marie-Hélène. *Féminisme et syndicalisme en France.* Paris: Anthropos, 1978.

# Index

www.ingramcontent.com/pod-product-compliance
Lightning Source LLC
Chambersburg PA
CBHW060025030426
42334CB00019B/2189
* 9 7 8 1 5 7 1 8 1 0 8 2 3 *